TEACHING FOR THINKING
Theory and Application

TEACHING FOR THINKING
Theory and Application
83089

Louis E. Raths
Newark State College

Arthur Jonas
Newark State College

Arnold Rothstein
City College of New York

Selma Wassermann
Simon Fraser University

Charles E. Merrill Publishing Company
Columbus, Ohio
A Bell & Howell Company

MERRILL'S INTERNATIONAL EDUCATION SERIES

Under the Editorship of **Kimball Wiles**
Dean of the College of Education
University of Florida

Library of Congress Catalog Number: 67-10851

International Standard Book Number: 0-675-09801-7

PRINTED IN THE UNITED STATES OF AMERICA

5 6 7 8 9 10 11 12 13 14 15-76 75 74 73 72 71 70

for Mildred

Man is but a reed, the feeblest thing in nature, but he is a thinking reed. The entire universe need not arm itself to destroy him. A vapour, a drop of water suffices to kill him. But were the universe to crush him, man would still be more noble than that which slays him, because he knows that he dies and the advantage which the universe has over him; of this the universe knows nothing.

All our dignity lies in thought. By thought we must elevate ourselves, not by space and time which we cannot fill. Let us endeavour then to think well; therein lies the principle of morality.

Blaise Pascal
1623-1662

INTRODUCTION

In this book *thinking* is associated with *the whole man*. It is not restricted to the cognitive domain alone. It embraces imagination, it includes thinking to some purpose, it invites the expression of values, attitudes, feelings, beliefs, and aspirations. Throughout the book there is a recurring emphasis on questioning of implicit and explicit assumptions, on generalizations, on the easy attributions to other people of motives, feelings and purposes. There is a stress on the meaning of the many ways in which life experiences may be clarified for their possible significance.

Through experiences with our family physician we are familiar with the distinction between *symptoms* and the probable underlying *causes* of those symptoms. We are helped by our medical advisor to realize that it is not enough to treat symptoms. It *is* important to investigate the causes of symptoms. For example, where a child exhibits unusual and persistent aggressive behavioral symptoms potentially or actually harmful to other children, we have come to believe that there are underlying causes which relate to the frustrations of very important emotional needs. We now believe that when these needs are met, the aggressive behavior is likely to diminish in frequency, or intensity or both. Studies in the field of psychology have enabled us to gain insight into human behavior and to make generalizations which help us to understand the possible causes of behavior. This type of *theoretical* orientation is extended in this book to those human functions we ordinarily associate with thinking: certain behaviors of people reflect an incompleteness or inconsistency of thought. These behaviors reflect experience with thinking which has not been adequately rigorous in terms of what is set forth in these pages.

Deprivation of certain kinds of experiences has consequences of a behavioral kind. Impulsiveness, for example, is generally associated with the function of thinking: one did not stop to think. A second illustration is reflected in the characterization that a student doesn't concentrate: at some moment in time he is not paying attention to what he is doing and hence meets failure in his work. It is commonly assumed that this is a neglect of rigor in the thinking processes. Where there is an emphasis upon thinking in the curriculum students tend to modify their behaviors. Where there is frequent opportunity to engage in a great variety of processes which involve thinking, the frequency of impulsive behavior tends to decline.

It is important to note that we are not suggesting that teachers can or should teach children *how to think*. There is no "one way" of thinking. We tend to assume that in the normal population of the human family the capacity to think is present and that what is needed most are *opportunities to think,* and opportunities to discuss the thinking which is done. The book, therefore, has many, many suggestions for teachers at various levels of instruction for ways to provide opportunities which involve thinking.

In this book we are concerned with *theory* and *its applications* in an area that focuses upon thinking. In this context *theory* is taken to mean a statement of relationships between two or more variables where effort is made to define the variables. In this book the variables under consideration are *thinking* and *behavior*. It is maintained that a relationship exists between thinking and *some* kinds of behavior. Incompleteness or inconsistency of thought or limited experience with thinking is often reflected in certain kinds of human behavior which can be observed in the classroom. A theory is also thought of as an attempt *to explain* the connections between variables or throw light upon a problem. The thinking theory presented in this book is defined in terms of its ability to explain the behavior in question.

Another criterion often associated with a theory is that hypotheses may be drawn from it and put to the test. The theory set forth in this volume is amenable to such testing. Children with certain thinking-related characteristics may be identified. These children may be given many opportunities over a period of one semester to think and then an assessment of their behaviors can be carried out a second time. To the extent that positive changes occur the theory is supported; to the extent that very little happens, doubt is thrown upon the theory. In other words, every teacher can be in a position to test what is here proposed as a workable theory.

We ask of a theory that it meet certain common sense notions. Is it reasonable to suppose that if we are given many opportunities to think we might become different in our behavior? The theory has been discussed with thousands of teachers and has stood this test very well. There is substantial agreement that an emphasis upon thinking activities will encourage thinking and result in a decrease in what may be termed "immature" behavior. A theory that is worth its salt tends to grow out of observed facts. This theory has developed from classroom observations, from long years of work with teachers, and from experimental evidence.

At appropriate places in the text we suggest the tremendously significant role which physical health plays in influencing behavior. We also point out how significant emotional security seems to be in its influence on behavior. We suggest that where there is a serious problem in learning which seems to relate to thinking, it is wise first to make some investigation of physical fitness and of emotional security. Mention is also made of the time and patience needed for application of this particular theory. Overnight results are out of the question. It is suggested that a minimum of one entire semester is needed to give the theory an adequate trial.

With these qualifications one might infer that the theory does attempt to explain too much. There is little doubt that it represents an over-simplified explanation of some complex behavior problems. Isn't it true, however, that in the early stages of its publication practically every theory in all fields is an oversimplification? One of the great values in formulating a theory is to bring it before the public of one's peers for experimental verification and for theoretical examination. Trials of the theory in many different situations, conducted by different experimenters, tend to subject the theory to very critical appraisal. Under these circumstances the theory may be modified or rejected. This is why, perhaps, theories are the subject of frequent debate: they challenge critical scrutiny; they open up channels for experimentation and for the exchange of data; they add zest and life to the related profession. In presenting a theory which relates clearly to the practice of education, what we have presented here will invite wide-spread criticism.

A further point bears mentioning. Wide-spread amongst educational leaders is the assumption that teachers *must* take responsibility for changing the behavior of children. In this book stress is given to the idea that teachers *must* take the responsibility for providing experiences which open up opportunities for students to change, if that is their desire. In other words, the teacher tries to create situations in which students have experiences which may or may not facilitate change. The teacher's job, his professional responsibility, is to provide richness of experience. The test of good teaching does not consist alone of changed behavior on the part of students. Good teaching is recognized, in part, by the quality of the experiences which are going on in the school. If students do *not* change, this does not mean that worthwhile experiences have not been provided. If students do not change, it means only that students have not changed. Other kinds of evidence are needed to answer the question: have excellent experiences been provided?

If teachers provide a school life which is very rich in its opportunities for thinking, it is very probable that most children will reconstruct their own behavior. We are familiar with the fact that teachers often say to children: you should, you ought, you must, as ways of getting changes in behavior. Students learn what the teacher wants and they give it to him. In this book we have tried to show that where children have opportunities for thinking, where these opportunities are so much a part of the curriculum that they are present day after day and week after week, they begin to change their own behavior. They are not told to change it. They are not penalized for not changing it. In the overwhelming majority of cases they do change it.

In the same vein teachers are not heartbroken if the students do not change. Teachers get satisfaction out of knowing that they are presenting rich opportunities for children to experience decision making, comparing, summarizing, and the other operations mentioned in this book. While they hope for change, they do not demand it. While they look for change, they do not manipulate children in order to get change. The teachers are looking for change which is self-directed on the part of students. The responsibility for change lies with the students. The responsibility for richness of experiences lies with the teachers. Where change is taking place under these circumstances, progress on the student's part is evidence of his achievement and it is also evidence that the curriculum is providing experiences which enable him to make decisions about his behavior.

It is *experience* which contributes most significantly to the process of maturing. Teachers cannot guarantee that any particular activity will become an experience for students in the classroom. Teachers can and should guide in the continuing process of developing a curriculum which seems to be rich in the qualities associated with the concept of experience. Opportunities to think belong in this category.

Perhaps something more should be said about the many subtle and not so subtle ways of manipulating students to get changes in behavior that are wanted. Those of us who have observed teachers at work have been surprised by the tendency of teachers to make judgments about what sudents say and do. Instead of accepting an explanation, an example, a dissent, a rebuttal, or a question as part of an encounter with the child's life, there is the tendency to use praise or blame for almost everything a student might say or do. Under these circumstances it becomes very clear to students what they "should do". In this book there are hundreds of examples which illustrate opportunities for students to think. If, in using these examples, teachers are going to make judgments, favorable or unfavorable, about every response made by students, a disservice will be done to the larger concept of providing opportunity for freedom to think. Instead of approving or disapproving, it is hoped that the teacher will relate what is being said to the purpose which is governing the encounter. There is no need for distributing applause or disapproval for what children say and do. In unusual circumstances it is appropriate. Where adults are exchanging ideas, or raising questions, or dissenting, we do not think it necessary for a continuing presentation of praise and blame for what is being said. Where we live with students in situations that have meaning for them and for us, we diminish the significance of those encounters by the over-use of praise and blame. It is high time that we respected these students more and respected ourselves more.

If we focus upon the thinking which is being done and raise questions about it at times and accept it at times we shall be doing what is required by the situation.

In this book *thinking* is conceived as processes associated with inquiry, and decision making. Where the process of *comparing* is purposeful, we see it as one way of acquiring facts about likeness and difference; we see it as a step toward weighing similarities and differences in preparation for choosing. Where *summarizing* is taking place we see the process as involving analyzing, abstracting, ordering, organizing, and synthesizing. And so too with the other operations discussed in the pages which follow. The emphasis is upon *opportunities to think,* so that inquiry may go forward, and so that decisions and conclusions may be more soundly based.

With John Dewey we believe that one of the most important aims of inquiry is to arrive at warranted assertability. Most of us want to make assertions that will stand critical scrutiny; we want a minimum of holes in our arguments. In a great many life situations we do not expect "to prove" something as absolutely true or false. Most often we do not have the time or the facilities; and quite often we may not have the needed training or experience in the area under discussion. A child in Grade IV may find a way to estimate the area of a circle. An acceptable *proof* might involve the use of the calculus. For *his* purposes, the method used by the child may be satisfactory, and the conclusion *warranted* in terms of that purpose. The thinking operations described in this volume represent activities which involve many kinds of thinking. Little or no attention, however, is given to rigorous proofs; or to designs of research appropriate to the exact testing of clearly formulated hypotheses. We are emphasizing *opportunities to think,* and opportunities *to share our thinking* as inquiry is carried forward in terms of purposes important in these situations.

The thinking operations emphasized in these pages, all of them, can be used to develop habits of thoughtful inquiry. Where they are consistently employed to enrich the experience of young people, we are entitled to hope that a contribution will be made to the maturity of our world.

The theory underlying this book and the many thinking operations set forth have been explored for several years. During that time many questions have been asked about the theory and the materials. We have lived with these questions and have tried to answer them to our own satisfaction, and we share a number of them with our readers.

Are we concerned purely with the intellectual processes? We believe that emotional security is very important and a necessary condition in the learning processes associated with school life. It is a necessary but not a sufficient condition to explain human behavior in total. Not *all* behavior can be explained by the weaning processes carried on in early childhood! We have emphasized the importance of physical health and emotional health and we have stressed the importance of thinking. We have suggested that thinking enters into many facets of life; that man is not compartmentalized; that thinking must be thought of in its relationship to values, and that values must be looked at in terms of choices and consequences. As we see it, young people have not been given many opportunities to think in our schools. We suggest that children and grown-ups have great capacities for thinking, and that if thinking is stressed in our schools, there will be an increased tendency to use thinking operations in the solution of many life problems.

Why have we not given much more space to the many people who have written about thinking? The reason is a simple one: we have restricted ourselves to a theory which relates thinking to a number of behavioral symptoms, and to a number of thinking operations. We have tried to bring together the materials relevant to this theory, and we have reported a number of the researches which bear upon the theory. The book is intended to clarify this theory and to illustrate it.

After long and intensive work with the materials and operations relating to the theory, some teachers have asked: what is new about this . . . . doesn't everybody know this? A new theory often is greeted in this way. When it is clearly formulated, many people wonder why it was not formulated years earlier! The newness is associated with a different organization of materials, with clear-cut hypotheses which can be tested by classroom teachers, and with many illustrations of thinking operations which are applicable to almost any type of organization of the curriculum. One might turn the question around: if the theory and its applications are so obvious, why shouldn't we find many evidences of its use in normal classroom functioning? Perhaps educators have given a lot of lip-service to thinking in the past without concommitent emphasis on thinking in the classroom.

Ideally, shouldn't a book that emphasizes thinking also emphasize the problems that should be thought about? We have many examples in the book which have bearing upon important problems, but we do not believe that we should be prescriptive about curriculum content. The book emphasizes method, student behavior, and operations. The stress is upon teaching for thinking and how to go about it. A very large number of problems become significant as these operations are used and the processes applied. Where the faculty has a voice in policy making which is concerned with curriculum, where teachers are free to think, and where thinking operations can be applied to curriculum development, progress can be made.

As more work is done with this theory and its applications we certainly anticipate that changes will be recommended. Some of the categories may not stand up; others may and probably will be added. Many other thinking operations may be suggested as appropriate for trials of the theory. The thinking operations overlap considerably. Some of the behavioral manifestations overlap. We do not consider this too serious in the actual applications of the ideas to classroom practice. We do not offer the materials as a syllabus to be adopted. We offer a series of suggestions to teachers as a basis for their further thinking.

In Webster's Twentieth Century Dictionary, Unabridged, second edition, thinking is defined in a number of ways. The first meaning is:

"to bring the intellectual faculties into play; to use the mind for arriving at conclusions, making decisions, drawing inferences, etc., to perform any mental operation to reason."

The second explanation for the word *think* is:

"to judge, to conclude; to decide; to hold as a settled opinion; to believe; as to *think* nobly of a person."

The third meaning says:

"to purpose; to intend; as I *thought* to help him."

A fourth interpretation:

"to muse; to meditate; to reflect; to weigh something mentally."

When we are asked to define a term, ordinarily we try to give boundaries to the term; to fix limits to it. We aim to be precise. We hope to make clear what is included and what is excluded. Where we describe, we intend accuracy and perhaps vividness. As we look again at the definitions quoted we are perhaps puzzled by the vagueness, by the lack of precision, the lack of clarity, the comprehensiveness of what has been suggested as the meaning of *thinking*. The authors of this book are unable to define thinking in a brief paragraph which would suggest the breadth and the depth of the concept as it is used in the pages which follow. We agree that man is a thinking being and that thinking is inextricably mixed with feeling and valuing and purposing. We see it as being influenced considerably by chemical and physical reactions within our bodies.

Instead of trying "to fix" a definition of this large concept in a small space we have devoted many, many pages to a clarification of some of the many things which we associate with thinking. By and large our efforts are two-fold:

(1) We suggest that many examples of our behavior are indicative both of thought and lack of thought. With respect to the latter we emphasize eight rather common behavioral syndromes as associated with an habitual disregard for thinking processes.

1. Impulsiveness	5. Dogmatic, assertive behavior
2. Overdependence upon the teacher	6. Extreme lack of confidence
3. Inability to concentrate	7. Missing the meaning
4. Rigidity and inflexibility	8. Resistance to thinking

Many instances are given throughout the book of positive evidences of thought: caution in generalizing; recognition of assumptions; grounding inferences by reference to data which are publicly available. There are dozens of these instances in the pages which follow. The point being made is that we make inferences about thinking from the behavior of people. We make inferences about "the mind" by the traces available of a mind at work. In much the same way we make inferences about the thinking of an individual. In part, therefore, thinking is defined as having a relationship to examined behavior.

(2) Our second effort at a definition of thinking is embraced by the listing of many thinking operations. We say explicitly that the listing is not complete. We say in clear fashion that when these operations are carried on, a favorable situation has been created for the *"eliciting"* of thinking by those who participate. We say that *comparing, interpreting, observing,* and *summarizing* are some thinking operations in the sense that their intelligent use elicits thinking. We give fifteen such categories of action for use in teaching with an emphasis on thinking.

Our definition is behavioral in part, procedural in part, conceptual in part. While it cannot be pin-pointed, it can be clarified in terms of emphasizing the objective in school practice. The reader can probably incorporate these suggested operations in his teaching practices and as he applies them, will probably agree that he is eliciting and emphasizing thinking. In the utilization of these processes he is apt to experience and to conceptualize what he means by thinking and what students mean by the term. We could not ask for more.

Part I of this volume deals with an exposition of a theory of thinking. Part II deals with application of the theory on the elementary school level. Part III deals with the application of the theory in the secondary school. Part IV is concerned with the role of the teacher in the application of the theory. Part V contains a recapitulation of the theory, research evidence, case studies, and some final comments. There are appendices which contain tests and instruments and selected readings.

High school teachers may wish to by-pass Part II, which deals with the elementary school, and go directly to Part III, where they will find a brief statement of theory and an extended discussion of applications. Those readers who make use of the entire volume will encounter some repetitions and perhaps redundancies in Part III. The repetition was intentional and was designed to serve the special interests of secondary school personnel. In the remaining parts of the book there is a recurring emphasis upon a number of the thinking operations and upon thinking-related behavior of students. We hope the several treatments are sufficiently varied and informative to merit the intensive emphasis given to these points.

The book was written primarily for classroom teachers and for those who are preparing to teach. It should also prove informative and useful to members of boards of education and to administrators and supervisors who prize emphasis upon thinking, and who are seeking practical ways of bringing that emphasis into being.

Louis E. Raths
Union, New Jersey
1967

CONTENTS

part one   **THEORY**   1
Introduction
Thinking Operations
Behavior and Thinking
Some Qualifying Comments
Conclusion

part two   **APPLICATION:**   31
THE ELEMENTARY
SCHOOL
Introduction
Using the Activities
Thinking Activities for Pre– and
    Beginning Readers
Thinking Activities for Children Just
    Gaining Fluency in Reading
Thinking Activities for Children
    Who are Fluent in Reading
A Climate for Thinking
Using the Thinking Activities
Conclusion

part three   **APPLICATION:**   113
THE SECONDARY
SCHOOL
Introduction
Thinking Operations
Some Final Considerations

part four APPLICATION: 241
THE TEACHER
Introduction
Occasions for Teaching for Thinking
Thinking in Various Fields
Process and Product
The Classroom and Thinking
Selecting Activities
Thinking Activities
Thinking Experiences
Focusing on Particular Behaviors
Implications of Teaching for
    Thinking
Conclusion

part five RECAPITULATION 291
Theory and Hypotheses
Research Related to the Theory
Case Studies
Additional Research Findings
Final Comments
Conclusion

SUGGESTED READINGS 339

INTRODUCTION

It has been said that for hundreds of thousands of years the primary aim of man was to survive, and most of early man's thinking probably served this end. And then a time came when man could plan not just to live — but to live better. And this called for the recognition of new alternatives, for the dreaming of dreams and the alteration of the environment in pursuit of the dreams. Man became social, and in that process he also created social problems. These problems in turn called for solution, and man's thinking was again challenged. There was, and there continues to be, no end to the problems which confront mankind, and the need to emphasize thinking in the education of children was never so urgent as it is today.

There is widespread verbal recognition of the importance of thinking. We want our children to be able to think for themselves, to be self-directing, considerate, and thoughtful. We don't want them to be rash or hasty in their judgments. In situations which are new to them, we hope they will be able to apply knowledge which they have gained in the past. We hope that they will be able to see through the propaganda which is directed toward them. We hope that they will come up with new ideas, new inventions, new dreams. We hope they will have an attitude of thoughtfulness in many situations which are problematic in character.

Why do we want all of this? Partly because we think that survival depends upon it. Perhaps because we realize that men cannot be both stupid and free. The free society which we have been trying to build demands a free intelligence. A population which cannot or will not think about its problems will not long remain free and independent. Respect for the personalities of others, a readiness to share, and faith in the use of intelligence are the cornerstones of a democratic society.

All of the social institutions of a society play an important role in the shaping of that society. As they create purposes, devote their energies to certain projects, reward and penalize certain kinds of behavior, they are engaged in creating a certain kind of society. Means and ends are thus integrated. As you sow, so shall you reap. Every hour of every school day we are not only living through that hour; we are helping to create a world. Will it be a thoughtful world? A free world? A sharing world? A world that has respect for the personality of each individual?

Schools contribute to the development of a society as they work with children. The United States has led the world in the direction of free, public education for all children. We spend a great deal of money and time on education, and we do so in the belief that it will make a better world to live in. If thinking is emphasized, will this probably enhance the contribution which schools make?

As children grow older they mature physically. It is our hope that they also mature emotionally, socially, and intellectually. We have learned much about the requirements for good physical development, and we are doing our best to find out what contributes most to the all around maturity of young people. We used to assume that it was learning itself which matured people: if we could make children learn, we were contributing to their maturity! We are beginning to see the great importance of experience in the maturing processes. We are beginning to believe that it is experience which matures people, and we are examining the role of the curriculum in providing those experiences most likely to contribute to maturity.

There are a great many words and phrases in use to describe immature behavior. It is not surprising to learn that many of them are associated with thinking activity or, more properly, its neglect. We may say of a person that he is like a child, forever leaning upon an adult for help in thinking; or again, we might say that a person is very impulsive and doesn't take time to think and that in this respect he seems not to have grown up. Or we say that he has never learned to concentrate, and we imply that in this respect he hasn't matured. There are many such phrases used, and more will be said about them later. All of them suggest the absence of those experiences which discipline behavior. There is also the subtle implication that if the experiences had been lived through, had been endured, the behavior of the individual would have been different.

We do not mean to suggest that the solution is a simple *either-or* choice: either learning or experience as the only basis for maturity. We are talking about *how* one learns. Some teachers have the idea that a student must *learn the facts first,* and *then* be asked to think about them. These same teachers often assume that learning the facts is largely a process of memorizing, of repetition and drill, until the facts are firmly fixed. They overlook the importance of the many processes by which facts may be acquired. When we are in a situation where a choice between two objects is necessary, we compare them and evaluate them in terms of the purposes they serve. *As we compare* we are acquiring facts, and if our purpose is to make judgments of better, or worse, or equal, we are discovering facts which are of great importance for making the final decision.

Thinking is *a way* of learning. Thinking is one way of inquiring for facts, and if the thinking is to some purpose, the facts so found will be relevant to that same purpose. We then have purposeful learning, and a person is maturing when his activities are disciplined by purpose.

If we grant the importance of thinking for the growth and maintenance of a free society, and if we acknowledge the contributions which thinking experiences make to maturity, we may well ask why the schools do not spend much of their time in efforts to extend greatly the opportunities for thinking.

There is no easy answer to this question. For different communities, for different schools, for different teachers, the answers may vary greatly. Superintendents and principals may be chosen because they have a reputation for stressing memorization, drill, homework, the three R's. If the elite positions of a system go to those who do not stress thinking, an example is being set for the teachers and the students. If promotions and praise go to those who most neglect thinking, this fact too will be learned by all those who work in the schools. If the rewards go to those teachers who keep the children quiet, who raise no questions about the curriculum or about experimentation, teachers will soon learn that inquiry, reflection, the consideration of alternatives are frowned upon.

Why should this be so? There is something unsettling about thinking. It raises questions about the status quo. It suggests that the text, or the teacher, or the superintendent, may not have considered adequately all of the alternatives. It suggests that the learners will have an opportunity to add alternatives of their own, before they make a choice. If alternatives are to be considered and weighed and chosen, this takes time. The so-called course of study may not be completed, and if pages in a text or topical headings have the highest importance, then thinking experiences may be sacrificed to subject matter coverage. Here again, the choice is not necessarily *either-or*, but it is often assumed to be, and many school systems elect to emphasize the so-called factual content. This is sometimes rationalized by saying that the children or the students are not yet mature enough to think about these matters! Can we deplore the immaturity of children and contribute to it at one and the same time? When will they be mature enough?

Another reason given for the lack of emphasis on thinking in our schools is associated with the work and attention that are involved. Where thinking is stressed the teacher must of necessity supplement the existing texts by exercises which call for thinking. The available text books are notably deficient in their attention to thinking. Developing curriculum materials is a difficult task, and it is easier to follow the book. Moreover, if thinking is to be stressed, one must pay close attention to what the children say and write; a teacher must also pay close attention to what he is saying and writing. How does one read a paper with attention to the thinking which is expressed? What does one listen FOR, as he listens to children?

Under-emphasis upon thinking may also be related to ideas of power and authority. If children are allowed to think, indeed, are encouraged to think, perhaps they will think some things that they shouldn't! If children raise alternatives, if they criticize, they may be questioning power which properly belongs to those in authority. This suggests that we may prefer to encourage docility and meekness, obedience to the power figures. It also suggests that day by day, we are not zealous in our efforts to create a free society. It may also imply that we are afraid to face up to the consequences of thinking.

Still another reason given for our neglect of thinking processes in our schools may be associated with a lack of skill and appreciation on the part of teachers. We have talked with hunderds of teachers about this matter, and the overwhelming majority have indicated that their college education prepared them most inadequately for appraising and encouraging the processes of thought. This was as true of the liberal arts graduates as it was of the graduates of teachers' colleges. If teachers are not well prepared by their own education to put an emphasis upon thinking, one can understand the neglect of thinking operations in the lives of school children.

In several ways the educational testing movement has influenced the trend toward under-emphasis on thinking. It has been easier to improvise tests of information that have statistical evidence of reliability. A kind of snowball effect has taken place: as more of these tests were used, more and more were asked for. Educational accomplishment tended to be measured in objective type, short answer test questions. Leaders in the field concentrated largely upon simple questions of fact derived from analyses of widely used texts. Teachers, children, and parents soon discovered that it paid to learn what was regarded as the most important kind of information. Curriculum and instruction quite naturally began to be oriented to the testing.

The post-World War II society displayed a very conservative trend, and this influenced the teaching of thinking in two very powerful ways. In the first place, there was a desire for simple solutions to very complex problems. If there was something wrong with society, it probably had its origins in the schools; and if the schools were at fault, it was probably because of the way that schools taught reading! Hence, it followed that more and more attention must be paid to the mechanics of reading, to the testing of reading, and to the methods by which reading was taught! As a matter of fact, so far as test scores were concerned, the available researches showed that children were reading as well or better than comparable samples of ten, twenty, and thirty years ago. This is not to say that the teaching of reading should not be improved. It is to say that if there is anything wrong with the schools, the causes are probably multiple and complex, and solutions will not be found in a new approach to the teaching or testing of reading. With the greatly increased emphasis upon reading, there was not much time or interest for a new emphasis on thinking.

The post-war era with its emphasis upon simple solutions to complex problems carried with it a disdain for intellectual processes. The term "egg-head" came into being, and it was almost always used derisively. A thoughtful person was often called a "longhair." There was much evidence of belief in guilt by association; a great deal of name-calling and labeling took place. Society wanted action, action, action. It wanted desperately to go backward, to a time of peace, quiet, and order; it looked about for scapegoats and found them. In these circumstances it was hard for many school officials to come out openly for a greatly increased emphasis upon thinking.

For all of these reasons, and probably for many more, thinking continued to be neglected in our school curriculum. Now the decks.seem to be clear again. We are ready for a new look at the place of thinking in our schools. In the long interval there has been considerable research into ways of encouraging thinking. There has been a serious examination of the relationships between certain kinds of behavior and thinking. In the pages which follow, an attempt is made to clarify what is meant by an emphasis upon thinking and what is meant by probable changes in the behavior of children when thinking is emphasized.

What can we do to put an emphasis upon thinking? What kinds of assignments can we make which will call for thinking, or which will probably evoke thinking? What kinds of questions can we ask which stress thinking?

THINKING OPERATIONS

Perhaps most people will agree that thinking is an important aim of education and that schools should do all that they can to provide opportunities for thinking. How can this be done? What are some of the ways that excellent teachers do it? What kinds of assignments and class activities tend to put an emphasis on thinking? Many of the suggestions which follow are not at all new to teachers everywhere. What may be instructive is the organized focus. The headings below can be used by teachers as a check list to monitor their own teaching. At the end of a morning, and again at the end of the school day, a teacher might look at the list and ask himself to what extent he has practiced any of the listed suggestions. It is not implied that the listing is complete; nor is it implied that every single morning and afternoon should include some of these activities. The list is suggestive rather than inclusive. It does, however, contain many ideas that are widely used for giving emphasis to thinking.

Comparing.

When we ask children to compare things we are putting them in a situation where thinking can take place. Children have the chance to observe differences and similarities in fact or in contemplation. They examine two or more objects or ideas or processes with the idea of seeing what relationships one has to another. They seek points of agreement and of disagreement. They observe what is present in one and missing in another. What they see and report will often depend upon the purposes underlying the assignment. As purposes vary, it is highly probable that the reports of comparisons will vary.

The assignment, *to compare,* can vary tremendously in difficulty and scope —from a comparison of two integers to a comparison of modern music with modern art, from a comparison of two coins to a comparison of two philosophies. One may ask high school students to compare the early Hemingway novels with the later ones, or to compare Hemingway with Joyce. One may ask mathematics students to compare two proofs; in science one may ask students to compare two scientific experiments; in foreign languages, to compare two translations or two styles of literature. Each subject is rich in possibilities for comparing. And the possibilities are as great at the level of kindergarten and first grade as they are at the level of senior high school and college.

If there has been the same assignment to a class of students, it is sometimes interesting *to compare* the comparisons! Children can learn from each other. As they see others noting likenesses or differences which they overlooked, their sensitivity may increase.

This process of comparing involves abstracting and holding the abstraction in the mind while attention is paid to the objects being compared. Where it is done superficially and only *for the sake of doing it,* it can be almost as dull as ordinary routine lessons. But where there is real purpose in the analysis, where there is a real motive for this searching for likes and dislikes, the quest proves to be interesting and stimulating both to teachers and to students. It should perhaps be noted that the comparisons of even trivial objects probably yield more in motivation and content learnings than the assignments which put great emphasis on recall alone. As an item in a check list the reader may ask himself: Have I asked my students to make significant comparisons in recent days?

Summarizing.

If you were asked now to summarize what has been presented thus far in the chapter, you would quite likely agree that to summarize requires thought. The idea of a summary is to state in brief or condensed form the substance of what has been presented. It is a restating of the gist of the matter, of the big idea or ideas. There is a requirement of conciseness without the omission of important points.

To do this one begins by reflecting upon the experience. One thinks back, and this can be done in a great number of ways. It is possible to recollect in terms of a time sequence: what came first, second, third, etc. One might start with an enumeration of the big ideas, and then briefly report on each one of them. One might summarize a discussion by indicating which individuals stood for certain points of view. There is no one way of summarizing, and different students may do the same task in different ways.

When children are asked to tell about a trip they have taken, when they are asked to report on a TV program, when they are asked to review a story or a book, when they are asked to tell briefly their experiences at a concert, they have opportunities to communicate in summary form.

Some children seem to have great difficulty in carrying out this kind of assignment, and they need help. This is sometimes given by showing them how to outline what they are going to say or write. Emphasis is given to the point that one puts down the big ideas, the important concepts, and then talks about each of them. A last paragraph might then consist of recounting the main ideas.

Frequently there is opportunity to combine the operations of summarizing and comparing. The latter is often done in terms of a series of specifics, and children can be asked to sum up what has been said about likenesses and differences. This training in sensitivity to what goes together, what is relevant and what is irrelevant, what is of greater and of lesser significance, is a contribution to development of discrimination. It is a slow process, but teachers can make daily efforts to add to each child's growth and development in this area.

Thus far two kinds of thinking assignments have been briefly discussed. Assuming that they are important points in a check list of thinking activities, do you use them regularly?

Observing.

Behind the assignment to observe, there is the idea of watching, of noting, of perceiving. Usually we are paying strict attention; we are watching closely and for a purpose; we are involved in something, and we have good reason for noting carefully. On some occasions we concentrate on details; at other times on substance or on procedures, and sometimes on both. Sometimes we are concerned with great accuracy of observation, and sometimes only with approximations.

When children are asked to compare objects of most any kind, observation is involved. Observations can also be focused upon an event. One may observe an experiment, an art exhibit, a sculptor at work, one's mother baking a cake. One may observe another student who is solving a problem. One may go to the window, look out, and tell what one sees. One may observe animals at play, an aquarium or herbarium. One may observe exhibitions and demonstrations. One may go to another classroom and make an observation. One may observe techniques of swimming, batting, painting, throwing, weaving. There are literally countless opportunities to *observe* what is going on in the world around us.

Are we teaching young people to make use of their eyes and ears? Are they employing all of their senses as they grow through our schools? Is it important that they should have opportunities to check on the accuracy and comprehensiveness of what they see, hear, feel, smell, and taste? Perhaps we are over-emphasizing the bookishness of learning? To observe is a way of discovering information, a part of the process of reacting meaningfully to the world. As we share our observations with others, we notice our blind spots and the blind spots of others. We learn to see and to note what we had not perceived before. We develop discrimination, and it is very important that we should have opportunities to grow in this area. It leads toward maturity.

We must be sure that observations are worth-while. We should rarely assign them as busy-work. There should be important reasons for making the assignment: there may be crucial points to observe and at particular times. On most occasions there should be opportunities to share the observations made. One should be careful about not prodding too much by saying: and what else did you see; what else, what else? If there is a long pause one might ask if there is anything more; one might sum up what has been said and ask if the child wants to add to it. If the purpose of the observation is clear, children are less apt to clutter up their reports with a lot of irrelevant detail.

The idea of keeping notes of one's observations, of making an outline from the notes and then summarizing, is a common method that incorporates comparing, summarizing, and observing. They tend to go together rather naturally. There is a discipline to observing, as there is to comparing and summarizing; the process should be disciplined by purpose. Our observations should be directed by purposes. This does not mean, of course, that other observations should always be excluded. It does mean that the reasons for their inclusion should be weighed.

Should you include assignments dealing with observations if you are stressing thinking? Should *observing* be an item on a checklist for monitoring your own teaching? Think back on the classroom activities of the past several days. Did you give your students opportunities to compare, to summarize, and to observe?

Classifying.

When we classify or sort things, we put them into groups according to some principle that we have in mind. If we are asked to classify a collection of objects, or ideas, we begin to examine them, and when we see certain things in common, we start by putting those objects or ideas together. We keep at it until we have a number of groupings. If the remainder seems unclassifiable according to the system we are using, we are apt to say that a different system might have to be used if they are to be included, or that they may be thought of in a grouping called "miscellaneous."

Children are exposed very early in their lives to systems of classification. The kitchen cabinets and the china closets are organized in certain ways: the plates go here, and the cups go here, and the saucers here, and the glasses here. In putting away the silver, the forks have a special place; so do the knives and the spoons and the ladles. The rooms of a home have different labels and functions: a dining room, bedrooms, kitchen. Oftentimes things "belong" in a room. Clothing has its groupings: clothes to play in, to sleep in, to work in, for school wear and for party wear, for summer and for winter. The idea of "what's mine and what's thine" is a simple *either-or* classification and sometimes difficult to teach!

In preschool, in kindergarten and first grade, children have opportunities to work with blocks, paper and beads in differing sizes, shapes, and colors, and as one observes them at work and play, he sees them improvise schemes of classification. In subsequent years of schooling, children have fewer opportunities to make their own systems of classification. Usually they are set forth by the text, and one has "to learn" them!

In the earlier years teachers sometimes give the groupings or headings or categories to children and supply the children with a collection of objects or words to be distributed within the given classification system. Sometimes the collections alone are given and the children are asked to work out ways of grouping the items. Here again, as children share their ideas for groupings, they learn from each other. They perceive new and different ways of handling the data which have been given.

In the junior and senior high school, requirements of a classification system can be developed and more rigor applied to the task of devising a system. Seeing what belongs and what doesn't, the work involved in "thinking up" possible headings, the business of trying things out and discarding them when they do not work out—these are purposeful exercises.

To classify is to bring order into existence; it is to contribute to the meaning of experience. It involves analysis and synthesis. It encourages children to make order out of their own world, to think on their own, to come to their own conclusions. It is an experience which can contribute to the maturing of young people.

In other chapters of this volume there are many examples of possibilities for classifying at all the levels of public education. Thoughtful teachers will use these as guides and will soon see in their own curriculum many other opportunities for providing this kind of experience. There is general agreement that an exercise of this kind should be included in a program that stresses thinking. Do your students have experiences in observing, summarizing, comparing, and classifying?

Interpreting.

When we interpret an experience we explain the meaning it has for us; interpreting is a process of putting meaning into and taking meaning out of our experiences. If we are asked how we got a particular meaning out of our experience, we give supporting details in defense of our interpretation. Children may have presented to them graphs, tables, charts, pictures, cartoons, caricatures, maps, reports, and poems. When they are asked: what meaning do you get out of this experience, they are being asked to interpret. Meanings are also the outcomes of interpreting trips and excursions, of making comparisons and summaries, of relating rewards and punishment to behavior. Wherever there is reaction to experience it is possible to check one's inference against the facts to see if the data support the interpretation.

Many inferences need qualification. We accompany the meaning with such words as *probably, perhaps, it seems,* and other such words. At other times an inference is much more sure, and our language conveys this degree of conviction. On occasion there is little clear-cut meaning which can be ascribed to or drawn from an experience. Under these circumstances we indicate that the data are too limited.

There is a tendency for children (and for adults, too) to generalize on the basis of insufficient evidence. Also, there are tendencies to attribute causation, validity and representativeness to data where these qualities are in doubt. On occasion children will use unwarranted analogies and metaphors. They sometimes extrapolate far into the future, and often they attribute meanings to words with a conviction that is not supported by the given data.

Sometimes when we interpret, we first describe and then explain the meaning we have received. Often we separate our interpretations into those that are reasonably sure, those which we think are probably true, and those that seem to us "hunches"—meanings which are possible but which go much beyond the available facts.

Some teachers take brief articles which contain data, and the authors' conclusions, and make copies of them for use by the children. Before distributing them, the teacher makes sure that the children receive only the facts and a statement of the purpose of the study. He then asks the children to write out the meanings which they see in the data. Later, he hands out a sheet which gives the author's inferences from the same evidence. The students now have a chance to compare their interpretations with those of the author. They begin to see the limits of what can be said from a given set of facts. This is excellent training for intelligent living. It disciplines us and makes us more respectful of facts and of the need for facts.

In this connection it may be worth noting that in a number of school-type experiences children may be taught *not* to respect facts or the need for them. In some science laboratories students will carry through a prescribed experiment and if their results do not agree with the answer in the lab manual, they are apt to change what they themselves have discovered. Students have learned that they are "expected" to get answers very similar to those in the manual. In other words, they are apt to have little respect for what they themselves have seen, weighed, or measured. The very fact of difference, of disagreement with the lab manual or text, sets the stage for further thinking, but all too often it is not so interpreted.

Most text books are out of date. They need to be supplemented by currently valid materials. Evidence pertaining to the local community, to its incomes and expenditures, to its products and what is imported and exported, to its population trends, to its budgets for human welfare, to its growth or decline—all these and many more are possibilities for exercises in interpretation. As students interact with data of these kinds, they are acquiring facts which can be of great importance to their own lives and to the life of the community.

The accumulation of meaning in life adds to the richness of living. To ask children to interpret trivia, to have them do it more as an exercise than as a chance to organize their own thinking, is to miss the significance of this thinking operation. Under a competent, informed, patient teacher, learning how to interpret life's experiences is an important milestone along the road to maturity. We may well ask ourselves how often we give our students opportunities to interpret significant data.

Criticizing.

When we criticize we make judgments; we analyze and make evaluations. We do this in terms of some standards that are implicit in our statements or we state the standards explicitly. Criticizing is not a matter of finding fault or of censuring. It involves critical examination of the qualities of whatever is being studied; hence, it is a designation of elements of worth as well as an indication of defects or shortcomings. Ordinarily we have a basis for any criticisms that we make. This basis represents the standards by which we judge. Where we have little or no basis for judging, our criticism is weakened.

Children like to criticize. They like to be asked for their judgments, for their appraisals of objects, of processes, of people's work. They are often able to criticize stories and comics and TV programs; they have a background for criticism of movies, of radio programs, of assembly programs. They may criticize the write-ups of sports, letters to the editor or editorials. They often have judgments to offer about political, social and scientific events.

On the occasion of any criticism it is well to ask for evidence in support of the comments made, to search for the standards which the critic is using and to contrast them with alternative standards which could be applied. It is well to accept criticism from children and to encourage them to reflect upon and to examine the critical comments which they have made. Children should be heard as well as seen, and we can profit much by listening closely when criticisms are being made. In our relationships with children, we should convey the impression of respect for them, and this includes an acknowledgment of their right to criticize, their right to share in formulating the values which will direct their lives.

Some attempt should be made for a comprehensive examination of the subject under scrutiny. We should not lead children into indiscriminate fault-finding as if this were a process of criticism. It is not *balance* in the pros and cons which is sought, but a search for the qualities which are present, and this searching must include the good and the worthy and the average, as well as the poor and unworthy.

Should this be included in your check list of thinking operations? If you were to criticize a book, or a play, or an educational experiment, as you see it, is thinking involved? Is it an activity that should be present frequently in the life of the school children? Where it is done often, and done well, children learn that they should have a basis for what they are saying. As they share with each other, they also learn about the existence of a variety of standards, and the evaluations of these standards by their classmates. Here again, there is a probable contribution to the development of discrimination and sound judgment which, in turn, lead toward greater maturity.

Looking for Assumptions.

In the elementary school these words are not often used, but the underlying idea is operative. By definition an assumption is something that is taken for granted. We may, for example, take for granted that something is probably true, or that something else is probably false. We think of a fact as true, as obvious, as not to be questioned in a particular context. An assumption, on the other hand, may be true, or probably true, or false or probably false; we don't know for sure, and hence, our need "to assume it" in the absence of factual support. We may be *unable* to investigate the relative truth or falsity of the assumed statement; it may take too long to investigate it, and we may need to assume it in order to go ahead with our plans.

The simplest example to come to mind relates to the boy who went to a store and bought two pencils for ten cents. The question is asked: How much did each pencil cost? If we limit ourselves to whole numbers, the answer may be represented by pairs of numbers which add up to ten. If we are to accept five cents as the appropriate answer, we have assumed that the pencils cost equal amounts. It doesn't say so in the statement of the problem. Unless we make some sort of assumption, we cannot emerge with one answer.

In this instance, as in many others, the assumption is concealed or implicit in the solution. We may say that a motorist went 100 miles in two hours, and then ask how far he went each hour. Unless some assumption is made, it is quite impossible to answer the question.

In *every* situation where a conclusion is drawn, one or more assumptions are being made. On occasion it is great fun to look for them. When we buy things, the decision to buy is based on facts and needs and assumptions of one kind or another. We may be assuming the integrity and sincerity of the vendor or the advertiser or the manufacturer. We may be assuming the competency and experience of those who are advising us; we may be assuming that their use of certain words and phrases is the same as ours; we may be assuming causal relations of one kind or another. Always, always, always — there are assumptions involved in the decision making process. We can help children to gain skill and competence in recognizing assumptions.

When we make critical judgments, usually there are standards which have been assumed. When we compare two things, we have assumed that they should be compared in terms of the qualities we have chosen. When we say that something is better because it costs more, we are assuming a relationship between quality and cost. When we measure the educational accomplishments of children by standardized short-answer tests, we are making a number of assumptions.

In mathematics we may look at a proof and analyze the assumptions which are being made. We can look at translations and see the assumptions which a translator probably made. We may look at a scientific experiment, and its conclusions, and look for the assumptions. Usually, assumptions represent gaps in what would constitute proof. They are the things which we take for granted when we accept the conclusion.

The American public is thought of as gullible, as easily persuaded by rather shoddy propaganda, as lacking in critical acumen. Perhaps if the schools spent more time in a critical search for assumptions, the students would develop more discrimination, more discernment, and more resistance to propositions that are poorly based.

What about this assignment of looking for assumptions? Does it have a place in a check list of thinking operations? Should it be a part of a steady educational diet that emphasizes thinking? It should be added that a number of teachers eschew the word completely. Sometimes a phrase like the following is used: If you believe this answer is true, *what else* do you have to believe? Occasionally an arithmetic problem with its solution is presented to children. They are asked to examine it and to answer the above question. Children see it as a game, at first, and then see its tremendous import in the decision making process. Sometimes too, they spend much time on listing what seem to be rather silly assumptions.

These, however, have to be listed, looked at, and evaluated. Through a process of respectful scrutiny children come to see which assumptions are critical; it is this kind of discrimination which is important. Here again there is the possibility of a significant contribution to maturity.

Imagining.

To imagine is to form some kind of idea about that which is not actually present; it is to perceive in the mind what has not been wholly experienced. It is a form of creativeness. We are released from the world of fact and reality and are free to roam where, perhaps, no one has ever been or ever will be. But we roam in fancy. We make mental pictures. In other words, we imagine.

Is this a form of thinking? Do we sometimes describe thinking as imaginative? And do we mean much the same thing when we say: to think creatively? Imagining takes a readiness to leave what is prosaic; it involves inventiveness and originality, a freedom to entertain what is new and different.

When we ask for the release of the imagination we then cannot ask for supporting data. The imagination goes beyond data, beyond our experience. It takes flight from reality. We may ask children in an art class to draw a headache! We may ask for an imaginative account of life in outer space. We may ask what one would do if he had twenty-four hours to live. We may ask for imaginative accounts of the daily life of a cavewoman. We may ask children to project themselves one thousand years into the future and write about the life of that time. We might ask them to imagine history if some event had NOT taken place. We might ask children to invent a language and to try to use it.

To imagine, to invent, to pretend, to create, are ways of liberating us from the demands of the day. We should not want a steady diet of imagining, but surely it has a place in our total scheme of things. It is difficult to defend as a "thinking" operation, but, intuitively, many of us sense that it is associated with and allied to thinking in a larger sense. Whatever is imagined should be accepted as "imagined." The sharing of what we imagine may introduce flexibility into our ways of thinking. What's more, it's fun.

Collecting and Organizing Data.

We seldom give students an opportunity to do independent work. By "independent" we mean work that starts out with a student's own curiosity, his own questions, his own seeking. There is a tendency for us to supply the student with information and to ask him to assimilate it. There are times, of course, when our assignments require him to examine several books and to collate the findings. This is one example of collecting and organizing data. Sometimes a problem may require interviewing, and this in turn may require planning a series of questions. It also requires some planning to determine how the replies to the questions are to be treated. There are occasions when students may formulate some simple questionnaires to distribute to a population from which information is sought. When the questionnaires are returned there is the problem of how to organize the materials and how to present them. There are times when students collect information which is relevant to a long span of time, and the data tend to be organized chronologically. Wherever data are collected, however, there are a number of ways of organizing them, and students should have an opportunity to be confronted with problems of this kind. In the very first section which dealt with *comparing,* students would have an opportunity to see different objects, or processes, or people. When they abstract from each and begin to summarize, they are getting into the problem of organizing the data. Sometimes the audience for whom one is preparing the materials will suggest methods of organization. If we are preparing the report for publication, we might think of several ways of organizing the data. If we are to make an oral report to the class, we might use exhibits. If we have a great deal of time, we might organize our data in great detail. Collecting and organizing data presents challenging thinking situations, and our students need many more opportunities for both. Do you provide opportunities for your students to collect and to organize data?

Hypothesizing.

An hypothesis is a statement which is proposed as a possible solution to a problem. It suggests a way of going at something. Very often it also represents an effort to explain why something will work, and it operates as a guide in going ahead with the solution of a problem. It is tentative and provisional. It represents a guess. Sometimes we restrict the term as in "a working hypothesis." When we are faced with a puzzling situation, an obstacle, a block of some kind, it is almost natural for us to conceive some way out of the dilemma. These hunches or ideas constitute hypotheses. As we become resourceful in suggesting possible solutions to our problem, we become more self-reliant and more independent in our work. Instead of depending upon others for direction, we ourselves suggest possible directions through the formulation of a guiding hypothesis. A resourceful teacher oftentimes presents a problem to a class and asks them to suggest various ways of attempting to solve it. He writes these hypotheses on the blackboard, and students are then asked to consider each of them or some combination of them. Students try to anticipate what would be involved if each were tried and what the consequences might be. This constitutes a preliminary intellectual testing of the idea. If one or several hypotheses seem sound by this testing, further steps are taken. We may have hypotheses about solutions; we may also have hypotheses about sources of data, about the length of time necessary to work on the matter at hand, about the availability of personnel or money, about the relative values which are at stake with different problems. There is little doubt that this imaginative projection of possible solutions to an enigmatic situation is thought provoking. Those who use this kind of assignment find it challenging and interesting to the students. They find also that it emphasizes thinking.

Applying Facts and Principles in New Situations.

This is one of the most common ways by which we now emphasize thinking. The text books are somewhat helpful in this area, and some help is also to be found in a few of the workbooks which are available. A situation is presented in which a solution to some problem is required. Some data are given. The student is "to work it out." Math and science problems come to mind almost immediately as classical examples of this kind of assignment.

In general, a student is supposed to have learned certain principles, rules, generalizations, or laws. He is also supposed to be familiar with relevant facts. The situation which is presented to him is supposed to be new and supposed to be a challenge. Does the student know which principles are applicable here? Does he know how to apply them? Can he supply the relevant facts, if any are missing? Can he disregard irrelevant data if the teacher has purposefully included some?

Sometimes a situation is described, and a student is asked to predict what will happen in the given circumstances. After making his prediction, the student is asked to give his reasons. Presumably, these reasons are the principles and the relevant facts. Sometimes the student is given a description of some past event, and is told the result. He is asked to explain the result in terms of any principles or facts with which he is familiar.

Situations relevant to language and literature, to social studies and the arts, may be improvised in much the same manner. Generalizations or principles from these fields are then supposed to be applied to the solution of the problems.

In general this type of thinking tests our ability to apply facts and principles in situations which are new to us. We have learned them in one context, and we are now being tested to see if we can make use of what we have learned in another context. This involves seeing relationships; noticing what "belongs together" in this new context; discriminating what is relevant from what is irrelevant.

It requires *thought* to see the relevance of principles in a new situation and to be successful subsequently in applying a principle is a valid measure of a sound understanding of the principle. Do your students have opportunities to apply principles in new situations?

Decision-Making.

This is much like the previous operation, with one major exception. In the previous section much emphasis was placed upon laws, principles, generalizations, or rules. In decision-making, these are not omitted, but increased emphasis is given to the role of values. What *should* be done and why? In this case the WHY is supposed to be revealing of the values which the student cherishes. Some teachers, when presenting opportunities for decision making, say to their students: "No matter how this problem may be solved, what *values* do you wish to protect in the solution?" This assumes that values are as, if not more, important than facts in problems which are related to social matters and to personal matters.

Thus far in the history of mankind, we have not paid very much attention to the roles of values in the solution of all kinds of problems. Since the time of the Greeks and before, we have been aware of the possibility (at least) of creating a society in the image of values which we cherish. We have gone beyond the stage of living better and are in a position to create a world after our heart's desire. What do we really want? What are the values we hold dear? What do we prize? Few of us really know what we prize most. Few of us really know the kind of a world we want. And schools pay little or no attention to the clarification of the values held by students.[1]

It is here assumed that if we were to present more decision-making situations to students, if we were to ask more frequently for those values which the student wants protected in the problematic situation, and if these could be shared and examined in a free give-and-take classroom discussion, we might be helping to create a world in which values have a chance to operate.

Are values important in the thinking operations? We think that they are. Our desires, our hopes, our purposes most often generate the power to think. We think in order to achieve ends we hold precious. But all too often, we are unaware of the goals we prize, or we conceal the motives of our actions. It is here assumed that strong lights should be shone on the values which impinge upon problematic situations. These are matters of choice, and choosing is often best served by comparing, observing, imagining, and all the other

---

[1]Louis E. Raths, Merrill Harmin, and Sidney B. Simon, *Values and Teaching* (Columbus, Ohio: Charles E. Merrill Books, Inc., 1966).

operations heretofore mentioned. Certainly decision-making deserves a place among the thinking operations and should be on our check list for monitoring our own teaching practices.

Designing Projects or Investigations.

This assignment may be thought of as more appropriate for junior and senior high school students, but it is also given in the upper grades of the elementary school. A project is a large-type assignment. It usually involves many different activities, takes longer to complete, and is complex enough to call for some kind of preliminary outline before work is started on it. Sometimes a committee assignment is made for the completion of a project, and this involves the planning of a division of labor and the integration of the timing of the several tasks.

A project involves a design for execution of the task, and children, for the first time, get a good idea of the importance of design. If certain questions are to be answered, certain kinds of data have to be gathered. If these data are not gathered, the question cannot be answered. Hence, the project starts out by an attempt to formulate a problem. One way of beginning is to list a series of questions which seem to be worthy of investigation. After some time an attempt is made to sort or to classify these questions. A cluster or group of questions sometimes transforms itself into one large problem.

If this happens, the individual or the committee, is asked to study the problem further. If it is to be solved, what are *all* of the questions which have to be answered? These questions are then analyzed in terms of locating the sources of information which are available. The library in the school is almost always one such source. Newspaper files often constitute another. Appeals are sometimes made to other students in terms of finding out if there are materials available in home libraries.

Sometimes a question cannot be answered by appeal to written sources. Authorities have to be found and letters have to be written to them. If the authorities are local, plans can be made to interview them. Where this is a necessary part of the project, children are taught something about interviewing: how to formulate their questions clearly, how to open the interview by introducing themselves and indicating the purpose of the visit and the investigation, how to close the interview and to thank the authority for his time and trouble.

Before the student goes out for the interview, the teacher goes over the questions and asks the student how he will use the responses when he writes up his results. Does he just want *"Yes* and *No"* types of answers? If so, perhaps he could formulate a short questionnaire and mail it to the authorities. Is he going to quote the authority? If so, what about taking notes? Will he read back the exact statement to the authority before the close of the interview, or will he write back later, and ask permission for a quote which he is enclosing?

Some investigations involve the polling of students and teachers. Usually people are not asked to sign their names and this brings up a question of a facing sheet. Should each respondent indicate his sex, grade level, and other information which might be useful in interpreting the results?

Where students are required to make a preliminary outline of the work of the project, where they are asked to indicate the order in which the separate tasks are to be attacked, where some due-dates are established for completing different parts of the investigation, the work is apt to proceed smoothly.

As the data-gathering nears completion, questions are raised about planning the final report. How will it be done? Is it to be an oral report? If oral or written, how will it be organized? If it is a committee report, who will lead off and who will follow and who will sum up? Are comments to be solicited from the class? Should it be presented to an assembly? If the report is a written one, can it be filed in the library for use by other students in the school?

Some teachers find this kind of curriculum activity exciting, profitable, and very stimulating so far as thinking is concerned. If students are working on a project which is their own, which involves *their* purposes, they are apt to work hard and long at the task. Almost always a significant project involves all of the other operations of thinking which have been discussed—comparing, summarizing, observing, interpreting, looking for assumptions, applying principles, and decision-making, imagining, and criticizing. There is no doubt that designing projects and investigations is very rich in its potentials for engaging in many thinking operations.

Coding.

When students hand in written *work,* it is a common practice today *to correct it* and *to grade it.* Under these circumstances, what are the children learning? Mistakes are found by the teacher and are pointed out to the student. He is asked to correct them, to supply the preferred response. In some situations this is an acceptable procedure. However, it should not be the only way of marking the written papers of students. Assume that we wanted to increase the responsibility which students take for their own thinking. Instead of *grading* the paper, or red-penciling it, could we code it?

If so, how shall we code it? Most of us are familiar with codes which are short-hand methods for indicating various and sundry stylistic shortcomings. How could it be done for thinking?

All-or-None:

We may be interested in the extreme statements used by a student in his writing. As we read his paper, we will be alert to such words as *all, every, each, always, never, nobody, everybody;* we will also look for superlatives: *the best, the worst, the biggest, the nicest, the tallest,* and so forth. We might place an X near the word, or in the margin of the line where it occurs. We could ask the students to take a clean sheet of paper and copy down each sentence with which an X is associated. The student is to answer two questions: 1) does he wish to change any of the sentences, and if so, which ones and how; and 2) in what way are the sentences alike?

Some students may not wish to change any of their "extreme" statements and will say so. *We should accept this decision without objection.* We have given to these students a *second* opportunity to read what they have written, and they have judged it to be appropriate. Each is saying to his teacher: "I will take full responsibility for what I wrote. I want to leave it as it is. I do not wish to change anything."

These students may be embarrassed by the coding and express this feeling by being defiant. Some may not be sensitive to the extremes which have been coded. Some may not care. A class sharing of reactions tends to be positive. The common response is to wonder why such an important matter has not been called to their attention before. Teachers who have used this approach report that subsequent papers reflect a more serious consideration of "extreme" statements.

Either-or's:

We look for the little word *or* and perhaps circle it. We look for such expressions as "there are two ways of doing . . . or three ways or four." Sometimes students will use the expression: *"The other way* of doing it," and this is a concealed *either-or* type of statement. The statement is not marked wrong. It is called to the attention of the student. Does he want to change it? Will he take the responsibility for the statement as it stands? We are trying to teach him to be responsible for what he says. If he is to learn to take responsibility, he must be given the responsibility to decide for himself. In the previous section concerned with extreme statements, the students might have used the word *only* and the teacher may have placed an X beside it. If the student believes it to be appropriate, he does not change it, and *the teacher accepts this decision,* even if at the moment he believes that the student should change it.

It is important for the teacher to code *all* of the extreme statements and *all* of the *either-or's*; not just the ones about which he has some doubts.

Qualifying words and phrases:

In their writings students use such words and phrases as: *it seems, it appears, it's my opinion, perhaps, maybe, might, probably,* and many others. These might be coded with the letter Q, signifying qualifying words. Again, the student is asked to recopy the sentences with which the Q is associated and to indicate how the sentences are alike and any changes he wishes to make. Some students will raise the question: why are these words coded at all, when you seem to be opposed to all (?) kinds of extreme statements? One has to say often that the code does NOT indicate that the teacher opposes the word or phrase. The code suggests that the student should take a second look at what he has written.

Another way of reacting to qualifying words is to have someone make a tabulation of all the qualifying words used by the class and to classify them into groups which have approximately the same meaning so far as degree of conviction is concerned. Under these conditions of self-examination, some students will find that they use certain qualifying words or phrases over and over again to the point of monotony. Some will find that they have a three point continuum noting that things are either *true, false,* or qualified with the expressions *it seems* or *it appears.*

The teacher may draw a long, horizontal line on the blackboard. At the extreme left end of the line he writes the words "absolutely true and absolutely false." At the extreme right end of the line he writes: "complete uncertainty." He asks the class for phrases or words which are very close to these extreme positions and then works the process toward the middle of the line. Students begin to see the meaning of such expressions as *almost without exception, with very few exceptions, almost always, in the large majority of instances, in general, in more cases than not,* and so forth. The idea is to say what we believe and to believe what we say. If we are more sure, our words should indicate that degree of sureness. If we are less sure, we should qualify our statement the more. We should use words with care, so that we communicate our thinking as best we can. We should be developing habits of accuracy of expression, not habits of slovenliness in communication. As teachers we can pay close attention to the ways students use qualifying expressions. We can help them to take a second look at their work, and we can give them the responsibility for deciding upon possible changes.

Value Statements:

Very often students will indicate what they like or dislike, what they want or don't want, what they prefer and what they do not prefer. Value expressions are usually associated with nouns. A teacher might place a V near the word which stands for the value. If something is disliked it might be a V minus (V—) and if it is liked it might be a V plus (V+). The student is to list these words and classify them; then he is to write a summary paragraph about the value expressions he has used. Sometimes he is asked if he has been consistent all the way through. Often he is asked if he has omitted some important values which he would now include.

On many occasions students will not be aware that they are revealing value indicators. They may have been writing a report of an observation in which they were supposed to restrict themselves to sense impressions. Value judgments expressed by students demand attention. What do our students cherish?

When the value indicators are placed on the blackboard, students get some idea of what others cherish. More alternatives come out into the open, and sometimes there is debate about their *value*. It is also a way of getting to know more about one's self. If the teacher helps a student to see what he stands for, he may, on reflection, reject his own stand, but even if he reaffirms his stand, he knows a little more about himself.

Where there is a paucity of value statements in the writings of students, a different type of assignment may help. The decision making kind of assignment is apt to yield many affirmations and denials. As one reads papers with special alertness for value expressions, one begins to know the students better. This is one way of finding out "what makes them tick." If the problems and issues are of great importance to them, they will reveal much about themselves. This is especially true in circumstances where their values are not criticized, or marked wrong — where they are accepted for what they are: value expressions.

Attributions:

In their writings students often give attributions to others. They attribute motives, causes, preferences, feelings, attitudes, beliefs, hopes, aspirations, authority, responsibility, skill, sincerity, hypocrisy, and scores of other human strengths and weaknesses. They are seldom aware that they are "attributing." It seems to them that they are stating "facts." After examination they see how difficult it is to be reliably informed about motives or feelings and how greatly such expressions need to be qualified. These attributions may also be thought of as assumptions and examined for their reasonableness. Teachers code these expressions with an A plus or an A minus and ask the students to list and classify their attributions and to comment upon their expressions.

Where this is started in the elementary grades and carried forward, students will have many opportunities to examine their habits. As with the other codings, in an atmosphere of acceptance and self-examination, children may become much more discerning, discriminating, and responsible in their use of language. This leads to more self-direction towards maturity.

Other Codings:

Some teachers want students to be sensitive about their use of generalizations. Wherever students generalize, the teacher codes the sentence with a G. Some teachers have used special codes for analogies and metaphors. Codes are sometimes used for vague and ambiguous constructions. Some look for the little word *if,* which usually is followed by *then.* Such a statement is often a great oversimplification of the case. Upon re-examination the student may see that the *then* does not logically follow if the *if* is fulfilled. It may take many different *if's* to meet the situation. Some teachers look for statements indicative of suspended judgment. Some look for carefulness in defining terms. Some look for direct correlation statements such as: "to the extent that a student studies, to that extent he will get high grades."

In the elementary grades some teachers code nouns, or adjectives or verbs, and have students examine their use of these terms. In higher grades infinitives and gerunds may be coded and reflected upon. The opportunities are almost unlimited, and what a teacher decides to use will be guided by his own cherished aims and the needs of students.

Coding Other Papers.

When students have become somewhat familiar with a few coding symbols, they may be asked to code some paper which has been selected by the teacher. This may be part of an editorial, a page from a text or a novel, a selection from a children's newspaper or magazine. He is directed to look for the extreme statements in the article, for the value statements, for the *either-or's* and *if-then's*, for the attributions and generalizations, for name-calling and propaganda statements. After he has coded the paper, he is asked to write a critical summary paragraph. This type of assignment teaches observation, summarizing, interpreting, criticizing, and, of course, responsibility. The student is held responsible for the coding he has done and the criticisms he has made.

One cannot make use of this coding operation on *every* paper that a student turns in. Like most assignments, over-use can produce boredom and monotony. There is little doubt, however, that its selective and discriminating use makes a contribution to a program which aims to stress thinking. To respond to the coding made by a teacher, and to code the writings of others, puts an emphasis upon some of the cruder and more common errors of thinking. It deserves a place in a check list for a teacher to use in monitoring his own curriculum materials and his own teaching.

BEHAVIOR AND THINKING

What are some symptoms of human behavior which reflect inadequate experiences with thinking? How significant are these "symptoms?" Do they tend to cut off opportunities to learn and to grow? Are children at all aware of these traits in themselves? Can the present habits or dispositions to act be modified? We have some evidence to indicate that certain behaviors of children change after the introduction of a program which emphasizes thinking. We shall begin by discussing some of these behaviors.

Impulsiveness.

There are some children who seem to react on the spur of the moment to many kinds of stimuli. Teachers often say of them that they go off "half-cocked"; they jump the gun. They begin to respond before the question is asked. In the minds of many teachers, this behavior is closely related to thinking. They say that impulsive children should stop to think, that they should take time to consider the problem and its alternatives. In this volume it is hypothesized that if children had many opportunities for thinking, the tendency toward impulsiveness would diminish. There is research evidence to support the hypothesis that this behavior can be modified. (See Part 5).

Over-dependence upon the teacher.

In practically every classroom there is the child who seems to be forever stuck. The teacher gets the group started, and this child's hand is raised. He indicates that he needs help. The teacher usually tells him how to do steps 1 and 2. A short time later his hand is up again. He now tells the teacher that he has completed steps 1 and 2, but that he needs help on how to go ahead. When this happens again and again, the teacher is quite apt to warn the child that in his life there will be many occasions for thinking when a teacher will not be present, and that he had better soon learn to think for himself. Here again, the teacher relates this over-dependence to a lack of experience and training in thinking. Research evidence suggests that when thinking is given an emphasis in the classroom work, this kind of behavior is modified. The child makes changes in his habits.

Inability to concentrate.

There are children who seem to start off all right in their efforts but soon something happens. Their minds seem to wander; sometimes they seem to be wool-gathering; they do not "pay attention" to their work. Connections between means and ends are missed. A rather thoughtless slip may ruin what was otherwise a good piece of work. Teachers often say of these children that they can't concentrate. It is common for teachers to tell these children over and over again that they should keep their minds on their work, that they should THINK about what they are doing. Notice that teachers connect the behavior directly with thinking. What is needed is a curriculum that puts an emphasis on thinking. *Telling* a child to think doesn't seem to work. We need classroom activities which require thinking operations, and we need to emphasize them year after year.

Missing the meaning.

Teachers say that some children get very little meaning out of their work. If these children are asked to give the gist of a story, they are quite apt to tell the whole story in great detail, or to sum it all up by a sentence or two which does not convey much sense. If a joke has been told and many children are smiling or laughing, these children are apt to ask: What are they laughing at? These children don't seem to see meanings in their experiences; they have little sense of big ideas. Teachers say that they are superficial, not thoughtful; that thinking is over their heads; that it's too deep for them. Yet, when a child so characterized has had frequent opportunities to think under the guidance of an informed teacher, he begins to change. A start has been made on the reconstruction of a habit that has interfered with maturation. Notice again the direct way in which teachers relate this behavior to thinking.

Dogmatic, assertive behavior.

In almost every class there is a child who seems to have all, or almost all, of the answers. He is a frequent user of *either-or's*. Sometimes he is thought of as the class "loud mouth." When he encounters a difference, he is quite apt to try to outshout the opposition. He seldom qualifies a response. Many of his statements are of the *all-or-nothing* kind. He is not sensitive to nuances of expression, to shades of meaning. Where things are probably true, he is apt to assert their unconditional truth. He may be equally assertive about propositions where evidence is lacking. He is sure, in situations where thoughtful people entertain a doubt. This child knows in some way that what he does is not quite right; he knows that he needs help, that something needs to be changed. The teacher knows this, too. The need is for curriculum materials and methods which stress thinking. This kind of child needs a concentrated diet of thinking activities. The research evidence indicates that a semester of work in which almost every day puts forth a requirement for varied kinds of thinking results in noticeable change in behavior.

Rigidity, inflexibility of behavior.

These children seem to be little old men and women long before their time. New ways of doing things seem to frighten them. If the teacher attempts to show one of these children another way by which he might subtract, the child is apt to respond by asking if he can't do it the way he was shown last year. He likes to act in terms of a formula, and he persists in a rigid manner. Some of these children, when asked to redo problems that were incorrect, even repeat their previous mistakes. There is a resistance to new ideas, new materials, new ways of doing things, new situations. There is a preference for the old ways, the known ways, the familiar ways. To think suggests a fresh look at a new situation; to think involves an examination of alternatives and often means the trying of a new hypothesis. These children are in great need of help in meeting situations which involve thought. Teachers relate this behavior to thinking habits and are aware of the need for a continuing emphasis on thinking.

Extreme lack of confidence in one's own thinking.

In this group are the children who almost never volunteer a response to a question which involves thought. If there has been a discussion in class, one of these children is apt to come to the teacher after it is all over and say that he wanted to say something, but he didn't know if it was correct, or he didn't know what the other children might say in criticism. There is a misunderstanding of the purposes of sharing our thinking. There is the idea that one's thoughts must be absolutely true or they should not be uttered. There is a timidity about revealing one's self; a lack of confidence in self. As this child experiences many thinking situations, sees others respond to them, is guided daily in many kinds of thinking operations, he will be apt to share his thinking with colleagues. Extreme lack of confidence in one's own thinking is here regarded as a symptom that is modifiable by a curriculum which emphasizes thinking operations.

Unwillingness to think.

Most of us have had experiences with children who just don't seem to want to think. They want the teacher to outline for them what is to be done, and then, they will do it. They detest independent work, projects, discussions, research. They are the lesson learners of our school society. They don't want to be in any doubt about standards of accomplishment. They believe that the teacher should do the thinking, and that children should give the right answers which are to be found in the texts. These children have habits which tend to make them resistant to change and difficult to work with if the curriculum emphasizes thinking. Steady exposure to many kinds of thinking operations, rewards judiciously applied, and informed, thoughtful guidance all help in getting the processes of change started.

SOME QUALIFYING COMMENTS:

Only eight categories of behavior were listed in association with lack of thinking experience. These were the most frequently mentioned by classroom teachers when so-called thinking-related behaviors were discussed. Are there more? Almost surely there are many more, and thoughtful teachers will recognize relationships between those other behaviors and thinking. Are these categories offered as iron-tight, with no over-lapping? Not at all. We do not have categories of behavior of that kind. These categories represent a rather crude way of going about a diagnosis. A child does not fit exactly into one of the categories; he approximates it. He is not *just like that* all of the time and in all situations. Teachers, however, have found these categories helpful in pointing a direction for teaching.

Is it certain that the "cause" of the foregoing behaviors is always and in every instance related to thinking? The contrary is probably true. Wherever a child is having difficulty in learning, the first step should be a careful physical examination by competent, thoughtful, informed medical doctors. We should rule out from our "non-thinking" group those children who are ill. In the second place, some children have deep emotional needs which are not being met, and these children too should be ruled out as having thinking-related behaviors. Where children are unusually and abnormally aggressive, hostile, or belligerent, where they are excessively shy and withdrawn, where they are submissive and meek, and where there is evidence of frequent regression to behavior that represents an earlier stage of development, we infer the presence of un-met emotional needs.[2]

In the preliminary trials of the materials and methods which receive extended treatment in the next two chapters, a number of teachers commented on the necessity for developing a feeling of security in children before emphasizing assignments relating to thinking. This seems to be sound advice. Thinking is sometimes unsettling; doubt is often disturbing; the trying out of new ideas has suspense and anxiety as correlates on many occasions. Where children are emotionally insecure, emphasis should first be placed upon the meeting of emotional needs.

The eight categories of behavior are associated with inadequacies in thinking. Children whose behavior seems to coincide with the descriptions in one or more of the categories have probably practiced these particular habits for a long period of time. Helping a child to change a habit is not the work of a moment, or an afternoon, or a week. It is a cooperative venture that may take many months. It requires a continuing exposure to thinking situations. In addition, it is also the thoughtful, friendly, patient, careful work of a competent teacher who identifies with the child in need of help. On the other hand, a teacher with all of these qualifications may experience frustration unless he is familiar with materials and practices which relate to the thinking processes. It is the integration of the two which promises most in terms of change.

---

[2]Louis E. Raths and Anna P. Burrell, *An Application to Education of the Needs Theory* (South Orange, N.J.: Economics Press, 1951).

Why is it that one child in a family may show one or more of the behaviors described in these eight categories, while brothers and sisters will not? We have no good answer for this question. Though children in the same family are said to have the same environment, this is questionable on many grounds. The same question is unanswered with respect to illnesses and particularly to communicable illnesses. It may be that without our being aware of it, some children miss frequent opportunities to carry on thinking processes.

What happens to children if no special emphasis is placed on thinking? We cannot answer the question with respect to a particular child, but there is evidence which indicates that a child who is impulsive, for example, will probably be categorized the same way, the following year, by his new teacher. In some schools where comments about children's habits and character are solicited from teachers annually, there is a surprising amount of repetition. In some quarters this is accepted as evidence that the child is not yet ready for change!

Piaget and others have been much interested in the changes which take place from year to year in the ways children think. Their conclusions are often generalized by age levels and by stages of development, and in several instances have been associated with the history of human development from the earliest time. It should be quite clear that the evidence pertains to children who have had little or no instruction in thinking and little guidance in the development of habits which stress thinking. Probably the results have more to do with neglect and chance, than with the "natural" evolution of man.

Isn't it true that in human development good things tend to go together? Aren't those who remember the facts the best more likely to be the best thinkers? At the college level the correlations between scores on information tests and scores on thinking tests tend to be low. At the elementary school level even the scores on intelligence tests tend to correlate with thinking test scores at a level of .50 or below, and oftentimes at the level of .30. As a matter of fact, when teachers begin to emphasize thinking operations, they find that certain students who were not doing well with the routine exercises now begin to excel and some students who have excelled at memoriter tasks need much help in assignments that emphasize thinking. There is probably some correlation among the "good" traits and habits, but it is not so high as is generally posited. Certainly one cannot take for granted that a person who does well on a factual type exam will also do well on a test which requires thinking.

Is it the responsibility of teachers to change the behaviors of children? What about the parents? What about other social institutions which have contacts with children? In one sense, to aim at the changing of children suggests that we will manipulate them in ways to satisfy our own ends. Who is to decide if and how children are to be changed? Shall we consult with parents and get their consent to our aims? Should we ask them how they want the schools to change their children?

Schools and teachers don't do just as they please. Through a Board of Education, in cooperation with educational leaders, broad policies are determined. Almost always such statements of educational aims include items associated with self-direction and independent thought. As we see it, teachers have a real responsibility to develop a curriculum which provides many opportunities for thinking. This is a major task. The school need not take responsibility for change; the child will take that responsibility if the educational diet is rich in experiences associated with a variety of thinking operations. It is hard to see how a child can take this responsibility if the school does not have trained, insightful, thoughtful, considerate teachers, who supply thinking opportunities.

There is much evidence from research into test results that children forget a great deal of what they learn in school. R. W. Tyler[3] and James E. Wert[4] conducted some studies into the lack of recall of college students. They found that the thinking skills which were learned — interpreting data and applying principles — were not forgotten, but the specific fact type of learning was not retained very well. This may be another reason for putting an emphasis upon thinking: it is a skilled habit which is likely to be retained.

CONCLUSION

Fifteen ways of emphasizing thinking have been presented in this chapter. Nowhere has it been suggested that this is an all-inclusive listing. While many thinking operations are frequently used in our classrooms, it is also probably true that few teachers consistently emphasize their use. On the other hand, in typical school practices, one is apt to see as much emphasis upon these operations in the kindergarten as in a junior high school or college classroom.

It is not uncommon to find high school teachers who will say that their students are not ready to think about problems; hence, these same teachers tend to emphasize a teaching function which puts great emphasis upon imparting information. The concept of *higher mental processes* may suggest to some that the mental processes operative in high school youth are quite different from those carried on by children in the elementary school. When one finds, however, that nearly all of these operations may be observed in the very early grades of elementary school, it raises a question about what is meant by higher mental processes. It probably means processes which distinguish human beings from lower orders of animals. It does not mean uniquely different processes for different age levels in the development

---

[3]R. W. Tyler, "Permanency of Learning," *Journal of Higher Education,* IV (April, 1933), 203-204.

[4]J. E. Wert, "Twin Examination Assumptions," *Journal of Higher Education,* VIII (March, 1937), 136-140.

towards maturity. Children in the elementary school, adolescents in our secondary schools, and the older students in our colleges all need continuing practice in these thinking operations.

If we emphasize these operations more in the early years of education, we shall develop students who employ more caution in making judgments and drawing conclusions. We shall have students who see more than one course of action. We shall have students who are looking for alternatives and delving for assumptions. We shall have students who prize doubt. They will be more open-minded and perhaps more ready for change in a great number of areas. They will probably have a more experimental outlook on life, and instead of being resistant to problems, they will probably welcome them. There is little doubt that the beginnings of a great university are to be found in the public schools of a nation. The better our base the more we can look forward to the flowering of a compassionate and intelligent study of man and his problems. To put an emphasis upon thinking is to take a first long step toward an improvement of the human situation.

part two

APPLICATION: THE ELEMENTARY SCHOOL

INTRODUCTION

Bob walked to the sink in the back of his classroom. The drain was clogged with plaster of Paris, and Bob groaned with dismay.

"Look here, at this sink," he said. "You know why this thing's clogged? It's cheap!"

Later on that day, during a class discussion, Bob said, "You know, we eat protozoa."

When asked how he had determined this, he volunteered, "Well, you said that meat has cells and we eat meat, so we eat protozoa."

A few days later, Bob approached his teacher with a science textbook in his hand, saying, "You see, I was right. Dinosaurs are not reptiles. It says in this book here that there are about 5,000 kinds of dinosaurs. The word *dinosaur* means *terrible lizard*. But dinosaurs were not lizards. They were not even close relatives of the lizards — so you see, they're not even reptiles."

During a class discussion on problems existing for the African in the Union of South Africa, the following interchange was recorded between this sixth grade student and his teacher:

Bob: "There's something I don't understand."

Teacher: "What's that, Bob?"

Bob: "Well, when there was a slavery problem down south in our country, the northern states fought them and won the war, and the slaves were freed. So why don't the people in North Africa go to war against South Africa and free the slaves there?"

How many times have you, as a teacher, been confronted with a question or a statement that has almost defied response because the reasoning behind it was so illogical? In the face of reasoning of this type, how do you react? Do you become utterly frustrated? Do you sit down at your desk and throw

your hands up in despair? Do you want to get your hat and leave the classroom — perhaps forever? Maybe you wish that just for one moment you
could pick the child up by his feet, shake him like a salt cellar, and restore
his logic by the simple rearrangement of the blood cells in his brain! Perhaps
you want to point out to the child the faulty reasoning in his statement.
Taking the last illustration as an example, how might you begin to show Bob
that the situations which he saw as analogous really have no relationship?
At that moment how could you help him to understand that his statement
is illogical? If you've tried it, you have probably found that Bob doesn't
understand your explanation at all. He doesn't really see why the situations
in America and Africa are not parallel.

Bob is in the sixth grade. How has he gotten so far in school with such poor
ability in thinking? An examination of his school records reveals that his I.Q.,
as measured by a standard group intelligence test, is 116. His report cards
and achievement test scores for previous grades show average performance.
What does it mean?

In this particular case, Bob was found to be a boy who lacked experiences
in thinking. His reasoning, as shown in the above examples, was often
illogical. Apparently, this did not affect his grades or his I. Q. score — or
did it? What might his I. Q. score and his scholastic performance be if Bob
could apply principles of logic?

Bob had been a "behavior problem" since the first grade. His first grade
teacher stated that his work habits and general attitude were poor and that
although he had done sufficiently adequate work for promotion to second
grade, she felt that he could have been near the top of the class if he had
only applied himself. His second grade teacher indicated that she was constantly after him to get his work done, and that he just wasn't trying. His
third grade teacher revealed that he was a behavioral disturbance in class.
In the fourth grade, his teacher felt that he was capable of doing his work
quickly, but that he procrastinated and was the last to finish. Bob's fifth grade
teacher, a man, exercised considerable control over him, with the threat of
severe punishment. He stated that Bob was not a behavior problem in his
class. The sixth grade teacher, however, found that Bob needed close supervision and structuring and that he seemed totally unequipped to function
independently.[1]

Upon investigation, it was determined that Bob was extremely "impulsive,"
extremely "loud, dogmatic and assertive" and that he "actively resisted thinking" (These behavioral types have been discussed in detail on pages 24-26.)

Bob was not able to apply principles of logic in his school work. He lacked

---

[1]Selma Wassermann, "A Study of the Changes in Thinking-Related Behaviors in a
Selected Group of Sixth Grade Children in the Presence of Selected Materials and
Techniques" (Unpublished Ed.D. dissertation, School of Education, New York Uni-
versity, 1962).

experiences in thinking. Had he been exposed to many exercises requiring comparisons, he might, perhaps, have been able to see how the North and South in the United States differed from Northern and Southern Africa. Had he been given many experiences in which he was required to suggest hypotheses, he might, perhaps, have seen other reasons for the sink being clogged. Had he been more skilled in observing and classifying, he might, perhaps, have understood the relationship between meat and protozoa, the relationship of dinosaurs to lizards and reptiles.

Educators today are paying a great deal of attention to the development of thinking skills in our schools. Yet, in spite of much discussion on the merits of programs which emphasize thinking, how many teachers can say, "These are some ways in which I am developing thinking processes in my children?" When an elementary teacher plans his day, he is likely to include some work in reading, in math, in spelling, creative writing and grammar, in science, in social studies, and perhaps some music and art. These subject areas are usually allotted blocks of time in the teacher's plans and often, as with reading or math, a page number accompanies the subject specified to indicate to the teacher just where in a specific text the work for that day is to begin. In how many teachers' daily plans is there a block of time allotted to the development of thinking skills? Ideally, teaching for thinking should occur within the framework of any given subject. But do we know precisely — as precisely as we know the steps of a developmental reading program, for example — *how* to teach for thinking?

When approached on the subject of teaching for thinking, teachers have responded in a number of ways, expressing various points of view. The following five statements have been found to be those most representative of teachers' reactions:

Teacher A: Believes that thinking should be developed within the subject matter through the use of specific techniques which promote thinking.

Teacher B: Believes that when he does a first-rate job of teaching a particular skill, increased thinking ability comes about simultaneously, as the child learns the skill.

Teacher C: Believes that there are some moments which arise in teaching when thinking is promoted. These are usually unplanned.

Teacher D: Believes that thinking skills are developed in children simply because they are human, and the teacher, therefore, need not be concerned about focusing the curriculum on thinking at all.

Teacher E: Would like to place more emphasis on teaching for thinking, but does not know exactly how this can be done.

Let us pose several questions which come to mind for some of the above teachers to consider.

Can Teacher A tell us what techniques can be used to promote thinking within the subject matter?

Can Teacher B tell us how it is possible that a sixth grade boy like Bob, who has shown good academic skills in reading and math, has such difficulty reasoning logically? If good teaching in the subject areas will automatically increase thinking ability, what has happened to this boy and others like him?

Can Teacher C tell us if unplanned teaching episodes, however successful and inspired, would be considered adequate for the development of a successful math program, or a science program? Is it reasonable to expect that this type of teaching is adequate for the development of thinking skills?

Can Teacher D cite reasons for the immaturity in thinking in a boy like Bob and the many children like him in the elementary schools, the high schools and even the colleges?

For Teacher E, there are no questions posed, but rather a suggestion to read on. For it is the intent of this part of the book to provide the elementary classroom teacher with specific and practical suggestions which will help him to focus on thinking in his teaching.

USING THE ACTIVITIES

If teaching for thinking is to succeed, it must be a planned part of the elementary school program; without such planning we are in danger of producing a crop of future citizens who — like Bob — have grades which reflect adequate scholastic achievement, but who reveal immaturity of thought. Teaching for thinking can occur in the elementary classroom, and this may be done within the framework of the existing curriculum. It is not necessary to revise the curriculum. Existing curriculum may serve as a basis for a planned program of teaching for thinking.

In Part 1 it was noted that there are a number of operations which relate to thinking. (See pages 6-23). It is suggested here that the elementary teacher develop classroom activities for his students which involve the operations of *observing, comparing, classifying, hypothesizing, looking for assumptions, criticizing, imagining, collecting and organizing data, coding, problem solving, decision-making, summarizing,* and *interpreting.* If children are given, daily, some opportunities to compare, to criticize, to decide, etc., they will be acquiring experience in thinking which will help them to mature.

Should the reader now consider the remainder of this part a manual of instruction, guaranteed to produce "thinking" children by the end of the school year, he is cautioned and asked to reflect upon the following.

The activities listed in this section are based upon hypothetical children in hypothetical classes. For that reason alone, they should *not* be considered by the teacher as the *only,* or *best,* procedures to be utilized in a given grade. The activities in the following pages represent examples. A teacher may adopt them for use with children when he finds the activity appropriate to need, to interest, and to ability. The teacher may modify some. He may use some as a guide to develop activities of his own, he may reject some completely in favor of those he himself develops as more suitable for his particular class. It is hoped that the activities to follow will be used by the resourceful teacher in many of the above ways.

The modern teacher is aware that in most classes the interests and capabilities of the children form the basis for the selection of curriculum materials. It is for each teacher, then, to determine the wisest use of the thinking activities. Perhaps some of them will be applicable to the entire class. Others might be considered for use with individual or small groups of children. Hopefully, each teacher will design an infinite number of thinking activities which revolve around the curriculum for that grade and which reflect the different needs, abilities, and experiences of his own group of children.

The activities to follow are presented in three different groupings. Each is based upon the reading abilities of the children for whom the activities are intended. The first group of activities has been constructed for children who cannot read and for those who are just beginning to read. The second group is meant for children who are just beginning to gain fluency in reading. The final group of activities is designed for those children who are skilled readers. There has been a deliberate attempt *not* to assign grade levels to these groupings, since we recognize that in many grades there exists a wide range of reading abilities among the children. It is suggested that the teacher consider activities from each section for possible use with his class.

THINKING ACTIVITIES FOR PRE- AND BEGINNING READERS

Observing.

When we ask children to make observations, we are, in a sense, asking them to obtain information in many different ways. In giving primary children experiences in observing, the teacher seeks out those tasks which are designed to give practice in *noticing* and *describing*. These tasks may include noticing and describing objects, conditions, events, pertinent details, etc. In the descriptions, the children are helped to ascertain the difference between what is *actually* observed, and what is *assumed*. For example, the teacher might ask the children to notice what he is doing and then to describe it. If the teacher gets up from his chair, walks over to the window and closes it — and the child describes the teacher getting up from his chair, walking over to the window, closing the window *because the teacher was cold* — the teacher helps the child to see that he has made an assumption. This might be done through skillful questions, such as, "How did you know I was cold?" or "For what other reasons might I have closed the window?" In this way, the child might be led to understand the difference between what he actually saw and what he assumed to be true.

Not all observations need be visual. Some may involve listening, some touching, or feeling, some smelling or tasting. In each case, the children are helped to understand the difference between what was *actually* observed and what assumptions, if any, were made from the observation. (For a more detailed description of this operation, see pp. 7-8.) The following list of *Observing* activities is suggested for use with children who have minimal reading skills.

1. Show a picture from a magazine or book. Ask the children to name *all* the things they see.
2. Show a picture of a person. Ask the children to describe him.
3. Show a picture of an animal. Ask the children to describe it.
4. Show a picture of something occurring. Ask the children to tell what is happening.
5. Ask the children to look around the room. Ask them to describe what they see.
6. Ask the children to look outside. Have them describe what they see.
7. Have the children observe the weather each hour for one day. Ask them to tell what they saw.
8. Show a picture of someone at work. Ask children to describe the work. Ask the children to tell what equipment the person needs for his job.
9. Show a picture that has several small details. Ask children to tell what they see.
10. If there is a class pet, ask children to observe his behavior during a specified time, and describe what they saw.
11. Ask children to observe and describe proper care for a pet.
12. Plant some seeds. Ask children to observe daily what they see and to describe it.
13. Ask children to observe and describe care of plants.
14. Place an onion (potato, lima bean, sweet potato, or other vegetable) in water. Ask children to observe and describe daily what they see.
15. Arrange for a trip to the boiler room of the school. Ask children to describe what they saw. Ask them to describe what they heard. What did they smell?
16. Visit the principal's (nurse's, assistant principal's) office. Ask children to describe what they saw and heard.
17. Take a walk around the school building (inside, outside). Ask children to describe their experiences.
18. In a walk around the outside of the school, taken at least once a month, children may observe and note differences (if any) produced by seasonal weather conditions.

19. Ask children to watch mother preparing dinner (or baking a cake) and describe what they saw.
20. Ask children to tell what they saw on the way to school.
21. Some first graders will be able to look at the structure and the letter make-up of a word and describe it.
22. Ask children to observe the sky. (Different children may observe at different times of the day, or on different days.) Ask them to describe what they saw. Perhaps some comparisons could be made by children who observed at different times.
23. Ask children to observe their shadows at different times during the day. Ask them to describe what they saw.
24. Play a musical record. Ask children to describe what they heard.
25. Ask children to close their eyes for a few moments. Have them describe the sounds that they heard.
26. Give the children an opportunity to touch various kinds of materials (such as velvet, silk, muslin, burlap, etc.). Have them describe what they saw and felt.
27. Ask the children to sample various kinds of spices (such as salt, pepper, cinammon, nutmeg). What do they notice about the taste of each? What do they notice about the smell?
28. Ask the children to describe the taste of such foods as candy, apple pie, lettuce, bread. What do they notice about the smells of these foods?

Comparing.

In providing opportunities for children to compare, the teacher first clarifies for the children the concept of comparing. When a person compares two things, he not only looks for similarities, but dissimilarities as well. For example, one first grade teacher asked her class to think of many ways in which trains and airplanes were alike. She then asked them to tell some ways in which trains and airplanes were different. Here again, it would be important to help the child to ascertain the difference between what is demonstrably true and what he assumes to be true. If a child were to say that trains and airplanes were alike because they both had wheels, this would be true only if seaplanes were excluded from the comparison. Otherwise, the concept of planes with wheels would have to be qualified — e. g., planes landing on hard ground have wheels. In selecting items for comparison, the tendency is often to choose things that have some apparent relationship to each other, such as two books, two cars, two toys, two people, etc. When a person is asked to compare two things which have no apparent relationship, such as a *train* and a *book,* he might say, "You can't compare them," or "They defy comparison." However, upon examination and reflection, it is possible to find similarities as well as differences between two seemingly very alien items. Furthermore, many teachers are often surprised by the perceptive observations of children who make these comparisons. (For a more detailed description of the operation of comparing, see page 6.) The following is a list of some of the many things which might be compared by primary children.

1. Compare two animals in a story read by the teacher (such as Father Bear and Baby Bear in *The Three Bears*; two of the *Three Little Pigs,* etc.).

2. Compare two people in a story read by the teacher (such as Snow White and Sleepy, in *Snow White and the Seven Dwarfs*; Cinderella and Step-Mother in *Cinderella*).

3. Compare two characters from different stories read by the teacher (such as Cinderella and Snow White; Goldilocks and Sleeping Beauty; Peter Pan and The Little Prince).

4. Compare two stories which have been read by the teacher.

5. Compare two songs which the children sing.

6. Compare two pieces of music which the children dance to.

7. Compare two pictures from a magazine.

8. Compare two paintings by famous artists.

9. Compare two photographs.

10. Compare two wild animals (two domestic animals, a wild animal and a domestic animal).

11. Compare two leaves.

12. Compare two plants.

13. Compare two flowers; a plant and a flower; a leaf and a flower.

14. Compare a flower and a painting.

15. Some children in this group will be able to compare two words. Some may be able to compare two sentences.

16. Compare two holidays (Christmas and Washington's Birthday; Thanksgiving and Easter).

17. Compare two poems which have been read by the teacher.

18. Compare two numbers (such as 4 and 7).

19. Some children in this group may be able to compare two math examples (such as *2 plus 2* and *1 plus 3*).

20. Some children may be able to compare a ruler with a measuring cup.

21. Some children may be able to compare a $\frac{1}{2}$ pint milk container with a quart milk container.

22. Compare winter and summer; fall and spring, etc.

23. Compare a butterfly and a bird.

24. Compare mother's work and father's work.

25. Compare two tools (used in class) such as a scissors and a paintbrush; a hammer and a saw; a pencil and a paintbrush.

26. Compare the teacher and the principal.
27. Compare a bird and an airplane.

Classifying.

In the process of classifying, the children are asked to arrange a variety of items according to categories, or groups. It is essential that the categories have a relationship to each other. For example, if a child were classifying the books he had read during the school year, he might set up one of the following classifications:

BOOKS I LIKED; BOOKS I DID NOT LIKE.

or

FUNNY BOOKS; ADVENTURE BOOKS; MYSTERY BOOKS; SAD BOOKS.

or

BOOKS ABOUT ANIMALS; BOOKS ABOUT BOYS; BOOKS ABOUT SPACE;
BOOKS ABOUT AIRPLANES.

or

FICTION; NON-FICTION.

A more sophisticated child might think of a number of additional ways in which he might classify his books. However, the teacher must be alert to point out to a child that his categories are not related if, for example, he should classify his books as follows:

BOOKS I LIKED; BOOKS ABOUT ANIMALS; NON-FICTION.

For first experiences with classification for primary children, it is advisable at the outset for the teacher to set up the categories and ask the children to place the items in the appropriate groups. For example, if the teacher had a collection of pictures from a magazine, he might invite the children to group them according to:

THOSE WHICH SHOW PEOPLE PLAYING; THOSE WHICH SHOW
PEOPLE WORKING.

The same pictures might be used again and again for different kinds of groupings. After the children have had many varied experiences grouping according to categories set up by the teacher, they might then be initiated to the kind of classification in which they themselves set up the groups.

It is believed that the *setting up* of the categories, or groupings, is a more complex process while the placing of the objects into the groups is a more routine, or menial, task. Therefore, it is advisable for the teacher to set up the groups for the children primarily as an *initiating* experience into the operation of classifying.

An important element in setting up groups is to determine whether the grouping is *purposeful*. The child may be asked to defend his classification, revealing *why* he has made *those* groups. In other words, he is helped to understand that grouping objects into categories ought to be purposeful to him. Different kinds of groupings might serve different purposes. His purpose, therefore, will determine the nature of the categories.

For example, if the child is asked to classify an assortment of blocks, he might group them according to which ones fit on the wider shelf and which fit on the narrower one. This type of grouping might suit one purpose. Or he might group them according to the shapes, like *rounds* and *rectangulars*, if his purpose is to use them in building. (See page 9 for a more detailed description of this operation.)

The following is a list of some of the many things which might be found in school and at home which can be grouped by primary children.

1. Pictures (cut from magazines)
2. Story books
3. Crayons
4. Buttons
5. Blocks
6. Classroom tools (such as pencils, scissors, crayons, paintbrushes, etc.)
7. Reading vocabulary words
8. Foods
9. Jobs of the fathers of the children in class
10. Airplanes
11. Boats
12. Cars
13. Vehicles used for transportation
14. Animals (this can be further broken down into categories of each of the classes, such as birds, mammals, reptiles)
15. Pets of children in class
16. Weather
17. Musical instruments (from rhythm bands)
18. Numbers
19. Toys
20. Activities children engage in after school
21. The teacher might himself group a number of items and then ask that the children determine how those items were grouped.

Collecting and Organizing Data.

This operation involves the accumulation of information on a given topic and the arrangement of that information according to a logical pattern or sequence. In the middle and upper grades, where most children are fluent in reading and writing, the mechanics involved present little problem. Pre- and beginning reading children, however, need not be kept from participation in this operation because of their limited reading and writing skills. They may collect information orally, from a resource person (such as mother, father, teacher, librarian) and they may orally relate that information in an organized form for the benefit of the class. Here the teacher's role is to help and guide the child in the arrangement of the information in an orderly pattern or developmental sequence. This may be accomplished by asking questions, such as, "What came first?" or "What happened then?" (See page 15 for a more detailed description of this operation.)

The following topics suggest themselves as possibilities wherein very young children may collect and organize data:

1. Ask children to find out what materials are needed to paint a picture. Ask them to suggest ideas for the organization of these materials.
2. Ask children to find out what materials are necessary to make puppets. Ask them to plan the working procedure once the materials have been assembled.
3. Ask the children to discover what materials would be needed to construct a boat of wood. Ask them to plan the sequence of the project.
4. Ask the children to determine what would be necessary to make a collage. Help them to determine the sequence of carrying out this project.
5. Ask children to find out what foods make a "balanced" breakfast. Is there a generally accepted sequence of eating these foods?
6. If there is a child whose parent plays a musical instrument, he might be asked to find out what he can about that instrument and tell the class about it.
7. Some children might be asked to think about certain characters in stories which are familiar to them and prepare to tell the class about a sequence in a story which they found funny, or sad, or exciting, etc.
8. If a school library or neighborhood library is visited by the class, the children might be asked to find out what they can about the library and to organize their information back in the class in an experience chart story about the library.
9. Some primary graders might be able to get some information on the telephone and talk about how to use the telephone successfully.
10. Several possibilities exist for collecting and organizing data in the curriculum area of science. The ability of the children in the group should guide the teacher in making appropriate selections from the following topics:
    10.1 How does the weather affect our dress?
    10.2 How does the weather affect our play?
    10.3 How does the weather affect our food?

10.4 How do we take care of plants? (Some teachers may want to use those plants which are growing in the classroom and are cared for by the children. Other teachers, who work in rural or suburban schools may want to include those plants growing in the gardens of the children's homes.)

10.5 How do we take care of animals? (Some children may want to "report" on the care of their pets. If there is a class pet, this may easily be utilized. A trip to the zoo or the farm would also provide many experiences for the children to discover information on the care of animals.)

10.6 What can we find out about airplanes? trains? boats?

10.7 What can we find out about the wheel?

11. Ask children to find out about holidays celebrated by their families. Perhaps small groups of children could work together to find out about different holidays and their traditions and then relate their information to the class.

12. Many primary children will be able to obtain information on the various communications media (TV, radio, telephone). Each of these could be discussed from many viewpoints such as, "How we use it at home," or "What it would be like without it."

13. Many children might be asked to find out about their father's job and tell about it in class. This might be the basis for a social studies unit on Daddies!

14. "How we travel" might be a topic of interest for some children to collect information about.

15. Perhaps a child would like to instruct a group in the rules of a new game which he has learned outside of school.

16. Ask children to find out about what happens when certain foods are cooked, such as rice or noodles.

17. Ask children to find out and tell how butter is made. Perhaps a plan for this could be worked out and butter made in class.

18. Ask children to find out how mother makes cookies. What are the steps that she follows? If baking facilities are available in school, perhaps these steps could be carried out by the children.

19. Ask children to find out how Jello is made and tell the steps involved. Can Jello be made in class?

Summarizing.

Because of the limited reading and writing ability of most primary grade children, the activities involving summarizing must be essentially oral in character. When a teacher asks young children to summarize, however, the major task he will face will be to help the child to relate only those facts which are essential and significant. Any teacher who has worked with highly verbal primary children will readily testify to their verbosity and their reluctance to pare down a story to its essential facts. Often a primary child will not only relate a story in great detail, but will add his own embellishments. A teacher who wishes to develop the skill of summarizing in primary children not only must help the child to recognize the essentials of content and structure, but also must do this without hurting the child's feelings by cutting off his fanciful embellishments. One way to initiate experiences with summarizing is to read a story to the group, then work together with the group to elicit (or tell outright, if need be) what was important, which were the key episodes, and what irrelevant material could be discarded for the sake of the summary. (For a more detailed description of this operation, see page 6.) The following list is suggested for use with children at the pre- and beginning reading levels.

1. Ask children to summarize a story read to the class.
2. Have children draw, in a four-picture sequence, the major events of a story.
3. Ask a child to summarize the part of the story that he liked best.
4. Ask the children to summarize the funniest (saddest, most exciting) part of the story.
5. Ask the children to think of a title for a story read to them.
6. Ask the children to summarize a movie shown in class.
7. Ask the children to summarize a television program which they enjoyed.
8. Sometimes there is a television program which the teacher suggests that the children view. They may then be asked to summarize that program.
9. Ask the children, at the end of the school day, to tell the key events of that day.
10. Ask the children to summarize what they did on Saturday or Sunday at home.
11. Often a picture tells a story. Children may be asked to suggest captions, or titles for pictures.
12. Some first and second grade children subscribe to classroom magazines, such as *News Pilot* or *News Ranger*. Articles in either magazine may be used as the basis for requesting summaries.
13. A science demonstration performed by the teacher may be summarized by the class.
14. If the children have participated in a field trip, they might be asked to summarize the events of their experiences.

Looking for Assumptions.

In developing in primary children the ability to determine the difference between assumption and fact, the teacher helps them to understand the meaning of the word *assumption* and the nature of making assumptions. While this might present more of a problem to the kindergarten teacher than it ordinarily would to a sixth grade teacher, for example, it is still possible for many kindergarten children to understand this concept. The teacher might, for example, phrase this idea in words which are more familiar to the young child, such as, "What is really true here?" and "What did you guess to be true?" The teacher is urged, at this point, not to *reject* the assumptions of children, but only to help the children understand that assumptions are being made. Actually, we adults go through life making numerous assumptions, almost without question. A critical-minded person, however, recognizes that he is making assumptions and does not treat his asumptions as facts.

When children are provided with many opportunities to look for assumptions, it is reasonable to suppose that they may develop greater skill in recognizing assumptions which they themselves make. (For a more detailed description of this operation, see page 12.) The following is a list of some of the many different experiences which children may have in looking for assumptions.

1. Show the children two differently-shaped containers each holding a quantity of water. Ask which contains more water. (Help them to understand that the only accurate way to determine which container holds more water is to measure it.)
2. Show the children a candy bar. You are going to divide this candy bar between Peter and Hildegarde. How much will each have? (If children say that both Peter and Hildegarde will have equal shares, you may break off $\frac{1}{8}$ and give it to Peter, giving the rest to Hildegarde. Ask them if they guessed or how they knew that each child would have an equal share.)
3. Show children the good side of a wormy apple. Ask if this is a good apple. Ask how they can tell if it is good.
4. Put twelve blocks in a box. Have four children pick out two blocks each. Ask children how many blocks were in the box. For those who say "eight" ask how they knew that.
5. Show children a larger box and a smaller one. Ask which one is heavier. (The larger one may be empty and the smaller one may contain two books.) Ask the children how they could really decide which box was heavier.
6. Ask the children to look at a picture of a dog (or cat). Ask them if they can really tell if the animal is happy or sad.
7. Show the children a picture of a man dressed in a business suit. Ask them if they can tell what his job is. (Actually he is a carpenter, but this is Sunday and he's going to church!)
8. Ask the children to tell what they see in the classroom. Help the chil-

dren to understand the difference between what they really see and what they are assuming is there.

9. Ask the children to look at the sky and to predict the weather. Help them to understand that these are guesses. Perhaps a discussion about qualifying words would help to clarify here. There's a difference between saying, "It's going to rain" and "It looks as if it might rain!"

10. Often children are quick to assume that someone (person or pet) is responsible for some damage when they have not actually seen the act, but have only seen the results. If a picture can be obtained of a cat surveying a pile of broken pottery, you might ask the children "Who broke the dishes?" and "How do they know?" (Actually, the dog broke them and he was smart enough to run away!)

11. Ask the children what's wrong with the following kinds of statements:

    11.1 Billy (substitute a child's name from your class) came late to school this morning because he overslept.

    11.2 Harry doesn't have a dog because he doesn't like dogs.

    11.3 Peter is painting because he is tired of building with blocks.

Hypothesizing.

The primary objective in giving the children experiences with this operation is to help them to understand and consider the variety of possibilities which may be involved in arriving at the solution of a problem. If the primary teacher does not wish to work with the word *hypothesis,* alternate possibilities are available which might bring the concept into sharper focus for the children. For example, in dealing with the following problem—

> The block corner had not been properly cleaned up after playtime and there were a number of blocks left on the floor.

—the teacher might ask the children to think about the problem for a few minutes and to suggest several *guesses,* or *possibilities* as reasons for this occurrence. The children should be helped to recognize that each suggestion is only one of several possibilities and not necessarily the actual reason for the occurrence. Children must also be helped to understand that it will take further examination (or, in later grades, we might say *testing*) of each hypothesis or suggestion before we can ascertain its appropriateness. To help the children gain this perspective, the teacher might ask them to stipulate verbally that their responses are simply suggestions, by adding qualifying words, such as the following:

1. *It might be* because there wasn't enough time . . .
2. *Maybe* it was because the children playing there forgot to clean up . . .
3. *Perhaps* it was because the blocks had fallen down . . .

Above all, the teacher should understand that a hypothesis is an educated guess. Any reasonable possibility given by the children is acceptable.

The children should be encouraged to think of as many hypotheses as possible. It is also important to note that *several* hypotheses might be appropriate to a given problem. (See page 15 for a more detailed description of this operation.) The following list of activities may provide primary children with many opportunities for hypothesizing.

1. The children are very noisy this morning. What do you think is the reason for this?
2. We are going on a trip:
   2.1 How shall we get there?
   2.2 What will we need to do before we go?
   2.3 What will we have to take with us?
   2.4 What arrangements will have to be made?
3. We cannot find a paintbrush. What do you think might have happened to it?
4. The paste jar was left uncovered. Why do you think this happened?
5. David's pet is not feeling well. What do you think might be the reason for this?
6. From the literature:
   6.1 Cinderella was very unhappy. Why do you think her stepsisters treated her that way?
   6.2 Peter Pan could fly. How do you think this happened?
   6.3 Why do you think Jack sold his cow for only a few beans?
   6.4 Why do you think that the duck and the dog and the cat did not want to help the Little Red Hen plant her wheat?
   6.5 Why were Hansel and Gretel sent off to the forest?
7. A plant kept in the classroom is dying. Why do you think this is happening?
8. What do you think are some good ways to keep the books in the library corner?
9. The class pet (a parakeet?) is not singing today. What do you think might be the reason?
10. Show a picture of a man dressed in a business suit. What do you think his job is?
11. What are some ways in which children could help mother? (father? teacher?)
12. The paint (left opened overnight) dried up. What do you think is the reason for this?
13. Jack just came from the dentist and he has five cavities. What do you think is the reason for this?
14. Paul's milk spilled. Why do you think that happened?
15. We have a new girl (boy) in class. What are some of the things we can do to make him feel welcome?
16. Why do you think some children are afraid of thunder?

17. Where does the light go when you turn it off?
18. What are some ways to have fun with a dog?
19. For those children who are already beginning to read, the teacher might use the readers and the characters in the stories as bases for questioning, such as:
    19.1 What kind of boy do you think Tom is?
    19.2 What kind of girl do you think Susan is?
    19.3 How do you think Dick felt (in a given situation)?

Applying Principles to New Situations.

Many teachers think of this operation solely in connection with the curriculum areas of mathematics and science. While both of these curriculum areas offer many possibilities, activities for this operation need not be restricted to math and science alone. Upon examination of other areas, the thoughtful teacher may see many opportunities to develop activities which will give children experiences in applying principles to new situations.

The process of applying principles to new situations requires the ability to transfer learning from old experiences to those situations which are new to us. It requires the ability to see relationships, to apply facts and principles previously learned to new problems. It requires the ability to determine *which* previously learned criteria are appropriate in the new situation, as well as the ability to apply them. Sometimes this is called *problem-solving*.

There are two types of situations in which children can exercise problem-solving abilities. In the first type, the teacher might *present a situation* which requires a solution to a problem. In addition, he also would *provide some data*. The student is then required to work out the solution. In the second type, the teacher would *describe a situation* and then ask the student to *predict the outcome* in given circumstances. The student is then asked to give his reasons for his prediction.

Can the student apply facts and principles which he has learned to these new situations?

Type 1. A. *Situation needing solution:* We would like to get two cookies for each of the children in the class.
   B. *Data given:* There are twenty-five children in the class.
   C. *Student works out the problem:* How many cookies do we need?

Type 2. A. *Situation given:* We have only three colors of paint today—red, yellow and blue.
   B. *Student asked to predict what will happen:* What will happen if we mix red and yellow? Yellow and blue? Red and blue?
   C. *Student asked to give reasons for prediction:* Why did you guess what would happen?

The following activities encompass both types of experiences for primary children. In many of them, *several* solutions are possible. (See page 16 for a more detailed description of this operation.)

1. We want to find out if this library book will fit on that shelf. The shelf is 8″ high.
2. Is it colder today than yesterday? Yesterday it was 45°.
3. Who lives closer to school, Harold or Peter? Peter lives on South Street and Harold lives on North Avenue.
4. John, Frank, and Ellen want to share a candy bar. They need to cut or break it into three equal parts.
5. How many crayons does Bob have? He had six and his mother bought him a box containing twelve.
6. Who has more cookies? Betty has four in her desk and six in her lunch pail. Charlie has eight in his pocket and two in his hand.
7. What objects in this room contain iron and steel? A magnet picks up objects of iron and steel.
8. Each child in the class will have an ice-cream cone today. The flavors to choose are chocolate, vanilla and strawberry. How many of each flavor will be needed?
9. What would happen if we did not water this plant for one day? (one week? one month?) Why do you think so?
10. What would happen if we left the paste uncovered all night? Why do you think so?
11. What would happen if you went out of doors on a winter day without your coat? Why do you think so ?
12. What would happen if you left the window open during a thunderstorm? Why do you think so?
13. What is the best way to move those blocks from one corner of the room to the other? Why do you think so?
14. What would happen if you planted a sunflower seed? Why do you think so?
15. What would happen if three children were late to school? Why do you think so?
16. What would happen if we made a lot of noise during the fire drill? Why do you think so?
17. What would happen if the teacher was absent tomorrow? Why do you think so?
18. What would happen if we put some lima beans in water? Why do you think so?
19. What would happen if there were only 20 cookies and 25 children in the class? Why do you think so?
20. What would happen if you dropped a magnet into a box of tacks? Why do you think so?

Criticizing.

Children, among others, are often freely critical (when this is permitted) and will need little prodding when they have strong feelings about something in particular which they do or do not like. Criticizing, however, requires deeper thought than simple statements of feeling, such as, "I don't like it" or "It's not good." When one criticizes, he should have a *basis* for what he is saying; he ought to have a position that has been thought about.

As the teacher helps the child to examine his reasons for or against something, he is giving the child an opportunity to establish some evaluative standards. This might be done simply by asking "Why do you like it?" or "Why do you think that isn't any good?" Sometimes a child will reply that he doesn't really know. If the teacher feels that it is wisest to drop the matter at this point, then he should not hesitate to say, "You like this, but you really don't know why you do—is that right?" And if the child does not wish to pursue the matter, and acquiesces, the teacher might simply indicate that he understands, showing that it is all right for the child not to respond further. Sometimes there are factors operating, unknown to anyone but the child himself, that make it difficult or impossible for him to respond at a particular time. A sensitive teacher who understands and responds to the needs of his students will realize at which time it is better not to push a child by forceful questioning. At other times, when the teacher feels he can pursue the questioning, he might suggest one or two possibilities for the child to consider, such as, "Do you like this story because it has pretty pictures?"

Creating a climate in the classroom in which children are free to express their opinions is an important factor in drawing out their criticisms. A child would, of course, have to feel that he could express his opinions, however different from the teacher's, without penalty. He would also have to know that teacher approval is not meted out only to those who express the same point of view as the teacher. The following list gives several topics about which primary children could voice their criticisms: (See page 11 for a more detailed description of the operation of criticizing.)

1. How do you feel about painting? What's good about it? What's not so good about it?
2. What is your opinion about having a class pet? Why do you think it is a good (bad) idea?
3. How do you think the clean-up went today? What were some things that were good (bad) about it?
4. How do you think the class behaved during music time? What were some things that went wrong? How do you think we could have improved?
5. How did you like that story? What were some of the things that made it a good story?

6. What did you think of the way Cinderella acted in the story? What was good (bad) about it?
7. What do you think of the way in which the library (science, block, etc.) corner is set up? How can we improve it?
8. How do you think you (personal) acted in school today?
9. What did you like best in school today? Why?
10. What did you like least? Why?
11. What do you like to do best at home? Why?

Decision-Making.

The objective in this operation is to help a child look at his own feelings or beliefs, attitudes or thoughts on a given situation and to let him decide for himself those values which he cherishes. The situations chosen for the children to reflect upon should provoke some introspection, and when the child responds, he should be given the opportunity to examine what he has said and thereby conclude, "This is what I stand for," or "This is not me at all." In this way, it is hoped that the values which a child holds are both revealed and accepted. In order for a teacher to provide experiences in decision-making, two rules need be applied. If neither of these is in effect in the teacher-pupil relationship, the activities could become meaningless.

One rule is that the teacher create a climate in his classroom in which children are free to decide for themselves their beliefs, thoughts and opinions, and to express them without fear of penalty. Another is that the teacher not attempt to impose his own beliefs, attitudes, and values upon the children.

There are similarities between the operation of decision-making and that of applying principles to new situations. The major difference, however, is that in applying principles, we ask children to be guided by principles, rules, generalizations, and laws in solving problems. In decision-making these obtain as well, but greater emphasis is placed upon the *values* the child may wish to protect in the solution.

When a child expresses his thought or feeling, it is the teacher's task to create a verbal image of what the child has said. He can do this by using one of the following procedures developed by Raths, called value-clarification technique:[2]

1. Say back what the child has said.
2. Paraphrase the child's statement.
3. Distort or read into the child's statement.
4. Ask for examples.
5. Ask that a term be defined.

---

[2]Louis E. Raths, Merril Harmin, and Sidney Simon, *Teaching and Values* (Columbus, Ohio: Charles E. Merrill Books, Inc., 1965), pp. 51-82.

 6. Ask another child to explain what was said.
 7. Ask the child to summarize his statements.
 8. Ask if there is an inconsistency.
 9. Ask if something is being assumed; bring out assumptions.
10. Ask where it will lead. What are the consequences? What comes next?
11. Ask if everyone should believe the statement.
12. Ask how good it is.
13. Ask "Where did you get that idea?"
14. Ask if this is something the child cares a lot about.
15. Ask if the child has thought a lot about it.
16. Ask if the child does this often.
17. Ask if this is what the child believes.
18. Ask how this affects the child's life.

When the teacher has, in one of the above ways, held up this verbal image for the child, and the child has responded to it, the teacher then indicates to the child that now he understands what the child means. In effect, the child has now made it clearer for him. Some examples of how this might work are shown in the brief interchanges below. Other clarification episodes might be somewhat longer.

Example A.

> Bobby: "There are two things that are important in my life, and they are drawing and thinking of the future."
>
> Teacher: "As I understand it, Bob, you are saying that the two most important things in your life are drawing and thinking of the future."
>
> Bobby: "Yes, those are the things I feel are important to me."
>
> Teacher: "Well, I see now what you mean."

Example B.

> Harold: (speaking to his teacher): "I don't think it is right for a teacher to give a zero when a boy doesn't do his homework."
>
> Teacher: "Are marks something you care a lot about, Harold?"
>
> Harold: "Well, if you don't get good marks then you won't be able to go to college."
>
> Teacher: "Oh, I see what you mean."

The following topics have been suggested by Raths as appropriate for eliciting value decisions in children: (See page 17 for an additional description of this operation.)

1. If I had $100. . . ?
2. If I could go wherever I pleased on Saturday, Sunday, in the summer, instead of school. . . ?
3. If I could do anything I pleased today. . . ?
4. What would I like to be when I grow up?

5. Who is my favorite person in radio, television, movies, sports, history stories, in the news, etc.?

6. What people in stories, movies, radio, etc., would I like to invite to a party?

7. What is the most beautiful thing I have ever seen?

8. What is the ugliest thing I have ever seen?

9. What was the most fun I ever had?

10. What was my most embarrassing moment?

11. What was the spookiest time that I've ever had?

12. What is the scariest thing that I know of?

13. What was the worst thing I ever did?

14. What was the nicest or kindest thing I ever did?

15. What was the best dream I ever had?

16. What was the worst dream I ever had?

17. What is the most fun to do in school?

18. What is the worst part of school?

19. What is the most fun to do after school, Saturdays, Sundays, summer?

20. What is the least fun after school, Saturdays, etc.?

21. What part of the world would I like most to go to? Least?

22. What does God look like? What does God do?

23. Why do we have war?

24. What is right? What is wrong?

25. Who tells us what's right? Wrong?

26. How do we know they are right?

27. How do we know about God?

28. Why does the world have people in it?

29. What are people for?

30. Why are there good people and bad people?

31. Who says they are good or bad?

32. Why are there men? Women?

33. Where do we come from?

34. Why are we here?

35. What is being happy?

36. What is being sad?

37. What was the saddest time for me?

38. What is mother for? What is father for?

39. Who would I like to be like when I grow up?

40. Who is the meanest person I know of in movies, radio, TV?

41. What does red mean?

42. What does black mean? White? Yellow? Blue?

43. What is a Negro?

44. What is punishment? Why am I punished? What for? Why do we have it? Who punishes me? Others?

45. What is crime? Who says so?

46. Who am I? What am I like?
47. What's good about where I live? What's not good about it?
48. What is a friend?
49. What is love?
50. Why do we love? What makes us hate?
51. Why do we get mad? What makes me mad?
52. Why do people fight? When is it right to fight? When not?
53. What would I do if I were the teacher?

In addition to the above, there are a number of other problems, specifically related to classroom situations, which would involve decision-making. These, too, are examples in which a child's *values* would be protected in the decision-making process.

1. Classroom management problems

    1.1 What would be the most suitable way to arrange the chairs and tables in this room?

    1.2 What would be the best ways in which to decide on classroom helpers?

    1.3 What would be some good ways in which we could clean up after activity periods?

    1.4 What would be some good ways in which we could remind the class that it is getting too noisy in the room?

    1.5 What are some good ideas for ways by which we could line up?

    1.6 What are some good ways by which we could keep our library (science, block) corner looking nice?

    1.7 What are some ways by which we could take good care of our class pet?

    1.8 What are some good procedures to follow for going to the bathroom, taking drinks, sharpening pencils?

    1.9 How could we decide if the clean-up job has been done properly?

2. Mathematics problems

    2.1 How could we find out which piece of wood (piece of material, pencil, etc.) is bigger (smaller, wider, narrower)?

    2.2 How could we tell which book (story) is longer?

    2.3 How could we find out which container has more water (milk, juice, etc.)?

    2.4 How could we decide how to cut the candy bar so that Peter, John, Frank, and Ellen each have the same amount?

    2.5 What would be some good ways by which we could count the milk money collected in class?

    2.6 How could we remember that at 10:30 A.M. we must go to the library?

    2.7 How can we tell if today is colder (warmer) than yesterday?

2.8 How can we tell what is the shortest way to walk from Harold's house to school?

2.9 How can we tell how far it is from school to Peggy's house?

3. Science problems

3.1 How can we find out what is the best kind of food for our class pet?

3.2 How can we tell if the food we choose for our pet is good for him?

3.3 How can we tell what is the right amount of water for our plant?

3.4 How can we tell if plant food makes the plant grow more quickly?

3.5 Why does the paste dry up when it is left uncovered overnight?

3.6 How can we tell why the paint dries up when it is left uncovered overnight?

3.7 How do animals protect themselves during the cold winters?

3.8 What are some things we would like to know about water?

4. Social Studies Problems

4.1 How can we decide how to share our things?

4.2 What are some things we can do to get along better with each other in school?

4.3 What are our individual responsibilities to the group?

4.4 What are some good ways to make new friends?

4.5 Going on a trip?

4.5.1 How shall we decide about the method(s) of transportation?

4.5.2 What rules do we need to set up for our behavior?

4.5.3 What are some things a person could do if he got lost?

4.5.4 What time factors are involved? How can they be worked out?

4.5.5 What money factors are involved? How shall we work this out?

4.5.6 What other arrangements have to be made? How shall we work these out?

4.6 What are some ways by which we can learn how to use the telephone?

Imagining.

One operational area that seems just made for primary children is imagining. In these activities the teacher asks the children to fancy freely what they would do if . . . Some of the most treasured responses from children have come in activities in which they are asked to use their imaginations. The

following list represents just a few of the activities in which primary children
may participate. An imaginative teacher might develop hundreds more.
(See page 14 for a more detailed description of this operation.)

1. How would you feel if you were the Little Prince?
2. What would you do if you had a hundred blocks?
3. What would you do if you were the teacher?
4. How would you act if you were Cinderella?
5. What would you do if you were a tiger?
6. How would you feel if you were chocolate ice cream?
7. What would you do if you owned the candy shop?
8. What would you get if you could buy twelve toys?
9. Where would you go if you could take a trip?
10. How would you feel if you were the first astronaut on the moon?
11. What would you do if you could fly?
12. What would you do if you could make yourself invisible?
13. How would you act if you were the principal?
14. What would you do if you had three wishes?
15. What would you do if you had $5.00?
16. What would you do on a camping trip?
17. What would you do if you were lost in the woods?
18. What if today were a day in which gravity didn't work?
19. What if today were a day that fish could talk?

Interpreting.

Developing skill in interpreting involves having many kinds of experiences
followed by practice in deriving meaning from those experiences. One of
the best ways in which a teacher can create activities to develop this skill
is to use the material which is readily available in his classroom — the equipment, the teaching tools (such as pictures, books, records, blocks, etc.) and
the classroom environment itself. Children who lack reading skills will of
necessity have to utilize primarily oral and pictorial materials. Essentially, the
teacher should present a body of data (for primary children this could be a
picture, or a statement of fact) and then pose some questions or statements
to the children. The object is for the children to be able to tell whether the
statement is true, not true, or not susceptible to evaluation, depending *solely*
upon the evidence presented. (See page 10 for a more detailed description of
the operation of interpreting.) Some examples of activities follow:

1. Show a picture of a red apple.
   Ask: This is an orange. (Children should respond *true, not true,*
   or *you can't tell from the picture)*
   Ask: This apple is round.
   Ask: Some apples are red and some are green.

2. Show a picture of four children working.
     Ask: There are four children in the picture.
     Ask: The children are happy.
     Ask: The children are at home.
3. Show a picture of a lion.
     Ask: The lion is hungry.
     Ask: The lion is tired.
     Ask: The lion has a mane of fur around his neck.
4. Show a picture of some children on swings.
     Ask: The children are at home in their backyard.
     Ask: The children are at school.
     Ask: The children are smiling.
5. Show a picture of an elephant.
     Ask: This is a gray elephant.
     Ask: The elephant is in the zoo.
     Ask: The elephant is the largest animal in the zoo.
6. Show a picture of children sitting near a teacher who is reading a story.
     Ask: A teacher is reading the story.
     Ask: The children like the story.
     Ask: It is a good story.
7. Show a picture of a dog.
     Ask: Dogs make good pets. (Can you tell this is true merely from looking at the picture?)
     Ask: This dog is a good dog.
     Ask: This dog is brown.
8. Look at the sky (from classroom window)
     Ask: Can you tell the color of the sky?
     Ask: Can you tell if it is cold?
     Ask: Can you tell if it is going to rain?
9. Hold up a new book.
     Ask: Can you tell if this is a funny story?
     Ask: Can you tell if it is about a fish?
     Ask: Can you tell if it is a good story?

These exercises presented so far have been designed for those children who have little or no ability to read. The section which follows presents exercises for children who are just beginning to gain skill in reading.

THINKING ACTIVITIES FOR CHILDREN JUST GAINING FLUENCY IN READING

Observing.

When we ask children to make observations, we are, in a sense, asking them to obtain information in many different ways. In giving upper-primary children experiences in observing, it is suggested that the teacher seek out those tasks which are designed to give practice in *noticing* and *describing*. These tasks may include noticing and describing objects, conditions, events, pertinent details. In the descriptions, the children are helped to ascertain the difference between what is *actually* observed, and what is assumed. For example, the teacher might ask the children to notice what he is doing and then to describe it. If the teacher gets up from his chair, walks over to the window and closes it — and the child describes the teacher, getting up from his chair, walking over to the window, closing the window *because the teacher was cold* — the teacher might help the child to see that he has made an assumption. This might be done through skillful questions, such as, "How did you know I was cold?" or "For what other reasons might I have closed the window?" In this way, the child might be led to understand the difference between what he actually saw and what he assumed to be true. Some upper-primary children might be ready to understand the concept of making an assumption. For those children who are able, the teacher might encourage the examination of observations and the identification of assumptions in them.

Not all observations need be visual. Some may involve listening, some touching, or feeling, some smelling or tasting. In each case, the children are helped to understand the difference between what was *actually* observed and what assumptions, if any, were made from the observation. (See page 7 for a more detailed description of the operation of observing.) The following list suggests several kinds of experiences wherein children may make observations.

1. Use pictures from reading textbooks:
    1.1 Ask children to describe what they see. Be on the lookout for assumptions and attributions of feelings and attitudes assigned by the children to the people in the picture.
    1.2 If a person in a picture is showing some facial expression as a smile, or a grimace, ask children what shows how the person is feeling.
    1.3 Ask children to describe details in a picture.
    1.4 Ask children to observe relative sizes of things in a picture.
    1.5 Ask children to describe the kind of coloring used in the picture.
    1.6 Some upper-primary children may be able to note the artistic style of the picture and describe it.
2. Ask children to observe the behavior of a person or an animal in a story. Ask them to describe this behavior.
3. Ask children to find words or phrases in the reading text that describe persons or things in the illustrations.
4. Ask children what they can tell about birds (fish, people in foreign lands, other countries, etc.) from the illustrations in a particular story of the reading text.

5. Show a picture of a man at work on a particular job. Ask children to observe the kind of equipment being used to carry out the work.

6. Show a picture of an animal in its natural habitat. Ask children what they can tell about this animal.

7. Take the children for a walk around the school in the spring (winter, fall). Ask them to describe what they saw.

8. Ask the children to look at the sky. Tell them to describe what they saw.

9. If there is a class pet, ask the children to observe his behavior during different times of the day (for example, before feeding, during feeding, after feeding).

10. If a child keeps a pet at home, ask him to observe its behavior during a specified time.

11. Ask children to observe what kind of treatment of their pet produces certain kinds of behavior.

12. Ask children to observe their shadows at different times of the day. Ask them to observe on sunny and cloudy days.

13. Visit the school nurse's office. Ask children to describe what they saw.

14. Arrange a visit to the principal's office. Ask children to describe what they saw.

15. Ask children to describe what they saw on the way to school that morning.

16. Ask children to observe and record the growth of plants in the classroom under certain conditions (ample water, too much water, lack of water, direct sunlight, no sunlight, etc.)

17. Plant an onion (potato, sweet potato, lima bean) in water or earth. Ask children to observe daily and record what they see.

18. Place a stalk of fresh celery in some water to which a drop of red ink has been added. Ask children to observe and describe what they see.

19. Bring in leaves from different trees. Ask children to observe and describe details.

20. If a variety of sea-shells can be obtained, ask children to describe what they can tell about the sea animals that lived within them.

21. Take children for a walk in the neighborhood. Have them observe and describe the different(?) kinds of residences seen and the different types of building materials used.

22. Take children on a trip to the supermarket. Ask them to describe what they saw.

23. Take children on a trip to the bakery (dairy, laundry, fire-station). Ask what they can tell about the jobs of the people working there.

24. Ask children to observe a mathematical computation. Let them describe what they saw.

25. Ask the children to listen to a record. Can they describe what they hear?

26. Have the children shut their eyes for a few moments. Can they describe the sounds that they heard? What assumptions were made?
27. Take the children for a walk around the school. What kinds of sounds did they hear?
28. Present the children with samples of various spices (such as salt, pepper, cinnamon, oregano). What do they notice about the smell of each spice? What do they notice about the taste of each?
29. What do the children notice about the smells and tastes of foods such as chocolate, apple, lettuce, lollipop, cupcake, milk?

Comparing.

When providing opportunities for children to compare at the second, third and fourth grade levels, the teacher might first help the children understand that comparing involves looking for *differences* as well as *similarities*. For example, a second grade teacher asked her children to think of many ways in which birds and butterflies were alike. She then asked the children to think of some ways in which birds and butterflies were different. As the child develops his ability to compare, the teacher may help him to become sensitive to the difference between what is demonstrably true and what the child might assume to be true. The response of a second or third grade child to the task set above might look like this:

Birds	*Butterflies*
have feathers	no feathers
bigger	smaller
fly	fly
have pretty colors	have pretty colors
eat worms	don't eat worms
don't come from caterpillars	come from caterpillars
make good pets	are not pets
fly faster	fly slower

Looking at the last item compared, the teacher would want to question the child to determine if this were really true, or if he were assuming this to be true. In the absence of specific evidence to support the assumption, the child might want to qualify his point by stating something like, *"It seems to me* that birds fly faster," or *"In my opinion* birds can fly faster."

When a child's response to a comparing activity is very limited, the teacher might want to help him find additional comparative points through skillful questioning. For example, the teacher might ask, "What can you think of that is different about the *heads* of birds and butterflies?" or "What is different about the *way* in which birds and butterflies get their food?"

In selecting items for comparison, the tendency is often to choose things that have some apparent relationship to each other, such as two books, two cars, two toys, two people, etc. When a person is asked to compare two things which have no apparent relationship, such as a *train* and a *book,* he might say, "You can't compare them," or "They defy comparison." However, upon close examination and reflection, it is possible to find similarities as well as differences between two seemingly very alien items. Furthermore, many teachers are often surprised by the perceptive observations of children who make these comparisons. (See page 6 for a more detailed description of this operation.) The activities listed below may provide children with many opportunities to compare.

1. Compare two people in a story read by the children.
2. Compare two people in a story read by the teacher.
3. Compare two characters from different stories (such as the Cat, from *Cat in the Hat*[3] and Angus, from *Angus and the Ducks*[4]).
4. Compare two books which the children have read.
5. Compare two stories read by the teacher.
6. Compare two paintings by famous artists.
7. Compare two folk songs; two melodies; two rhythms.
8. Compare two words from the reading vocabulary.
9. Compare two poems.
10. Compare the spelling of two words on the spelling list.
11. Compare two vowels; two consonant blends; two vowel digraphs.
12. Compare two flowers.
13. Compare two machines.
14. Compare the sun and the moon.
15. Compare ants and grasshoppers.
16. Compare two plants growing in the room (or out of doors).
17. Compare the teeth of dogs and the teeth of horses.
18. Compare bees and butterflies.
19. Compare a clock and a sundial.
20. Compare snow and wind.
21. Compare clouds and hail.
22. Compare a carrot and an onion.
23. Compare a seed with a bulb.
24. Compare frogs and goldfish.
25. Compare two holidays.
26. Compare two famous men.
27. Compare policemen and firemen.
28. Compare airports with railroad stations.
29. Compare factories with farms.

---

[3]Dr. Seuss, *The Cat in the Hat* (New York: Random House, Inc.) 1957.
[4]Marjorie Flack, *Angus and the Ducks* (New York: Doubleday and Co., Inc.) 1939.

30. Compare Chinese food and Mexican food.
31. Compare steak with apple pie.
32. Compare water and air.
33. Compare living on a farm to living in the city.
34. Compare winter with summer.
35. Compare the dairy and the bakery.
36. Compare the doctor with the railroad engineer.
37. Compare the park and the school playground.
38. Compare working in a group to working alone.
39. Compare two math problems.
40. Compare two numbers (such as 3 and 7).
41. Compare a yardstick and a ruler.
42. Compare two groups of objects.
43. Compare a dime and a quarter.
44. Compare clay and paint.

Classifying.

In the process of classification, the children are asked to arrange a variety of items according to categories or groups. It is essential that the categories have a distinct relationship to each other. For example, if the teacher put the following words on the blackboard, he might invite the children to group them according to:

           1. Those things we use for work, (and)
           2. Those things we use for play

| ball | hammer | toys | balloon | paint |
| paper | nails | doll | pen | pencil |

It is advisable, in most instances, to have the *children* set up the categories of classification. Very often, numerous possibilities for classification suggest themselves to the children. Wherever there is a relationship between the categories, the classification is acceptable. When the relationship does not exist, the teacher might help to point this out to the child. Where the children have suggested many possible types of classifications for groups of words, or pictures, or indeed anything set up for classification, the teacher is *urged* to welcome the various suggestions.

It is believed that the setting up of categories is a more complex task while the placing of objects into established groups is a more routine, or menial, task. Therefore, it is advisable for the teacher to set up the groups for the children primarily as an initiating experience into the operation of classifying.

An important element in setting up groups is to determine whether the grouping is *purposeful*. The child may be asked to defend his classification, revealing *why* he has made *those* groups. In other words, he is helped to understand that grouping objects into categories should be purposeful to him. Different kinds of groupings might serve different purposes. His purpose, therefore, will determine the nature of the categories.

For example, if he was asked to classify an assortment of books he might group them according to which fit on the larger shelf and which fit on the smaller. This type of grouping, by size, might suit his purpose of storing the books. Perhaps he might group them according to content. This would serve another purpose. He might group them in alphabetical order if his purpose was to locate them easily by the author's last name.

The following is a list of some of the very many things which might be found in school, at home, and in the neighborhood which can be grouped by upper-primary children: (See page 9 for a more detailed description of this operation.)

1. Books in the classroom library
2. Stories, or books the children have read
3. Vocabulary words
4. Spelling words
5. Stories written by the children
6. Poems written by the children
7. Poems dealing with one theme
8. Math examples
9. Math problems
10. Numbers
11. Occupations of fathers of children in the class
12. Stores in the neighborhood
13. Foods
14. Animals
15. Musical instruments
16. Toys
17. Kinds of work done by children in the class
18. Vehicles used for transportation
19. Implements used for communication
20. Games children play during/after school
21. Trees
22. Flowers
23. Bridges
24. Birds
25. Insects
26. Kinds of weather

The following pages contain examples of activities developed by teachers of upper-primary children for the purpose of classification.

Example A.
sun, rain, cold, clouds, ice, snow, warm, wind, hot.

Summer Days	*Winter Days*
sun	cold
rain	ice
clouds	snow
warm	rain
hot	clouds
wind	wind

Example B.

We Eat	We Put On	We Play
_____	_____	_____
_____	_____	_____
_____	_____	_____
_____	_____	_____
_____	_____	_____
_____	_____	_____
_____	_____	_____
_____	_____	_____

rubbers	cherry	bread	shoe	ball
dress	game	eggs	blocks	pancakes
balloons	hat	toy	clothes	drum
mitten	nuts	cake	coat	wagon
apple	muff	sled	honey	

Example C.

1. _____	1. _____	1. _____	1. _____	1. _____
2. _____	2. _____	2. _____	2. _____	2. _____
3. _____	3. _____	3. _____	3. _____	3. _____
4. _____	4. _____	4. _____	4. _____	4. _____
5. _____	5. _____	5. _____	5. _____	5. _____
6. _____	6. _____	6. _____	6. _____	6. _____
_____	_____	_____	_____	_____
_____	_____	_____	_____	_____

ball	mother	shoes	boy
dress	uncle	hat	top
bike	pie	cat	soda
school	fruit	church	cow
store	mouse	meat	cake

home	house	wagon	friend
dog	father	gloves	shirt
apartment	goat	girl	horse
milk	bat	pants	kite

Collecting and Organizing Data.

Although upper-primary children may have limited reading and writing skills, they need not be kept from participation in this operation. Children who have difficulty with written language may collect information orally, from a resource person (such as mother, father, teacher, librarian) and they may relate their information for the benefit of the class. Whether the information is collected orally, or in written form, it is suggested that the teacher help and guide the child in the arrangement, in logical pattern or sequence, of the information which he has collected. Questions, such as, "What is the first thing you want to tell?" and "What should come next?" might help the child to begin to see a sequence of events.

The following topics are suggested as possibilities for the collection and organization of data by the upper-primary child: (See page 15 for a more detailed description of this operation.)

1. Ask the children to find out what is necessary to make puppets. Ask them to plan a step-by-step procedure once the materials have been determined.
2. Ask the children to find out about magnets. Ask them to plan a presentation on magnets that encompasses what they have learned.
3. Ask the children to do research on some of the following topics: The Farm; The Dairy; Wholesale or Retail Markets; Airplanes and Airports; The Post Office; Trains; Ships and Cargoes.[5] Ask them to organize their information in an oral or written report following a prescribed outline.
4. Ask the children to find out about the chief occupations of the area in which they live. Have them organize their information according to a prescribed outline.
5. Some children might be interested in collecting and organizing information on various kinds of recreation.
6. Ask the children to find out about what holidays are celebrated by their families. Perhaps some children could work together in groups to gather this information and share it with the class.
7. If the class is going on a trip, the children may be asked to collect information on the way, or when there, with a specific problem in mind. For

---

[5]Lavone Hanna, Gladys Potter, and Neva Hagaman, *Unit Teaching in the Elementary School* (New York: Holt, Rinehart and Winston, Inc., 1960), p. 86.

example, if the children are studying about different communities, they might be asked to note what kinds of communities they notice as their bus goes from the school to a neighboring city.

8. Some children might want to do some research on a particular person. This may be either an historical or a contemporary figure. The information collected could be organized according to a specific outline.

9. Children might be invited to do research on the types of buildings in their communities. This information could be classified into related categories.

10. Some children might be asked to go to the library and obtain a number of books dealing with a specific theme.

11. Ask the children to find out how butter (cottage cheese, ice cream) is made. Plan a step-by-step outline to follow to make this in class.

12. The class may decide on obtaining a pet. Some children could be responsible for learning about the proper care and feeding of the animal. Perhaps this information could be placed on a chart and used by the entire class.

13. Some children might be asked to find out how certain foods are obtained in their community.

14. Ask the children to collect information on where the water comes from that is used in their community.

15. Some additional topics for the science curriculum are suggested below for the collection and organization of data. The children's interests and abilities might guide the teacher in making appropriate selections.

    15.1   Clouds
    15.2   Snow
    15.3   Wind
    15.4   Storms
    15.5   Seeds
    15.6   Trees
    15.7   Flowers
    15.8   Plants
    15.9   Birds
    15.10 Squirrels
    15.11 Farm animals
    15.12 Zoo animals
    15.13 Goldfish
    15.14 Frogs
    15.15 Bees
    15.16 Cocoons and moths
    15.17 Dogs and cats[6]

---

[6] J. Murray Lee and Dorris May Lee, *The Child and His Curriculum* (New York: Appleton, Century-Crofts, 1960), p. 429.

Summarizing.

These experiences for upper-primary children may be either oral or written. When a teacher asks young children to summarize, the major task he will face will be to help the child to relate only those facts which are essential and significant. Any teacher who has worked with highly verbal upper-primary grade children will readily testify to their verbosity and their reluctance to pare down a story to its bare essentials. Often a child will not only relate a story in great detail, but also add his own embellishments. A teacher who wishes to develop the skill of summarizing in upper-primary children not only helps the child to recognize relevant points in content and structure, but also does this without hurting the child's feelings by cutting off his fanciful additions. One suggested way to initiate experiences with summarizing is to read a story to the group, then work together with the group to elicit (or tell outright if need be) what was important, which were the key episodes, and what irrelevant material could be discarded for the sake of the summary. (For a more detailed description of this operation, see page 6). The following list is suggestive of possible summarizing experiences for upper-primary children.

1. Children may summarize a story read to the class.
2. They may summarize a story that they have read.
3. They may summarize their day's activities in school.
4. A child may summarize parts of a story, such as the part he liked best, the funniest part, the saddest part, the most exciting part.
5. Children may be asked to find a good title for a story.
6. Children may summarize a movie or film strip shown in class.
7. Children may summarize their experiences on a field trip.
8. Some children may summarize a day's activities outside of school.
9. Children may summarize a social studies or science experience.
10. A child may summarize a math lesson.
11. Children may assign a title to a picture, or a photograph.
12. Some children subscribe to classroom magazines which deal with current events, such as *News Trails,* or *News Explorer.* Articles in these magazines may be summarized.

Looking for Assumptions.

As upper-primary children begin to engage in thinking activities of this type, the teacher can help to explain the concept of assumptions. We need to help the children understand that to make an assumption is not necessarily wrong; the important thing is for them to see that an assumption is being made.

Some events, relationships, and qualities are quite clearly evident. Sometimes we say that they are true. For example, we look at an apple and we say,

"It is red." We recognize this as clearly observable. Some assumptions we make are based upon strong bits of evidence. The strength of the evidence gives greater support to the assumption — nevertheless, it remains an assumption. For example, we look at the same apple and we say, "It has seeds." We cannot see the seeds on the inside of the apple, but we can be pretty certain that they are there — unless they have been removed in a manner which cannot be detected, or this is a new form of seedless apple. It would be a reasonable assumption, therefore, to look at an apple and conclude that it has seeds, *recognizing the possibility* that this may not be so.

On the other hand, many assumptions are based upon very little evidence, and it is these that are most subject to question. For example, to look at the same red apple and to conclude that all or most apples are red would be a rather broad assumption. When children make assumptions, the teacher might ask if they are *guessing* that something is true. Again, the teacher might ask for some *evidence,* or *support,* of a statement which a child has made to help him see that he has made an assumption.

To summarize, then, the teacher should keep in mind that to make assumptions is not necessarily wrong. It is the ability to identify statements as assumptions that we wish to develop in children. The following list contains a number of activities in which upper-primary children can look for assumptions: (See page 12 for a more detailed description of this operation.)

1. Show the children a picture of a cat (or dog). Ask them if it is a good (bad) cat (dog). Ask them if they can tell how it is feeling. Help them to see that any responses to the above questions would *have* to be assumptions without additional information or evidence.

2. Two automobiles are in a race. Car A reaches its destination ahead of car B. Can we conclude that Car A is faster? (Perhaps Car B had a flat tire?) To conclude that Car A is faster would be an assumption. We would need further evidence before we could determine which car was really faster.

3. Two pencils cost 6¢. Therefore, each pencil costs 3¢. What assumption has been made? Is this a valid assumption? (Actually, one pencil costs 5¢ and the other costs 1¢!)

4. Farmer Brown had a basket of eggs. He put his hand into the basket two times and each time brought out two eggs. How many eggs were in the basket? (Can we really tell the answer to this problem without making an assumption?)

5. We planted an avocado seed, and it did not grow. To conclude that it did not grow because of insufficient water would be a rather broad assumption. We would need more information before reaching a conclusion about the avocado seed.

6. Ask the children to look at the sky. Ask them to predict the weather. Help them to see that these predictions are assumptions.

7. Paul came to school late this morning. When Sally saw him come into the room, she said, "Paul, you are late because you overslept." Is this an assumption?
8. Jerry got up in the morning and looked outside through his window. He said, "It must be very cold today." Is this an assumption?
9. Tomorrow will be a lovely, warm day. Is this an assumption?
10. Ask the children to write about an experience they have had. Help them to find any assumptions they made.
11. Show the children a picture of a neatly dressed man in a business suit. Ask if they can tell from what country he comes.
12. Show the children a map of the United States. Ask them to make observations about what they see. Be alert to point out what is fact and what is assumption.
13. Have the children examine some pictures from a reading text or library book. Ask them if they can draw any conclusions about the characters in the story.
14. Show the children a worn out, shabbily jacketed book. Ask them if they can tell if this is a good book.
15. Ask the children who is the tallest (shortest) in the class (when all are sitting down).

Hypothesizing.

The primary objective in giving children experiences with this operation is to help them to understand and consider the variety of possibilities which may be involved in arriving at the solution of a problem. If the upper-primary grade teacher does not wish to work with the word *hypothesis,* alternate possibilities are available which might bring the concept into sharper focus for the children. For example, in dealing with the following problem —

> The block corner had not been properly cleaned up after playtime and there were a number of blocks left on the floor.

— the teacher might ask the children to think about the problem for a few minutes and to suggest *several guesses,* or *possibilities* as reasons for this occurrence. The children may be helped to recognize that each suggestion is only one of several possibilities and not necessarily the only reason for the occurrence. Children need also to be helped to understand that it will take further examination (or in later grades we might say *testing*) of each hypothesis or suggestion before we can ascertain its appropriateness. To help the children gain this perspective, the teacher might ask them to stipulate verbally that their responses are simply suggestions by adding qualifying words, such as the following:

1. *It might be* because there wasn't enough time . . .

2. *Maybe* it was because the children playing there forgot to clean up . . .

3. *Perhaps* it was because the blocks had fallen down . . .

Above all, the teacher should understand that a hypothesis is an educated guess. Any reasonable possibility given by the children is acceptable. The children may be encouraged to think of as many hypotheses as possible. It is also important to note that *several* hypotheses might be applicable to a given problem. (See page 15 for a more detailed description of this operation.) The following list of activities may provide children with many opportunities for hypothesizing.

1. One of the library books is missing. What might have happened to it?
2. It is easier for some children to learn the word *submarine* than it is for them to learn the word *what*. What do you think the reasons might be for this?
3. Some children do not like to come to school. What do you think might be the reasons for this?
4. We could not see the moon last night. Why do you think this was so?
5. David's hamster has very glossy fur. Why do you think this is so?
6. We can grow a potato (or sweet potato) in soil. We can also grow it in water. Why do you think this is so?
7. There are two plants in the classroom. One is growing and the other is dying. What might be the reasons for this?
8. A dog barks, but a cat meows. What might be the reasons for this?
9. A giraffe has a very long neck. What might be the reasons for this?
10. Roses are red, violets are blue. What might be the reasons for this?
11. You added 5 and 2 and 3 and got 11. What might be the reasons for that?
12. You had a candy bar and wanted to share it with your three friends. How might this be done?
13. You want to add 43 and 62 and 127. How might this be done?
14. John is taller than Suzy. What might be the reasons for that?
15. Percy is having a bad day in school today. What might be the reasons for this?
16. Some people do not like dogs. What might be the reasons for this?
17. Some children do not like poetry. What might be the reasons for this?
18. Some children love reading. What might be the reasons for this?
19. Some children do not like to paint. Why might this be so?

Applying Principles to New Situations.

Many teachers think of this operation solely in connection with the curriculum areas of mathematics and science. While both of these curriculum areas offer many possibilities, activities for this operation need not be restricted to math and science alone. Upon examination of other areas, the thoughtful teacher may see many opportunities to develop activities which will give children experiences in applying principles to new situations.

The process of applying principles to new situations requires the ability to transfer learning from old experiences to those situations which are new to us. It requires the ability to see relationships, to apply facts and principles previously learned to new problems. It requires the ability to determine *which* previously learned criteria are appropriate in the new situation, as well as the ability to apply them. Sometimes this is called *problem-solving*.

There are two types of situations in which children can exercise their problem-solving abilities. In the first type, the teacher might *present a situation* which requires a solution to a problem. In addition, he also would *provide some data*. The student is then required to work out the solution. In the second type, the teacher would *describe a situation* and then ask the student to *predict the outcome* in given circumstances. The student is then asked to give his reasons for his prediction.

Can the student apply facts and principles which he has learned to these new situations?

An example of an activity for each type of situation described above is as follows:

Type 1. A. *Situation needing solution:* We would like to find out how many dimes there are in one dollar.
B. *Data given:* There are 100 pennies in a dollar. There are 10 pennies in one dime.
C. *Student works out the problem:* How many dimes are there in one dollar?

Type 2. A. *Situation given:* Mary got caught in the rain and she got very, very wet.
B. *Student asked to predict what will happen:* What do you think will happen to Mary?
C. *Student asked to give reasons for prediction:* Why do you think so?

The following activities include samples of both types of experiences for upper-primary children. In many of them, *several* solutions are possible. (See page 16 for a more detailed description of this operation.)

1. How much will the total amount of milk money be? Milk costs 5¢ and 15 children have paid their money.
2. Paul needs a desk that he can sit at comfortably. His foot to knee length is 14″. How high would his desk have to be?
3. Does Mary or Alice have a larger piece of pie? Mary has ⅓ of the pie and Alice has ¼.

4. Who lives closest to school, John, Bob or Eddy? John lives on Maple Street, Bob lives on Elm Street and Eddie lives five blocks from school.
5. How much taller is John than Susan? John is 40″ tall.
6. How many children weigh more than Peter? Peter weighs 50 lbs.
7. Can we find out how many quarts of water the pitcher holds if we have a measuring cup (8 oz.) and we know that a quart is equal to 4 measuring cups?
8. Each child in the class wishes a piece of candy. There are 16 candy bars and 30 children in the class.
9. How many grapefruits will fit into that basket? We know that the basket will hold 60 oranges and that one grapefruit takes up the space of three oranges.
10. This plant needs a room temperature of 80° to grow. That temperature is too hot for a classroom. How could we solve this problem?
11. What is the fastest way for Bob to get from school to his house? He lives on Hudson Boulevard.
12. How do you think a potato (sweet potato, onion) would grow best? Why?
13. What kind of food do you think squirrels (cats, dogs, fish, etc.) like best? Why?
14. Why do you think there are no longer any dinosaurs?
15. What would it sound like if this song were played only on a drum? Why do you think so?
16. We need a good student to build a wagon. Whom would you pick? Why?
17. There are only two colors of paint (black and red). What do you think a picture with these two colors would look like? Why?
18. What would happen if the President visited our school? Why do you think so?
19. Suppose your teacher was absent tomorrow? What do you think might happen? Why?
20. What would happen if the school had to close down for repairs? Why do you think so?
21. What would happen if a great snowfall kept each of us snowed in at home for one week? Why do you think so?
22. Suppose you were offered two books and you had to choose only one. Which would you choose? Why?

Criticizing.

Children are often freely critical (when this is permitted) and will need little prodding when they have strong feelings about something in particular which they do or do not like. Criticizing, however, requires deeper thought than simple statements of feeling, such as, "I don't like it" or "It's not good."

When one criticizes, he should have a basis for what he is saying; he ought to have a position that has been thought about.

As the teacher helps the child to examine his reasons for or against something, he is giving the child an opportunity to establish some evaluative standards. This might be done simply by asking "Why do you like it?" or "Why do you think that isn't any good?" Sometimes a child will reply that he doesn't really know. If the teacher feels that it is wisest to drop the matter at this point, then he should not hesitate to say, "You like this, but you really don't know why you do—is that right?" And if the child does not wish to pursue the matter and acquiesces, the teacher might simply indicate that he understands, showing that it is all right for the child not to respond further. Sometimes there are factors operating unknown to anyone but the child himself that make it difficult or impossible for him to respond at a particular time. A sensitive teacher who understands and responds to the needs of his students will realize at which time it is better not to push a child by forceful questioning. At other times, when the teacher feels he can pursue the questioning, he might suggest one or two possibilities for the child to consider, such as, "Do you like this story because it has pretty pictures?"

Creating a climate in the classroom in which children are free to express their opinions is an important factor in drawing out their criticisms. A child would, of course, have to feel that he could express his opinions, without penalty, however different from the teacher's they may be. He would also have to know that teacher approval is not meted out only to those who express the same point of view as the teacher.

When children have been encouraged to express criticism freely, the tendency sometimes occurs to carry criticism to an extreme. For example, one teacher recalled with mixed horror and pleasure the polite but unmistakable criticism, voiced by several of his children, of a new art teacher—*during the art lesson!* Whether the art teacher deserved to be so openly critized by the children is irrelevant to this discussion. More to the point, perhaps, would be to question whether children should be permitted, or encouraged, to criticize a teacher. There are several answers which might be considered, depending, of course, upon the particular objectives and values of the individual teacher. However, taken beyond the "what is right and what is wrong" stage, we might remember that if we are to encourage criticism in our classrooms, we cannot suddenly become inconsistent and discourage the very kind of behavior we are seeking to develop. Rather, we must teach children to temper the expression of their criticism with *good judgment*. It is also wise to use great caution in encouraging children to be freely critical about the ideas and efforts of other children in the class. (See page 11 for a more detailed description of this operation.)

The following list gives several topics about which upper-primary children might voice their criticisms.

1. What do you think about using water colors (or another art medium) in painting? What are the disadvantages? The advantages?
2. What do you think about your drawing (painting)? What are some good things about it? What are some things you don't like?
3. Did you like that book, story, poem? Why? Why not? What did you like about it? What did you dislike?
4. What do you think about the homework we had last night? How could the assignment have been improved?
5. How was that science demonstration? What was good about it? How could it have been more successful?
6. How do you think our pet is being cared for? What are some good things about its care? What would you like to see improved?
7. How do you like the community in which you live? What are the good features? What would you like to see improved? Why?
8. How do you like the arrangement of this classroom? What are some good things about this arrangement? How might we improve the things we don't like?
9. What are some things we like about our reading (social studies) group? What are the things we would like to improve?
10. What do you like, dislike about our school? What suggestions would you make to the principal?
11. What class routines would you like to see improved? Why?
12. What is the best subject in school? Why?
13. Which subject do you dislike the most? Why? How could we improve it?
14. How did the social studies (science) unit turn out? What were the good things about it? What could have been improved?
15. What did you think of the class' behavior during the trip (fire drill, assembly, etc.)? What do you think was good about it? How might we improve it?
16. What do you think about the science (social studies) textbook? What are some good things about it? What are some of its poorer features?
17. How did you like that play? Why do you think it was so good?

Imagining.

Most children, no matter what the grade, seem to enjoy and participate most enthusiastically in activities which ask them to do some imagining. Here, in a fanciful world, a child can be a king, a jet pilot, or take a trip to Venus. In these activities, the teacher merely asks the children to fancy freely what they would do if . . . There are few, if any, qualifications which a teacher would impose upon a child's imaginings. After all, we have invited him to explore, to create, to fancy, to ponder what is beyond his real world. Some of the most treasured responses from children have come from activities which ask them to use their imaginations. The following list represents just a few of the activities in which upper-primary children may participate. An imaginative teacher might develop hundreds more. (See page 14 for a more detailed description of this operation.)

1. What would it be like to be a strawberry?
2. How would you draw a picture of love? anger?
3. What would it be like to be number 6?
4. If you could make yourself invisible, what would you do?
5. If you could do anything in the world you wanted to on Saturday . . . ?
6. If you were 7 feet tall . . . ?
7. If there were no TV. . . ?
8. If Columbus hadn't discovered America . . . ?
9. If summer vacation came in December . . . ?
10. If you were a puppet . . . ?
11. If you lived in the city (or on a farm) . . . ?
12. How does it feel to be a tiger in the jungle?
13. If you were all alone on an island . . . ?
14. If you had $100 . . . ?
15. If you were the President . . . ?
16. If you were the teacher . . . ?
17. What if today were a day in which people could fly?
18. If you had a birthday every month . . . ?
19. If you could live wherever you wanted to . . . ?
20. If you had three wishes . . . ?
21. What if today were a day that dogs could talk?
22. What if you were suddenly all grown up?

Interpreting.

To develop skill in interpreting requires having many kinds of experiences followed by practice in deriving meaning from the experiences. When children are asked about the meanings of an experience, they are being asked to interpret. When a teacher asks a child how he got that particular meaning from an experience, he is being asked to give supporting details in defense of his interpretation. When we ask children to interpret, we must judge whether:

1. the data of the experience supports the interpretation,
2. a generalization is being made on the basis of insufficient evidence.

In providing opportunities for children to interpret, the teacher may use maps, charts, graphs, illustrations, and photographs. For example, the children might be asked to interpret meanings in the following illustration.

It is important to remember that the data given in the illustration must support the interpretation. With that in mind, the following statements, or meanings would be appropriate.

1. The dog is in the water.
2. Two men are trying to get the dog out.
3. They are using a ladder.
4. Several people are watching.
5. There is ice on the water.

The following types of statements, or meanings, would *not* be appropriate because to draw these meanings from the data in the illustration would be going beyond the evidence in the illustration.

1. The dog fell into the water (he might have jumped in, or been thrown in).
2. The firemen are trying to get him out (they might be policemen, or ASPCA, or other civic servants).
3. It is a cold day (perhaps the ice is melting or cracked because the day is warm).
4. The dog is in the lake (it might be a river or a pond).

Should the child draw inferences from the illustration, he would need to use some kind of accompanying qualification. The following examples would be appropriate in this case:

1. The dog *probably* fell in, or the dog *might have* fallen in.
2. The men *seem to be* firemen.
3. It is *probably* cold, or wintertime.
4. They *seem to be* using the ladder as a safety device.

The following examples are presented as possible exercises from which children can draw meanings: (See page 10 for a more detailed description of this operation.)

1. How Much Do Hamburgers Cost?

Year	Ground Beef (per lb.)	Bread (per loaf)	Onions (per lb.)
1957	42¢	19¢	10¢
1959	55¢	20¢	11¢
1961	51¢	21¢	10¢
1963	52¢	22¢	10¢

Are the following statements true (T) or false (F) or is there not enough information (?) in the chart to determine whether the statement is either true or false?

a. In 1957, a loaf of bread cost 21¢.	T	F	?
b. A pound of onions cost most in 1959.	T	F	?
c. In 1965, ground beef will increase in price.	T	F	?
d. The materials for a hamburger sandwich cost most in 1963.	T	F	?
e. In 1957, bread cost almost twice as much as onions.	T	F	?
f. Ground beef is very expensive.	T	F	?

2. Are the following statements true (T) or false (F) or is there not enough information (?) in the graph to determine whether the statement is either true or false?

a. In 1961 the cost of equipment bought by the U. S. railroads was about $63 million.	T	F	?
b. The railroads spent $5,800,000,000 in 1959.	T	F	?
c. The greatest amount spent was in 1957.	T	F	?
d. Railroads were better in 1957 than in 1955.	T	F	?
e. No money was spent in 1962.	T	F	?
f. More money will be spent in 1965 than in 1963.	T	F	?
g. About 2 billion dollars more was spent in 1963 than in 1961.	T	F	?

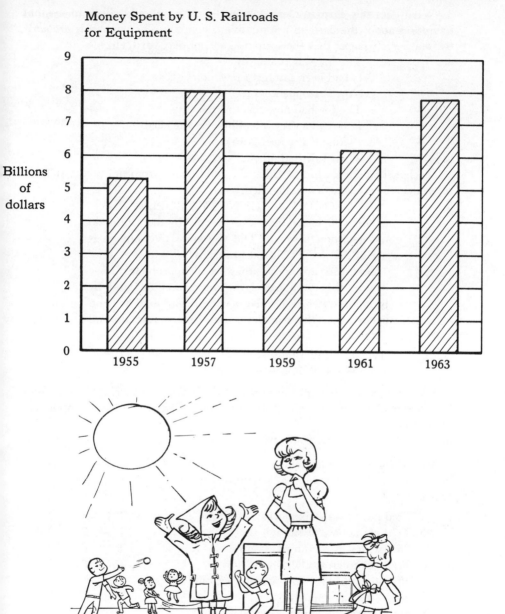

But Miss Hamilton, my mother says that *every time* my father washes the car it rains!

3. What does this cartoon mean to you? (Teacher should check to see that inferences about the cartoon are qualified, such as: The woman is *probably* the teacher; It *seems* that the scene is a school play yard, etc.)

4.   The fog was rolling in,
            It had been raining a few moments ago,
            Now it stopped.
            The fog had now reached the city,
            It spread a dreary feeling over the earth.
            I struggled to keep awake,
            Then I drifted off . . .[7]

Teacher should ask what meaning the children get from this poem. (Check to see that the inferences are qualified.)

5.   FOOD FOR HUNGRY PEOPLE
            Did you know that most people in the world do
            not get enough to eat? Did you know that hunger is
            one of the world's biggest problems?
            Scientists are trying to solve this problem. They
            believe that man can grow more food on land by
            bringing water to dry places with irrigation. They also
            believe that the sea can supply many animals and
            plants which are good food. Someday perhaps there
            will be enough food for all when we use the land
            and the sea to feed many more people.

Ask children to interpret the information in the article. Have them *check* their statements against the facts in the article to see if the data support the interpretation.

6. This map shows one route from Fred's home to school.

Are the following statements true (T) or false (F) or is there not enough information (?) in the map to determine whether the statement is either true or false?

a. Fred has to walk six blocks to school.	T	F	?
b. Fred cannot walk through the park.	T	F	?
c. The school is on Third Avenue.	T	F	?
d. Fred has to cross Oak Street.	T	F	?
e. If Fred walked on First Street, he would get home just as quickly.	T	F	?
f. Fred passes the library every day.	T	F	?

---

[7]Original poem by Paula Wassermann, age 9.

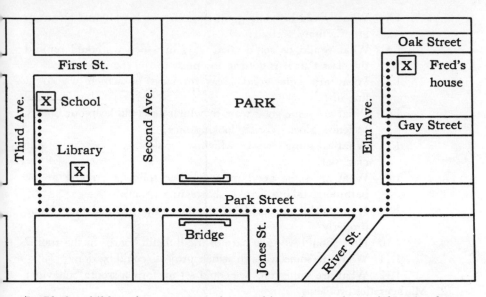

7. If the children have compared something, the teacher might ask what meaning they got from that experience.
8. After a trip or an excursion, the teacher may ask what meaning the children got from that experience.
9. If the children were punished for some infraction of class rules, the teacher might ask what meaning they derived from this experience.

In each of the last three examples, it is suggested that the teacher make certain that the interpretation is supported by the data. Wherever possible, the teacher is urged to develop exercises in interpretation from the real-life experiences of the class.

Decision-making.

The reader is referred to the operation of *Decision-making* on pages 50-54. Activities listed in these pages are also suitable for children who are just gaining fluency in reading. In addition to these, other problems specifically related to classroom situations are presented below. These, too, involve the decision-making process and require the protection of the child's values.

1. Classroom management problems

    1.1   What would be a suitable way to arrange the chairs and tables in this room?

    1.2   What would be the best ways in which to decide on classroom helpers?

1.3   What would be some good ways in which we could clean up after activity periods?

1.4   What would be some good ways in which we could remind the class that it is getting too noisy in the room?

1.5   What are some good ideas for ways by which we could line up?

1.6   What are some good ways by which we could keep our library (science, block) corner looking nice?

1.7   What are some ways by which we could take good care of our class pet?

1.8   What are some good procedures to follow for going to the bathroom, taking drinks, sharpening pencils?

1.9   How could we decide if the clean-up job has been done properly?

1.10 How should we take care of the bulletin boards in the room?

1.11 What are some ways in which projects could be done?

1.12 What are some rules we could set up for classroom behavior?

2.   Mathematics problems

2.1   How could we find out if one thing is bigger than another?

2.2   How could we find out how far it is from the front of the room to the back, from one side to the other?

2.3   How could we find out how far it is from Dick's house to school?

2.4   How can we find out who is the tallest in the class (the shortest)?

2.5   How can we find out who weighs the most? Least?

2.6   How can we find out if the quart container or pitcher holds more milk?

2.7   How can we find out what time it is (if the clock has stopped)?

2.8   How can we find out what zero means?

2.9   How can we tell how to divide the cake so that each of four children will have an equal share?

1.10 How can we tell how many apples will fit into that basket?

1.11 How many things can we find out about the number 12?

3.   Science problems

3.1   How can we tell about the different kinds of sounds we hear?

3.2   How can we tell about tomorrow's weather?

3.3   How can we tell if January is a colder month than February?

3.4   How can we determine the best kind of care for our plant? Class pet?

3.5   How can we tell the best conditions under which a potato (sweet potato, onion) will grow?

3.6 How can we tell if a hamster or white mouse would be better as a class pet?

3.7 How can we tell what kind of food squirrels (cats, dogs, fish) like best?

3.8 How can we tell why a balloon filled with air takes longer to float to earth than one without air?

3.9 Why is it that there are no longer any dinosaurs?

3.10 Where does our water come from?

4. Social studies problems

4.1 What are our individual responsibilities to the group?

4.2 What rules do we need about sharing?

4.3 How can we decide what are the best practices for group living?

4.4 How can we tell which children make good leaders?

4.5 Going on a trip

4.5.1 How shall we decide about transportation?

4.5.2 What rules should be set up for the group?

4.5.3 What are some things a person could do if he got lost?

4.5.4 What time factors are involved? How shall we work this out?

4.5.5 What money factors are involved? How shall we work this out?

4.5.6 What other arrangements need to be made? How shall we work these out?

4.6 Ask the children to list all foods they had for dinner last night. How can we tell where these came from?

4.7 What are the recreational facilities available for children in our community? What restrictions do they have?

4.8 How can we tell who lived in this area before we did?

4.9 What is it like to live in the tropics? Hawaii? Alaska? New York City? Texas?

4.10 What are the responsibilities of a citizen in our community?

4.11 How many different uses can you make of a brick?

4.12 What goes into mashed potatoes?

4.13 How can you tell if Brand X is better than Brand Y?

Coding and Coding Other Papers.

It is the belief of this writer that these two operations are best left for those children who have attained fluency in reading and writing. Activities that involve these operations have, therefore, not been included in this section for upper-primary grade children who, generally speaking, are just beginning to gain fluency in each of these skills. In many upper-primary groups, however, a number of children are both fluent readers and prolific writers. For these exceptional children the teacher is asked to refer to the examples of activities in the intermediate grade section which follows.

The exercises presented in this section have been designed for those children who are just beginning to gain skill in reading. The examples of activities to be found in the next section are for the use of those children who are skilled readers.

THINKING ACTIVITIES FOR CHILDREN WHO ARE FLUENT IN READING

Observing.

It should be kept in mind that observations may be *visual, auditory,* may involve *touch* and *smell.* In other words, children engaged in making observations may be obtaining information in multi-sensory ways. The objective of the observation is *not* the accumulation of isolated facts, but rather the accumulation of facts as a means to a general intellectual conclusion.

When children participate in making observations, they are getting practice in *noticing* and *describing.* In the descriptions, however, the children can be taught to differentiate between what *actually* was observed and any assumptions made from the observation. When a child has made an assumption, he has gone beyond the data and drawn a conclusion that is not supported by the details of the observation. Children who have had frequent opportunities to observe and who have had much practice in separating the facts from the assumptions have a tendency to become very cautious about making assumptions. For example, several children were asked to look at a reproduction of a painting by Modigliani. Some of them described the colors of the painting. Some of them described the elongated head and neck of the woman in the painting. Others noted the fine detail. One boy described the woman in the painting as sad. It was brought to his attention that she might only have posed this face for the artist, that what appeared to be sadness might only have been serenity. In writing up the descriptions of their observations, the children are asked to look for any assumptions they might have made. (On page 7 the reader will find a more detailed description of this operation. The intermediate grade teacher is also referred to page 164 dealing with the operation of observing in the secondary school.)

Some observations that intermediate grade children might be asked to make are suggested below.

1. Put a boiled potato on a saucer in the corner of the room. Ask the children to describe what they see after 3 days, after 6 days, after 2 weeks. What olfactory observations can be made at these intervals?
2. Bring in an assortment of various foods. Have the children taste the samples to determine the extent of sweetness in each.
3. Have the children find their own pulse. What do they notice about the

rate? Ask them to do ten push-ups and take their pulse immediately afterwards. What do they notice about the rate?

4. Have the children describe, both visually and by touch, an assortment of rocks.

5. Ask the children to shut their eyes for several minutes. Then ask them to describe what they heard.

6. If there is a class pet (such as a garter snake), ask the children to record its reactions to certain stimuli (such as food, noise, touch).

7. Ask children to make observations about the local newspaper, a "slick" magazine, the city newspaper.

8. Ask the children to record the details of the behavior of a prominent person (such as the President) from daily articles in the newspapers.

9. Have the children walk outside of the school in the fall (winter, spring). Ask them to make visual, auditory, and olfactory observations from this experience.

10. Have the children visit the school or public library. Ask them to describe what they saw.

11. Play a record of classical (popular, folk) music. Ask children to describe what they heard.

12. Ask children to describe the details of a football (baseball, basketball) game.

13. Ask children to describe life in India (Greece, Japan, Hawaii)—depending upon unit of study in class.

14. Have the children carefully observe a plant. Ask them to note details of size, color, texture, smell.

15. Have the children study a painting by a well-known artist. Ask them to describe what they see.

16. Ask the children to observe the structure of a specific part of an animal (reptile, bird, insect). Ask them to describe the details of their observation.

17. Ask the children to look at the sky. What observations can they make about the clouds?

18. Have the children look at a map. What can they tell about the country (or other location) from this map?

19. If a trip can be taken to a construction site, have the children observe and then describe what they saw.

20. Ask the children to describe what goes wrong when there is negative individual or group behavior.

21. Have the children observe the computation and solution to a math problem. Ask them to describe what they saw.

Comparing.

When providing opportunities for children to compare in the intermediate grades, the teacher might first help the children understand what steps are involved when comparisons are made. First, there is the element of observing, of noting details. Then, there is a mental sorting of these details, so that both *similarities* and *differences* of the objects being compared are noted. For example, a sixth grade teacher asked his students to think of many ways in which the life of an eleven-year-old boy in a suburban New York community was the same as, and ways in which it was different from, the life of an eleven-year-old boy in the Congo. The response of one student was as follows:

1. An 11 year old boy in the suburbs is more civilized than an 11 year old boy in the Congo. (I am referring to a primitive boy.)
2. An 11 year old boy in the suburbs is much smarter in arithmetic, spelling, reading, etc.
3. An 11 year old boy in the Congo knows how to hunt better than an 11 year old boy in the suburbs.
4. An 11 year old boy in the suburbs has a much more balanced diet than an 11 year old boy in the Congo.
5. An 11 year old boy in the Congo lives in a hut and an 11 year old boy in the suburbs lives in a house.
6. An 11 year old boy in the Congo can take care of himself better than an 11 year old boy in the suburbs.
7. An 11 year old boy in the Congo hasn't as much opportunity as an 11 year old boy in the suburbs.
8. An 11 year old boy in the Congo is much more interested in survival than anything else.
9. An 11 year old boy in the suburbs has more entertainment and activity than an 11 year old boy in the Congo.

In the above response, only differences were noted. Another sixth grader compared two girls in her class. Here, both similarities and differences were noted:

Anita	*Stefi*
1. blue eyes	1. hazel eyes
2. thin	2. chubby
3. dirty blond hair	3. brown hair
4. wears a brass (sic) on teeth	4. wears a brass (sic) on teeth
5. small in height	5. big in height
6. very cute and pretty	6. pretty
7. nice	7. a little fresh sometimes
8. good personality	8. good personality
9. pretends a lot	9. doesn't pretend so much
10. is very tender	10. is very tough
11. enjoys everyone	11. enjoys only some people
12. works well	12. takes a while to make friends

In examining each of the comparing responses, it is important for the teacher to help the child to understand the difference between what is demonstrably true and what the child might have assumed to be true. Hence, in the first of the above two examples, the teacher might question the child with regard to items #1, #2, and #9. In the absence of specific additional evidence to support these points, the child might want to qualify his statements by stating that, "It *seems to me* that suburban boys are more civilized" or "An 11 year old in the suburbs is *probably* smarter in arithmetic, spelling and reading." In the second example, the teacher might question items #9 and #11. In any of these instances, the child may be able to give some valid evidence to support his statements. It remains, therefore, for the teacher *not* to judge these comparative points *right* or *wrong,* but only to question for additional supporting evidence.

When a child's response to a comparing activity is very limited, the teacher might want to help him, through skillful questioning, to find additional comparative points. For example, he might ask, "What else can you think of that is different about the *activities* of a boy in the Congo and one in suburban New York?" or "What is *similar* about the *family structure* of a Congolese and a suburban boy?"

In selecting items for comparison the tendency is often to choose things that have some apparent relationship to each other, such as two books, two cars, two toys, two people. When a person is asked to compare two things which have no apparent relationship, such as a *train* and a *book,* he might say, "You can't compare them," or "They defy comparison." However, upon close examination and reflection, it *is* possible to find similarities as well as differences between two seemingly alien items. Furthermore, many teachers are often surprised by the perceptive observations of children who make these comparisons. (See page 6 for a more detailed description of this operation. The intermediate teacher is also referred to page 132 dealing with comparing for secondary school students.)

Below are several suggestions for comparing activities for intermediate grade children.

1. Two paintings by famous artists on the same theme
2. Two paintings by famous artists on different themes (e. g., a still life and a rural scene)
3. A folk song with a classical work
4. A folk song with a popular modern song
5. Life in India with life in your particular community
6. Life in India with life in Mexico
7. Reptiles and mammals
8. The growth and development of a frog and the growth and development of a butterfly
9. Two short stories
10. Two books
11. Two films

12. Two TV programs
13. Two newspapers
14. Science and social studies
15. The platforms of two candidates campaigning for the same office
16. Two poems
17. The writing styles of two poets
18. Two science demonstrations (or experiments)
19. Editorials and news stories
20. Cartoons and comic strips
21. Comic books and library books
22. The eye and the ear
23. The respiratory system and the digestive system of a human
24. The flute and the piano
25. An insect and a flower
26. Two children in class
27. Two teachers
28. Two methods of teaching
29. Saturday and Sunday
30. Christmas and Valentine's Day
31. An alligator and an automobile

Classifying.

In the process of classifying, the children are asked to arrange a variety of items according to groups or categories. It is essential that the categories have a distinct relationship to each other. Since it is believed that the *setting up* of the categories, or groupings, is a more complex task, it becomes advisable, in most instances, to have the children themselves determine the categories of classification. Should the teacher present to the class a list of geographical locations and then ask the children to group them according to cities and countries, he has, in a sense, done the children's thinking for them, and he is merely asking them to do a routine job of listing. There are, of course, children who cannot set up classifications or related groupings by themselves. In these instances it becomes necessary for the teacher to *show how,* to *explain,* and perhaps initially to *set up some sample groupings* for these children.

Very often, numerous possibilities for setting up related groupings suggest themselves to the children. Wherever there is a relationship between the categories, the classification system is acceptable. When the relationship does not exist, the teacher should help to point this out to the child. When the children have suggested many possible types of classifications for groups of words, or pictures, or, indeed, anything set up for classification, the teacher is urged to welcome the various suggestions.

An important element in setting up groups is to determine whether the grouping is *purposeful*. The child may be asked to defend his classification, revealing *why* he has made *those* groups. In other words, he is helped to understand that grouping objects into categories should be purposeful to him. Different kinds of groupings might serve different purposes. His purpose, therefore, will determine the nature of the categories.

For example, the child might be asked to classify an assortment of books. He might group them according to size, if his purpose is to store them on various-sized shelves. He might group them according to author's last name, in alphabetical order, if his purpose is to set up a library system. He might group them according to spheres of interest, if his purpose is to be able to locate a particular kind of book easily. (See page 9 for a more detailed description of this operation. The intermediate teacher is also referred to page 151 dealing with classifying in the secondary school curriculum.)

The following list contains suggestions of classifying activities for intermediate grade children.

1. Geographical locations
2. Animals
3. Books
4. Stories
5. Vocabulary words
6. Contemporary people
7. Famous historical men and women
8. Musical instruments
9. Sports
10. Foods
11. Math problems
12. Math examples
13. Science experiments
14. Proverbs
15. Occupations
16. Poems
17. Flowers
18. Plants
19. Games
20. Birds
21. Customs
22. Toys
23. Machines
24. Fish
25. Substances, such as animal, vegetable, mineral
26. Elements and compounds

27. Bodies of water
28. Islands
29. States
30. Countries
31. Holidays
32. Learning experiences
33. Activities of a school day
34. Activities of a week-end
35. Articles in a newspaper
36. Numbers

The examples which follow are samples of classification exercises done by sixth grade children.

Example A.

Classify the following items:

3, 5, .73, .01, 1/9, 12, 100, 1/3, .633,
17, III, 13, 3/4, .2, IX, X, 7/8

One student grouped the numbers in the following ways:

Whole numbers	*Fractions (proper)*	*Decimal fractions*
3	1/9	.73
5	1/3	.01
12	3/4	.633
100	7/8	.2
III		
13		
IX		
X		

Obviously, several other types of groupings are possible.

Example B.

Classify the following words:

compare	intricate	classify	curriculum
evaluate	propaganda	atomic	tired
ethnic	observe	molecule	summarize
orientation	delightful	committee	

One student grouped the words according to parts of speech:

Verbs	*Adjectives*	*Nouns*
compare	ethnic	propaganda
evaluate	intricate	orientation
summarize	atomic	molecule
classify	delightful	curriculum
observe	tired	committee

Again, several other types of classification are possible.

Collecting and Organizing Data.

Many teachers have, at one time or another, complained about the quality of "research" done by elementary school children. It seems that when some children are given an assignment to locate information on Louis Pasteur, for example, they head straight for the encyclopedia, select the P volume, locate Pasteur, and proceed to copy, word for word, the information contained therein. Next morning in class, the unsuspecting teacher asks, "Who has found the information on Pasteur?" Tommy enthusiastically waves his hand in the air (he has indeed found the information and spent perhaps one or two hours laboriously copying it — exercising the small muscles of his hand rather than his mind) and, in the innocence of youth, begins to read, *verbatim,* what he has copied. Of course, there are many words which he does not understand, and his performance is interrupted frequently by his stumbling over words he cannot read and by his having to ask the teacher, "What does this word say?" The benefits which Tommy and the class receive from this experience are questionable.

It seems that teachers ought to insure against such an eventuality by instructing children in library techniques as early as the intermediate grades. There are a number of guidelines that a teacher might consider and some rules that should be insisted upon.

1. If the topic happens to be Pasteur, the teacher might help the children to discover the numerous references which they might consult for information.

2. Children should be encouraged to consult various sources to determine the validity of the data as well as to uncover any inconsistencies in it.

3. The students should be helped to develop an outline. For students new to this experience the outline might be developed before the information is obtained. For example, the teacher might ask the students to decide what they wanted to know about Pasteur. A general outline, suggested by the students, might include:

I. The early life of Pasteur
    A. Home
    B. Family
    C. Schooling
II. His chosen profession
    A. Early experiments
    B. Frustrations and successes
III. His major scientific contributions
    A. What they were
    B. His experiences during their discoveries
IV. The effects of his work on our life today

Then, the student going to the literature will have some *focus* and some specific purpose for his collection of data. Of course, he may want to amend, to modify or even to expand his outline as his data is being collected.

4. Finally, it should be made very clear to students that to take material from the literature and use it as one's own is not only highly unethical, but illegal as well.

Let us then give students many opportunities to work independently, to collect information from various sources, and to organize this information into developmental and sequential written work, no matter how rudimentary their first efforts are. Let us prize these efforts even in their most primitive forms.

The following topics are suggested as possibilities for the collection and organization of data. This work may be carried out individually or in groups. It is strongly recommended that most topics come from the particular curriculum of a class. (See page 15 for a more detailed description of this operation. The intermediate teacher is also referred to page 208 which deals with problem-solving in the secondary school curriculum.)

1. Social studies topics

    1.1   The growth of our city (town, community)

    1.2   The history of our state

    1.3   The first settlers of New England

    1.4   Exploration and settlement of the West

    1.5   The growth and change of the South

    1.6   The effect of the geography of our state on the way we live

    1.7   The emergence of the independent African nations

    1.8   Life in India (Japan, Mexico, etc.) today

    1.9   The work of the United Nations

    1.10 Our relationship with the U.S.S.R.

    1.11 A comparative study of early Greek and early Roman civilizations

    1.12 The history of mathematics

    1.13 Alexander the Great

    1.14 Albert Schweitzer

    1.15 Winston Churchill

    1.16 Nehru

    1.17 John F. Kennedy

    1.18 U.N.I.C.E.F.

    1.19 The Supreme Court

    1.20 The President's Cabinet

2. Science topics

    2.1   How the respiratory (digestive, circulatory) system works in the human body

2.2   The evolution of life on earth
2.3   Harmful and helpful bacteria
2.4   Insects
2.5   Solar energy
2.6   Albert Einstein
2.7   Photosynthesis
2.8   Simple machines
2.9   Hurricanes and tornadoes
2.10 A mathematical process (reciprocals, for example)

Summarizing.

These experiences for intermediate children may be either oral or written. When a teacher asks his children to summarize, he is asking them to determine what is *significant* and what is not, what is *relevant* and what is irrelevant, what is *pertinent,* what is *essential.* Several skills are involved in this operation. There is the *synthesizing* of the material, there is the *determining* of what is important, and there is the *restating* of these essential points in a meaningful and sequential presentation.

Summaries may be made from various types of material and need not relate only to written work. The following suggestions are given for possible summarizing activities for intermediate grade children. (See page 6 for a more detailed description of this operation. The intermediate grade teacher is also referred to page 174 dealing with summarizing in the secondary school curriculum.)

1. Articles from reading workbooks, such as a basal series workbook, *Readers Digest Skillbuilders, Reading Skilltexts,* and others.
2. Films seen in school and outside of school
3. A day's activities in school
4. The activities of a week-end
5. A book
6. A story
7. A child's learning from a particular lesson
8. A child's reflections about an experience
9. A particular TV program
10. A newspaper article
11. An article from a children's weekly news magazine, such as *NewsTime,* or *Junior Scholastic*
12. A point of view expressed in a lecture or discussion
13. A lecture by the teacher or a visitor
14. A completed unit of work
15. A science experiment or demonstration
16. The experiences of a social studies or science unit of work.

Looking for Assumptions.

As intermediate children begin to engage in thinking activities of this type, the teacher might help to explain the concept of assumptions for them. We need to help children understand that to make an assumption is not necessarily wrong; but the important thing is for them to see that an assumption is being made.

There are some things that are quite clearly evident. Sometimes we say that they are true. For example, we look at an apple and we say, "It is red." We recognize this as clearly observable. Some assumptions we make are based upon strong bits of evidence. The strength of the evidence gives greater support to the assumption — nevertheless, it remains an assumption. For example, we look at the same apple and we say, "It has seeds." We cannot see the seeds on the inside of the apple, but we can be pretty certain that they are there — unless they have been removed in a manner which cannot be detected, or this is a new form of seedless apple. It would be a reasonable assumption, therefore, to look at an apple and conclude that it has seeds, *recognizing the possibility* that this may not be so.

On the other hand, many assumptions are based upon very little evidence, and it is these that are most subject to question. For example, to look at the same red apple and to conclude that all or most apples are red would be a rather broad assumption. When children make assumptions, the teacher might ask if they are *guessing* that something is true. Again, the teacher might ask for some *evidence, or support,* of a statement which a child has made to help him to see that he has made an assumption.

To summarize, then, the teacher should keep in mind that to make assumptions is not necessarily wrong. It is the ability to identify statements as assumptions that we wish to develop in children. The following list contains a number of activities in which intermediate grade children can look for assumptions. (See page 12 for a more detailed description of this operation. The intermediate teacher is also referred to page 196 dealing with the analysis of assumptions in the secondary school curriculum.)

1. Look for assumptions in responses to observations made by children.
2. Look for assumptions in responses to comparing activities.
3. In the illustration on p. 93, which contains more water? (Has an assumption been made?)
4. Two automobiles are in a race. Car A reaches its destination ahead of Car B. Can we conclude that Car A is faster? (Perhaps Car B had a flat tire?) To conclude that Car A is faster would be an assumption. We would need further evidence before we could determine which was really faster.

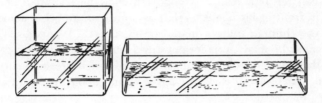

5. Three pencils cost 18¢. Therefore, each pencil costs 6¢. What assumption has been made? Is this a valid assumption? (Perhaps one pencil costs 10¢, one 5¢ and one 3¢?

6. Farmer Brown had a basket of eggs. He reached into the basket six times and each time brought out four eggs. How many eggs were in the basket? (Can we really tell the answer to this problem without making an assumption?)

7. Have the children check their math textbooks. Can they find any problems similar to those stated in items 5 and 6 above where assumptions need to be made before an answer can be found?

8. An airline company, in a popular advertisement, showed a picture of a jet plane in flight. The caption of the ad read, "You deserve the best on your flight to Miami." What assumption are they asking you to make?

9. Brand X claims that if you use their toothpaste you will have 32% fewer cavities. What assumptions are they asking you to make?

10. Ask the children to look in a magazine for advertisements. What assumptions do they ask you to make?

11. Have the children report on commercials seen on TV. What assumptions do they ask you to make?

12. Ask the children to write about an experience they have had. Help them to find any assumptions they made.

13. If you have read two very good stories by the same author and eagerly seek out a third, what assumption are you making?

14. Some money is missing in class. Peter is the likely suspect because he "hangs out" with those boys of questionable character. What assumption is being made here?

15. Arthur was late to school this morning. When he came into class, Anita said, "If you didn't stay up so late at night, you wouldn't have such trouble getting up in the morning." What assumptions might she be making? What assumption are you making about her?

16. "It doesn't snow as much in the wintertime as it did in the good old days." Is this an assumption?

17. "Spare the rod and spoil the child." What assumptions are underlying this statement?
18. "You can tell if a man is a good citizen if he has an American flag flying in front of his house." What assumptions are being made here?
19. Have the children study a map (graph, chart). What observations do they make? Be ready to point out any assumptions made.
20. Have the children look at an illustration of a well-dressed man (shabbily dressed man). Ask if they can tell anything about his occupation? His country or origin?
21. Have the children look at a picture of a person manifesting a particular facial expression (smile, frown). Ask if they can determine how this person is feeling. Ask if the evidence in the illustration is sufficient to support those conclusions.

Hypothesizing.

The primary objective in giving the children experiences with this thinking operation is to help them to understand and consider the variety of possibilities which may be involved in arriving at the explanation of a phenomenon. To orient intermediate children to the concept of hypothesizing is not difficult. Most intermediate children not only learn the concept rapidly, but are enchanted with the prospect of adding to their vocabularies so impressive-sounding a word.

In providing opportunities for hypothesizing the teacher needs to acquaint the children with the nature of an hypothesis. They may easily understand that an hypothesis is an *educated guess,* a *reasonable possibility,* suggested as a tentative explanation of something they have observed or have been told about. After the initial introduction, it is usually a good idea to give the children several examples in which they are permitted to arrive together at a number of hypotheses to explain a given situation. This type of experience may help the teacher to see how well the concept is being learned, and which children may need additional guided exercises in formulating hypotheses.

In addition, the children can be helped to understand that often *many* possibilities, or hypotheses, may be suggested for a problem, and that it will take further examination or *testing* of each hypothesis before they can ascertain its appropriateness. Implied in hypothesizing, therefore, is the notion of being able to *test* the various hypotheses presented. It is also important to note that *more than one* hypothesis may provide an appropriate explanation of a given phenomenon.

To further the idea that each hypothesis is a reasonable possibility, it is suggested that the teacher ask the children to stipulate this by the use of qualifying words, as in the following problem and the hypothetical statements below it.

Alfred did a problem involving the division of fractions. It was a problem of a mixed number being divided by a fraction. His answer was incorrect. What do you think the trouble might have been?

a. It *might be* that he forgot to invert the divisor.

b. *Perhaps* it is that he was feeling ill and could not think clearly.

c. *Maybe* Alfred was not taught how to do this.

d. He *might* not have read the problem correctly.

As the teacher works with children, *he should be ready to accept any reasonable possibility offered by the children as an hypothesis. The children may be encouraged to think of as many hypotheses as possible.*

Children who participate in many exercises requiring hypothesizing and who are given frequent opportunities to see many possible explanations of a given phenomenon become habituated to the kind of thinking which involves seeing many alternatives in problem-solving. (See page 15 for a more detailed description of this operation. The intermediate teacher is also referred to page 208 which deal with problem-solving in the secondary school curriculum.) The following list may provide children with several opportunities to hypothesize.

1. Why do you think that civilizations arose in river valleys?
2. What events might have caused the crisis in Vietnam (or another country currently in the news)?
3. Why do you think the author ended his story in that way?
4. What would be some ways in which we could increase our speaking vocabulary?
5. If Susan did not like poetry, how might we help her change her mind?
6. Frank is a very poor speller. How might we help him to improve?
7. Sally gets 100% in almost every spelling test, yet her spelling in her compositions is not good. Why do you suppose this is so?
8. If we wanted to study the difference between chemical and physical changes, how might we do it?
9. If we wanted to demonstrate how the earth turns around the sun, how might we do this?
10. If we wanted to study the phases of the moon, how might we do this?
11. If we wanted to study the weather, how might we do this?
12. How might we study the operation of the human circulatory (digestive, respiratory) system?
13. How might we measure the size of our classroom? our school? our playground?
14. How might we determine how many 1″ cubes will fit into a 6″ cube?
15. How can we determine the best method for solving a math problem?
16. How can we find out which is the shortest (fastest) route from the school to the public library?

17. Why do you think Columbus really set sail for America?
18. What do you think were some of the things that provoked the Civil War?
19. Why do you think that the colonies fought the War of Independence?
20. What do you think were some factors which helped the colonists to win the War for Independence?
21. Why do you think that California has so rapidly increased its population?
22. What do you think were some of the things that made Alexander the Great so "great"?
23. How do you think that Alaska could attract a larger population?
24. You are having a bad day at school. Your self-discipline is not working. You can not get any work done. The room seems to be very noisy. What do you think may be the trouble?
25. Your social studies group is not going well. You are all having problems deciding on what is to be done and how to do it. The other groups seem to be going ahead full steam. What do you think might be the trouble?
26. Your dog suddenly stopped eating. You are very worried about him. The vet cannot be reached. What do you think may be the trouble?
27. You have been doing very well in math. Your test scores have been very high. Suddenly, your marks begin to go down. You have not passed a math test in two weeks. What do you think may be the trouble?
28. Your teacher has been with your class for eight months. One day you come to school and find that you have a new teacher. What do you think might have happened?
29. Your stock has been declining steadily for two weeks. What do you think may be the trouble?
30. You wake up one morning and you find that your hair has turned purple. What do you think might have happened?
31. Peter behaves badly in class. He is often thoughtless and inconsiderate of others. His manners in the lunchroom are terrible. Suddenly there is a very great change in his attitude and behavior. What do you think has caused this?

Applying Principles to New Situations.

Many teachers think of this operation solely in connection with the curriculum areas of mathematics and science. While both of these curriculum areas offer many possibilities, activities for this operation, it need not be restricted to math and science alone. Upon examination of other areas, the thoughtful teacher will see many opportunities to develop activities which will give children experiences in applying principles to new situations.

The process of applying principles to new situations requires the ability to transfer learning from old experiences to those situations which are new to us. It requires the abilty to see relationships, to apply facts and principles previously learned to new problems. It requires the ability to determine *which* previously learned criteria are appropriate in the new situation, as well as the ability to apply them. Sometimes this is called *problem-solving.*

There are two types of situations in which children can exercise problem-solving abilities. In the first, the teacher might *present a situation* which requires a solution to a problem. In addition, he also would *provide some data.* The student is then required to work out the solution. In the second type, the teacher would *describe a situation* and then ask the student to *predict the outcome* in given circumstances The student is then asked to give reasons for his prediction.

Can the student apply facts and principles which he has learned to these new situations?

An example of an activity for each type of situation described above is as follows:

Type 1. A. *Situation needing solution:* How can we determine which of two containers is the larger?

   B. *Data given:* Container X is 2′ long, 4′ wide and 3′ deep. Container Y is 3′ long, 4′ wide and 2′ deep.

   C. *Student works out the problem:* Which container holds more milk?

Type 2. A. *Situation given:* Suppose we permitted each student in the class to have unrestricted access to the art supplies in the room.

   B. *Student asked to predict what will happen:* What do you think would happen?

   C. *Student asked to give reasons for prediction:* Why do you think so?

The following activities include samples of both types of experiences for intermediate grade children. In many of them, *several* solutions are possible. (See page 16 for a more detailed description of this operation. The intermediate teacher is also referred to page 208 dealing with problem-solving in the secondary school curriculum.)

1. How many yards long is our room? Our room is 540″ long.
2. Each child would like an equal share of pie. There are 25 children in the class. We have 5 pies.
3. What is the shortest walking route from the school to the public library? (Show children a city-block map of the area.)
4. What is the shortest driving route, in miles, from New York to Chicago? (Show children road map.)
5. How would you demonstrate wind power (water power, muscle power, solar power)?

6. What data would be needed to determine if tornadoes or hurricanes were more dangerous?

7. What data would be needed to discover the best kind of diet for white mice?

8. What evidence can you supply to demonstrate the stages of evolution?

9. How would you demonstrate that certain foods contain protein (starch, sugar)?

10. How can we tell if January is colder than February? If July is hotter than August?

11. How can you demonstrate that plants obtain food through their roots?

12. What would happen if you could sit next to your best friend in class? Why do you think so?

13. Who would be your choice for class president? Why?

14. What would happen if each student in the class had unlimited access to the art supplies? Why do you think so?

15. What would be the results if we spent two hours each day on math (reading, penmanship)? Why do you think so?

16. What would happen if the teacher did not "discipline" the students? Why do you think so?

17. How would it work if each child was permitted to choose his own book for reading? Why do you think so?

18. How would it work if we asked Alfred to take charge of distributing supplies? Why do you think so?

19. What would happen if we did not do spelling every day? Why do you think so?

20. What would the results be if we had to write a composition every day? Why do you think so?

21. Suppose a piece of music was played by an orchestra consisting of all trumpets. How do you think it would sound? Why do you think so?

22. (Show road map.) What would you guess to be the easiest automobile route to travel between New York and San Francisco? Why do you think so?

23. What do you believe to be the best art media for making a relief map? Why do you think so?

24. What reference do you believe will give you the information you need about gasoline engines? Why do you think so?

Criticizing.

Children are often freely critical (when this is permitted) and will need little prodding when they have strong feelings about something in particular which they do or do not like. Criticizing, however, requires deeper thought than the simple statements of feeling, such as, "I don't like it" or "It's not good." When one criticizes he should have a basis for what he is saying; he ought to have a position that has been thought about.

As the teacher helps the child to examine his reasons for or against something, he is giving the child an opportunity to establish some evaluative standards.

This might be done simply by asking "Why do you like it?" or "Why do you think that isn't any good?" Sometimes a child will reply that he doesn't really know. If the teacher feels that it is wisest to drop the matter at this point, then he should not hesitate to say, "You like this, but you really don't know why you do — is that right?" And if the child does not wish to pursue the matter and acquiesces, the teacher might simply indicate that he understands, showing that it is all right for the child not to respond further. Sometimes there are factors unknown to anyone but the child himself that make it difficult or impossible for him to respond at a particular time. A sensitive teacher who understands and responds to the needs of his individual students will realize at which time it is better not to push a child by forceful questioning. At other times, when the teacher feels he can pursue the questioning, he might suggest one or two possibilities for the child to consider, such as, "Do you like this story because it has good illustrations?"

Creating a climate in the classroom in which children are free to express their opinions is an important factor in drawing out their criticisms. A child would, of course, have to feel that he could express his opinions without penalty, however different from the teacher's they might be. He would also have to know that teacher approval is not meted out only to those who express the same point of view as the teacher.

When children have been encouraged to express criticism freely, there is sometimes the tendency to carry this criticism to an extreme. For example, one teacher recalled with mixed horror and pleasure the polite but unmistakable criticism, voiced by several of his children, of a new art teacher — *during the art lesson!* Whether the art teacher deserved to be so openly criticized by the children is irrelevant to this discussion. More to the point, perhaps, would be to question whether children should be permitted, or encouraged, to criticize a teacher. There are several answers which should be considered, depending, of course, upon the particular objectives and values of the individual teacher. However, taken beyond the "what is right and what is wrong" stage, we must remember that if we are to encourage criticism in our classrooms, we cannot suddenly become inconsistent and discourage the very kind of behavior we are seeking to develop. Rather, we must teach children to temper the expression of their criticism with *good judgment.* It is also wise to use great caution in encouraging children to be freely critical about the ideas and efforts of other children in the class. (See page 11 for a more detailed description of this operation. The intermediate teacher is also referred to page 220 dealing with evaluating and criticizing in the secondary school curriculum.)

The following list gives several topics about which intermediate grade children might voice their criticisms.

1. What do you think about this science (social studies) text book? Why?
2. What do you think about the safety patrol program in this school?
3. What do you think about a teacher's special monitor?
4. What are your feelings about being represented by class officers?
5. What are some suggestions for the improvement of the running of this class?
6. What do you think about the quality of your work this term in reading (math, spelling, etc.)?
7. What are some suggestions you might make for the improvement of the school lunch program?
8. What are your thoughts about your own prejudices?
9. In what ways do you think you might improve your own behavior?
10. What are your thoughts about the use of capital punishment?
11. What do you think about this country's policy towards Cuba?
12. Did you like the play? What were some good things about it?
13. How do you like our reading program? Do you have any suggestions for its improvement?
14. What did you think of _____ TV program?
15. How do you like that painting? What are some things that you like (dislike) about it?
16. How did you enjoy the trip? What were some of the good things about it? What are some things that you would like to see improved for the next trip?
17. What did you think about the science demonstration? How might it have been more successful?
18. What classroom routines would you like to see improved? Why?
19. What are some of the favorable features of our community? What would you like to see improved?

Imagining.

Most children, no matter what grade, seem to enjoy and participate enthusiastically in activities which ask them to do some imagining. Here, in a fanciful world, a child can be a king, a jet pilot, or take a trip to Venus. In these activities, the teacher merely asks the children to fancy freely what they would do if ... There are few, if any, qualifications which a teacher would impose upon a child's imaginings. After all, we have invited him to explore, to create, to fancy, to ponder what is beyond his real world. Some of the most treasured responses from children have come from activities which ask them to use their imaginations. The following list represents just a few of the activities in which intermediate children may participate. An imaginative teacher might develop hundreds more. (See page 14 for a more detailed description of this operation. The intermediate teacher is also referred to page 231 dealing with imagining and creating in the secondary school curriculum.)

1. What if today were a day in which gravity did not work?
2. What would you do if you were Tom Swift (Nancy Drew)?
3. What would it be like to be a snowflake?
4. How would you feel if you were the fraction ¼?
5. What would it be like if you could make yourself invisible at will?
6. What would you do if you could talk to animals?
7. What if you could fly?
8. What would it be like to live on Mars?
9. What would it be like if you were a famous baseball player (ballet dancer)?
10. What would you do if school were closed for a year?
11. What would it be like to be a trombone?
12. Suppose you were the color green?
13. What if you could go anywhere in the world on Saturday?
14. What if you woke up one morning and found that your hair had turned blue?
15. What if summer vacation came in December and January?
16. What if you found yourself all alone on a desert island?
17. What if the Wright Brothers had never invented the airplane?
18. What if Ferdinand and Isabella had not given Columbus the money to sail to America?
19. What if oil were discovered in your backyard?
20. What if Manhattan Island still belonged to the Indians?
21. What if the United States and Russia suddenly became very friendly to each other?
22. What if there was no TV?
23. Suppose you had three wishes?

Interpreting.

The reader is referred to the operation of *Interpreting* on pages 74-79. The activities listed in these pages are also suitable for children who have good reading and writing skills.

Decision-making.

The reader is referred to the operation of *Decision-making* on pages 50-54. Activities listed in these pages are also suitable for children who are fluent readers. In addition to these, other problems specifically related to classroom situations are presented below. These, too, involve the decision-making process and require the protection of the child's values.

1. Classroom management problems
   1.1 What would be a suitable way to arrange the chairs and tables in this room?
   1.2 How could we decide on job responsibilities?
   1.3 What would be the advantages and disadvantages of having class officers?
   1.4 How would we find a suitable way to elect class officers?
   1.5 What would be some good ways of working out classroom routines?
   1.6 How shall we arrange for space for displays?
   1.7 How can we arrange for additional room to carry out project work?
   1.8 What might be some good ways to handle the bulletin board displays?
   1.9 What do we want to do about the general appearance of our room?
   1.10 What would be some good rules to set up about behavior in the classroom?
   1.11 What might be some ways by which we could improve the behavior of the class?
   1.12 In what ways might we attempt to control the noise level in the room?
   1.13 What might be some good ways to set up the distribution of supplies?
2. Mathematics problems
   2.1 How can we find out if equal weights of liquids and solids have the same bulk?
   2.2 How can we measure the size of our room?
   2.3 How can we measure the size of a container?
   2.4 How can we tell which of two containers is the larger?
   2.5 What is the best way to cut a pumpkin pie into seven equal pieces?
   2.6 How can we find out the differences between decimal and common fractions?
   2.7 What are some ways in which we can understand the use of reciprocals?
   2.8 How can we determine the shortest (fastest) route from the school to the public library?
   2.9 How can we find out what is the best route from our school to destination_____?

2.10   What is the best route, by automobile, from New York to San Francisco?

2.11   How can we find out how many blocks can fit into a given container?

3. Science problems

3.1   How could we find out how a steam turbine (gasoline engine, jet engine, diesel engine) works?

3.2   What kinds of demonstrations can we set up to show wind power (water power, muscle power, solar power)?

3.3   How can we find out the differences between tornadoes and hurricanes?

3.4   How can we determine which factors influence the weather?

3.5   How can we determine the best kind of diet for white mice (for hamsters, for cats, for humans)?

3.6   How can we demonstrate that erosion is constantly taking place?

3.7   What demonstrations can we set up to show the stages of evolution?

3.8   What demonstrations can we set up to show that foods contain protein (starch, sugar)?

3.9   How can we tell if January is colder than February? If July is hotter than August?

3.10   How can we tell whether the soil outside of the school would be good for planting a vegetable garden?

3.11   How can we tell which vegetables would grow best outside of the school?

3.12   How can we tell how flowers obtain food?

4. Social studies problems

4.1   What are our individual responsibilities to the group?

4.2   How can we decide on the best practices for group living?

4.3   Going on a trip

4.3.1   How shall we decide on transportation?

4.3.2   What rules should be set up for the group?

4.3.3   What time factors are involved? How shall we work these out?

4.3.4   What money factors are involved? How shall we work these out?

4.3.5   What other arrangements need to be made? How shall we work these out?

4.4   Doing a social studies unit on ancient civilization

4.4.1   What would we want to find out?

4.4.2   What would be some good ways in which to set up groups?

4.4.3 How would we go about determining the learning experiences involved in doing group projects?

4.4.4 How would we evaluate the effectiveness of the group work? Of what we learned in the unit?

4.4.5 How would we go about finding suitable reference material to obtain needed information?

4.4.6 What are some effective ways of obtaining information?

4.5 Doing a class play

4.5.1 How shall we decide on a play?

4.5.2 What would be some good ways in which to distribute parts?

4.5.3 What plans would have to be worked out for the production?

4.5.4 How would we go about obtaining costumes?

4.5.5 How would we do the scenery?

4.6 How can our class make a significant social contribution to the school? To our community? To our state? To the U.S.?

4.7 Could our class adopt a foster child? How would we work this out?

4.8 How might we make our studies of other countries more real to us?

4.9 How might we go about inviting a guest speaker to our class?

4.10 What trips could we plan which would bring more meaning to our class work?

4.11 Making a project

4.11.1 How can we determine the suitability of the project as a learning experience?

4.11.2 What materials would we need?

4.11.3 How could we obtain these materials?

4.11.4 Where would the work be carried on?

4.11.5 What would be the individual responsibilities of each member of the group?

4.11.6 How would we demonstrate the project to the class?

4.11.7 How would we evaluate what we learned from experience?

4.12 How could we find out more about the Peace Corps?

Coding and Coding Other Papers.

The operation of coding has as its purpose the increasing of the student's awareness of the relationship between his thinking and his writing. Two processes are involved here. In the first, the teacher codes the student's papers, in an attempt to have him scrutinize his own thinking. In the second, the student is asked to code material that has been written by others. This material may be made up of editorials, newspaper articles, letters to the editor, magazine articles, textbook excerpts, and the like. Here too, the purpose of the coding is to reveal to the student some of the more common errors in thinking.

In both types of coding activities, specific symbols are used to represent specific kinds of thinking. Thus:

1. X is used to mark extreme statements, such as those containing *all, none, always, never*. It is also used to call attention to superlatives, such as the *best,* the *worst,* the *nicest,* the *biggest,* etc.

2. The letters "E-O" are used to mark *either-or* statements.

3. A "Q" is used to mark qualifying words, or phrases, such as, *in my opinion, it seems to me, perhaps, maybe,* etc.

4. "V" is used to note value statements — those words or phrases used by the writer to indicate what he likes or dislikes, what he favors or does not favor, what he wants or does not want. The symbol V — may be used for a negative value statement and V + for a positive statement.

5. "A" is used to mark attributions which writers have made to others. Attributions might relate to feelings, hopes, beliefs, causes, motives. A — may represent a negative attribution, A + a positive one.

6. "G" may be used to note a writer's generalizations.

When a teacher codes a student's paper, or asks a student to code his own paper, he should make clear that the coding symbols do not indicate *errors* that the student has made. In other words, the student is not marked *wrong* for the types of expressions he has used. Instead, the teacher simply brings these expressions to the student's attention. He then asks the student to re-examine these statements and to decide if the statements truly and accurately represent the student's thinking. It might be that a child has written, "Every boy in this class has read *The Phantom Toll Booth,*" and that this is *exactly* what he means to say. In this case, the teacher accepts the student's decision to keep the statement intact. If the teacher's coding of an "X" over the word *every* causes a youngster to re-examine and then modify his statement, the teacher has helped the student to express his thinking more clearly in his writing.

Coding, like any good teaching technique, should not be carried to an extreme. In other words, the teacher need *not* make use of the coding operation on *every paper* that the student writes. (See page 19 for a more detailed description of this operation. The intermediate teacher is also referred to page 121 dealing with the operation of coding in the secondary school curriculum.)

Some examples of the coding of students' papers follow.

X

I learned that there are a lot of different places in New York City. I never heard of Washington Square but I saw it on the day of the field trip. I also learned that a bookshop run by a beat is the same as one run by a business man. I thought that
G   V+
beatniks only like jazz, but they like folksongs too (and they sing pretty good). I learned that the United Nations was planned by eleven men (from different countries). I saw gifts given to the U. N. by Holland, Russia and Greece. I saw
X   X
all the flags of different countries and the U. N. garden. I learned what all the rooms were for and the countries that took parts in the meetings and why they
                       X
took parts in the meetings. I learned that there was a dark room for anyone who wanted to think or pray before meetings. I learned who planned the different rooms and furnished them. I learned that the U. N. has all kinds of people working for it. And I learned there are four rooms, but I forget their names. I also
                 V
learned that the U. N. has a very expensive gift shop.

Myself. I think I'm tall and long. I think I'm a normal thinker, what I mean is,
               E-O   V+
I'm not dumb and I'm not brilliant. I am a good drawer sometimes, but there are
                                V+
days when I can't even draw a straight line. I think I'm good in social studies
                                V−
off and on in science (it all depends on the subject), but in spelling, oh brother!
V+ X   X
I like most sports and enter most events, but there are times I can't even kick a
  V+
ball. I like hobbies such as putting together models and collecting odds and ends
              V+
which my mother calls junk! I like to read about famous generals of the past and
              V+
wars and countries. I like school for one reason. I learn there and another is if
              X
there were no school I wouldn't have anything to do and I would soon get bored.
V+   V+
I like to travel and I've gone to a lot of places in the country. I like animals and once in a while I find an animal I like in the woods or the pet store (but that's
              V+
very rare that I get one). I like my friends (that's because I've been playing with
                   V+
them for ten years) and go to many places with them. I like many things, but
X
best of all I like my parents and brothers.

If I had to choose between buying my mother a gift and buying myself a bicycle

V+

tire, I would not buy the tire for this reason. My mother should get something for

X   X

her birthday because it only comes once a year. My mother always buys me a

X   A

present for my birthday, and never thinks of herself. I will not buy the tire because
I should not think of myself first and I will buy her the present for this reason.

A CLIMATE FOR THINKING

If a teacher is to be concerned with teaching for thinking, he will discover
that it takes more than a conglomeration of activities to bring it about. He
will know that as he assigns the exercises, and while they are being carried
out, he must create a climate in the classroom that permits freedom for
thinking. Unfortunately, the climate in some elementary classrooms has the
opposite result — that of placing obstacles in the path of this freedom.

In talking and working with numerous groups of teachers, we have found
that teachers themselves are often guilty, however inadvertently or unintentionally, of obstructing a "climate for thinking" in their classrooms. Several
statements listed below are illustrations of teachers' comments about teaching
for thinking. They are typical remarks made to the authors which reveal
teachers' reactions on the subject.

1. *"I'd like to spend some time on developing thinking, but the day is
already so full of work that we barely finish."* Certainly the development of
any skill requires time for explanation, time for reflection, time for practice,
time for evaluation. When we ask a child to *think about something,* to *reflect
on alternatives,* to *decide,* we need also to provide the time for him to do
this. Of course, in an already crowded school day, this is going to be difficult.
Think for a moment of the teacher who suddenly found that it was 10:05
A.M., and the class was scheduled for a music period at 10:00 (what will the
music teacher say!); a paint jar had been knocked over, leaving intricate
patterns of red on the newly polished tile floor (what will the custodian
say!); a boy from the class next door stood at his desk demanding, "Mr.
O'Brien said I was not to leave until you returned our stapler" (what will
Mr. O'Brien say!); and Mark, his own student, politely asked, "What do you
think I ought to do about this, Mr. Rogers?" Of course, *it takes time* to use
this opportunity to say to Mark, "Now Mark, what do *you* think about it?"
What is really important here?

2. *"Thinking is important, I grant, but we just have enough time to cover
the curriculum."* This again seems to be a question of time, but another
aspect has been added — that of having to *cover the curriculum.* This means,
to so many teachers, the going over of certain prescribed content material for
that grade. Does it also mean that thinking is to be sacrificed on the altar of

content? Does the mastery of curriculum mean the negation of reflection? Might we, perhaps, examine again our purposes in teaching and our objectives in education?

What is really important here?

3. *"After all, I'm the teacher here!"* This remark is frequently made by those teachers who truly believe that the teacher is the omnipotent being in the classroom, that his opinions are the "right" ones, that his authority is not to be questioned. These teachers resent questions. They object to differences of opinion — particularly when it is a mere child who has the temerity to differ with the teacher's authority. These teachers want agreement rather than controversy. The following anecdote is to the point: A nine-year old girl found a problem in her math homework in which an assumption had to be made before an answer could be determined. With encouragement from an incorrigible mother, she approached her teacher on the following morning, indicating the fault in the problem. What was the teacher's response? "Never mind about *that,* Paula. Just *do* the problem." A climate *for* thinking?

What is important here?

4. *"I like to do things in my own classroom myself. In that way, I know that they get done right."* This statement came from a third grade teacher of many years experience, who had the most sincere objectives in teaching. She wanted things to be "just right." There was no room for error. Therefore, she did not permit her children to *explore,* to *discover,* to *experience,* since they were apt to make too many mistakes. It was so much better for her to do the thinking herself. A climate for thinking? Fertile ground for reflection?

What is important here?

5. *"To develop a curriculum in which children can be given frequent opportunities for thinking takes additional work, planning and time. I already spend two to three hours after school each day merely on routine tasks."* It is true that to focus on thinking in teaching takes additional planning on the part of the teacher, but if we were to total the amount of additional work for each week, it would most likely be a negligible amount. It also takes *thinking* on the part of the teacher. Is this, perhaps, the prospect that is the most threatening of all? Have our own teaching techniques become so automated that the prospect of doing something different becomes frightening?

What is important here?

6. *"That's not the answer I'm looking for."* Often without realizing it, a teacher stifles thinking in an attempt to have the children discover what he has in mind. He asks a question, receives several possible and plausible responses, yet *rejects each,* in search of the single response which he had in his own mind. The rejection of plausible answers is a stifling of thinking. True, there are occasions when *only one* answer is the correct one. But very often we ask questions for which many answers might be considered. An

illustration concerns a math lesson in which a child had demonstrated how he had obtained an answer to a particular problem. When the answer had been verified as correct by the teacher, another student raised his hand and said, "I got the same answer, but I did it in another way." A wave of a hand by the teacher dismissed the child. The answer had been found — what more needed to be said! A climate for thinking?

What is important here?

    7. *"What should I do here, Miss Peters?"*

      "This is the way you do it, Billy."

Miss Peters is the teacher who unwittingly does the children's thinking for them. She is the teacher with the automatic response. One of the hardest lessons for some teachers to learn is that of holding back that automatic response. Because of the various pressures of everyday living in an elementary school classroom, because of the variety of problems, of concerns, of activities, of requests, of questions, of decisions that have to be made, that seem to go on simultaneously, many teachers seem to be prone to dispatch children — to send them on their way with "the answer." *We,* the teachers, need time to reflect on what *we* are *doing* and *saying* to our children. We need to develop the skill of causing children to ponder about problems for themselves. When Billy asks, "What do I do here, Miss Peters?" It seems so simple to say, "Now, what do *you* think about that, Billy?" Try it!

    8. *"Elementary school children are too young to think."* Some teachers believe that the development of thinking processes can proceed profitably only after the age of twelve or so. But is this idea consistent with the major objectives of elementary education? Almost any proud parent will certainly give evidence to support the notion that thinking occurs even in pre-school age children!

    9. *"Teaching with an emphasis on thinking is too dangerous!"* What are the results of developing thinking skills? Children become more questioning. They are less apt to accept things at face value. They become more critical and consequently more aware of existing faults. Certainly children become less apt to accept assumptions and more skilled in interpreting experiences. This probably would tend to cause more *critical debate* in a classroom, more skepticism and less reliance on the teacher as an authority. In other words, the myth of the teacher as an all-knowing, all-powerful person might be shattered. If we wish to continue this myth, if we wish children to be accepting, without question, if we wish little criticism, if we want children to do things simply because we tell them to, then, certainly, *thinking is dangerous.*

    10. *"Thinking disrupts my classroom."* Some teachers become terribly unsettled by any attempt at disturbing the status quo. They are threatened by questions, by lack of agreement, by suspension of judgment. They want their classrooms to be in order — with almost everything reducible to *yes* or *no, true* or *false.* If a teacher believes that "thinking disrupts," what kind of thinking is *he* doing?

The foregoing examples give an indication of some of the very real problems faced by teachers who are concerned with teaching for thinking. In each, the primary question has been "What is important here?" For a teacher who *truly values teaching for thinking as a primary objective of education in the elementary classroom,* what is the answer?

USING THE THINKING ACTIVITIES

Given a "climate for thinking" the teacher needs to consider three other aspects of the use of the thinking activities in the classroom. These are the orientation of the children to the thinking operations, the consideration of the responses of children, and the evaluation of the responses. Each of these aspects is dealt with briefly below.

1. The orientation of children to the thinking operations

In undertaking almost any new teaching task, there is usually a period of orientation—a time of *initiation,* of *explanation,* of *demonstration.* Such a period is important when the children are introduced to many of the thinking operations. When giving children activities in observing, the teacher might first *initiate* them to this task. He may *explain* the different senses involved in making observations. A *demonstration,* a sample exercise in observing, might be performed. This kind of orientation is to be planned carefully for each thinking operation, so that the children will know clearly what is expected of them.

2. The responses of the children

In the sections of Part II where the activities are listed, many samples are given of children's responses to these activities. The teacher's reactions to such responses, as well as to any others a child might make are of the utmost importance to the success of a thinking-oriented program.

If the teacher agrees that the program's purpose is to cultivate thinking processes and not to stifle them, he wants to be sure that the things he says to children, when he looks at their work or listens to them speak, will fulfill his objectives. Therefore:

a. When the teacher asks questions with the intention of promoting thinking, he ought to do this in a *gentle* way, rather than in a tone of voice or manner that implies pressure.

b. When children respond very slowly at first, it would be wise for the teacher not to *insist* on more comparative points, or more hypotheses, for example, but rather to encourage these through the further use of demonstrations, examples and exploratory questions.

c. Teachers might acquaint themselves with the types of questions that are most thought-provoking, most helpful in causing a child to reflect more deeply. Specific questions can help the child to focus on a particular aspect of a problem.

d. Teachers need to become alert to those questions or comments which tend to "cut off" thinking. As the teacher grows aware of these, he can abandon their use.

3. Evaluation of responses

Many teachers have asked, "How do you mark the responses of children to these activities?" If a teacher begins to judge these responses by number or letter, he is missing a major point of this work. Would the reader think of putting an 89 or a B— on a child's drawing? To put a mark on a thinking activity would serve an equally absurd purpose.

In evaluating a child's response, then, the teacher's purpose is best served when he looks for quality of thought, for creativity of thought, for depth of thought. Sometimes it is a good idea to "'mark" on a child's paper that it is *Good*. Sometimes we may note "Good Thinking" on a paper to compliment a child who has really put his mind to work. In other instances, perhaps we can write, "This is a good try," or, "You are really making progress." Where you feel that the child has not done the best he is able to do you might "mark" the comment, "What else might you have considered in this problem?" on his paper; or, where the wrong tack has been taken, "You need some help here. Let's sit down and talk about it."

The "positive" approach is likely to be far more successful in assuring continued progress.

The initial responses of many children in undertaking a new thinking operation are often limited. But with encouragement, questioning, and many exposures to the same operation, teachers may expect to find considerable improvement in the quality of response.

One way in which a teacher might "evaluate" the children's responses to the activities is to observe the children's behavior. Is their behavior less impulsive? Are certain children more willing to try things out on their own? Do more children seem to have a greater understanding of events around them? Do they begin to see many alternatives? Do they seem to value inquiry? Are they skeptical, questioning? Do they suspend judgment? If you see these signs appearing in your children, then it would be reasonable to assume that they have profited from their work.

One word of caution should be raised at this point. Teachers, like children, need to feel a sense of success in what they do, to have some tangible evidence of their success in teaching. It pleases us immensely when a child who has been struggling with reading becomes a skilled reader, when a lad suddenly gains insight into the process of division of fractions, when Alice, that shy little eight-year-old, is helped to emerge from her shell. What about tangible evidence of increased skill in thinking? The clues given in the preceding paragraph may help to measure the teacher's success. There is also the likelihood that certain types of undesirable behavioral patterns—those manifestations of behavior which are related to lack of experience with thinking will become modified (see page 23). This is another way of determining the teacher's success in his task. However, like other skills, thinking skills *take time* for development to show itself. In some children, results will begin to appear after about six to eight weeks. In others, results may not appear in as many months. As different children learn other skills at varying rates, so will they vary in the time it takes for them to learn comparing, observing, classifying and the others.

CONCLUSION

The examples, statements, events, responses, even many of the activities themselves shared with you in Part II are not fictional. Most of them come from the authors' work with children in the elementary classroom. Some came from observations and discussions with other elementary school teachers. It is from these real experiences with teachers that this concluding statement is recalled.

Teaching for thinking is not a simple job, but neither is any other good teaching a simple job. Those who *value* good teaching will practice it. Those who *value teaching for thinking* will seek out the ways to practice it. Teaching for thinking can be the most exciting kind of teaching you have ever done. It is exciting to find children enthusiastically responding to comparing activities—and to find them comparing when you have not even asked them to do so. It is exciting to see children working out solutions to problems on their own. It is exciting to find children *challenging, inquiring,* and *suspending* judgment. It was exciting to find Mark—the child who was "always stuck" and overly dependent—becoming more independent and trying new things out for himself. It was exciting to find Debbie finally able to find means which were consistent with her aims. It was so very exciting to find even Bob —who was loud, dogmatic, and overly assertive, resistant to thinking *and* impulsive, the boy whose illogical statements were used to open this part of the book—become more thoughtful, less impulsive and easier to work with. When a special service teacher remarked that Bob did not seem to be the same boy anymore, *it was exciting.* But perhaps most exciting of all was the day that twenty-five former sixth-graders who had been exposed, by their teacher, to a year of thinking activities, visited with that same teacher's college classes. Almost 100 sophomore education students pummeled these children, now seventh graders and in their first year of junior high school, with questions about their sixth grade experiences. "How do you think that your work in the sixth grade helped you to adjust to the new experiences of junior high school?" one student asked. Eddie, identified at the beginning of his sixth grade career as being "in-a-rut," a child who was most comfortable doing things always in the same ways, replied enthusiastically, "Well, you see, we're such independent thinkers that we are really able to handle new situations much more easily."

part three

APPLICATION: THE SECONDARY SCHOOL

INTRODUCTION

Thinking is one of the safe words, even though in intensity, it can equal the powerful affective connotations of words like freedom, democracy, justice, love and integrity. One may ask, why not? Each time a practical problem is solved—*thinking how* to get into our house—thinking is going on. When we muse pensively *thinking of* thousands of things so that it seems as if we are thinking of nothing, thinking is going on. If we are busy marshaling our defenses—*thinking up* reasons for our behavior and beliefs—thinking is going on. As we delay making a judgment or decision—so that we can *think about* the matter—thinking is going on. And when we are searching and examining, investigating and analyzing an elaborate synthesis of ideas or a classification scheme—*thinking through* the system to check for order and interrelationship—thinking is going on.

Thinking *how*, thinking *of*, thinking *up*, thinking *about*, thinking *through* seem to be part of human equipment. We all spend some time on each, though some of us become adept and skilled at one or the other "varieties" of thinking, perhaps because we devote time to it. Then too, we all spend much time changing our minds, *i.e.*, exchanging one thought or idea for another. We do this sometimes almost casually. Seemingly, like a good trader, we are interested in swapping as well as collecting, but usually only when *we* are in the mood. Somewhat like the collector of rare treasures, we are proud of our showcase and become alarmed if someone threatens to remove one of our jewels. Although we ourselves often replace the items in that showcase, and though from time to time, we might even empty the whole thing out somewhat impulsively and heedlessly, or even reluctantly, this is something which we regard as a personal right. After all, it is we who determine whether additions to the showcase will fit in with the existing collection. Trouble sometimes ensues when we urge one of our treasures on someone else or when the other person is insistent upon our acceptance of one of his gems.

It has been suggested that the term *thinking* is safe; by definition, non-controversial. And the *fact* of thinking, as far as the individual is concerned, is also not debatable. That is to say, thinking is popular because everybody does it! Moreover, not only is there egalitarian distribution of the particular commodity, but even the acquisitive instinct of man, normally intensely operative when it comes to other goods of the world, here is quiescent. It would seem that our beliefs on the matter tend towards a natural and pristine communism. "I have a terrible memory" [usually said with pride], "but I have plenty of good old horse sense," is a saying which should be, by now, firmly established in the folklore. Rooted as the belief is in our psyche, to deny that sense is common to us would be tantamount to a denial of the selfhood, our identity, our human-ness. It would be similar perhaps to an admission that we lack a "sense" of humor.

If one were to talk about education and its objectives and the relationship to thinking, we might see controversy entering the arena. There seem to be very few persons who are really interested in someone else's musings and dreams, or his mental habits which help him to perform the operations of daily living, or his rationalizations and his "good reasons." Traditionally, however, teachers have been believed to be interested in the reflections of students, thoughts that have been arrived at through deliberation and with deliberateness; yet reflection, time-requiring as it is, sometimes annoys to the point of hurrying the person "off the fence." "Make up your mind" is often heard as an injunction *not* to think. There is an accompanying notion that students somewhere have learned and should now somehow know how to come up with a judgment upon demand; more often than not, the demanded judgment is one that happens to be coincident with an accepted view.

Perhaps it is a truism that teachers are concerned with the thinking of students or, as some would have it, the lack of it, for it is generally believed that teaching operations should induce thinking. An embarrassing question would ask to what extent teaching activities actually reflect concern with thinking *how*, thinking *of*, thinking *up*, and thinking *about*. It seems to be fairly obvious that thinking *through* is of some concern. Yet, one even hears a questioning voice asking if thinking (even thinking *through*) should be a feature of teaching and learning?

Though a common saying is "to think for oneself," redundancy becomes obvious when one considers that thinking has to be for oneself or it is something else. It is necessarily personal and creative; it cannot be *re*-creative and *re*-productive. As Dewey has said so well, thoughts and ideas cannot possibly be conveyed from one mind to another, only facts can be transferred. Incidentally, the ease with which it is possible to transfer facts may be related to the forgetting rate, which is enormous.

Thus, though teachers might imagine that they are teaching for thinking by teaching someone else's thinking, what they are actually doing is teaching the product of someone else's thought. In so confusing product with process we are led astray. To try to transfer full-blown the interpretations and syntheses from one mind to another is *not* to teach for thinking.[1] It seems that mankind has traditionally valued the products of thought while not caring too much about the processes. Perhaps conventional knowledge assumes that the process is a collective possession which comes about sooner or later while the product of thought is believed to be a matter of individual contribution.

Schools seem to reflect conventional knowledge. A traditional position has been that since the processes, or methods, of thought cannot be taught, let us teach the products, the results of someone else's thoughts. Thus, the aphorism, "when one teaches information, one teaches all that it is possible to teach," has been a beacon light for schools, teachers, and test makers.

We might know more about this matter had there been numerous attempts to teach processes. There is not an abundance of evidence on this point. If one is to judge from tests in widespread use from elementary school through college, one finds that there is little direct instruction in thinking processes and skills. At the same time, there is a tacit assumption and, if the law of equal distribution hold, an expectation that thinking processes and skills should somehow exist ready for use. Surely, an attempt at cultivation can yield some information on the question.

For teachers to provide opportunities for thinking would be to advance citizenship education. Some believe that the creed of the American people is well-expressed in the saying: "You can't fool all the people all the time." Now, if we subscribe to this as a maxim, we also subscribe to its antecedent and corollary, that the people, *en masse,* in the long run, are capable of making right judgments. Ostensibly, there is faith in self-determination; the individual should make choices. That the schools "should" concern themselves with teaching for judgment-making is an old, old story. That in the main, they do not do so is also an old, old story.

Perhaps there is prevalent a belief that minds are wax, something to be molded, something upon which teachers can leave their imprint. Sometimes, teachers stack the cards to make sure that the judgments of the young agree with theirs. At other times, adults make judgments for the young upon the assumption that the collective judgment of mankind in the past is sure. There

---

[1]Perhaps the relationship may be expressed in terms of literary art. A task of the historical novelist is to help the reader imagine that the past is the present. Despite the novelist's artistry in transcending time, the reader can never really leave the present.

is also the simplistic notion that judgment-making is best learned by *accepting* other people's judgments. Joined to it is the naive idea that the process of judgment-making is learned by watching and imitating someone else doing it or by studying the products of other people's "judgings." Sometimes, the assumption is made that the young must be shielded from the consequences of errors in judgment-making. Yet the young do become adults. Few of us are prepared to "go whole hog." We do not suggest disfranchising legislation for adults who make errors in judgment. No doubt, there is faith that somehow life, maturation, or common sense will work to the rescue of society, and our faith in democratic processes will be justified. Four centuries ago, Montaigne asked a question which is still insistent today: "I should like to see one who can teach us to throw a spear, play upon the lute, or judge, without any exercise in each of these skills."[2]

There are so many exercises which focus on the products of someone else's thoughts and which call forth the lower mental processes of recall, recognition, and association. Exercises are needed which are less concerned with product and which will call forth processes classified in the higher mental grouping like interpreting, evaluating, analyzing.

The invention of such exercises is not as difficult as might be supposed. As a beginning, teachers may ask themselves certain check questions: How many judgments have my students made today? How many times have I asked students to compare, to summarize, and to interpret? How often do my students observe and report? How many times have they classified and criticized? Have they been alerted to look for unstated assumptions or to distinguish between fact and inference? In short, how many opportunities have I given my students to see *how* knowledge is created and to participate in the creation of knowledge? Moreover, how do these foregoing opportunities compare with the number of times I am asking my students to commit to their depository the knowledges created by others? In my pursuit of data-gathering, is such harvesting seen as a link in the chain of a method of science, of coming to know?

Few of us will deny that we need respite and surcease from the *ex cathedra* utterance, the obeisances to the gods that are offered as part of public devotions. Loyalty oaths publicly sworn, genuflections, and talk about thinking are weak substitutes for demonstration of activities, procedures, and processes. What is needed are many examples at the grass roots level. Hopefully, this is what this book is all about.

Sometimes, however, despite our protestations to the contrary, teachers really do not want thinking to ensue as a consequence of teaching. Almost unconsciously, they adopt tactics and attitudes which are effective inhibitors. If thinking processes are to be nurtured, an awareness of attitudes and tactics

[2]*Of The Education of Children*

which inhibit thought on the one hand and those which promote thought on the other needs to be developed. In this regard, a few basic ground rules are set forth:

1. Some teachers seem to make a career of asking the question: "Guess what I have on my mind?" Perceptive students soon learn that to find out what the teacher wants and then to give it to him brings its rewards. The teacher beams and says, "Good thinking; that's the answer I was looking for!" Such paternal pats on the head often condition students away from thinking. Whether or not the teacher consciously attempts to seduce and to cultivate docility, the results are often the same; he becomes shepherd to a flock of sheep.

2. The teacher who asks what the data are (the *who, what, when, where* questions) is concerned with a lower mental process, albeit he elicits the responses with pedagogical flourish. The teacher who gives the student some data and then asks what they mean is concerned with a higher mental process. In the lower mental process, there is emphasis upon receiving material and reproducing it relatively unchanged. Faithfulness to the original is the watchword. In the higher mental process, there is a reworking of the material into something not there before; there is contribution on the part of the individual to that which is presented. Change of the original is the watchword of the higher process.

3. There is, then, a distinction between asking a student what he thinks and what he remembers. To think, in the foregoing sense, is to see what others may not see. To remember is to recollect knowledge which is held in common. It is perhaps important here to note that it is self-defeating to teach students techniques for interpreting and evaluating and then to test them on what they can recall. Students have a way of finding out what it is that they will be tested on and then studying for that purpose. Teachers, of course, often have a way of teaching to that purpose.

4. Some conceive of mental processes as being contained within two compartments of "pure" reason and "pure" emotion. "Now one thinks and now one feels." Instead the situation more nearly approximates *e pluribus unum*. Mental activity often consists of reflection *and* reverie, of concern with practical problems *and* defense of the organism. To hold that thinking processes are orderly or easily compartmentalized into a single faculty is, in the long run, probably hurtful.

Mental processes are not synonymous with the word *logic* or with scientific method or with steps in problem-solving, all of which imply orderliness. As has been suggested, they are overlapping, intertwined, and even messy and unsystematic. The subject matter of logic deals with the products of thought, with a procedural summary, a *post mortem* as it were, and it helps in the analysis of a position already advanced; it is not confused with the means by which the particular position was origi-nally established. Hence, listings of *the* problem-solving method or steps in *the* scientific method are viewed critically, problem-solving method being seen as the method of hindsight, an inference or historical inter-pretation about a situation.

For example, if one does a technical experiment as outlined in a typical laboratory manual, he is finding out what someone else did and how he did it. But in the ongoing research experiment, problem-solving *as method* is being created. In other words, to list steps in *the* scientific method is to pick out, in retrospect, features of the way a series of experiments, sometimes lasting two hundred years, was conducted so that it can be retraced or redrawn. (The germ theory of disease might be a good example.) Somewhat like Alice's Cheshire Cat, the appear-ance, but not the substance remains.[3]

5. Thinking, expressed as a challenge to old forms, seems to fit in with the emotional patterns of the adolescent youngster. Hence, criticism of the teacher and other authorities will probably be a consequence of teaching with an emphasis on thinking. This critical attitude is not only a matter of chronological age or endocrinological ferment, but also may be related to the number of opportunities which the youngster has had heretofore for expressing his thoughts. Where thinking has been encouraged, there may not be a compelling need for hypercriticism. On the other hand, if its outward expression has been generally suppressed heretofore, and then suddenly it is made available, certain youngsters tend to become inebriated with a new found power. It may then be expected that at first, a certain amount of argumentative arrogance and even "smart aleckism" will be manifest. As the youngster acquires skill and under-standing of purposes, there will be a tendency for initial exaggeration to abate.

6. To face the results of inquiry and reflection takes courage and fortitude. It is frightfully easy to be critical about the "other" fellow and the "other" idea. It is perhaps even easier to be critical about neutral or objective matters. If thinking means criticism at all, it means criticism of the self. Teachers especially will be ready to accept the criticism of stu-dents, for indeed, criticism is the life of life itself as it certainly is the life of science and art. Thus, it has been well said that doubt is a hand-maiden to inquiry. Teachers might forewarn themselves that that which

---

[3]"To the onlooker, who makes a study at an advanced stage of the work, the experi-menter's thinking must often appear wasteful, directed so far as specific stages are concerned, but wandering in relation to final issues, remarkably uneconomical in the sense that what may take the experimenter years to establish may take the expositor only a few minutes to describe." F. Bartlett, *Thinking* (New York: Basic Books, Inc., 1958), pp. 132-133.

the mind seizes and dwells upon with particular delight is to be held suspect.

7. There may be some who will confuse an emphasis on thinking with teaching students tricks and stunts to use as a means for winning an argument or for showing someone up. A higher morality may prevail— that of facilitating understanding which leads to self-understanding; debating or arguing for the sake of winning, or learning tricks wherewith to demolish an opponent would then be seen as a monstrous caricature.

8. It has sometimes been said that thinking is only worthwhile in "objective" matters, in closed systems, where the answer is compelled by an internal logic; that no fruitful results can be obtained in open systems where the subjective enters in. To concentrate thinking activities exclusively on closed systems simply because it is easier to come to agreement is to overlook possibilities for greater challenge. *Because* the subjective enters in and because it is not easy to work in the open system, redoubled efforts for thinking activities may be worthwhile.

Some have indicated that thinking in open systems is beset by yet another difficulty. Open systems are often found in "closed" areas: morality, politics, sex. Surely, if choices and alternatives are not present, one can hardly talk about thinking, for with the erection of tabu topics comes an effective throttling of thought. One is reminded of the school superintendent who cautioned a young teacher against the teaching of controversial issues—as if there were any other kinds! It is hoped that the foregoing will not be interpreted as an argument against the teaching of mythology. By mythology, we do not mean that special kind of language, quite distinct from historical or scientific language, that symbolizes certain realities in poetic and allegorical form. As a means of introducing us to fabulous wonder, of fostering sensitivity to the beautiful, mythology is often overlooked and sadly misinterpreted. We *do* mean, however, the subverting of the purposes of mythology whereby there is a cultivation and ensconcing of fiction rather than fact: "it is a crime to examine the laws of heat because it is a duty to worship the sun." The notion of closed areas is noxious to thinking as is the latter destructive of the former; one or the other usually prevails.

In the section which is to follow, operations, procedures, tactics, and activities are offered as illustrations of possible ways of emphasizing thinking processes. As has been indicated, thinking is an omnibus term which includes several mental processes. Some of these, especially the lower processes of recall, recognition, and association receive extensive practice from elementary school through college; the higher mental processes seem to receive only occasional and incidental stress. By many they are looked upon as by-products of the lower processes. A few reasons are offered for this state of affairs: 1) Many teachers seem not to know *how* to put an emphasis on higher mental processes. 2) There is a notion that first one needs to focus on lower mental processes to prepare the groundwork for the higher processes. 3) Much of testing reveals a concern for the right answer, hence, teaching is absorbed with developing right answers.

The cliche, "walk before you run," has just enough truth in it to be false. The analogy, usually offered as proof, implies that *the* facts come first and thinking comes second. Correctly understood, thinking is a *means of acquiring facts*, relevant facts. Moreover, there is considerable evidence that higher mental processes are strengthened as opportunities for exercise are increased. Perhaps of greater concern to some is that the lower processes are strengthened as there is focus on the higher processes; rather than a loss of content there is a gain. As William James once said, science or rational order is the perfect mnemonic system. Furthermore, exposure to years of teaching which focuses almost exclusively on lower processes conditions the mind to uncritical acceptance. Is not a lack of opportunities which engage the higher mental processes related to mental sluggishness? The teaching of facts, the gathering of information, is properly seen as a response to thinking.

"But," it is argued, "a teacher must teach the curriculum, mustn't he?" The operations which will be described below do not comprise a syllabus which is to be "covered"; neither are they intended as a pattern which must slavishly be followed. While the operations may be applied within the framework of an existing curriculum, *i.e.,* their application requires little actual revision of curriculum, they do ask of the teacher that he develop the curriculum. It is hoped that the next section will provide enough illustrations so that teachers may be guided towards the invention of their own materials in developing the curriculum.

A final word of introduction is in order. It is the process that is important and not the conclusion as such. For some teachers of secondary school subjects, patterns of teaching, which are largely variations of "test-prepping," are so indelibly tatooed as to preclude new avenues of thought. Given such conditioning (perhaps one may say traumatizing), the operations herein may well be converted into tests for which there is only one acceptable answer. The authors can only make a plea for the teacher to focus on the process and not to treat the operations as stunts nor the exercises illustrating them as a syllabus or test.

THINKING OPERATIONS

In this section and in succeeding sections of this part, there will be an identification of ten operations relating to thinking. Each operation will be described, and exercises and suggestions for exercises will be set forth with illustrations drawn from various subject areas. Included in the exposition will be some pedagogic guidelines. The operations that have been selected are reacting to coding, comparing, classifying, observing and reporting, summarizing, interpreting, analyzing assumptions, problem-solving, criticizing and evaluating, imagining and creating.

The foregoing is not a listing of the only operations in existence relating to thinking. Neither is it a list whose groupings are sacred or whose descriptive terms are the only possible ways of describing the operations. Furthermore, the order in which the operations are presented represents a convenience. Elsewhere in this book, the reader will perhaps encounter a different listing of operations. In this regard, the examination of the differences and the similarities may be of interest.

It is strongly urged that the contents of these sections *not* be considered as a course to be covered or as examples *of* thinking; the examples are rather designed to elicit thinking. Again it is emphasized that curriculum revision is not called for but that curriculum development is. No subject area as such has been identified, although applications to a subject organization of studies may be apparent. (This is not intended to convey the impression that core studies, experience curriculum, or other plans of curricular organization are thereby excluded.) Each subject area has within its existing content rich resources for use within each of the operations.

1. Reacting to Coding

"As a man thinketh in his heart so is he" is an aphorism with which many can agree. Literally, a man is what he thinks. And the incarnation of what he thinks and the way he thinks is found in the way he speaks and writes, for conceptualization is impossible without language. For the teacher, attention to the words students use will aid in revealing their thinking processes. The teacher can help the student "see what he thought" by getting him to look at what he wrote. If thinking is seen in part as a matter of disciplining the self, a fruitful place to begin disciplinary activity is with language and word usage in speaking and writing; no school subject can avoid these two manifestations of thinking. Yet, there is little direct instruction in dealing with expressions relating to thinking processes. Why is this so?

Not many teachers take the time for the careful analysis that would be necessary. Perhaps there is a prevalent faith that such work belongs within the domain of a teacher of logic or at least within the purview of an English teacher. As a corollary, analysis of expressions relating to thinking processes may be thought of as a matter of content organization rather than as method which might pervade all courses. Curriculum development is sometimes seen as: "Let's add a course in . . ."

Then too, it is not uncommon to hear that the ability to discern and to analyze carefully is a skill which results from mere aging. If this is so, perhaps one has a right to expect college students to have attained a measure of intellectual maturity. In an investigation, into the written expressions of college students, it was found that not much attention was given to manifestations of thinking.[4] Upon tabulation of the types of markings found on student term papers, it was seen that mechanics of writing, form and style, endorsement or criticism of the writer's views, and the assignment of a grade appeared to occupy the attention of the instructors who read the papers. (This was true regardless of the course for which the paper was written.) Yet, opportunities for marking papers in such a way as to call attention to thinking processes were disregarded at an average ratio of 5:1.

It may be observed that the need for practice in differentiating between that which is observational and that which is inferential and the tendency to confusion between the ascriptive and the descriptive are not the exclusive property of the uneducated. To go even further, this tendency to attribution and imputation is so bound up in the psyche of the human being, that unless one is on guard, attribution of cause and feeling falls from our lips routinely, "as a manner of speaking." Semanticists have pointed out the symbiotic nature of ways of speaking and prejudice of all varieties. Certainly, the attribution, loosely applied, is a rock upon which prejudice can rest.

Previously, it had been said that the teacher can help the student see what he thought by having him examine what he wrote. How is this to be done? In the several pages which follow, expressions relating to some thinking processes are first identified. Expressions of attribution, of generality, of value, of analogy, among others, are delineated and illustrated. A code symbol appears alongside each expression indicating that it represents a form of thinking.

Following the presentation of expressions relating to thinking processes, a sample paper has been coded with the symbols to indicate a possible application. On p. 128 some recommendations are made for the teacher regarding presentation and use of coding to elicit the reactions of students. Finally, some more samples of coded papers are offered.

Below appears the listing and explication of expressions relating to thinking processes. The reader may wish to consult Parts 1 and 2 of the text for variations in order and treatment.

1.1   *Attributive Statements*   *(Code A)*

These are statements which are ascriptive rather than descriptive. Usually, they impute feeling to another person. They also commonly ascribe causation or motivation to a person and, in some cases, to an idea. In the typical context, the word *because* is the signal for a possible attribution: "The reason

---

[4]Arnold M. Rothstein, "Marks on Term Papers in the Liberal Arts," *Journal of Teacher Education* (June, 1965), pp. 249-50.

they are poor is *because* they don't want to work." Here, motivation and reason are being attributed. Or, "if they were not so lazy, they might get somewhere." Here, a feeling or temperamental outlook is being ascribed.

Some see the confusion between description and ascription essentially as the confusion between observational and inferential terms. That is to say, instead of using terms which are "camera-like" in their objectivity in that they point to matters which others can verify, very often individuals will substitute the inference in the honest, but mistaken, belief that it is observation. For example, upon noticing a man staggering, some persons will say, "That man is drunk!" They will be fully satisfied that the statement is indeed an observational one. The fact of the matter is that it is clearly an inference despite the form and even the *sound* of factuality. As an inference, it may or may not be true; hence, a qualification ("probably") is in order. The ease with which we make attributions may be seen in our casual comments. For instance, in describing our reactions to a play, we tend to say, "*It* was a good play," whereby we attribute our feelings to the play and fuse external fact with internal feeling. The more accurate, though probably more difficult, statement to make would be, "*I* liked the play."

1.2   *Extreme Statements*   *(Code X)*

These are the superlative words, the words that permit no exceptions—*all, none, always, never, ever, no difference, the same, completely, entirely.* In a sense, they are usually exaggerations and overstatements; they bespeak a redundancy despite their frequent use for color and emphasis.

> "*Nothing* is *ever* learned."
> "This has *no* value *whatsoever.*"
> "This method is *identical* with the other. It is
>   *exactly* the *same.*"
> "He does it *constantly.*"
> "I *never* generalize."
> "There are *no* absolute truths."

Some persons refer to the above-mentioned expressions as generalizations. They are more than generalizations; they are absolutes. As absolutes, sometimes paradoxes are created as in the last two examples.

1.3   *Generalities*   *(Code G)*

Great systems of thought are built on generalizations; without the generalization, a system is impossible. However, generalization is the result of accumulation of data and their analysis. It differs some from the generality which implies a loose statement carelessly strewn about. Generalities, though implying a great number, are less than absolutes; somewhat less than all is implied. Expressions may be grouped under the headings, "in general words" or "generally speaking words." For example, *people, they, them, we, groups, countries, nations, Negroes, Jews, Puerto Ricans, Mexicans, Italians,* may be classified as generalities. Such words as *many, most, much, majority,* though implying generalness, are here classed as words which indicate a quantity. As such they are found under the heading below.

1.4   *Qualifications*   *(Code Q)*

Words and expressions in this grouping are usually statements of caution. They are frequently intended to hedge in or restrict the scope of the statement. Sometimes, the person using the qualification is trying to be precise by employing words which really indicate a rough quantity. Then too, the qualification may reveal an excessive caution where it is not warranted. ("That's *just* an exception," or "that's *merely* another way of putting it.") Under the grouping *Qualification,* three subgroups are identified.

The first is represented by those expressions which are colloquially referred to as weasel words, or words of caution; that is, they tend to cast doubt on a proposition: *maybe, perhaps, it seems, apparently, might, probably.*

The second subgrouping is represented by those terms which indicate quantity: *many, most, some, few, usually, rarely, at times.* A distinction is here noted between the extreme *all people,* the generality *people,* and the qualification *most people.* Perhaps some would argue that the latter represents a generality as well. As catalogued here, *most* indicates a rough quantity as would *some people* or *few people* and, hence, is included among the qualifications. In point of actual number, the qualification *few* can exceed many, to wit: "Few people in the world starve." "Many people in this room are happy." There are, of course, qualifications that are very specific. They limit by referring to a specific reference frame; for example, "the people in this room." Or, sometimes, the qualification is precise, 52.7 per cent of the people, rather than *some* people.

The third subgrouping under qualifications includes those terms which indicate a quality. Like the terms expressing quantity, they approximate. Though not actually denoting a quantity, they do imply, however loosely, an amount. Thus, the *better* people, the *finer* styles, the *cheaper* goods, *great* significances, *little* meaning.

Presumably it has been observed that qualifications have the effect of a delimiting and narrowing of the area of reference. They can be seen as important clues to the mental processes of the individual.

1.5   *Either-Or's*   *(Code O)*

In one sense, the *either-or* may be grouped as a subheading of the extreme statement. There is an erection of absolutes, a polarization of possibilities and alternatives which circumscribes the area of choice. As a manipulative and argumentative device, it may be seen as supremely helpful in invoking the combative spirit: "You're either for us or against us." The usage, of course, reveals a two-valued orientation, "we or they," "good or bad." In situations calling for the competitive and combative spirit and delimitations of the areas of choice, for example, games, wars, political campaigns, *either-or's* serve as powerful underpinning and as spurs to action. In situations calling for the study of a problem and the consideration of views, *either-or's* tend to interfere with reflection; often they are used to intimidate. Moreover, the narrowing of solutions to problems to but two possibilities is typically found in speech patterns given to the frequent use of extremes. The word *problem,* by definition, suggests alternatives. With no alternatives, with but one course of action open, there can hardly be a problem. In proportion to the number of alternatives that are available as solutions to a problem, possibilities for reflection are increased. As the teacher reveals the *either-or* to the student, he raises the question of appropriateness of a two-value system in a multi-valued world.

Perhaps the persistence with which we are prone to express ourselves in two-value terms is a carry-over from the world of pre-science. Upon careful analysis, terms like *up-down,* and *healthy-sick* reveal their historic past. These simple polarizations often incapacitate us because of the way they restrict and rigidify our thinking. One is reminded of the honest man who divided humanity into two classes: law-breakers and law-abiders. When asked what a law-abider was, he replied, "Someone who keeps *the* [one, some, most, all?] law." When asked what a law-breaker was, he replied, "Someone who breaks *the* [one, some, most, all?] law." No matter which he chooses, one law, some laws, most laws, all laws, our honest man is in trouble logically and is in an indefensible position. Now, it is probably clear that all of us are in some sense law-abider *and* law-breaker. Fortunately (unlike our honest man), our legal code recognizes multiple values. It has multiple categories for law-breaking (misdemeanor, offense, felony) and degrees of violation within each type (e.g., burglary, petty larceny, grand larceny, embezzlement, and armed robbery). Yet, some of us prefer simplicity: "They're all crooks." Perhaps it makes it easier to deal with the matter.

Suffice it to say, however, that we usually put ourselves into an untenable position when we employ terms with but two values. Indeed, many illustrations of logical fallacies cluster around the erection of a two-value system; no doubt it is evident how relatively easy it would be to reveal the inconsistency in the division of society into law-breakers and law-abiders. Sometimes, as in our usage of true or false tests (and even in our multiple choice tests), our students rightly point out a degree of falsity in what is called true and a degree of truth in what is called false.

1.6   *Analogies*   *(Code An.)*

Analogies express a relationship. Though properly used for color and for illustrative purposes, they are often misused as demonstrative proofs. In a sense, the analogical words, *like, same as, you might as well say, just like,* are forms of the extreme statement. "This is the same as that" permits no exception. "This is similar to that" (a qualification) does permit an area of difference. In identifying analogies, the teacher is helping the student to ask how appropriate to the given situation his analogy is.

1.7   *If-Then's*   *(Code I-T)*

Here too, a relationship is being expressed that is causal. In typical hypothetical statements, sometimes the *then* is omitted but is understood. Sometimes also, the *if* is omitted as in "Had the nation not permitted this, the results would have been different." Some examples are,

> "If he weren't what he is, this wouldn't have happened."
> "How could it be there if I didn't see it?"
> "How could it be any good if it's not advertised?"
> "If you're so smart, why ain't you rich?"
> "If the good Lord wanted us to fly, he would have given
>   us wings."

The task of the teacher is to help the student to see whether or not the *then* follows from the *if*.

1.8   *Value Statements*   *(Code V)*

These are the *good* and *bad* words, the *like* and *dislike* words. Value terms may further be distinguished by the label V+ and V−, the former indicating a positive attitude and the latter a negative one. As a rule, value statements afford clues to the person's feelings and attitudes and, sometimes, his behavior. They are indicators of possible behavior; they do not necessarily imply behavior. Among the intellectually immature, there is often a confusion of the value statement with a descriptive statement. As a matter of common speech idiom, this substitution in thought is often taken for granted. Though typically ascriptive, the form of expression, and usually the tone as well, present the external qualities of description: "the play was *bad*"; "this is an *excellent* book"; "the ideas expressed are positively abominable." Here too, the teacher seeks to have the student examine the appropriateness of his value expressions to a given situation.

1.9   *Superfluous Words*   *(Code A+)*

Some teachers use an A+ as a grade. Actually it has the effect of destroying the *A* if A is considered the top grade. When one establishes a *non plus ultra,* it is weakened by an attempt to strengthen it. Some gestural language which attempts to strengthen a superlative includes table thumping and vigorous head and facial movements. The examples below are intended to indicate what is meant by superfluous words.

"I *really* believe . . ."	Are there things he does not really believe?
"My *own, personal* opinion . . ."	Does he have opinions that are not his own or that are not personal?
"I *personally* think . . ."	Can he think impersonally?
"It is my *firm* conviction . . ."	Does he have convictions that are not firm?
"This is *very, very* good . . ."	After two *very*'s, one would need new A+ words like *stupendous* and *colossal* to replace the superlatives that are destroyed.

One could extend this category to include other types of redundancies like *controversial issues, red-blooded American, singularly unique,* a *brief summary,* a *funny joke,* a *new innovation,* a *free gift.*

In the example which follows, a paper of a college student has been coded to show how the system may be applied.

Jacques Barzun's statement: 'Thinking is inwardly a haphazard, fitful,
                                                                                X
incoherent activity' is described by the author of our text exactly when he recounts as an example what passed through the mind of someone during
                                                                                                                Q
some problematical situation in the form of a power failure. It appears
              A+   An.
that straight-forward scientific thinking is no more natural than daily
                                                    An.
calisthenics are to the average person. Just as we can set up a daily physical exercise regime, we can attempt to deal with specific limited problems on
A+   Q   An.   Q
a purely logical basis. But for more normal activities, just as exercise is apt
                                    Q
to be of a sporadic nature so do we tend to jump around in our minds in
      Q
considering most situations that require thinking. The key application of this is in abductive thinking where the author tries to show how with very
                                                                                X
few facts to go on, one can hypothesize purely by conjecture at first and
                                                                                X
then come to logical conclusions by casting out any obviously false guesses.

G

The random wanderings of the mind serve the purpose of turning up new faces of possible interpretations and approaches to a problem and, according to the author, the source of invention.

Q

According to the author, we tend to deviate from the problem under consideration to possibly day-dream or recall past experiences or consider other problems or situations that have occurred. If a problem appears

I-T

unsolvable or it temporarily baffles us, the mind will jump in unpredictable

X

directions at the slightest excuse. The ability to concentrate and focus the

X   G

mind on any one thing is not normal and actually is not particularly

V—   G   X

desirable. It requires this continuous upheaval to develop any creative solutions. The problem is to control this random thinking and direct it towards desired goals.

In effecting and using the coding system described in the foregoing pages, it is perhaps best for the teacher not to introduce the entire system at one time nor to present any part of it didactically. Instead, he might proceed as follows. When looking at written assignments, the teacher puts an *x* over all extreme words (even those with which he happens to agree). Papers are returned to students who are asked to copy out the sentences where words have been checked. They are instructed to note how the words or sentences are similar on the assumption that they discover ways in which the words are all-inclusive. (It is much better if the students themselves arrive at this and somewhat less effective if they are told.) The act of copying out the words and sentences permits them to see what the sentences have in common and to react to the coded words.

On a later assignment, the teacher continues to use the code *x* and introduces the code *G* over generalities. Again the students are asked to react and are led to discover and discern the similarities between the words that have been coded. The system is introduced in this fashion, one part at a time, with allowance for several weeks of assimilation of the old before the new is presented. The teacher's duty has not been discharged with the mere presentation of the system. Consistent instruction takes place during the year. (It sometimes happens that the teacher begins to notice changes in the way *he* talks and writes!) To be sure, this type of analysis is time-consuming, but students may participate in the analysis by coding each other's papers as well as their own.

Coding is used to get students to take another look at what they have written. As the teacher questions the appropriateness of the students' expressions, he is asking them to reflect on their thoughts. If the student desires it, he makes changes in what he wrote. Should he not desire to alter his expressions, he does not do so. Sometimes, the student is not ready to change the expression of thought patterns; he needs more time to reflect on his usages. Sometimes, for color, perhaps, he meant to say just what he did say.

Teachers may use coding as a diagnostic instrument. The dogmatism and absolutism, the confusion of values with description, the illogicality of the *if-then's* are not marked wrong; the student is not scored by having to pay penalty points. Instead, a sample of his writing is taken at the beginning of the term and marked, perhaps, on a five point scale as to its appropriateness and restraint. How sweeping are the student's assertions? How relevant are his statements? Do his expressions of certitude match the data he has been able to muster? A sample of writing taken at the end of the term is similarly treated, and the amount of growth, as a result of consistent instruction, may then be noted.

Below are some selections to which coding has been applied.

1.

The President's Illness[5]

      X

The entire world will await the outcome of President Eisenhower's ill-
        A

ness with sympathy and with hope.   V
      G

The hope will be based upon the fact that in his two previous and very
           Q

serious illnesses he showed remarkable powers of recovery.
                                   Q

It will be further based upon the fact that after the slight cerebral
           Q

occlusion and a resulting mild hesitancy in his speech, he showed considerable improvement in the course of the same day. And there is
further hope in the White House bulletin which states: 'The outlook for
      X   G

complete recovery within a reasonable period of time is excellent.' It is
      V

good news too that hospitalization is not required and that a later bulletin said 'his present disability is mild and transitory in nature.'

One of the ironies of these complex and difficult times — in which the
        Q

V President has done so much to create a climate of conciliation, as at the
summit meeting in Geneva — is the fact that he suffered his chill which
led to the attack while waiting bareheaded at the airport to greet King
Mohammed V of Morocco.

---

[5]*New York Herald Tribune,* November 27, 1957.

    X   A

V   The world will regret that this illness may delay the NATO meeting of

          A   V

the Allies. But it can also be glad that in the interim ahead the President's system of running the government by creating teams to which he

                  V   X

can delegate certain areas of his authority, will now prove to be a reassuring strength. So will the fact that Vice-President Nixon has been

   X   X   X

trained from the beginning to shoulder all the full responsibilities of a

                    X   X

Deputy President. He is not only thoroughly familiar with all the prob-

          X   X

lems now confronting the world but is a man completely equipped by character to act upon them, and to act intelligently and forcefully.

We wish the President well in his recovery and in the period of conva-

        X   Q   A

lescence ahead. No President since Washington has been more beloved

  X   An.   X

by all the American people. And like Washington he stands unique as a

             X   X   X

soldier, hero and statesman, first in war, first in peace, and first in the

          X

hearts of his countrymen as well as all the peoples of the world.   A

2.

A Student Report of Her Observations

          G

The principal spoke to us of the benefits of the vocational-technical high

            G

school. I noticed as the boys came in late, they were very well-mannered   V

            X

and looked neat even though they wore no ties. I found they were not obliged to. To me this seems sensible since it does not force them to come looking as gentlemen and have to change clothes to work in shop.

V   The classroom had very good equipment, There were diagrams around for the boys to see and study. The boys were helpful in explaining the workings of the machines and the jobs they were doing. In fact they   G

     A

were eager to share their talk with someone who was as eager as they to

                                         Q

listen. They were happy to show off their work. From the first to the

     X

last room visited all the boys began from scratch and worked up to the finished product as in the case of making tables, sheet and metal works and carpentry. A good thing also was that the boys were allowed to take

                    Q

V   their finished works home. I think this makes a boy work better because he is proud to do his work and show it to his family and friends. It is something others can see as hard work.

The school gave an insight into technical-vocational schools showing
V   Q
they just don't educate the hands but the mind as well. Some go to
               Q
V college immediately upon graduation, others go later, but eventually
Q   V —
almost all go. The boys were not roughnecks or ill-mannered. They are
V   X
well-disciplined in school. The only problem is the increasing number of students entering this type of school. There is not enough equipment
                                                A
for each student and they have to share with others. Because of this some have to work faster to allow others to use the machines.

V To me a boy can be very neat looking even though he does not wear a
I-T suit. If they are neat looking usually they are also well-mannered. A few asked if they could help and asked a few questions about college, inter-
                       G   A
est in classes, and courses offered. They were amazed that girls would
                   A
be interested in their shopwork and then discussed happily their work. They began from diagrams and figured out scale modeling, then cut the sheet metal or wood to the appropriate size and at the end of the course,
                                                I-T
they had made a filter, table or house. This is difficult to do otherwise more people would do it. Even though the school is vocational-
                       V
technical it provides a basis for going on to college. Unfortunately so many students' work is held up by not enough equipment. The school is
V
indeed useful in a busy city such as New York.

It may be seen that coding can be applied to various types of writing: editorials, political pamphlets, letters to the editor, student reports of observations, among others. It is well to note that this is but one of several coding systems that are possible. In two other parts in this book, the reader will find some differences in the systems presented. He may use those guides, he may use the system presented here, or he may add to them, and he is certainly advised to make up his own.

As indicated earlier, the use of coding does not require curriculum revision; one need not add a special course wherein this operation is carried on. The existing materials of existing courses are organized in such a way so that coding becomes one of the teaching operations and reacting to coding, a learning operation. For those teachers who rarely give written assignments, coding can be applied to passages from books, including textbooks, or to oral statements made by both student and teacher.[6] It is difficult to imagine a school subject where students are not required to make reports of their observations of an event, a demonstration, a picture, a diagram, a sketch, a model, a film, a slide, an experiment, a trip. In these instances, coding may be used to call attention to the thinking expressions of students.

While liberalization seems to be a desideratum of educative systems and while parochialization might be the goal of training and conditioning, there are some who view liberalization as a mere by-product, an automatic result of emphasis on *other* things; more often than not, it is the result of direct instruction such as is urged here. With a developed awareness, increasing sensitivity to the uses of language, more precise thinking, and an increasing liberalization of outlook are more likely. One can hope that, as the ability to use language more precisely goes forward, skill in such operations as comparing, observing and reporting, summarizing, interpreting, and analyzing will be enhanced.

2. Comparing

Perhaps one of the simplest ways for a teacher to stimulate thinking is to ask students to compare things, to discern likenesses and differences. But one may ask why? Discernment may be understood as the acquisition of standards which in turn results from exposure and exploration. As opportunities for comparison are increased, the bases for judgment are broadened. An ability to judge rests on a well-filled larder of references. The professional critic in the fine arts builds up a background, a storehouse of experiences, by which he judges (in actuality, compares) a present performance with a previous one. Thus, as we ask students to compare, we are helping them build up such a storehouse by which future discernments will be increased and refined and by which the growth of discriminative judgment, taste and appreciation may be aided.

The common expressions, "yes, but that's different," or "what's *the* difference," may give some clue as to the frequency with which comparing, sorting out differences and similarities, goes on. When one forms concepts, arrives at generalizations, or fashions a new idea, the creation, in each case, is a result of at least one and, in some cases, countless comparisons.

At times, some persons will confuse the terms equate and compare. When we equate things, we are saying that they are equal or identical; the similarities are in focus. However, when we compare them, we are saying that there are similarities *and* differences; both are in focus. When we contrast things, we focus only on the differences. Thus, the conventional saying, "those two things are as different as night from day; you can't compare them," probably

---

[6]One teacher had his graduate students code passages from a rather widely used text on thinking.

intends to convey the impression that they cannot be considered equal. With provision of opportunities for comparison, students can be led to see that similarities and sameness are differentiable.

Sometimes when we compare, we see the differences as greater in number or more crucial than the likenesses. We then tend to use the expression, "that's *completely* different." We mean, of course, that the number of differences outweighs the number of similarities. When similarities are greater in number or are more crucial, we tend to use the expression, "that's the same; there's *no* difference between them." Here too, of course, we mean that the differences are fewer in number.

Perhaps this becomes clearer as we refer to purpose. When no choice is to be made, we tend to ask: "what's *the* difference?" If no choosing is involved, differences between apple, pear, plum, and peach, for example, may disappear into "they're all fruit." Similarly, a collection of words of mixed parts of speech can be made undifferentiable — "they're just a bunch of words" — if purpose in choosing or identifying adjectives, for example, is absent. When "it makes no difference," we minimize distinctions and indeed swallow them up by moving on to the next larger category. When "it makes a difference," we maximize distinctions, small and refined ones as well as the gross ones. Whether or not differences are greater than likenesses or more crucial would relate to purpose, in making the comparison.

In pedagogic technique, the teacher may select two items and present them for comparison. He may have to show students that comparing can be approached atomistically, a reaction to partiality, or globally, a reaction to totality. Students can be led to discover such differences in approach if they are asked to compare two sets of comparisons, for example, a comma and a period, and then the game of ping pong with the game of badminton. In the former set, there will be a necessity to compare the totality while in the latter, the comparison will probably contain a mixture of reaction to totality and partiality. Some reflection will reveal why this is so. The former, as physical objects with more specific functions, cannot be as readily subdivided as the latter.

It may be worthwhile to elicit lists from students labeled "similarities" and "differences" and then to have them compare the listings item by item. Sometimes, a reaction to the totality is desirable and sometimes to the partiality; at times these may be grouped separately. At the outset, the checking idea — looking to see whether what is in A is also in B — is recommended because it is relatively easy to manipulate. Perhaps, at the outset, too, concretes may be kept together. For example, a pin is compared with a thumb tack and a poem with an essay rather than a mixture of a concrete term with an abstraction.

It is recommended that the teacher elicit similarities first since there seems to be a tendency to focus on differences. A list may be written on the blackboard, or it may serve some purpose to have students try to retain the list in mind. Then differences are elicited. At this point, students may be asked to report accurately what has been said or to summarize the listings as a unit. Several other procedures are indicated. Similarities may be tallied. With the absence of purpose, there is no necessity to choose one or the other. If purpose is defined and a choice is to be made, the critical point of difference is selected in relation to that purpose. Thus, students may be given the opportunity to offer an interpretation, evaluation, or generalization at the conclusion of a comparison.

Below are several illustrations of exercises which employ, among others, the operation of *comparing*. It may be seen that several subject areas are represented. It may also be observed that the operation of *comparing* does not involve the addition of a new course to the curriculum nor the change of existing content. It does involve the adaptation of materials and perhaps an adjustment in the teacher's pedagogic techniques. It is useful to remember that each subject area provides enough rich and meaningful materials for the exploitation of the operation; artificial, trivial, titillating, and nonproductive materials need not be employed.

2.1

Often the reporting of an event is of historical significance. Here are two versions of a now rather famous telegram. Some people consider that one version was *the* cause of a war, the Franco-Prussian War of 1870-71.

Compare, and see if you agree that the differences are sufficient or significant enough to cause a war. Which version provoked excitement do you think? Why?

Heinrich Abeken Text

(Heinrich Abeken was German

Councilor of Legation at Paris.)

Ems — July 13, 1870.

To the Federal Chancellor, Count Bismarck.

No. 27, No. 61 eod. 3:10 P.M. (*Station Ems*; Rush!)

His Majesty the King writes to me:

'M Benedetti intercepted me on the Promenade in order to demand of me most insistently that I should authorize him to telegraph immediately to Paris that I shall obligate myself for all future time never again to give my approval to the candidacy of the Hohenzollerns should it be renewed. I refused to agree to this, the last time somewhat severely, informing him that one dare not and cannot assume such obligations *à tout jamais*. Naturally, I informed him that I had received no news as yet, and since he had been informed earlier than I by way of Paris and Madrid, he could easily understand why my government was once again out of the matter.'

Since then His Majesty has received a dispatch from the Prince [Charles Anthony]. As His Majesty has informed Count Benedetti that he was expecting news from the Prince, His Majesty himself, in view of the above mentioned demand and in consonance with the advice of Count Eulenberg and myself, decided not to receive the French envoy again but to inform him through an adjutant that His Majesty had now received from the Prince confirmation of the news which Benedetti had already received from Paris, and that he had nothing further to say to the Ambassador. His Majesty leaves it to the judgment of Your Excellency whether or not to communicate at once the new demand by Benedetti and its rejection to our ambassador and the press.

Signed A [beken] 13.7.70

Otto von Bismarck Text

After the reports of the renunciation by the hereditary Prince of Hohenzollern had been officially transmitted by the Royal Government of Spain to the Imperial Government of France, the French Ambassador presented to His Majesty the King at Ems the demand to authorize him to telegraph to Paris that His Majesty the King would obligate himself for all future time never again to give his approval to the candidacy of the Hohenzollerns should it be renewed. His Majesty the King thereupon refused to receive the French envoy again and informed him through an adjutant that His Majesty had nothing further to say to the Ambassador.[7]

1. In what ways are the telegrams alike?
2. In what ways are they different?
3. Which is more crucial, the likenesses or the differences? Why?
4. How would each version be received by a Frenchman? By a German?

2.2

Compare the solar system with an atom of fluoride. (Listed below is a compilation of student responses.)

Similarities	Differences
1. Both are systems	Atom micro; solar system. macro
2. Both contain a central nucleus	Atom has nucleus as center; solar system has sun
3. Both have nine elements in orbit	Atom has electrons in orbit; sun has planets
4. In both, the elements which orbit rotate and revolve around the nucleus	Spatial relationships between two systems vary tremendously
5. Both are affected by gravity	Electrons have negative electrical charge; planets have no charge

---

[7]Both texts are from Louis L. Snyder, ed., *Documents of German History* (New Brunswick: Rutgers University Press, 1958), pp. 215-216.

6. Both have weight and mass	Atom nucleus can be split; sun cannot
7. Both systems have stimulated much thought	We can manipulate the atom more directly
8. Both systems are parts of a whole	Atom refers to elements; solar system refers to universe
9. Both systems represent organic or inorganic substances	Nucleus of the atom contains charged particles; nucleus of solar system contains atoms

10. Both systems may be represented by models.

Some questions for you:

1. Which differences may be put in the similarities column?
2. Which differences are the "ones that count"?
3. What do we mean when we say things are different?
4. Using a beam balance, compare the two systems above. In one pan, put the similarities; in the other, the differences.

2.3

Compare the two columns of words: How are these words alike and how are they different?

1.	2.	1.	2.
dancer	Tänzer	forest	forêt
devil	Teufel	festival	fête
door	Tür	priest	le prêtre
drink	Trunk	school	école
father	Vater	stamen	étamine
God	Gott	state	état
knead	kneten	stole	étole
knee	Knie	stranger	étranger
knob	Knopf	strangler	étrangler
boy (knave)	Knabe	strap	étrape
knuckle	Knöchel	stop	s' arrêter
thick	dick	study	étudier
thief	Dieb	stuff	étoffes
thing	Ding		
this	dies		
thistle	Distel		
thunder	Donner		

2.4
Lincoln's First Inaugural Address — March 4, 1861

Apprehensions seem to exist among the people of the Southern States that by the accession of a Republican administration their property and their peace and personal security are to be endangered. There has never been any reasonable cause for such apprehension. Indeed, the most ample evidence to the contrary has all the while existed and been open to their inspection. It is found in nearly all the published speeches of him who now addresses you. I do but quote from one of those speeches when I declare that 'I have no purposes, directly or indirectly, to interfere with the institution of slavery in the States where it exists. I believe I have no lawful right to do so and I have no inclination to do so.'

Lincoln's Emancipation Proclamation, January 1, 1863

That on the 1st day of January, A.D. 1863, all persons held as slaves within any State or designated part of a State the people whereof shall then be in rebellion against the United States shall be then, thenceforward, and forever free; and the executive government of the United States, including the military and naval authority thereof, will recognize and maintain the freedom of such persons and will do no act or acts to repress such persons, or any of them in any efforts they may make for their actual freedom.

Consider the two documents quoted above:
1. What differences do you find between the two statements? Are they significant differences? Why?
2. a. Find out the circumstances under which the Inaugural Address was made.
   b. Find out the circumstances under which the Emancipation Proclamation was issued.
3. In what way were these circumstances similar? Different?
4. How do you account for the seeming change in viewpoint evidenced in the two documents?

2.5

1. I warn John L. Lewis and his communistic cohorts that no second carpetbag expedition into the Southland under the Red Banner of Soviet Russia, and concealed under the slogans of the C.I.O. will be tolerated. If the C.I.O. attempts to carry through the South its lawless plan of organization, if they attempt to demoralize our industry, to corrupt our colored citizens, to incite race hatreds and race warfare, I warn him here and now that they will be met by the flower of Southern manhood and they will reap the bitter fruits of their folly.[8]

2. McCarthy's movement is made up of frustrated, insecure and frenzied elements of the middle class who are prey to the demogogic offerings of a scapegoat for all their difficulties and worries. 'Communism' is the scapegoat. The mass base

---

[8]Speaker: E.E. Cox of Georgia. Speech in U.S. House of Representatives, June, 1937.

of McCarthy's support includes every fascist and would-be-fascist group gnawing at the vitals of America. The rags and remnants of the Coughlin movement, the Silver Shirts, Christian Fronters, America Firsters, G.L.K. Smith's supporters, Legionnaires, Catholic War Veterans, scabs, F.B.I. stool-pigeons, professional red-baiters and strike-breakers, Ku Klux Klanners, lynchers, vigilantes, hooligans, and gangsters are in McCarthy's movement.[9]

1. How are these selections alike?
2. How do they differ?

2.6

Consider the following:

1. *The Times* of London — October 19, 1959[10]

Clashes occurred during celebrations in honor of the poet Schiller, which took place in Vienna last night. About 2000 neo-Nazi organizers and participants of the freedom torch procession were attacked by members of the *Bundesjugendring,* which includes about 400,000 members of different creeds and from all walks of life. The police, who appeared in considerable force, could not prevent serious disturbances, which resulted in a number of arrests and some injuries on both sides. The *Bundesjugendring* protested several days ago against the Schiller freedom celebrations by the 'gravediggers of freedom' and announced there would be counter-demonstrations against the neo-Nazis if the Government did not prohibit the torch parade.

2. *The New York Times* — October 19, 1959[11]

About twenty-five persons, some demonstrators wearing illegal swastika badges, and other 'anti-Fascists,' were arrested here last night when the police broke up fighting between Communists and youths who staged a torchlight procession.

3. *The New York Times* — June 6, 1960[12]

Windsheim, Germany: SEPP DIETRICH, former comander of Hitler's body-guard and ranking officer in the Nazi Elite Guard, was present, uninvited, at a reunion of 1,500 men of the unit here today.

4. *Associated Press* — June 6, 1960

Windsheim, Germany: About 1,200 diehard SS (Nazi Elite Guard) men marched through this old Franconian town Sunday night singing Nazi songs. And yesterday police said they had no grounds to stop them.

'We are the Black Guards that Adolf Hitler loved so much,' the former black-uniformed SS men roared. They then sang another song: 'If all become unfaithful, we'll stand by you.'

Many observers thought that by singing the latter song, the old ex-SS men wanted to show their allegiance is still with Hitler and his Nazi ideologies. Police didn't think so. They said that the former SS men, all members of the Sixth

---

[9]M. Weiss, *McCarthyism: American Fascism on the March,* New York: Pioneer Publishers (December, 1953), p. 16.

[10]Reprinted by permission from *The Times* of October 19, 1959.

[11]©1959 by The New York Times Company. Reprinted by permission.

[12]©1960 by The New York Times Company. Reprinted by permission.

Mountain Division were drunk when they sang the songs. 'Under the influence of alcohol, they may have thought they were back 20 years in their lives,' a police official explained.

Officially, the meeting was aimed at finding SS men still missing. World War II SS Gen. SEPP DIETRICH, the man who commanded Hitler's bodyguards and later the Leibstandarte Division, a crack SS unit, presided over the meeting as honorary guest.

1. Compare accounts 1 and 2 and list the similarities. Now list the differences.
2. Are the similarities more significant than the differences? Why?
3. Are the differences more significant than the similarities? Why?
4. How do you account for the differences which exist?
5. Do the same for selections 3 and 4.

After discussing the selections with the class, "for fun," the teacher may ask the class some questions dealing with recall of specific information. For example:

1. What are the dates of the news releases in 3 and 4?
2. What news media are involved?
3. Where did the incidents take place?
4. Who was the individual involved?
5. How many persons were involved in each account?

If one wanted, one could be even more picayune and ask for the name of the province in Germany and the name of the army division itself. The teacher may discover that most of the class will respond with a great deal of accuracy to the foregoing questions. The teacher may then want to ask himself why, without focus on "the facts," via the usual recall questions of "who," "what," "when," "where," such knowledge is readily available.

2.7

Read the two poems below:

Gefunden[13]	*Mondnacht*[14]
Ich ging im Walde	Es war, als haett' der Himmel
So fuer mich hin,	Die Erde still gekuesst,
Und nichts zu suchen,	Dass sie im Bluetenschimmer
Das war mein Sinn.	Von ihm nun traeumen muesst'.
Im Schatten sach ich	Die Luft ging durch die Felder
Ein Bluemchen stehn,	Die Aehren wogten sacht,
Wie Sterne leuchtend,	Es rauschten leis die Waelder,
Wie Aeuglein schoen	So sternklar war die Nacht.

[13]James Boyd, *Goethe's Poems* (Oxford: Basil Blackwell, 1947), p. 169.
[14]Joseph von Eichendorff, *Eichendorff Werke* (Stuttgart: J. G. Cotta'sche Buchhandlung Nachfolger, 1953), p. 306.

Ich wollt' es brechen
Da sagt es fein:
"Soll ich zum Welken
Gebrochen sein?"

Ich grub's mit allen
Den Wuerzlein aus,
Zum Garten trug ich's
Am huebschen Haus,

Und pflantzt' es wieder
Am stillen Ort;
Nun zweigt es immer
Und blueht so fort.

Und meine Seele spannte
Weit ihre Fluegel aus,
Flog durch die stillen Lande,
Als floege sie nach Haus.

1. Draw up a two columned list. Head one column, "Poems Are Similar to Each Other," and head the other column, "Poems Are Different From Each Other." Then answer the following questions and put your answers under *one* of the two headings:

   1. Wo befindet sich der Dichter?   Where is the poet in each case?
   2. Was tut der Dichter in diesem Gedicht?   What is the poet doing as described in the poem?
   3. Welche Tageszeit ist es?   What time of day is it?
   4. Welche Worte werden in beiden Gedichten gebraucht? Unterstreiche sie. Sind die Bedeutungen die selben?   Which words are used in both poems? Underline them. (For example, *"Haus."*) Are the meanings the same?

2. Which of the following characteristics or emotions seem to be expressed in either *Mondnacht* or *Gefunden* or in both or in neither?

	Mondnacht	*Gefunden*	*Both*	*Neither*
Freude				
Traurigkeit				
Sinnenfreudigkeit				
Wanderlust				
Heimweh				
Naturliebe				
Freiheitsliebe				
Ordnungssinn				
Konservativisimus				
Empathie				
Melancholie				
Sehnsucht				
Praktischer Sinn				
Traeumerei				
Verzweiflung				

Glueck
Unglueck
Zufriedenheit
Froemmigkeit
Liebe
Empfindsamkeit
Idealismus
Materialismus

2.8

1. Discussion of 13 billion dollars appropriated for the War Department and returned unused.[15]

Senator Barkley: "It is always impossible to sit down at a table and calculate to the fineness of a bat's eye just how much is going to be needed everywhere."

Senator Wheeler: "Mr. President, I do not wish to be understood as criticizing the War Department for turning back the money; but when the Senator talks about 13 billion dollars being what can be put in a bat's eye . . ."

Senator Barkley: "The Senator knows that I was not talking about putting 13 billion dollars in a bat's eye. I was talking about Army officers sitting down at a table and working out to the fineness of a bat's eye everything they needed in the way of supplies and equipment."

Senator Wheeler: "The Senator was talking about a bat's eye, and I say he was talking about putting 13 billion dollars in a bat's eye."

Senator Barkley: "I think the Senator is playing on words."

Senator Wheeler: "The Senator from Kentucky was playing on words."

Senator Barkley: "I do not understand that even the Senator from Montana thinks that 13 billion dollars can be put into a bat's eye."

Senator Wheeler: "The Senator was playing on words when he was talking about the 13 billion dollars which I mentioned. He said that Army officers could not sit down and work it out to the fineness of a bat's eye. I said that 13 billion dollars could not be put in a bat's eye."

Senator Barkley: "For once, the Senator and I agree. Thirteen billion dollars cannot be put in a bat's eye. That is settled." (Laughter)

Senator Wheeler: "I am glad to have the Senator agree with me once in a while."

2. "In your country, brother, what is the wage of a master bailiff, master hind, carter, shepherd, swineherd?

"Twenty-five milrays a day; that is to say, a quarter of a cent."

The Smith's face beamed with joy. He said:

---

[15]Congressional Record, November 22, 1943, Vol. 89, p. 9919.

"With us they are allowed the double of it! And what may a mechanic get —
carpenter, dauber, mason, painter, blacksmith, wheelwright, and the like?"

"Oh the average, fifty milrays; half a cent a day."

"Ho-ho! With us they are allowed a hundred! With us any good mechanic is
allowed a cent a day! I count out the tailor, but not the others — they are all
allowed a cent a day, and in driving times they get more — yes, up to a hundred
and ten and even fifteen milrays a day. I've paid a hundred and fifteen myself,
within the week. 'Rah for protection — to Sheol with free trade!"

And his face shone upon the company like a sunburst. But I didn't scare at all. I
rigged up my pile-driver, and allowed myself fifteen minutes to drive him into the
earth — drive him *all* in — till not even the curve of his skull should show above
ground. Here is the way I started in on him. I asked:

"What do you pay a pound for salt?"

"A hundred milrays."

"We pay forty. What do you pay for beef and mutton — when you buy it?" That
was a neat hit; it made the color come.

"It varieth somewhat, but not much; one may say seventy-five milrays the pound."

"*We* pay thirty-three. What do you pay for eggs?"

"Fifty milrays the dozen."

"We pay twenty. What do you pay for beer?"

"It costeth us eight and one-half milrays the pint."

"We get it for four; twenty-five bottles for a cent. What do you pay for wheat?"

"At the rate of nine hundred milrays the bushel."

"We pay four hundred. What do you pay for man's tow linen suit?"

"Thirteen cents."

"We pay six. What do you pay for a stuff gown for the wife of the laborer or the
mechanic?"

"We pay eight cents, four mills."

"Well, observe the difference: you pay eight cents and four mills, we pay only
four cents." I prepared now to sock it to him. I said: "Look here, dear friend,
what's become of your high wages you were bragging so about a few minutes ago?
— and I looked around on the company with placid satisfaction, for I had slipped
up on him gradually and tied him hand and foot, you see, without his ever noticing
that he was being tied at all. "What's become of those noble high wages of yours?
— I seem to have knocked the stuffing all out of them, it appears to me.'

But if you will believe me, he merely looked surprised, that is all! He didn't grasp
the situation at all, didn't know he had walked into a trap, didn't discover that he
was *in* a trap. I could have shot him, from sheer vexation. With cloudy eye and a
struggling intellect he fetched this out:

"Marry I seem not to understand. It is *proved* that our wages be double thine;
how then may it be that thou'st knocked therefrom the stuffing? — an I miscall not
the wonderly word, this being the first time under grace and providence of God it
hath been granted to me to hear it."

Well, I was stunned; partly with this unlooked-for stupidity on his part, and
partly because his fellows so manifestly sided with him and were of his mind — if

you might call it mind. My position was simple enough, plain enough; how could it ever be simplified more? However I must try:

"Why look here, brother Dowley, don't you see? Your wages are merely higher than ours in *name,* not in *fact.*"

"Hear him! They are the *double* — ye have confessed it yourself."

"Yes-yes, I don't deny that at all. But that's got nothing to do with it; the *amount* of the wages in mere coins, with meaning-less names attached to them to know them by, has got nothing to do with it. The thing is, how much can you *buy* with your wages? — that's the idea. While it is true that with you a good mechanic is allowed about three dollars and a half a year, and with us only about a dollar and seventy-five —"

"There — ye're confessing it again, ye're confessing it again!"

"Confound it, I've never denied it, I tell you! What I say is this. With us *half* a dollar buys more than a *dollar* buys with you — and *therefore* it stands to reason and the commonest kind of common sense, that our wages are *higher* than yours."

He looked dazed and said despairingly:

"Verily, I cannot make it out. Ye've just *said* ours are the higher, and with the same breath ye take it back."[16]

1. How are the two selections alike?
2. How are they not alike?
3. What seems to be the trouble?
4. How would you overcome the difficulty?
5. Do you suppose it is easy to teach someone something? Why?

2.9

Compare the following:

1. While the famous regiments of Charles V triumphantly overran Europe, off in the New World Spanish soldiers and sailors were discovering and conquering vast regions. Our country dedicated itself solely to the great task of Christianizing the trans-Atlantic world, sacrificing to this lofty historical end the ideals of political and religious liberty which the spirit of the times called for. To fulfill this civilizing mission, it was necessary to maintain the traditional monarchy and the Catholic Church as centers of power and guidance. Consequently the soldier who acclaimed the king and enlarged the fatherland was accompanied by the missionary who proclaimed his God and spread the Gospel . . .

   If we compared the scanty means of those explorers with the immense resources which Stanley, Brazza, and the rest of the African explorers had at their disposal, we should see how illustrious our magnificent forbears appear. For they were inspired not so much by desire for gold as by a noble yearning for fame and by a generous aspiration to carry the Cross in triumph over all the

---

[16]Mark Twain, *A Connecticut Yankee in King Arthur's Court* (New York: The Modern Library, Inc., 1917), pp. 323-326.

world. A race of sublime Quixotes, consumed by a passion for the unknown and the great, which made of the 16th century a poem of action, eclipsing the most exalted figures of ancient history, Greece would have ranked them among her demigods . . .[17]

2. It was the lust for gold that led on the Spanish adventurers ... it was the immense treasure from the New World that became the foundation stone of the great Spanish character and industry . . .[18]

3. . . . the Inca, as the ruler of these Indians was known, was taken prisoner and cruelly murdered even though he paid as ransom for his freedom a roomful of gold worth about $15,000,000.[19]

4. For all their expenditures of money and lives, the Spaniards, seventy years after Columbus' great voyage, had not a single settlement in America north of the Gulf of Mexico . . . they did not colonize this region as they did the West Indies, Mexico, and Central and South America. The provinces, or vice-royalties, which they set up in New Spain were governed quite despotically. All the trade was regulated by the 'India House' at Seville and forbidden to foreigners. The Roman Catholic religion was the only one allowed. The native Indians and imported Negroes were frightfully treated under the lash of the slave drivers. The land was in the hands of a few wealthy proprietors. There were no representative assemblies.[20]

5. Accomplished during a century that was as brilliant and hard as the steel of Toledo, the conquest of America lost its adventurous aspect when the clamor of arms ceased. The man to use the most somber colors in painting the violence and excesses inherent in that kind of conquest is Father Las Casas, a priest of Seville.

   Foreign authors have depended upon his testimony to loosen their tongues in insults against our country, without considering the fact that similar deeds were committed by the Portugese in the conquest of the Indies, and by the Englishmen, Frenchmen, and other European peoples in the American colonization.

   In the discovery and conquest of the New World, Spain showed herself as she was at the time, a nation with deplorable faults but also great virtues; and thanks to the latter, that continent came soon into the bosom of civilization. If there were crimes, 'the crimes were of the times and not Spain's,' as the poet said. To expect the discovery and conquest of America without war—and war without violence, ravages, and desolation—is the same as expecting parting without sorrow and life without death. Only the nation that has fought with tactics

---

[17]Alfredo Moreno Espinosa, *Compendio de Historia de España* (Barcelona: Editorial Atlante), pp. 339, 341, 343, as cited in Arthur Walworth, *School Historians at War* pp. 58-59. (Cambridge, Mass.: Harvard University Press,) Copyright 1938, by the President and Fellows of Harvard College. Reprinted by permission of the publishers.
[18]W. B. Guitteau, *History of the United States* (Boston: Houghton-Mifflin Company, 1937), p. 17.
[19]F. P. Wirth, *The Development of America* (New York: American Book Company, 1936), p. 34.
[20]D. S. Muzzey, *History of the American People* (Boston: Ginn and Company, 1936), p. 41.

different from those practiced by Spain is privileged to throw the first stone at Spain.[21]

6. After the taking of Mexico, Cortez divided the land among the conquerors, and on the ruins of the Aztec city he began to build the Spanish city of Mexico, proclaiming its future greatness. He organized a city corporation, established markets, repaired the aqueduct of Chapultepec, which had been cut during the siege, laid down moral laws, thus beginning the government of the colony whose wealth he protected by wise measures . . .

Then Pizarro showed his admirable gifts as organizer and colonizer; he divided the land into districts, he organized the administration of justice and the working of the mines . . . and in a short time, thanks to his energy and will, the church, town hall, palaces, and houses, formed a beautiful city (Lima) which grew and prospered.[22]

7. Pizarro, in imitation of Cortes, laid hands on the Inca, Atahualpe, and held him as security for the good behavior of his people. In return for his freedom the Inca promised to fill a large room with objects of gold to a depth of nine feet. Almost immediately porters began to come in bearing golden vases, goblets, and jars; miniature gold birds and beasts, golden leaves, flowers, beads, roots. Melted down, this mass yielded 1,326,539 pesos de oro, the equivalent of $15,-550,000 in American money. Having secured this treasure, the Spaniards treacherously led their prisoner out to the plaza of Caxamarca and strangled him with a bowstring.[23]

8. In order to govern such distant colonies, the mother country laid down the wise laws of the Indies, a code that gives us a claim to glory because of the noble humanitarian impulse by which it was inspired.

Thanks to the Laws of the Indies, all Spanish America was covered with universities and other centers of learning which spread culture among all those peoples, stimulating in some—Mexico and Peru for instance—a great flowering of literature.

While the colonial systems of other countries are concerned solely with material exploitation of the colonies, ours always was preoccupied especially with moral purposes. We strove to propagate learning in such a way that within a few years of its conquest all Spanish America was covered with universities and other institutions of learning. In this respect no other colonizing has outdone Spain's; and perhaps this explains why, the culture of the natives having been raised so considerably, Spanish America was soon able to free herself from our dominion and rule her own destiny. For this reason Senor Barrantes called our colonial system 'Generous and Christian, without doubt, but also suicidal.' Therefore, today, now that the old hates are dying out, all Americans of Latin blood are

---

[21]Espinosa, *Compendio de Historia de España,* p. 350, as cited in Walworth, *School Histories at War,* p. 61.

[22]Pedro A. Bleye, *Compendio de Historia de España* (Madrid: Espasa-Calpe, S.A., 1933), pp. 115, 123-124, as cited in Walworth, *School Histories at War,* p. 62.

[23]T. J. Wertenbaker and D. E. Smith, *The United States of America* (New York: Charles Scribner's Sons, 1931), pp. 18-19.

stretching their arms toward the mother country, proud to feel the noble blood of Spain coursing through their veins . . .

The discovery of America is the most transcendent episode of secular history since in a way it completed the work of God making contacts between lands and peoples separated by force of geological cataclysms, and triumphantly carrying them the Gospel of Christ and the word of Spain . . .[24]

1. Which accounts present Spain in the role of a civilizing mission?
2. Which accounts look upon the conquistadores as scourges of the devil rather than the emissaries of the Christian God?
3. The differences in the accounts appear to be crucial. Why do the accounts differ so much?
4. Which account is correct?

2.10

Compare: Hail and Sleet

(Listed below are some student answers)

Atomistic Differences

Hail	*Sleet*
1. four letter word	five letter word
2. hard	soft
3. heavy	light
4. formed in warm weather	formed in cold weather
5. melts more slowly	melts quickly
6. frozen layers of moisture	frozen rain
7. sometimes recirculated in the air	falls directly to ground
8. larger	smaller
9. formed while circulating in atmosphere	formed while falling to earth

Atomistic Similarities

1. Both words begin with a consonant
2. Produced from moisture or water vapor
3. Have ice crystals
4. Composed of two atoms of hydrogen and one atom of oxygen
5. Associated with meteorology
6. Fairly common in temperature climates
7. Colorless
8. Opaque
9. Solid form of matter
10. Become liquid when heated

---

[24]Espinosa, *Compendio de Historia de España,* pp. 350-51, as cited in Walworth, *School Histories at War,* pp. 62-63.

11. We can observe and touch forms
12. Fall to earth or evaporate in atmosphere

Global Similarities

1. Forms of precipitation
2. Formed in the atmosphere
3. Fall to earth because of the force of gravity
4. Formed in clouds
5. Forms of weather
6. Nouns

Points of critical Similarity:
1. Formed from the evaporation of water vapor
2. First fall as rain
3. Both contain tiny ice particles

Points of Critical Difference:
1. Sleet is rain which becomes partly frozen on its way to earth
2. Hail and sleet are formed differently

2.11

Compare Decimal System and Quinary System
(Some student responses)

Similarities
1. Digit symbols used to represent numbers
2. Place values used
3. Unlimited number of places
4. Can be written in fractional form
5. Place values before and after the decimal point
6. Numbers can be added, subtracted, multiplied, and divided
7. Both possess commutative, associative, and distributive properties
8. Both have an additive and multiplicative identity element

Differences
The Decimal System:
1. Uses only ten digit symbols: 0, 1, 2, 3, 4, 5, 6, 7, 8, 9.
2. Has place values based on the powers of ten.
The Quinary System:
1. Uses only five digit symbols: 0, 1, 2, 3, 4.
2. Has place values based on powers of five.
3. The digit five is never used or written.

2.12

Compare a Ditto Machine and a Mimeograph Machine
(Student Responses)

Similarities
1. Both make multiple copies

Differences
1. Mimeograph may produce quantity ten times greater

2. Electrical and manual machines are available

3. Inexpensive paper can be used

4. Information may be typed or drawn on master

5. Master copies are correctable

6. Both can produce copy on standard and legal size paper

7. Colored finished copy as well as black and white may be produced

8. Position of the master may be adjusted

2. Mimeograph uses ink. Ditto uses alcohol mixture

3. Mimeograph paper has a rough surface is absorbent. Ditto paper has smooth surface and is not absorbent.

4. Mimeograph uses a stencil master. Ditto uses a ditto master.

5. In typing on stencil, typewriter ribbon is disengaged. On ditto master, ribbon may remain in its usual position.

6. Finished mimeograph copy is more lasting.

7. Typing of ditto master can probably be done more quickly than stencil master.

8. Correction of errors on stencil require placing liquid wax on error. Ditto master may be corrected by scraping the chemical off with a razor or eraser.

Critical Similarities
1. Both machines make multiple copies from a master.
2. Both may be used to produce a variety of forms.

Critical Differences
1. Quantity produced on a mimeograph machine is ten times greater than that produced on a chemical duplicator.
2. The finished mimeograph copy is relatively permanent while the finished ditto material will eventually fade.

2.13

Compare Paint and Wood Stain
(Student Responses)

Similarities
1. They are liquids.
2. They impart color to wood.
3. They come in a variety of colors.
4. They are applied with a brush
5. They are stored in air-tight containers
6. They may be used decoratively.
7. Pigment on each determines the color.

Differences

	How Applied	*Coverage*	*Result*
Paint	Allowed to dry	Forms protective coat	Hides the wood
Stain	Excess wiped off	Penetrates into grain	Changes color of wood

2.14

Compare Heart and Lungs
(Some student responses)

Similarities
1. Body organs
2. Necessary to keep body alive
3. Located in upper half of body
4. Expand and contract
5. Made up of cells
6. Contain compartments
7. Have openings into tubes

Differences

Heart	Lungs
1. One organ	Paired organ
2. Contains blood	Contains air
3. Contracts itself	Forced to contract by pressure of diaphragm
4. No opening to outside of body	Open to outside of body
5. Made of muscles	Made of elastic tissue
6. Contains valves	No valves
7. Four compartments	Many compartments
8. Eight openings into tubes	Two openings into tubes

Summary: If either organ stopped functioning, the body would not survive. A critical difference lies in the material used by each organ to perform its life-maintaining function, the heart containing blood and the lungs containing air.

Thus far, the reader has seen exercises in comparing which have been used by teachers and students and through which thinking was stimulated. There follows a listing of suggestions indicating some possibilities which exist for comparing activities in various subject fields.

COMPARE

1. Fog and dew
2. Frost and rain
3. Snow and hail
4. Drizzle and sleet
5. Mist and glaze
6. Whirlwind and monsoon

7. Cyclone and hurricane
8. Tornado and typhoon
9. Fingers and toes
10. Skin and fruit peel
11. White blood cell and red blood cell
12. Earthquake and volcano
13. Halo and rainbow
14. Harmony and discord
15. Echo and reflection
16. Solar year and lunar year
17. Julian calendar and Gregorian calendar
18. French Revolutionary Calendar and Gregorian calendar
19. Pressure and force
20. Weight and height
21. Flower and vegetable
22. Sponge and clam
23. Fruits and nuts
24. Digestive system and circulatory system
25. Lord Kelvin's Cosmozoic theory of life with Ernst Haeckel's primeval sea hypothesis
26. Darwin's and Lamarck's theories
27. Latitude and longitude
28. Northern hemisphere and southern hemisphere
29. Torrid zone and temperate zone
30. Continent and island
31. Country and nation
32. Political and geographic
33. Economic and social
34. Chemical and biological
35. Physical and geologic
36. Geometric and arithmetic
37. Artistic and scientific

38. Beethoven and Strauss
39. Bach and Mahler
40. Harmony and counterpoint
41. Form and content
42. Vibrato and staccato
43. Trumpet and violin
44. Harp and piano
45. Valasquez and van Gogh
46. Picasso and Rembrandt
47. Shellac and varnish
48. Addition and multiplication
49. Fractions and integers
50. The *Odyssey* and *Robin Hood*
51. Peter the Great and Charles Stuart I
52. *Tale of Two Cities* and *Julius Caesar*
53. Oliver Cromwell and Robespierre
54. Vowel and consonant
55. Comma and period
56. Colon and semicolon
57. Number and numeral
58. Mean and median
59. Circle graph and bar graph
60. Circle and oval
61. Rectangle and square
62. Area and perimeter
63. Interest and dividend
64. Salary and wage
65. Profit and rent
66. Fee and royalty
67. King and dictator
68. Serf and slave
69. Peasant and proletarian

70.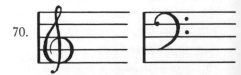

[25]Acknowledgement of indebtedness is made to graduate students for their contributions of items 2.2, 2.7, 2.10, 2.11, 2.12, 2.13, 2.14.

71. Music and noise
72. Compare two problem
    solutions

73. Compare two translations
74. Compare problem statements
75. Compare two comparisons

It has been stated that as the learner compares, he acquires standards, bases for discernment; that this skill, extended and refined, helps him to make appropriate judgments. If this is so, it would seem reasonable for the teacher to provide opportunities for the operation of comparing. Much of the value of the activity would be lost if the teacher were to do *comparing* for the learner. No one really can do this for someone else without vitiating the purposes for which comparisons are made. Informed judgments and the ability to make up one's mind have been recognized as marks of the educated man. An ability to make wise decisions rests on the quantity and quality of experiences in making comparisons; the broader and richer the comparisons, the greater the likelihood of worthwhile judgments.

In the ensuing pages, other operations are set forth. The interrelationship between *analyzing* and *criticizing* to *comparing* may become evident as these operations are explicated.

3. *Classifying*

Classifying may be conceived as an extension of comparing in which one looks for similarities and differences. When enough similarities are found, a grouping is possible; its characteristics are distinguishable from another grouping which represents a different cluster of similarities. Groupings themselves may be compared and put into even larger systems. Essentially, this is what goes on in the taxonomic process.

Ordinary language usage itself is already a form of classifying. For example, the word "cow" identifies an animal which has characteristics in common with other animals in its class. It eats grass, it produces milk, it has four legs. The grouping, "cow," is usually more meaningful to us than the larger category, "a brownish object." This larger grouping can include so many things where differences between them may be greater than resemblances. Thus, as we go on describing "cow" as spotted, or brown and hornless, we are putting it into smaller and smaller classes; by our continued differentiations, sub-groupings are themselves being sub-divided and sub-divided.

If we want students to classify, we ask them to develop groups or categories based on function, size, effect, form, or rank or some other criterion. In this operation, thinking becomes equivalent to correlating. When one correlates, one is apt to obtain a deeper and more lucid picture of "unlikes." Such clear pictures of unlikes are necessary for concept development.

A usual application of the *classifying* operation is to have students use established groupings. The groupings are predetermined and the student places the "pieces" in the right envelopes, as it were. For example, a teacher will have students pick out all nouns, all adjectives, and all verbs. Surely, at times, this is a necessary process and is used over and over again in so many different areas of knowledge. It is urged that the operation be carried a step further. This would mean the creation and development of groups and categories by the learners themselves. Of course, the operation will then be seen as related to *imagining and creating* since thinking is freed from established patterns. However, classifying will continue to be a search for similarities in a systematic way. The group may be established on the basis of function and use. Or it can be a personal categorization based on feeling or effect. Both of these represent what may be termed "new" systems. As has been said, the grouping can also be a formal well-established system. No doubt, students will learn that groupings are possible on several levels and with varying degrees of precision, complexity, sophistication, and purpose. It is important for them to discover that, on the one hand, though a convenience, a grouping is not arbitrarily or capriciously established; on the other hand, it is equally significant for them to realize that groupings are not indestructible truths. They are useful generalizations—almost a lexicographic system for storing larger quantities of information; they serve purposes and are subject to revision when purposes change.

Probably the greatest conflicts known to man have arisen in connection with groupings whose lines have hardened into rigidity, e.g. French versus German, Communist versus non-Communist, republican versus monarchist. In other words, the group classification is taken over by the mind and applied to all constituents within the group. Readers will no doubt recognize that this is essentially what happens in racial, religious, national, or hemispheric prejudice.

It has been said that groupings are based on similarity. It has also been said that in some sense they can *become* rigidified and arbitrary. In the groupings which human beings create to classify themselves as members of groups, sub-groups, and sub-sub-groups, we may note that it is *we* who determine the crucial point of similarity. We erect a quintessential element which will determine membership within the group while we tolerate other differences. Can we get students to see how one or two similarities become the crucial criteria? In a sense, we ask: what relationship is there between the promotion of international good will and the operation of *classifying?*

In pedagogic technique, the teacher permits students to discover that, although countless groupings are possible, each grouping is to have internal consistency; that that which is included within the group relates to the purpose for which the group was established. No doubt, students will find out that only one principle at a time is to be operative as groupings are established. For example, if one were to group the fruits in a large fruitbowl, one could categorize them on the basis of personal like and dislike. Or, one could group them on the basis of color, or flavor, or size, or even alphabetically.

But, only one principle at a time is operative. One may not group the fruits according to size and color and like-dislike at the *same* time. Similarly, to provide but one large category — fruit — I.E., to move into the next higher order of classification, would be to obliterate differences. The teacher may proceed as in comparing—having students note whether similarities or differences are crucial, the former determining inclusion in the group and the latter determining exclusion from the group.

Exercises which involve the *classifying* operation are offered below in several subject areas. Again it is emphasized that the operation of *classifying* requires no new course and no change of content, but that it does involve adaptation of existing content. As indicated heretofore, meaningful materials might be searched out while trite ones are eschewed.

3.1

Examine the list of words below. They have been selected because they contain all the simple vowel sounds of present-day English. You can find out what these sounds are by pronouncing the words aloud many times to determine which sounds are alike and which differ from one another. Remember that speech cannot be studied in silence. Besides, you can learn more about the English language from your own observations than from what an author can tell you because you are in a better position to examine your own speech.

1. Determine how many stressed vowel sounds there are in modern English as it is spoken in your locality. Rearrange the list, putting words of similar vowel sound together. For example, although *soul* and *boat* are spelled differently, they have the same vowel sound and hence, belong together.

soul	gnaw	full	sham	which
food	bid	cough	measure	cube
great	book	leave	think	ask
pass	word	bird	boat	ale
calm	top	bathe	chews	farther
rut	jerk	feed	hand	frost
let	son	rude	zinc	bead
long	heard	turn	yet	quay
tall	many	nap	take	bath
water	dawn	balk	use	of
golf	bade	have	just	none
palm	glass	branch	shoe	foot
heir	learn	fir	air	basket
song	wear	path	psalm	wool

2. How many vowel characters does the English alphabet provide for these vowel sounds? What vowel characters do not always represent the same sound?

3. Consult a dictionary to discover the symbols which are employed in indicating the vowel sounds in 1.

The foregoing exercise was tried with students who grouped the words according to the way *they* made the particular sounds. Despite "wrong" answers, the students had to listen to themselves and to others acutely. On the basis of dictionary investigation, they also discovered that there was not only one way to make sounds; there were certain accepted "groupings" each of which had its internal standards. When these standards are accepted in a particular locality, they are adhered to in the interest of intra-communication.

The following was worked on by a ninth grade class in home economics. It served as a basis for discussion of the appropriateness of the groups.

3.2

Below are listed some foods. Group them in a way you believe to be proper. Applesauce, baked apple, biscuits, chocolate-cream pudding, cinnamon toast, cranberry jelly-sauce, creamed dried chip-beef, cream of tomato soup, custard, egg nog, fruit-jello mold, hot chocolate, leafy salad, macaroni-supreme salad, melon, muffins, omelet, oven-fried chicken, popcorn balls, steak, vegetable-oil pastry, waffles.
(Student Responses)
1. Fruits, breads, meats, dairy, and vegetables.
2. Fruits, desserts, breads, meats, eggs, soups, salads.
3. Foods I like and foods I dislike.
4. Desserts, beverages, breads, proteins, and vegetables
5. Fattening foods and non-fattening foods
6. Breakfast, lunch, dinner, and snack foods
7. Solids and liquids
8. Foods that require cooking and foods that may be eaten uncooked.
9. Foods cooked on top of the stove and foods cooked in the oven.
10. Foods served cold and foods served hot
11. The basic four: breads and cereal, meat, dairy, fruits and vegetables

1. Analyze each of the above groupings. Can you determine on what basis or principle the groups were selected?
2. Look at the eleven groups themselves carefully. Do you see a way of grouping *them?*

3.3

Group the following any way you see fit:
Connecticut, Delaware, Georgia, Maryland, Massachusetts, New Hampshire, New Jersey, New York, North Carolina, Pennsylvania, Rhode Island, South Carolina, Virginia

Some Student Responses:
1. Middle states, New England states, southern states
2. Agricultural states—industrial states
3. Northern states—southern states
4. Union States—Confederate states
5. States with *New* in them and states without *New*
6. Proprietary colonies—self-governing colonies—royal colonies
7. States named after a monarch and states named after a lord
8. States with Indian names and those named after a section in England
9. Types of settlers settling in each state
10. States may be grouped according to products produced
11. States may be grouped according to size or population
12. Number of rivers and number of mountains
13. Which state produced the most leaders in government

Additional assignments could include the actual listing of the states within the grouping system.

3.4

The words in the exercise below seem to have some relationship to each other. Read each pair carefully, see if you can find additional pairs that can express the relationship existing between the two words in each ratio.

1. Carpenter: house
   Laborer: job

Criticize or justify these   Skilled: product
answers   Worker: product
                                   Laborer: product
                                   Means: end
                                   Man: job

2. Writer: book
   Author: work

Criticize or justify these   Creator: creation
answers   Thinker: product
                                   Means: product
                                   Cause: effect

Try now to differentiate specific from general classifications. That is to say, rank your groups, going from all types of relationship in the one group to very specific ones. For example, organism: animal: mammal: whale: bottle-nosed.

3.5

Below are twenty statements which reveal some attitudes. Group them according to the following scheme:

Which seem to make snap judgments? They reject the problem and introduce irrelevant material. Mark these *D* for dogmatic.

Which delay making a judgment and ask questions which seem to be pertinent to the problem? Mark these *C* for critical.

Which seem to accept the problem too readily? They show suggestibility or guillibility. Mark these *U* for uncritical.

Which sit on the fence? They will not even accept a temporary hypothesis. Mark these *H* for hypercritical.

PROBLEM: HOW CAN WE REDUCE HUMAN POVERTY?

—— 1. You can not tamper with certain social institutions or you upset the applecart.

—— 2. What type of experimental situation could we set up?

—— 3. Is poverty a natural thing or is it man-made?

—— 4. What would be necessary for the study of such a problem?

—— 5. The causes of poverty are probably related to human behavior. What is there in that behavior that would shed light on the issue?

—— 6. Poverty exists because of the greed of others.

—— 7. Poverty exists because people are lazy.

—— 8. To allow poverty is to be inhumane.

—— 9. Justice, simple justice, and it will triumph in the end, demands that the problem be solved.

——10. Human nature can not be changed; it is a waste of time.

——11. Might as well try to solve the problem of war.

——12. This problem has no practical value.

——13. Only poor people want this problem solved.

——14. There will always be poor people.

——15. Poverty is the easiest thing in the world to overcome if we only do something about it.

——16. It would be important for us to determine what we mean by poverty.

——17. We might have to study the causes of poverty.

——18. The evidence would have to be pretty substantial before we could act on it.

——19. How are we ever going to gather enough information to form any sort of hypothesis?

——20. There's no getting around it; poverty is here to stay.

3.6

Are the following opposites?

1. Riches and poverty
2. Red and blue
3. Republican and Democrat
4. Heads and tails
5. Fever and chills
6. Fat and slim

7. Protestant and Catholic   9. Round and square
8. Soft and hard   10. Tall and short

Compare this grouping:

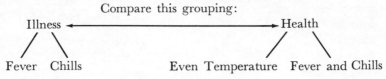

1. What does the above have to do with opposites?
2. How would you tell whether the other nine pairs on the list are opposites?

3.7

Listed below are some groups of stores. On what bases have such groups emerged? Can you list the distinguishing qualities that set off one type of store from another?

General store   Mail-order house
Neighborhood store   Discount house
Specialty store   Automatic vending
Department store   Roadside stand
Variety store   Pushcart
Supermarket   Itinerant store

1. In what way are all of the above alike?
2. What are some ways you could distinguish between each of the above?

(Some Student Responses)
1. How goods are sold
2. How goods are displayed
3. What services are offered
4. How the store is owned
5. What kind of ownership it is
6. Where the store is located
7. How the working personnel are organized
8. How goods are distributed

3. Take any one of the stores above and compare it to four others on the basis of distinguishing marks you have established. Then, on a scale running from small differences to great differences, indicate where you think the position of each of the ones you have chosen fits.

3.8

How many different ways can you group the following?

common water snake   turtles
sea horse   giraffe
penguin   mud puppy
ring-necked pheasant   cardinal

hippopotamus	shrew
bat	sailfish
moray eel	mice
flounder	ostriches
alligator	collared lizard
whales	pythons
common toad	tortoises
leopard frog	

1. Size
2. Mating habits
3. What it eats
4. Where it lives
5. How it protects itself
6. Fish-animals-birds-reptiles
7. Mammals — egg-laying

After a principle has been selected, students may work out the actual grouping.

3.9

A set is a collection of objects containing a common factor or element. Group the following set into as many subsets as you can. Place an x next to the number which would fit in the particular grouping as has been done for the prime numbers.

20 21 22 23 24 25 26 27 28 29 30 31 32 33 34 35 36 37 38 39 40

Integers
Real nos.
Natural nos.
Rational nos.
Irrational nos.
Even nos.
Odd nos.
Prime nos.   x   x   x   x
Negative nos.
Positive nos.
Cardinal nos.
Ordinal nos.

3.10

Here is a list of elements. Name as many categories you can under which they may be classified.

Hydrogen	Potassium
Uranium	Oxygen
Lithium	Aluminum
Magnesium	Mercury

Bromine   Carbon
Sulphur   Cadmium
Chlorine   Radon
Argon   Neon

Some Student Responses:

1. Solid, liquid, gas at room temperature
2. Solubility in water at room temperature
3. Metals, non-metals
4. Ionic, covalent
5. Density compared to water
6. Ability to form isotopes
7. Active, inert
8. Electron donor, electron receiver
9. Positive valence, negative valence
10. Ph value
11. Flame tests
12. Sulphide precipitates
13. Radioactivity
14. Supports combustion, does not support combustion
15. Flammable, nonflammable
16. Colorless, colored
17. Occurrence, free-combined
18. Odor, odorless, characteristic odor
19. Reducing agent, oxidizing agent
20. Found in organic compounds, not found in organic compounds

Further assignments might include the listing of the elements under each heading above and the grouping of the groups themselves.

3.11

Group the following words:

Elle, elles, vous, tu, nous, me, les, le, ils, il.

(Some Student Responses)

Groupings

1. Voice (first, second, third)
2. Gender
3. Case
4. Number

By Number		*By Case*	
Singular:	Elle	Subjective case:	Elle
	il		elles
	le		il
	me		ils
	tu		tu

Plural: elles   Objective Case: le
         ils   les
         les   me
         nous   Both subjective nous
         vous   and objective: vous

3.12

Group the following:

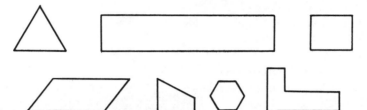

Some Student Responses

1. Quadrilaterals and polygons
2. Parallelograms and not parallelograms
3. Regular polygons and irregular polygons
4. Rectangles and not rectangles
5. Odd number of sides and angles and even number of sides and angles
6. Those containing only right angles and those with various size angles

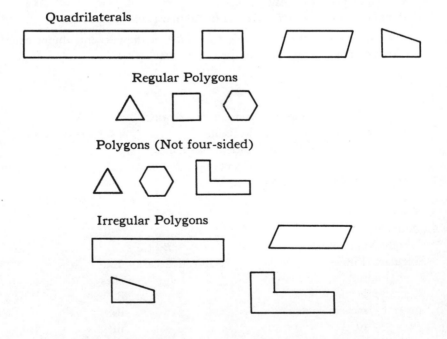

Quadrilaterals

Regular Polygons

Polygons (Not four-sided)

Irregular Polygons

3.13

Classify the following businesses:

Farmers' Cooperative Association
M. Johnson, Groceries
United States Post Office
Black and Grey Mfg. Company
Z and B Trucking
Tennessee Valley Authority
Great Lakes Lighting Company
Minnesota Mining Corp.

(Student Responses)

1. Ownership — public or private
2. Organization — sole owner, partnership, corporation, cooperative
3. Function — producer, manufacturer, wholesaler, retailer, distributor, public utility
4. Profit or non-profit making
5. Supplier of goods or services
6. Interstate or intra-state

Supplier of goods	*Supplier of services*
Minnesota Mining Corp.	Great Lakes Lighting Co.
Farmers' Cooperative Assn.	United States Post Office
M. Johnson, Groceries	Tennessee Valley Authority
Black and Grey Mfg. Co.	
Z and B Trucking	

Profit making	*Non-profit making*
Minnesota Mining Corp.	Tennessee Valley Authority
Z and B Trucking	United States Post Office
M. Johnson, Groceries	Farmers' Cooperative Assn.
Black and Grey Mfg.	
Great Lakes Lighting Co.	

3.14

Classify the following:

Light bulb, dry cell, generator, ammeter, voltmeter, storage battery.

(Some Student Responses)

1. Producer or user of electric current
2. Containing glass in its makeup
3. Containing a permanent or electro magnet
4. Containing movable parts
5. Presence of chemical action in its operation

Chemical action   *No chemical action*
Dry cell   Light bulb
Storage battery   Generator
                           Ammeter
                           Voltmeter

Producer of electricity   *User of electricity*
  Dry cell   Light bulb
  Storage battery   Ammeter
  Generator   Voltmeter

3.15

Classify the following:

Lion, whale, codfish, eagle, rattlesnake, frog, horse, canary, lizard
(Some Student Responses)

1. Air breathing
2. Warm blooded
3. Four legged
4. Terrestrial
5. Meat eating
6. Egg laying

Egg laying   *Non-egg laying*
1. Codfish   1. Lion
2. Eagle   2. Whale
3. Rattlesnake   3. Horse
4. Frog
5. Canary
6. Lizard

Warm blooded   *Cold blooded*
1. Lion   1. Codfish
2. Whale   2. Rattlesnake
3. Eagle   3. Frog
4. Horse   4. Lizard
5. Canary

3.16

Classify the following:

1,2,3,4,5,6,7,8,9,10

(Some Student Responses)

1. Odd numbers — even numbers
2. Prime numbers
3. Numbers evenly divisible by 4 and those not

4. Numbers with factors of 3 and 1 only and numbers with factors other than 3 and 1
5. Two digit numbers — one digit numbers
6. Numbers greater than or equal to 7 and numbers less than 7

Prime numbers:	Non-prime numbers:
2,3,5,7	1,4,6,8,9,10
Numbers with factors of 3 and 1 only:	Numbers without factors of 3 and 1:
3,9	1,2,4,5,6,7,8,10

Thus far, the reader has seen some exercises which were used by teachers and students in the operation of *classifying*.[26] Below is a listing of suggestions which will indicate some further classifying possibilities.

CLASSIFY

1. Latvians, Dutch, Bulgarians, Portugese, Hungarians, Rumanians, Swiss, Spanish, Ukranians, French, Slovenians, Poles, Slovaks, Italians, Czechs, Serbs, Germans, Croats.

2. 1776, 1941, 1917, 1812, 1839, 1861, 1898.

3. Prokofiev, Beethoven, Tschaikowsky, Schubert, Verdi, Mendelssohn, Brahms, Schumann, Scarlatti, Rossini, Purcell, Haydn, Shostakovich, Mozart, Gounod, Vivaldi, Wagner, Smetana, Bach, Dvorak.

4. Tennis, pool, golf, hockey, jai-alai, pingpong, volleyball, basketball, baseball, lacrosse, polo, football, soccer, badminton.

5. Matisse, Renoir, Picasso, Gainesborough, Dürer, Holbein, Vermeer, Rembrandt, Degas, Modigliani, Lautrec, Goya, Velasquez, Turner, Cezanne, Manet, Monet.

6. Meager, menial, mortify, demonic, domicile, needless, nocturnal, destitute, denounce, depradation, decry, mutual, mystify, negligent, nimble, monster.

7. Knox, Adams, Washington, Jackson, Lincoln, Marshall, Taney, Taft, Randolph, Tyler, Grant, Wm. Harrison, Taylor, Eisenhower, Jay, Seward, Jefferson, Hamilton.

8. Flute, violin, cymbals, tambourine, trumpet, harp, lute, clarinet, English horn, triangle, cello, viola, French horn, trombone.

9. Group the ways of earning a living.

10. Group the tools in a woodshop.

11. Group the parts of the body.

12. Group the countries of the world.

---

[26]Acknowledgment is made to graduate students for their contributions of 3.1, 3.2, 3.4, 3.7, 3.9, 3.10, 3.11, 3.12, 3.13, 3.14, 3.15, 3.16.

It is sometimes helpful for teachers to show how a classification system developed, how differentiations may be made if one can agree on the criteria for differentiation. For example, a system used by fruit growers to classify apples may be introduced: McIntosh, Delicious, Winesap, Golden Delicious, Jonathan, Stayman, Cortland, Baldwin, York Imperial. The tendency for students to say "they're all apples" will lessen as they see that function (cooking, eating raw, baking, pie), size, shape, color, and taste are criteria which are used to produce the classification.

Some variations in classification may be introduced. For example, students may list names of a dozen fish or a dozen animals. They may then be asked to group them as sportsmen, zoologists, or food connoisseurs would.

Complicated systems of classification and their social implications may also be presented. The socio-legal classifications for the act of killing are a case in point. For murder, society inflicts punishment; for accidental killing, usually compensation is expected; for psychopathic killing, institutionalization is often the result; for killing in self-defense, acquittal with no penalty is frequently a consequence; for killing under military command, society sometimes awards medals.

As students get opportunities to classify, they begin to see that purpose is crucial to the operation. They become aware that classifications are not revealed truths, nor are they the result of magic. Perhaps too, the rigid classifications which cause so much trouble in the social order will be seen in a different light. The teacher too comes to realize that neither he nor the textbook can perform the classifying operation for the student without depriving him of an important thinking operation. To present established classifications to the learner is to give him facts which others have created. To have him search out classifications is to have him ideate and order his thoughts. As continuing use is made of the operation of *classifying,* it will no doubt be observed how it suffuses nearly all thinking operations.

4. *Observing and Reporting*

Human beings are not mere intellects. We are often driven by impulse, passion, and routine to obtain satisfaction for our physical needs. Sometimes, we use our minds to further *these* ends. When this occurs, our reasoning can become unreasonable.

On such occasions, we have a tendency to overestimate our capacities and to underestimate our limitations. We talk of habit and prejudice but think these refer to others. We laugh at suggestibility and credulity and wonder how *people* can be like that. There are times when we even forget how we are hampered by our uses of language. What are our capacities and what are our limitations?

Our ultimate contact with fact is through our senses. We feel, see, hear, smell, or taste something. There have been some who have spoken of a sixth sense or a "common sense" which combines and unites the other five. Generally, our sense impressions are what we accept as evidence. As one wag put it, proof is what convinces *me*. We even call such evidence primary or eyewitness evidence. There are times when we go further and accept the evidence of the senses that other people give us. To be sure, we tend to put less faith in such evidence because it represents a secondary account, but if the person is accorded prestige, our faith in his evidence tends to reflect our faith in *him*.

How reliable are our senses? Furthermore, how reliable is the way in which we retain and recount our past experiences? In other words, how reliable is our memory? Does it retain our experiences without change? Look at the following for only one second:

Even at a fleeting glance, we can tell how many dots there are, perhaps because we have seen them on a die often enough. Now, look at the following for just one second:

Here, it is a little more difficult to tell at a glance how many dots there are without actually counting them out. Sense evidence, or perceptions, are affected by past experiences which include collected knowledge, thought habits and a tendency to see wholes, rather than parts.

Even though it is imperfect, sense perception is our basis of knowledge. It is the beginning of other mental processes. However, it is to be supplemented with *thought,* e.g., analysis, comparison. Thought is the check on imperfect perception. Without it, we are at the mercy of a cruel nature; we would have to believe in full the evidence of our senses. And this evidence, as we probably know, is not infrequently deceiving.

It has been said that sense evidence is the beginning of knowledge—sense evidence that is *checked for accuracy* and which reveals awareness of the distortions to which it is liable. Inaccurate sense evidence leads to misinterpretation and false inference. Our control of the universe depends upon our understanding of it, which in turn depends on checked observations. Perhaps this is what we mean when we say of someone, "He knows his 'stuff'." We mean he understands. An expert, whether an expert car mechanic or an expert physiologist, understands not only the way something is put together, but the functions of its parts; he sees not only the wholes, but the details.

How reliable is our memory? Does it retain our experience? The ability to recall and the ability to retain are commonly referred to as memory, but there is an important difference. Here are some things a teacher did to reveal that difference:

A student was asked to read the passage below and to write it out from memory. The teacher passed his version on to six other students who were asked to do the same. What do you suppose happened?

April 19, 1906[27]

Earthquake and fire yesterday laid nearly half of San Francisco in ruins. The fire is not yet under control. More than two hundred people were killed, one thousand injured, and the property loss, so far, is estimated at $200,000,000. Practically the entire business district was burned. Dynamite was used to check the progress of the flames.

The sweep of the earthquake was wide, deaths and large property losses marking its track in several cities to the north of San Francisco. Shocks were felt in the Far West, New York State, and Washington, D. C. and at the same time San Francisco quaked, a shock was felt in Austria.

Messages of sympathy and offers of aid were sent from all over the country immediately on receipt of the news, President Roosevelt and Congress sending messages and Boston subscribing $25,000 at once.

The teacher then showed the sketch below to a student for thirty seconds who was asked to reproduce it from memory. His reproduction was in turn shown to six others who were asked, one at a time, to reproduce it. What role do you suppose imagination plays in this?

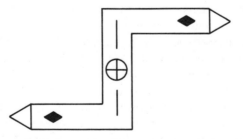

The teacher then asked his class to read the following selection. He challenged the class to write out in story form what they could remember, without reproducing actual wording. Each phrase between vertical lines repre-

---

[27]*The New York Tribune.*

sents a fact; there are a total of twenty-four facts. The teacher considered that fifteen facts recalled represented a good score.

Shortly before noon| Sunday| June| 28,| 1914,| Archduke| Francis Ferdinand,| heir-presumptive| to the thrones of Austria-Hungary,| and his wife,| Sophie,| were assassinated| by Gavrilo Printsip| in the Bosnian city| of Sarajevo.| Six weeks later| Austria-Hungary| and Germany| were involved in an armed struggle| with Serbia,| Russia,| France,| Belgium,| and Great Britain.|

"It has been said that one picture is worth a thousand words. Is this because the sense of sight is more accurate than the sense of hearing?" With these words, the teacher introduced his lesson. He then showed the picture below for ten seconds. Thereafter, he asked the class the questions below:

1. How many people are in the picture?
2. How many men are there? Women? Children?
3. What are the names of the intersecting streets?
4. How many people are wearing hats?
5. How many people are wearing coats?
6. What season of the year would you guess that it is?

7. How many automobiles are there?
8. How many automobiles are parked?
9. Does the traffic light say "stop" or "go"?
10. What kinds of businesses are there on the street?

If we were to try these little experiments, we would find that our memories, even regarding the immediate past, are remarkably short. What are they like after an interval of time has elapsed? What prompted Oscar Wilde to claim that the public has *no* memory?

One reason for "short memory" may be that its primary function is to aid us in the attainment of a *present* goal. Like perception, memory is intended to serve us, and like perception (see the square, triangle, and circle made of dots, p. 165), accurate recall of detail is not always necessary. Checking perceptions (perceivings) is much easier than checking recollections (rememberings). Most of us know how recollections blend in with imagination with the passage of time. Folklore and mythology are the usual result of collective perceptions and recollections. As an art form, sometimes, the product is very beautiful, and it may be recognized and preserved for what it is.

Generally, our ability to recall ("seeing" and "hearing") is unreliable because our perceivings and rememberings are related to practical purposes wherein accuracy is unnecessary. For example, for ordinary purposes, how many of us have to know or to remember how many spokes there are in a bicycle wheel or in the umbrella we use? Exactly what we recall depends on our attentiveness, which is influenced by our thought habits and patterns, as well as our needs.

While it is perhaps more desirable to see less and observe more, sometimes we *do* have to remember. For example, how reliable is our testimony as a witness to a crime? What effect does time have on our story? What effect does a gallery full of people have on us? How suggestible are we and what effect does our talking to others have? In some of the examples below, perhaps some answers to these questions are suggested.

This operation is listed as *observing and reporting* because it is believed that the two bear a symbiotic relationship to each other; reporting seems to follow naturally from an observation. It is well to stress that observing is somewhat different from just "seeing" or "hearing." As Poe tells us, "the necessary knowledge is that of what to observe."[28] Thus, observing is much more noting, discerning, taking in similarities and differences, and grouping.

When it comes to remembering what we have observed, sometimes it helps us if we can make a picture for ourselves (so we don't have to remember!). For example, a mnemonic device is actually a personal system so that individual parts of a whole may be recalled when one recalls the system. Acros-

---

[28]*The Murders in the Rue Morgue.*

tics are one of the common types of mnemonic devices, e.g., *vibgyor or Roy G. Biv* is supposed to represent the first letters of words for colors in the spectrum. No doubt, each of us has developed personal mnemonic devices so that larger bodies of information can easily be reduced.

It is hoped that the foregoing is not interpreted to mean that mnemonic devices are urged. Where they *are* used, it is better that they make sense and arise naturally rather than represent an artificial contrivance like *vibgyor*. A notorious example of the contrivance was *St. Wapniacl,* the acrostic solecism which stood for the names of the U. S. cabinet offices. Of a different sort is the memory aid which arises from within and is not superimposed.

A student who was having difficulty in distinguishing between horizontal and vertical was asked by his teacher to discover the *horizon* in the word horizontal. Thenceforward, the plague of confusion disappeared.

The following are some suggestions for exercises in observing and reporting:

4.1

The subject area of science generally comes to mind when one speaks of observations. Laboratory animals and plants are observed for certain characteristics, models are looked at carefully, the sky full of stars is studied. A nature walk offers a fruitful area for observation. Just a few possibilities for observation are mentioned here: fire, a snowflake, a rock, a leaf, a tree, ice, hail, a drop of water, chemical reactions, microscopic analysis.

4.2

The subject areas of music and art certainly have rich potential for observing from simple sound and color differentiations to the discernment of differentiations in pitch and intensity to an analysis of complicated constructions.

4.3

Fabrics like wool, cotton, linen, and substances used in daily living like glass, leather, paper, and metals offer possibilities for observing (with the eyes and with the hands). Similarly, objects which are made from the foregoing list of substances may be used.

4.4

In gym, students may put themselves in a position where they think they are in maximum balance, or in minimum balance.[29] Others may observe and report the various ways balance may be achieved. In addition to oral reporting, and perhaps as a more appropriate form of reporting, students may *demonstrate* their understanding of the concept of balance.

---

[29]Forms of movement may be used: sitting down, getting up, jumping, walking forward or backwards or sidewards, and other ways of moving the body. Seen in a demonstration by Muska Mosston at New Jersey Association for Supervision and Curriculum Development Annual Conference, 1965.

4.5

Illustrations are forms of reporting observations. Students may be asked to make a map of a given place (the school grounds, the classroom, the neighborhood, the city). Making a map offers some distinct advantages over copying or filling in a map. Or students may be asked to make a drawing, a figure, or a chart, which are all forms of reporting an observation.

4.6

Students may construct a vehicle by which observing may take place: carvings, modelings, resonating boxes.

4.7

Geoboard

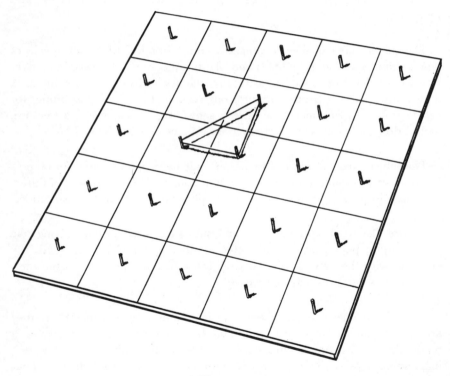

Figure 1

An example of the foregoing is the geoboard (see Figure 1). It is easily constructed. On a piece of 3/8 inch plywood, 11¼ inches square, draw a series of horizontal and vertical lines 2¼ inches apart to form a grid on the surface of the plywood. The grid will be five squares long and five squares wide. In the center of each square put in a nail. The only additional equipment needed is a box of different colored elastic bands.

Students may first be left to their own devices with the rubber bands and the board for a length of time. Initial instruction may include an explanation about the existence of squares of unit areas on the geoboard. By stretching a rubber band around four adjacent pegs, a square of the unit can be formed. By stretching a second rubber band between the diagonal of this unit square, the figure will be divided into two triangles. (Students can perhaps discover that these triangles are equal in area and that two of them form one square.) They may also discover that the area of one of the triangles is half the area of the unit square. They can perhaps go further to find areas of squares, rectangles and various shaped figures.

4.8

Students may be given a list such as the following, told to study it for a few minutes, and then asked to recall what they have "seen":

voice	choppy	low
singing	soprano	happy
short	smooth	music
full	alto	sad
light	beautiful	ugly
body	words	long
breath	high	slow
raucous	fast	pleasant

4.9

Students are told to go to the window, to look outside for a few moments, and are then asked to recall what they have observed. A variant of this procedure is to have a boy and girl stand in front of the room for a few minutes. They then step outside and the class is asked to describe what it has observed.

4.10

Pictures, diagrams, charts, or drawings of various types may be shown fleetingly and students are asked to recall. It may be noted that in exercises 4.8, 4.9 and 4.10, observing calls for much more than mere seeing. In his discussion of observation, Edgar Allan Poe said that "to observe attentively is to remember distinctly."[30] Remembering seems to involve ordering what it is that we see. In exercise 4.8, a system of some sort would no doubt be helpful in recalling particulars. In exercise 4.9, the system might be a little harder to devise. Exercise 4.11 below probably helps to illustrate how we are affected by perceptual bias; we see what we want to see.

---

[30]*The Murders in the Rue Morgue.*

4.11

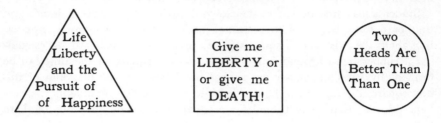

4.12

Various names have been given to the following exercise. It has been called "spy message" or "telephone." A message is written out for one person in each row to see. He passes on the message orally to the person behind him and he to the next person and so on until the last person in the row has been reached. When this person receives the message via the transmission process, he repeats it aloud or puts it on the blackboard. The original message is then read for comparison.

There are variations of the above. The rumor clinic idea, where one person looks at a picture and then "explains" it to another person who explains it to another and so on is suitable for use here also. So is the staging of a mock fight so that all may then report what they saw.

4.13

It should perhaps be pointed out that observing is not restricted to the eyes alone. Various spices may be brought in, smelled by one person or a group and then reported on. Different tastes—sweet, salty, sour, bitter—are "observed." Several qualities and shapes of material may be presented: soft, hard, round, square, fuzzy, silky, scratchy. With closed eyes, students may be asked to report on what they feel. Or, various sounds—high, low, short, long, rapid, slow—are made. Variations in pitch may be introduced on one instrument or on several.

In the illustrations cited thus far, it may be seen that there is a problem of reporting accurately what one sees, hears, smells, and feels. Using short cuts or systems to create a whole for purposes of recall will be seen as functional if the system is recognized as a mere convenience or mnemonic. This becomes important when we realize that some of us have erected fairly rigid cataloguing systems which are designed to evoke a specific mental image. Particularly lethal are grouping terms like swarthy, criminal-type, slimy, greasy, oily. Used indiscriminately, they have tended to create stereotypes of certain national groupings. In this regard, attention is called to the two-value systems which are frequently employed: "goodies" versus "baddies." Sometimes we catalogue by using virtue words and poison words to color our reporting and to give it "life." Students can be made sensitive to the differences between description and ascription. The exercise indicated below may be helpful in this regard.

4.14

A story is read or one or two pictures are displayed. Students are asked to write a report on what they have seen or heard in as factual a way as they can. It probably will be discovered that inferential statements will be included among the factual statements. The teacher might have students rate their own statements as observational or inferential, descriptive or ascriptive. A brief story like the following is intended:

> A man staggered into a drug store gesturing unsteadily. His speech was incoherent and his gait very erratic. A woman customer, in irate fashion, said to the clerk, "Jim, that man is drunk! Throw him out of here!" As the clerk responded, he noticed that the man was pointing to his pocket. He put his hand into the man's pocket and took out some chocolate cubes and put one into the man's mouth. The man later returned to the drug store; his speech was coherent and his gait steady.

1. Is the woman's statement, "That man is drunk," factual or inferential?
2. Are the following statements factual or inferential?
   1. The man was walking unsteadily.
   2. The man was suffering from insulin shock.
   3. Something was apparently wrong with the man.
3. Make up some statements which are factual. Make up some which are inferential.

It may be kept in mind that, in observing, students are asked to discern patterns, to note likeness and difference, as they do in comparing. In reporting, the student is asked to discern between what is observable by others and what it is that he adds to the situation—his interpretation. In other words, the student is to note distinctions between fact and opinion.

4.15

In the exercise below, students are given the reports of other people's observations and they are asked to react to them. While a detective story is here indicated, reports of various kinds may be used.

How does Watson see Jabez Wilson and how does Holmes see him?[31]

Watson's Observations	*Holmes' Observations*
baggy trousers	Chinese chain indicated man had
black frock	been to China
frayed cuffs	one hand larger than other indicated
red hair	man did manual labor
faded overcoat	man wore a tatoo
not overly clean	man was a Freemason
fat	right cuff shiny
slow	
pompous	

---

[31]Sir Arthur Conan Doyle, *The Redheaded League.*

1. What are the differences in Watson's observations and in Holme's observations?
2. Who is the better detective? Why?

It is probably apparent how basic to the other operations is this one of *observing and reporting*. It is of inestimable aid in sharpening perception; it enables the learner to see how perceptual bias colors observation. He becomes sensitive to the idea that personal experiences are interpreted with caution; they are not the same as universal proofs.[32]

It is hoped that observing and reporting are properly seen as a *means* of learning. Too often do we rely on secondary accounts as contained in books as a means of teaching, while we neglect a primary basis of knowing—firsthand observation.

It might be supposed that the operation of *observing and reporting* relates only to a science course where demonstrations are typical. Or perhaps some see its applications to a geography course, a music course, an art course, or one of the industrial arts or home economics courses where maps, charts, pictures, diagrams, blue prints and the like are in fairly frequent use. To incorporate the operation requires no curriculum revision, no addition of a course, no assignment of the operation to the aforementioned courses alone. On the contrary, within each subject area are meaningful materials which the teacher can search out and employ to promote observing and reporting. The operation is something which the students perform at regular intervals rather than something which the teacher does *for* the students.

5. Summarizing.

Summarizing is more than putting together a series of steps. It is more than recounting and reporting what has taken place. It is to discern and to evaluate what is significant and what is insignificant. Thus, it means a decision has to be made about what to put in and what to leave out; main ideas have to be brought together in a synthesis. Of all skills related to thinking, this is perhaps the least taught and the most assumed to be! Too many teachers think that the skill of summarizing can be taught by *their* doing the summarizing *for* the learners. Would that it were so easily transferable and susceptible to imitation. Unfortunately, the results of proceeding on such an assumption are the bore and the miser.

We are well acquainted with the verbal spendthrift; he lavishly puts *everything* in when he tells a story. Afraid that he will omit something important, he treats us to a labyrinthine recital of detail after detail. Is he a bore because he did not learn how to omit, how to distinguish the significant from the insignificant? At the other extreme is the curt and cryptic indi-

---

[32]Acknowledgement to a graduate student is made for his contribution of exercise 4.7.

vidual given to such parsimony that for him to put in detail is to be uneconomical. That it would make him less obscure seems not to be his concern. Is he laconic because he did not learn to distinguish the significant from the insignificant?

There is the implication that, although related to reporting, summarizing, like interpreting, requires not mere reproduction nor mere translation. Instead, as an extension of interpreting, it reads between the lines and moves beyond the given to abstract and filter out, to integrate and synthesize salient points. It deals with the question: what is to be put in and in what order? The amount to be included in a summary is usually determined by the purpose the summary is to serve.

In pedagogic technique, the teacher may provide students with materials and ask them to justify the bases upon which they have determined what is essential. It will probably become apparent that some students do not know how to determine what is essential. The teacher may have to go back and work with observing and reporting materials before asking students to abstract and extract the essence. It is important for the teacher not to assume that students have, or should have, the skill of summarizing. Instead of wishing that they *be,* he helps them *become.* He may discover that students may confuse summarizing with interpreting. He will lead them to see that, although the *summary* is itself an interpretation, the *act* of summarizing extends beyond interpreting. Similarly, though the summary as product is synthetic, the process itself is analytic. As with other skills mentioned herein, summarizing is best learned through repeated experiences.

Rather than pumping one student dry, the teacher may ask for summaries from several students. One need not cajole students to "put more into" a summary, nor need there be public evaluation of the students' efforts. Instead, the teacher may ask: "Who can summarize differently?" or, "How would you summarize the same thing?" Further, it is useful to have summaries compared. Items which have been omitted may be listed and students can be asked to defend their omissions. Beyond this, summaries themselves may be summarized!

Below are some suggestions for exercises which put an emphasis on summarizing:

5.1

1. Read the germ theory of disease, Locke's theory of government, or Darwin's theory (any theory may be used). Write a summary of the theory in three paragraphs.
2. From your knowledge of United States history at this point, write a one page summary called: "The Story of the United States."
3. Prepare a summary of a subject (or part of it) which you have studied. What is the subject all about? What are the most important

rules of that subject (or unit of it)? (e.g., geometry, chemistry, biology, a foreign language, bookkeeping, poetry.)

4. Prepare a summary paragraph of your life.

5.2 Titling is often a form of summarizing.
1. Teacher reads a poem, a story, or a news article and asks for an appropriate title.
2. A picture, diagram, chart, or graph is displayed and titles are solicited.
3. A problem, an experiment, a procedure, or a process is read. Students create a title and subtitles for it.
4. Sections and even chapters in a textbook are re-titled and evaluated as to their appropriateness.

5.3 Inventing captions is a form of summarizing.
1. Pictures and cartoons are given captions.
2. For variety, captions may be slanted to show a particular point of view.

5.4 Organizing data may be seen as a form of summarizing.
1. Students are given some loose data to organize under appropriate headings which they create.
2. Data may be organized in the form of a map, diagram, or chart. The preparation of adequate keys is a summarizing skill.
3. Preparing a table of contents or an index is sometimes useful as an organizing and summarizing experience.
4. In written reports of the term paper variety, students prepare initial outlines and then abstracts or summaries before the project is due. These can be used for guidance purposes as well.

5.5
Students may be working on a problem or attempting to apply principles to new situations. (See exercises 8.19 and 8.20 on pages 215 and 216.) After they have concluded work on the problem, they summarize the series of steps that they have taken towards solution.

5.6
Accounts of a series of experiments are read (e. g., the work of Galileo, Lavoisier, Faraday). Summaries are prepared.

5.7

Excerpts of a log or diary are read (e. g., the records of Columbus, Magellan, Lewis and Clark). Oral summaries are made.

5.8

See the illustrations under the operations *comparing and classifying* on pages 132 and 151. As the operation is completed, the teacher may call for summarizing.

5. 9

See the illustrations under the operations of *interpreting, analyzing, criticizing,* and *imagining* on pages 181, 196, 220, and 231. Under each of them, summarizing is appropriate.

5.10

Sometimes teachers assign group or committee work, and each group *reports* to the class. Frequently, boredom is a concomitant of such reporting. Instead of lengthy reports, can summaries be substituted?

The reader is referred to Part 2, pages 91-94 for additional listings of summarizing activities. In the examples which follow, there is an attempt to make summarizing the focus of the exercise:

5.11 Read the statements below. What connection do you see between each? You will note that they are themes or central ideas. As you read them, see if you can determine what a central idea is.

   1. General education is basic to the proper development of man's capacities.
   2. Herman Melville was the first important naturalist in the mainstream of American fiction.
   3. Society has robbed man of his economic independence.
   4. Effective communication is necessary in labor-management disputes.
   5. California produces more oranges than Texas.
   6. The American way of life is the result of interaction of both the Puritan and frontier influences.
   7. Effective communication is important in maintaining family unity.

From the foregoing statements which are examples of *central ideas,* extract some rules which might help you formulate a central idea or thesis statement of your own.

(Some student answers)

A central idea should:

1. Be stated in a simple declarative sentence.
2. Be stated so that the meaning is clear.
3. Be a summary of what is to follow; it acts as an introduction.

5.12

Here are some questions which a fur dealer might ask before he made a purchase:

1. From what animal was the fur obtained?
2. What was the sex of the animal?
3. How was the skin obtained?
4. What is the color of the fur?
5. How popular is the color?
6. How was the fur manipulated (for example, let-out is an expensive process)?
7. What is the style of the garment?
8. What is its cost relationship to other furs?

Now suppose you saw the following advertisement:

SALE!

GIGANTIC
FUR
CLEARANCE

NATURAL LET-OUT CERULEAN MINK STOLES $398.00

In a summary statement, show how you would evaluate the advertisement.

5:13

We generally like sales because we think we are saving some money. Sometimes, advertisements give us significant information; sometimes, they do not. Below are two advertisements. Study them carefully. If your parents were to purchase an air conditioner, which of the advertisements do you think would be of most value to them? Write a summary paragraph indicating reasons for your choice.

Advertisement #1

SAVE $60 WITH KOLD
NEW KOLD AIR CONDITIONER
REQUIRES NO COSTLY SPECIAL
WIRING $299.50

Originally $359.50
No down payment
As low as $3.23 a week

This new ¾ HP "KOLD" plugs into any outlet. 7.5 ampere motor uses only 862 watts, less than an iron or a toaster. Cools, filters, and dehumidifies an average 20 x 20 room. Automatic temperature control; grille allows easy air stream adjustment, eliminates drafts. Push-button exhaust-intake control. Installation optional.

Advertisement #2

SAVE $60 to $200 off

COLOSSAL SAVINGS

UP TO 25%
COOLE
AIR CONDITIONER

Relax in the coolness of your home with a COOLE air conditioner. Enjoy ocean-like breezes for just a few pennies a day. COOLE is the finest unit made.

This stupendous bargain is available for SEVEN DAYS ONLY.

COOLE is used in thousands of homes today. Be the first in your neighborhood to own a superb COOLE.

5:14

In gym class, students may put themselves in a position where they think they are in maximum balance or in minimum balance. Or various forms of movements may be demonstrated in various styles: sitting down, getting up, walking forward, and ways of moving the body. Students may observe various ways of performing each activity. Others may undertake to summarize either orally or by demonstration that which they consider significant.[33]

5.15

A selection in a foreign language is read. The story may be summarized in English with little emphasis upon literal or even loose translation.

5.16

Famous paintings are shown and impressions are solicited from a class. These impressions are listed on a ditto master and distributed. The class is divided into groups and asked to order the list in some way, to create summaries.

Perhaps some persons will see the thinking operation of *summarizing*[34] as being within the special purview of a teacher of English. This has long been the case with spelling and with language expression in general. Yet, knowing that a conceptual response is impossible without language places upon every teacher the responsibility for pulling his share of the burden. To cast about searching for those upon whom we can heap blame does not get the job done. If teachers want to put an emphasis upon a generalized ability called thinking, *summarizing,* one of the thinking operations, needs to be given practice in every subject. From what is known about transfer, *i. e.,* that generalized abilities are not transferable across content lines, it becomes imperative to emphasize the operation in all subject areas.

Within each subject area there is sufficient material to afford opportunities for the exercise of this operation. Special courses are not needed, nor is delegation of the problem to the English teacher a solution. Being able to abstract is a skill necessary to daily living. No doubt it may be seen how finding the essence of the matter is intimately involved in the operations of *comparing, classifying* and *observing and reporting* which have been discussed thus far.

---

[33]Seen in a demonstration by Muska Mosston at New Jersey Association for Supervision and Curriculum Development Annual Conference, 1965.
[34]Acknowledgement is made to graduate students for their contributions in constructing exercises 5.11, 5.12, and 5.13.

6. Interpreting.

The operation of *interpreting* is concerned with the inferences and generalizations which may be drawn from reports. Interpreting is not limited to mere translating; the latter is closer to reporting. Interpreting is to add meaning, to read between the lines, to fill in gaps, and to extend on given material *within the limits of that material*. To interpret is to understand reports: numerical, pictorial, graphic, artistic, and literary.

John Stuart Mill once said: "The great business of life is in drawing inferences." It is hardly conceivable that we could go through a day without making an interpretation from data. Sometimes, we have a tendency to leap beyond the data, and some of us may tend to distort the data through crude errors. At other times, we may exhibit over-caution, although caution is generally desirable. Not uncommon is the inability to interpolate and to extrapolate, to see inner meaning and extended meaning as well as to see the limitations of the data and to recognize when probability applies. Suffice it to say, learning to correlate cause and effect is an important thinking skill—one which seems to receive little attention in terms of school practices.

Like the other operations mentioned heretofore, interpretations may be "told" to someone, but the skills involved in the performance of the particular operation are not a mere matter of "telling." An observation of a lesson on what a teacher called *interpretation* is brought to mind. First came some questions which elicited facts—the data: "Who was he, what did he do, when did he live, where? What is the main character's name, where did he go, how and when?" After many minutes spent on collecting this information, the teacher then announced: "Take out your notebooks. I'll give you the interpretation of the story and you can write it down." The performance of the teacher does not help the learner very much in acquiring skill in interpreting. As with other matters, learning how to make interpretations comes with the making of them.

In this regard, an appeal is made not to deprive the student of his rightful role. In fact, the teacher might reverse the traditional roles. Instead of asking students to recall facts which are then evaluated, interpreted and synthesized by the teacher, the students are *given* facts by the teacher who, in turn, asks them to engage in the various thinking processes.

The learner is given some data and the teacher asks him what they mean: e. g., "On the basis of these data, what can you tell us? Can you predict anything with certainty? With probability?" The student is asked to say something not already said by the data, to go beyond the translation of the data, to extend upon them, fill in the gaps in the data. This is what is meant by a higher mental process; the student makes a contribution to that which is given; he does not merely reproduce it.

In building up skill in interpreting, it is perhaps wise to get the student to notice first what is in the data and when changes occur. After many experiences with mere translation, the student begins to compare parts of the data with other parts. Still later in terms of experiences, he is asked to fill in the gaps and to extend the meaning of the data.

In the illustrations and exercises offered, it may be seen that several varieties are possible:

1. Students are given data and set interpretations are prepared which the students evaluate as to accuracy. (6.6)
2. Students are given data and they make their own interpretations. These interpretations are then reproduced and re-submitted to the students, who may evaluate them for accuracy. (6.7-6.12)
3. Students are given data and asked to make interpretations. Such interpretations are then compared with actual interpretations made in the original case. For example:
   1. The experiment of a scientist is reproduced, but not the findings. Students interpret his data and then compare their interpretations with the findings of the scientist.
   2. The students are given some geographical data about a region and are asked to make some interpretations about the climate, people, and topography. These interpretations are then compared with the findings made by explorers who first charted the area. (The diaries of Lewis and Clark, Stanley and Livingstone, Champlain, and others may be consulted.)
4. Non-tabular materials are presented for interpretation.

The first exercise below is offered more as an example of translation. Succeeding illustrations deal more directly with interpretation as defined above.

6.1

Can you find the relationship between the number of sides of a polygon and the sum of its angles?

The sum of the angles of a triangle is 180°. Divide each of these polygons below into the fewest number of triangles possible. (When dividing the polygons into triangles, the lines must go between the angles of the polygons. Can you see why?) From the number of triangles obtained, calculate the sum of the angles in each polygon and complete the chart.

		Number of sides in each Polygon	Number of triangles (180°) in each polygon	Sum of the angles of each polygon
1.	Triangle	————	————	————
2.	Quadrilateral	————	————	————
3.	Pentagon	————	————	————
4.	Hexagon	————	————	————
5.	Heptagon	————	————	————

Answers:

1.	Triangle	3	1	180°
2.	Quadrilateral	4	2	360°
3.	Pentagon	5	3	540°
4.	Hexagon	6	4	720°
5.	Heptagon	7	5	900°

6.2

Read the following paragraph carefully. If you think the statements which follow it are true, write *T* in the space provided. If you think they are false, write *F*. If you think there is insufficient information, write *I*.

C'est jeudi. Il n'y a pas de classe aujourd'hui. Alice est chez son amie Louise. Elles écoutent les disques que Louise vient d'acheter. Il est midi et demi. Alice donne un coup de téléphone à sa mère. Elle lui demande si elle peut rester chez Louise pour dejéuner. Sa mère est d'accord. Mais elle demande à Alice d'acheter du pain et du beurre avant cinq heures.[35]

1. Alice est parasseuse.
2. Alice vient d'acheter des disques.
3. Les jeunes filles vont déjeuner chez Louise.
4. La mère d'Alice dit qu'Alice peut rester chez Louise.
5. Il fait froid.
6. Il est trois heures.
7. Sa mère demande à Alice d'acheter du chocolat.
8. Le jour de la semaine est dimanche.
9. Alice est laborieuse.
10. Louise n'est pas hereuse.[36]

6.3

In an experiment on the interaction of an acid and a base, the following data were obtained:

Trial No.	Volume of Acid Used	Volume of Base Used	Effect of Resulting Solution On:	
			Red Litmus	Blue Litmus
1	25 ml	18 ml	Turned blue	None
2	20 ml	8 ml	None	None
3	15 ml	5 ml	None	Turned red
4	90 ml	36 ml	None	None
5	7 ml	2 ml	None	Turned red
6	25 ml	50 ml	Turned blue	None

On the basis of *these data alone*, indicate whether the statements below are true or false. If the data alone do not warrant the statement, label it *I*— insufficient evidence.

1. An acid and base can react to neutralize each other.
2. The acid and base used in this experiment have unequal concentrations or normalities.
3. If the volume of the acid used is larger than the volume of base used, the resulting solution will be neutral or acid to litmus.
4. The products of the reaction of an acid and a base are a salt and water.
5. The reaction of an acid and a base evolves heat.
6. One milliliter of this base will neutralize 2.5 milliliters of the acid.

---

[35]*Audio Lingual Materials, French Level One* (New York: Harcourt, Brace & World, Inc., 1963), p. 59.
[36]1. I; 2. F; 3. T; 4. T; 5. I; 6. F; 7. F; 8. F; 9. I; 10. I.

7. A given acid and a given base react according to the law of definite proportions.

8. The solution resulting from trial number 2 would have no effect on methyl orange indicator solution.

9. The normality of this acid is 0.4 times the normality of the base.

10. The solution resulting from trial number 3 contains a greater weight of hydrogen ions (as acid) than the solution resulting from trial number 5.[37]

In the multi-valued world of today, we recognize the danger of teaching in terms of two values only. Yet, sometimes, the fixing of only two values in the minds of the young occurs because of years of conditioning. Our true or false tests, in no small measure, are responsible, as is our teaching, which persists in limiting choices to *either-or's*. On the one hand, it is suggested that we break with the true-false tradition and introduce the yes or no form. Thus, not, "An acid turns blue litmus paper red, true or false?," but, "Does an acid turn blue litmus paper red, yes or no?" At first glance, these two forms appear to be the same, but they are not. Careful examination will show why this is so. True and false forms might best be used *only* when the data are given to the student for him to refer to as in exercises 6.4 and 6.5 below. It is better not to use them in situations requiring mere recall or recognition.

Now, on the other hand, is it possible to do away with offering *only* two choices as often as we can? In exercises 6.2 and 6.3, three choices are given to the students. It is recommended that a three-choice exercise be used for a long period of time until a fair level of sophistication has been achieved. At that point, two additional choices, in the form of probability statements, may be introduced.

Probably true and *probably false* are assigned in those instances where there is a clear indication in the data, but *all* the data are not present; there is a gap to be filled (interpolation) or an extension to be made to the data (extrapolation). At the outset, students might tend to be over-cautious due to a training period which included only true, false, and insufficient data. In fact, they may have to be prodded a bit to employ *probably true* and *probably false,* since they may tend to equate the lack of all the data with insufficient data. The teacher may help students discover the differences in data requirements for a statement to be marked *true* and *probably true.* Students will see that *probably true* occupies the middle ground between *true* and *insufficient data* and that *probability* and *possibility* are not interchangeable terms.

The following exercises are somewhat more complicated. As one increases choices, it would seem that complication follows; answers become more difficult to secure.

---

[37]1. T; 2. T; 3. I; 4. I; 5. I; 6. F; 7. I; 8. I; 9. F; 10. T.

6.4

Read the following paragraph:

Depuis longtemps notre train électrique, comme d'ailleurs le sont tous ceux du Chemin de Fer du Midi, serpentait entre de petites montagnes, s'approchant peu à peu des Pyrénées qu'on appercevait déjà au loin. Enfin il s'arrêta à la gare de Lourdes. Je me sentis transporté d emblée dans un autre monde. La foule des pèlerins venus de tous les pays de l'Europe, parlant les langues les plus diverses, portant les costumes les plus variés, envahissait la petite gare. Partout on voyait des prêtres, des malades, des infirmières, des civières, des voiturettes, que sais-je encore?[38]

Having read this paragraph, fill in the spaces below according to the following:

T   These data alone are sufficient to make the statement true.

PT   These data alone are sufficient to indicate that the statement is probably true.

I   These data alone are not sufficient to indicate whether there is truth or falsity in the statement.

PF   These data alone are sufficient to indicate that the statement is probably false.

F   These data alone are sufficient to show the falsity of the statement.

1. Une personne traversait l'Europe en train.
2. Les choses que l'auteur a vues étaient très vielles.
3. Le train s'est arrêté à la gare de Lourdes.
4. L'homme est malade, et il espère aller à une des infirmières.
5. Le train est électrique.
6. Le train va au sud de la France.
7. L'auteur était étranger.
8. L'auteur voyage depuis longtemps.
9. Les pèlerins parlent des langues diverses .
10. L'auteur fait un voyage à Lourdes.[39]

6.5

Read the following article and then answer the questions below by inserting T if the statement is true, PT if the statement is probably true, I if there is no evidence in the article to support the statement, PF if the statement is probably false, or F if the statement is false. Use only the data given below and consider all the information contained therein to be true.

Dallas, November 22, 1963

President John Fitzgerald Kennedy was shot and killed by an assassin today.

---

[38]Arthur G. Bovée and David H. Charnahan, *Lettres de Paris* (Boston: D. C. Heath & Company, 1954), p. 59.
[39]1. I; 2. PF; 3. T; 4. I; 5. T; 6. T; 7. I; 8. PT; 9. T; 10. PT.

He died of a wound in the brain caused by the rifle bullet that was fired at him as he was riding through downtown Dallas in a motorcade.

Vice-President Johnson, who was riding in the third car behind Mr. Kennedy's, was sworn in as the 36th president of the United States 99 minutes after Mr. Kennedy's death.

Shortly after the assassination, Lee H. Oswald, who once defected to the Soviet Union and who has been an active member in the Fair Play for Cuba Committee, was arrested by the Dallas police. Tonight he was accused of the killing.

Oswald, 24 years old, was also accused of slaying a policeman who had approached him in the street. Oswald was subdued after a scuffle with a second policeman in a nearby theater.

Mr. Johnson, who was uninjured in the shooting, took his oath in the Presidential jet plane as it stood on the runway at Love Field. The body of Mr. Kennedy was aboard. Immediately after the oath taking, the plane took off for Washington.

1. President Kennedy was killed in a motorcade through downtown Dallas.
2. The man who assassinated President Kennedy disliked him.
3. John F. Kennedy was the 34th president of the United States.
4. Lee Oswald was a patriotic American.
5. Lee Oswald assassinated the President as part of a Communist plot.
6. Love Field is in or near Dallas.
7. Mr. Johnson became president 99 minutes after the death of President Kennedy.
8. The Fair Play for Cuba Committee is a Communist organization.
9. Oswald scuffled with three policemen.
10. Lee Oswald was an active member of the Fair Play for Cuba Committee.
11. A revolver bullet killed President Kennedy.
12. Oswald did not like the policies of the Fair Play for Cuba Committee.
13. Mr. Johnson flew to Washington in the Presidential jet plane.[40]

6.6

Based on the data supplied in the illustration below, identify the succeeding statements as:

T — if the data are sufficient to make the statement true.

PT— if the data are sufficient to indicate probably true.

I — if the data are insufficient to warrant any degree of truth or falsity.

PF — if the data conflict with the statement sufficiently to indicate probably false.

F — if the data clearly conflict with the statement so that it is false.

1. Because of the time-saving element, more people travel by plane today than by railroad.

---

[40]1. T; 2. I; 3. F; 4. PF; 5. I; 6. PT; 7. T; 8. I; 9. F; 10. T; 11. F; 12. PF; 13. PT.

TRAVEL TIME

FROM
PITTSBURGH

TO
PHILADELPHIA

1812

1834

1854

1920

TODAY

Each clock represents 4 hours of travel

2. A person traveling from Pittsburgh to Philadelphia today can save more than 140 hours of traveling time as compared to a traveler in 1812.

3. Between 1812 and 1854, travel by coach decreased while travel by railroad increased.

4. Different types of locomotives were used between 1834 and 1920.

5. Travel by rail was faster between Pittsburgh and Philadelphia in 1840 than in 1850.

6. Travel time between Pittsburgh and Philadelphia will continue to decrease.

7. The increase of speed in rail travel between Philadelphia and Pittsburgh between the years 1834 and 1920 was due to the use of better grade steel in the tracks.

8. Both Pittsburgh and Philadelphia have nearby airfields today.

9. The appearance of the two cities (Pittsburgh and Philadelphia) altered between the year of 1812 and today.

10. In every corner of the world today, travel time is decreasing.

11. Travel time by rail between Pittsburgh and Philadelphia increased by more than two days in 1854.

12. While travel time was decreasing between Pittsburgh and Philadelphia, it was also decreasing in other parts of the U. S. between 1834 and 1920.

13. Invention of the steam engine was the cause of the great saving of time in traveling.

14. The Philadelphia-Pittsburgh Railroad Company had faster trains in 1920 than in 1900.[41]

In the following examples, 6.7-6.13 data are given to the students, who are asked to make interpretations. These interpretations may then be reproduced and given back to the students for their evaluation.

6.7

On a scale of 100 points, here are the final grades of four high school boys in various subjects. What correlations, if any, do you see?

	Composition	Algebra	Geometry	History
Tom	90	10	20	80
Jim	20	80	70	30
Bill	60	40	30	10
George	40	70	60	70

Some additional information for you to consider:

1. A correlation is a measure of the extent to which variation in one variable corresponds with variation in another. For example, attendance

---

[41] 1. I; 2. T; 3. I; 4. T; 5. PF; 6. PT; 7. I; 8. PT; 9. T; 10. I; 11. F; 12. PT; 13. I; 14. I.

record and scholastic achievement are two variables which *may* be correlated.

2. High correlations *suggest* (but do no more than suggest) a relationship of cause and effect.

3. Variable factors in a situation may be correlated positively or negatively or not at all.

6.8

Here are some names of diseases and pests in the United States:

Spanish flu
Asian flu
German measles
French pox
Dutch elm blight
Mexican beetle
Japanese beetle
Mediterranean fruit fly

Here are some names of diseases and pests in other countries:

The French call syphilis English pox
The English call syphilis French pox
The Austrians call a cockroach a Swabian
The Germans call a cockroach a Frenchman
The Poles call a coachroach a Prussian
The French call a louse a Spaniard
The Czechs call a pimple a Hungarian

What are some of your conclusions?

6.9

A group of students were told to draw some inferences from *these data alone:*

November 1860 — Election of Lincoln as President of the U.S.A.
December 1860 to February 1861 — Secession of six southern states
March 1861 — Inauguration of Lincoln as President of the U.S.A.
April 1861 — War between the states

The following were some inferences drawn by college students, all of them majors in history. These inferences were then examined for validity and relationship to the data.

1. The election of Lincoln caused the secession of six southern states.

2. Inauguration of Lincoln caused the Civil War.

3. War between the states implies separate equal bodies fighting one another.

4. Lincoln's election ended the possibility of peaceful resolution of differences.
5. Lincoln did not cower in the face of the southern states.
6. The person of Lincoln was detested by the South.
7. War between the states indicates that there were two nations.
8. Secession was a result of a proposed plan, and war was a result of carrying out that plan.
9. Some action by Lincoln may have caused secession.
10. Lincoln was in favor of preserving the Union.
11. Southern states nullified the Constitution of the U.S.
12. Lincoln was elected by a minority.
13. In the absence of further data, interpretations which I make are in the nature of probabilities.
14. The South was responsible for the Civil War.
15. If Lincoln had not been elected, there would not have been a Civil War.

Which of these statements would you mark true or false; *i. e.,* they are supported by the data given above.

Which of these statements would you mark as insufficient data?

6.10
   Here are some data compiled from genetic studies of some families:
1. *The Jukes Family*
There were 709 descendants.
Fifty percent died in infancy.
Of the remaining fifty percent:
 310 were paupers
  30 were convicted criminals
The estimated cost to the government to prosecute and maintain these persons was in excess of three million dollars.
2. *The Kallikak Family*
First wife was feebleminded:
There were 481 descendants.
143 of these were feebleminded.
291 of these showed inferior mental ability.
 47 were normal.
Second wife was normal:
There were 496 descendants.
Two of these showed indications of subnormal mental activity.
494 were successful citizens.
3. *The Edwards Family*
By 1900, 1394 descendants were known.
295 of these were college graduates.

There were thirteen college presidents and school principals.

  60 were physicians.

100 were clergymen.

  75 were military officers.

100 were lawyers.

  30 were judges.

  80 were public officials, including one Vice-President of the United States.

1. Can you organize these data into any kind of pattern?

2. How do you interpret these data?

3. What conclusions is it possible for you to draw?

6.11

Here are some data. What inferences do you draw from them?

NOBEL AWARDS — 1901-1956

1901-1929

	Physics	Chemistry	Medicine	Literature	Peace	Total
1. Germany	10	11	5	5	2	33
2. France	5	4	3	4	6	22
3. England	7	6	3	2	2	20
4. Sweden	2	3	1	2	2	10
5. United States	3	1	1		5	10
6. Switzerland	1	1	1	1	4	8
7. Holland	4	1	2		1	8
8. Denmark	1		3	2	1	7
9. Austria		1	2		2	5
10. Norway				3	2	5
11. Italy	1		1	2	1	5
12. Belgium			1	1	2	4
13. Spain			1	2		3
14. Poland				2		2
15. Canada			2			2
16. Russia			2			2
17. India				1		1
18. Ireland				1		1

1930-1956

	Physics	Chemistry	Medicine	Literature	Peace	Total (1930-56)	Grand Total (1901-56)
1. U. S. A.	13	10	20	5	7	55	65
2. Germany	2	10	5		1	18	51
3. England	8	3	6	4	4	25	45
4. France		2		5	2	9	31
5. Sweden		1	1	2	1	5	15

6. Switzerland		2	3	1		6	14
7. Austria	3		1			4	9
8. Denmark			1	1		2	9
9. Holland	1					1	9
10. Italy	1			1		2	7
11. Belgium			1			1	5
12. Norway						0	5
13. Spain						0	3
14. Canada		1				1	3
15. Russia		1				1	3
16. Poland						0	2
17. India	1					1	2
18. Argentina			1		1	2	2
19. Finland		1		1		2	2
20. Chile				2		2	2
21. Hungary	1		1			2	2
22. Ireland	1					1	2
23. Japan	1					1	1
24. Iceland				1		1	1
25. Portugal				1		1	1
26. Puerto Rico				1		1	1

6.12

If R is true and R implies G, then G is true.

1. Using some geometric figures, can you give an illustration of the foregoing principles?
2. Translate the above principle using sentences.

In the following illustration this kind of non-tabular material is often given to students for interpretation.

6.13

Overthrow of the Radicals[42]

As the year 1870 drew to a close, conditions in South Carolina became more and more terrible. Crimes among the negroes — murder, burglary, and house burning — were frequent . . .

This dreadful condition of affairs forced the white people of the State to organize secretly for their own protection. They formed small bands called Ku Klux Klans whose purpose was to frighten the negroes from their evil doing . . . Many of the best men in South Carolina belonged to the Ku Klux Klan.

The negroes in the town of Union were the first to suffer punishment at the hands of the Klan. In January 1871, a one-armed Confederate soldier was cruelly beaten and then murdered by a company of 40 negro militiamen. The Klan forced the militia to disarm and put in jail thirteen of the negroes believed to

---

[42]Mary C. Simms Oliphant, *The Simms History of South Carolina* (Columbia: The State Company, 1932), pp. 245-246.

have taken active part in the murder. The negroes in Union became so threatening that the Klan visited the jail and shot the murderers except three who escaped.

Whenever the negro militiamen became intolerable, the Klan set itself to work to frighten or punish them. Seeing the determination of the white people to take justice into their own hands, Governor Scott finally disbanded the negro militia in the counties where they were giving the most trouble. The Ku Klux Klan then stopped its work.

Interpretation by a Student

According to the selection, the Ku Klux Klan seems to have been organized to prevent lawlessness and evil doing on the part of Negroes. It administers justice. It is a punishing organization, like a parent over a child. It disbands when its "good work" has been accomplished. The writer defends the Klan as an organization to which many of the "best men" in the state belonged. This would tend to create a favorable impression in the minds of readers. Some slanting is obvious: Negroes is spelled with a small *n* indicating an attitude that they are unimportant. In paragraph 3, sentence 3, it is assumed that 13 Negroes are involved in a murder. In sentence 4, there is no doubt about it; the writer convicts them, without trial, as murderers.

It would be unfortunate indeed not to see the operation of *interpreting* as part of such subject areas as poetry, music, and industrial arts, among others. There may even be some who see the operation as falling within the confines of a single course, or a part of a course. Often, a unit in mathematics, like statistics, is earmarked for "interpreting data," or sometimes geography and map reading are so slated. Then too, there may be a course called "Study Skills" in which interpretation of data is a unit. However, it may be observed that various materials can be used for interpreting: charts, maps, cartoons, graphs, poems, stories, pictures, demonstrations, exhibits, observations. Thus, interpreting is an imperative which pervades all subject areas; within each subject in the existing curriculum is sufficient material to afford manifold opportunities for adaptation.

Sometimes, those who are data oriented think that if only students have enough facts (whatever *have* means), interpretation is something that will inexorably ensue. Frequently the argument is presented in trite fashion: "Let's just get the facts first. After all, you can't think without facts." A rejoinder is fairly easy. *Which* facts should one *get?* Besides, is not the distinction between fact and interpretation itself not a goal of teaching and learning? Most often, in life, conflict arises not over what facts *are,* but over what they *mean.* The former is usually easier to determine, while the latter is the area of difficulty. One has only to read two newspaper accounts of the same incident or to listen to two analysts interpolate, extrapolate, and expatiate on the significance of the news to see that this is so. The classic witness stories in which several people viewing the same happening dispute loud, long and clear as to *meaning,* is another instance. Reproduced below is one part of an interchange between two professors which is relevant to the discussion here:

Professor Byrne Replies[43]

I have long agreed with Professor Hoffmann's contention that "all is far from well with testing," and am in fact one of the test users I spoke of in my review who "have cautioned against the glaring misuses" of tests. Thus not only have I not ignored what Professor Hoffman identifies as the crucial point of the book, but I am in general accord with it. What Professor Hoffman sees as "the crucial point," however, is not what I see as the crucial point for purposes of my review of his book.

The problem rests on the difference between facts and evidence. A fact may be used by a writer as his evidence for a stand and a program based on that stand, and what becomes "crucial" is whether the fact does indeed constitute evidence. Dr. Hoffman reported facts in his book—which I did not report in my review—not because I dispute the facts, but because I challenge Professor Hoffmann's use of them. I do not look upon them as evidence supporting Professor Hoffmann's argument. My review emphasized what I identified as the crucial point: the invalid use of facts as evidence supporting his major premise.

To present an analogy, an investigator may inform the governor of a state that a high state official has been involved in questionable contact "deals.' 'The Governor excuses the man, down-plays the charges, and in effect says that he is going to do nothing about removing the man from office; and the investigator responds by charging that everything he has uncovered is *evidence* of the "Tyranny of Democracy." The facts cannot be disputed. But the conclusion from those facts that democracy is a tyranny is scarcely valid. In short, there is no disagreement with the facts and no agreement with the general conclusions. Similarly, one can only regret the existence of inadequacies in testing, which, so far as I see them, are mostly in the misuse of tests and test results by unknowledgeable persons. But I find no evidence as yet presented by anyone, including Dr. Hoffman, that our culture is the victim of a tyranny of testing.

Perhaps, in addition to gathering facts, teachers may put an emphasis on how to derive meaning from them. As such emphasis is brought to bear, it may be seen that the operations of *comparing, classifying, observing and reporting,* and *summarizing* are engaged by a synthetic process which unites them all. As indicated earlier, it is not sufficient to provide practice in interpreting within a given course or part thereof. To hold that it *is* sufficient is to misunderstand the nature of thinking. It is to imagine the existence of a generalized ability unrelated to, and apart from an underpinning of, specific skills. It is also to believe that the generalized ability is transferable, and it is to foster a concept of mind that is alien to actual mental processes and their functioning.[44]

---

[43]Richard Hill Byrne, "Professor Byrne Replies," *AAUP Bulletin,* 49:3 (September, 1963), p. 288.

7. Analyzing Assumptions.

Human intercourse is marked by the observance of certain conventions, mutually understood and agreed upon, though usually informally. A culture produces a distinctive set of conventions or assumptions which are taken for granted by those who carry on interchange within the culture. Even in war and in competitive sports, there are unspoken but understood rules which support the continuance of the particular activity. (Children's games are an especially good example of an unwritten code.) Long having played a game according to rules handed down via oral tradition and common assumption, it is usually unnerving to discover that there may be other rules. Sometimes, we seem oblivious to the possibility that others do not share *our* conventions and *our* rules. Conflict may ensue when assumptions, unspoken and unshared, continue to guide our actions. Would it not be helpful to make them explicit and to examine them? Perhaps the experience of the blind men is instructive.

The Blind Men and the Elephant[45]

It was six men of Indostan
  To learning much inclined
Who went to see the elephant
  (Though each of them was blind,)
That each by observation
  Might satisfy his mind.

The first approached the elephant
  And happening to fall
Against his broad and sturdy side,
  At once began to bawl:
"God bless me, but the elephant
  Is very much like a wall."

The second, feeling of the tusk,
  Cried: "Ho, what have we here
So round and smooth and sharp?
  To me, 'tis very clear
This wonder of an elephant
  Is very like a spear."

The third approached the animal
  And happening to take
The squirming trunk with his hands,
  Thus boldly up he spake:

---

[44]Acknowledgment is made to students for their contributions of examples 6.1, 6.2, 6.3, 6.4, 6.5, 6.6, 6.7.
[45]J. G. Saxe, *The Poetical Works of John Godfrey Saxe* (Boston: Houghton Mifflin Company, 1882), pp. 111-112.

"I see," quoth he, "the elephant
Is very much like a snake."

The fourth reached out his eager hand,
    And fell upon the knee:
"What most this wondrous beast is like,
    Is very plain," quoth he;
" 'Tis clear enough, the elephant
    Is very like a tree."

The fifth who chanced to touch the ear,
    Said: "Even the blindest man
Can tell what this resembles most.
    Deny the fact who can,
This marvel of an elephant
    Is very like a fan."

The sixth no sooner had begun
    About the beast to grope
Then seizing on the swinging tail
    That fell within his scope,
"I see," quoth he, "the elephant
    Is very like a rope."

And so the men of Indostan
    Disputed loud and long,
Each in his own opinion
    Exceeding stiff and strong
Though each was partly in the right
    And all were in the wrong.

In this poem, imaginative teachers may see possibilities for a variety of uses: the "some equals all" fallacy, the relationship between data and conclusions. To us, who know what an elephant looks like, the conclusions of the blind men appear to imply certain assumptions. How can this help us to understand what an assumption is? What does it mean to analyze and look for assumptions?

The grammarian who diagrammed a sentence was easily recognized as an analyst. Similarly, the critic who "tears a presentation apart" is an analyst. Much like the chemist who analyzes a compound, there is an attempt to get at the constituents, to see what makes up the particular unit. The analytic function then is designed to afford an increase in understanding the totality. To look for assumptions is to look for what is *not* stated but *must* be believed if that which *is* stated is to be accepted and believed.

In the illustrations which follow, it can be seen that some exercises deal with assumptions which support a given conclusion (7.6-7.12). Other exercises seek to have students identify and distinguish between fact and assumption, whether the latter is considered pre-judgment, guess, or inference (7.1-7.5). It is recommended that teachers help students develop sensitivity to, and awareness of, the distinctions between fact and assumption, the distinction between *saying* and meaning.[46] Then teachers may introduce materials which will have students explicate unstated assumptions necessary to a conclusion. This order of priority is followed here.

7.1

---

[46]"Then you should say what you mean," the March Hare went on. "I do," Alice hastily replied: "at least—at least I mean what I say—that's the same thing you know."
    "Not the same thing a bit!" said the Hatter.
    Lewis Carroll, *Alice in Wonderland*.

You are a representative from New York, serving in Congress in the summer of 1807. You read the local newspaper which contains the above sketch, drawn by an artist at the scene, and the following news story:

> The British ship of war *Leopard* unlawfully attacked the U. S. frigate *Chesapeake* in Chesapeake Bay for refusing to submit to a search for British deserters. During the engagement, three American seamen were killed and eighteen wounded. Four men were seized by the British as deserters, although only one was a British subject.

Although President Jefferson has decided not to summon the Congress, you are anxious to learn all you can about the incident. The only information you have is the "artist's sketch" above drawn by him at the scene of the incident. Assume that the sketch faithfully depicts a frigate carrying an American flag, a ship of war carrying a British flag, and a British officer and an American seaman standing aboard the frigate.

On the basis of the information provided by the sketch, consider the following statements. If the sketch alone supports the statement, put an **F** in the space. This means that you believe the statement is a fact. If you think that the statement cannot be made on the basis of the sketch alone, put an **A** in the space. This means that you believe that the statement is an assumption.[47]

1. The British ship of war *Leopard* seizes the U. S. frigate *Chesapeake*.
2. The British officer's arrogance angers the American seaman.
3. An officer and a seaman are aboard the frigate.
4. Three of the men taken by the British as deserters are Americans.
5. The seaman has his arms raised.
6. The *Chesapeake* refused to submit to a search for British deserters.
7. The ship of war is flying a British flag.
8. The British are impressing American seamen.
9. The frigate is listing.
10. The dead and wounded are lying on the deck of the frigate.

7.2 Read the following selection carefully.

> Louis XIII était jaloux du Cardinal de Richelieu tout en ne pouvant pas se tirer d'affaire sans ses services.

---

[47]*Facts*—these statements are acceptable to you at face value, or with very minor doubts, if any. You are so sure of them you would not bother to investigate them. They seem self-evident to you. *The evidence in support of your conviction is publicly available.*
Assumptions—these statements are not acceptable to you at face value. You question them. You have some doubts about them. If you used them in this situation you would point out that they had not been verified so far as you know. They may be true—they may be false—you do not know. You need further information about them. They may be relevant or irrelevant to the situation. They are assumptions as far as you are concerned.

Dans un bal qu'on donnait à la cour, le roi, qui s'y ennuyait, voulut se retirer au moment meme où le cardinal se retirait également.

Tout le monde se rangeait pour laisser passer le ministre, et le roi remarqua qu'on rendait beaucoup plus de respect á ce dernier qu' à lui-même. Richelieu ignorait que le roi le suivait, mais voyant s'avancer quelques pages, il le devina et se rangea de côté, pour le laisser passer. Le roi, de son côté, s'arrêta et lui dit:

"Pourquoi ne passez-vous pas, monsieur le Cardinal? N'êtes-vous pas le maître?"

Le sens de cette réflexion n'échappa pas à Richelieu. Il prit un flamabeau des mains d'un page, et marchant devant le roi, lui dit:

"Sire, je peux passer devant Votre Majesté seulement en faisant les fonctions du plus humble des serviteurs."[48]

Read each of the statements below. If the paragraph alone warrants the conclusion drawn, place an F after the statement. If you have any doubts that the statement can be made on the basis of the paragraph alone, place an A in the space. This means you consider it to be an assumption.

1. Le roi et le cardinal étaient au bal en même temps.
2. Le roi avait besoin du cardinal.
3. Quand le cardinal partait, les invités s'écartaient pour lui faire place.
4. Il y avait beaucoup d'amis du cardinal au bal.
5. Un page marchait devant le roi.
6. Richelieu désirait se moquer du roi.
7. Le roi ne s'amusait point au bal.
8. Richelieu était le meilleur ministre de Louis XIII.
9. Le cardinal s'ennuyait au bal.
10. La foule n'a pas reconnu le roi.[49]

7.3

Desk Set By Sheapher

You've never sent your personal stock soaring so easily! Any client would be impressed with the striking new gift case, a Sheapher exclusive. But that's only the beginning!

Here are the real reasons Sheapher Desk Sets are the choice of selective gift-buyers: richly styled bases, to complement the most luxurious setting and famous Sheapher pens with cartridge filling action, superbly crafted with 14K gold points, kept writing-moist in exclusive humidor-sockets. The coup de grace—a personalized name plate.

When no other Christmas gift seems important enough for an important client, choose Sheapher, the most-given desk set in America.

---

[48]Eli Blume, *Workbook in French, Three Years* (New York: Amsco School Publications, Inc., 1963), p. 279.
[49]1. F; 2. F; 3. F; 4. A; 5. F; 6. A; 7. F; 8. A; 9. A; 10. A.

Below is a list of statements about the advertisement. If you were shopping for a gift for a friend or client and had read the advertisement, you might believe that some or all of the statements are true. If you think a statement is a fact, or can reasonably be believed, place an F alongside the number. If you think that the statement cannot be made on the basis of the advertisement alone, place an A next to the number.

1. Clients tend to judge you by the presents you give them.
2. Sheapher is the only manufacturer offering a desk set complete with gift case.
3. 14K gold is the best possible substance for a pen point.
4. Sheapher pens operate on the principle of capillary action.
5. For best writing, a fountain pen's tip should be kept moist.
6. Sheapher is the largest selling fountain pen in America.
7. Sheaper Desk Sets are the choice of selective gift buyers.
8. A personalized name plate tends to make an appeal.
9. The Sheapher pen is inexpensive.
10. Sheapher is interested in helping you send your personal stock soaring.

If you wanted to buy a Sheapher Desk Set, which two statements would you want to be most sure about before you made a purchase?

7.4

In the following chronology, you will note that some statements are of a factual type and others are interpretations (inferences) drawn from facts. Distinguish between the two by marking those which you believe to be factual with an F and those which you believe to be interpretations with an I.

1. 1776 John Hancock, Thomas Jefferson, Benjamin Franklin, and other delegates from the thirteen American colonies sign the Declaration of Independence.
2. 1776 By their victory at Trenton, the Americans prove to be better soldiers than the British.
3. 1781 The Articles of Confederation create a tie between the colonies.
4. 1787 Members of the Constitutional Convention draft a Constitution in secret session.
5. 1791 The Bill of Rights is ratified and becomes a part of the Constitution.
6. 1793 Eli Whitney's cotton gin makes southern agriculture more productive and creates a boom in the slave market.
7. 1798 Adams uses the Alien and Sedition Acts for the sole purpose of taking the vote away from his opponents.
8. 1803 Chief Justice Marshall's rulings in *Marbury vs. Madison* show that he intends to make the Supreme Court more powerful than the drafters of the Constitution intended it to be.

9. 1804 The Twelfth Amendment requires that the President and Vice-President be elected separately.
10. 1829 As the first popularly elected President, Jackson succeeds in making the government more democratic.
11. 1837 Van Buren defeats several Whig opponents and becomes President.
12. 1852 *Uncle Tom's Cabin* brings violent reactions in the South and moves the South closer to secession.
13. 1861 The Civil War in the United States begins with the Battle of Fort Sumter.
14. 1862 The battle between the *Monitor* and the *Virginia* showed that the North had better ship builders than the South.
15. 1215 This is the date that the Magna Charta was signed. It is the basis of democracy.
16. 15th and 16th centuries. The Renaissance occurred during this time.
17. 500-1000 These were the Dark Ages.
18. 1789 This marks the beginning of freedom and nationalism in France.
19. 1781-89 This was the critical period in the United States.
20. 1500 This was the beginning of the modern period of history.[50]

7.5

Based *only* on the excerpt below, write in the space before each statement an F if it is a fact or an A if it is an assumption.

All the negroes were friends of ours, and with those of our own age we were in effect comrades. I say in effect, using the phrase as a modification. We were comrades, and yet not comrades; color and condition interposed a subtle line which both parties were conscious of and which rendered complete fusion impossible. We had a faithful and affectionate good friend, ally, and adviser in 'Unc'l Dan'l,' a middle-aged slave whose head was the best one in the negro quarter, whose sympathies were wide and warm, and whose heart was honest and simple and knew no guile. He has served me well these many, many years. I have not seen him for more than half a century, and yet spiritually I have had his welcome company a good part of that time and have staged him in books under his own name and as 'Jim,' carted him all around—to Hannibal, down the Mississippi on a raft and even across the Desert of Sahara in a balloon—and he has endured it all with the patience and friendliness and loyalty which were his birthright. It was on the farm that I got my strong liking for his race and my appreciation of certain of its fine qualities. This feeling and this estimate have stood the test of sixty years and more, and have suffered no impairment. The black face is as welcome to me now as it was then . . .[51]

1. The Negroes were not discriminated against in Twain's boyhood.
2. In effect, all Negroes were Twain's comrades.

[50]1. F; 2. I; 3. I; 4. F; 5. F; 6. I; 7. I; 8. I; 9.   F; 10. I; 11. F; 12. I; 13. F; 14. I; 15. I; 16. I; 17. I; 18. I; 19. I; 20. I.

3. Unc'l Dan'l served as the model for "Jim."
4. Mark Twain admired and respected Unc'l Dan'l.
5. As a child, Mark Twain did not discriminate according to color.
6. Unc'l Dan'l lived in the Negro quarter.
7. The characteristics that Mark Twain admired are all found in Unc'l Dan'l.
8. Life on the farm helped shape Mark Twain's attitude towards the Negro.
9. The word "condition" refers to a slave-like status.
10. By "complete fusion," Twain meant complete acceptance and equality.
11. In older age, Twain still felt admiration and liking for the Negro.
12. Unc'l Dan'l has been a source of literary study for Mark Twain for many years.
13. Twain qualifies his acceptance of the Negro.
14. Twain always regarded the Negro as separate but equal.
15. Twain does not discriminate against the Negro socially.[52]

Thus far, excercises have stressed the distinction between fact and assumption. In those which are offered now, the focus is on explicating those assumptions upon which a conclusion rests.

7.6

Read the following paragraph and list the assumptions necessary for the statement to be judged true or probably true.

Some unfamiliar type of force must hold the protons and neutrons together in the nucleus. They cannot be held by electrostatic attraction because the similarly charged protons would repel each other; and neutrons, being neutral, are not subject to electrostatic attraction. The force cannot be gravitational either because calculations show it would be too weak. The forces between nuclear particles have very short range, somewhat smaller than the diameter of the nucleus.[53]

(Some Assumptions Listed by Students)
1. An atom can be divided into smaller particles.
2. Some of these particles must be concentrated in a nucleus.
3. Two of the particles which are concentrated in the nucleus are protons and neutrons.
4. Some of these particles carry an electric charge.
5. All protons carry the same charge.
6. All neutrons are uncharged.

---

[51]Mark Twain, *The Autobiography of Mark Twain,* ed. by Charles Neider (New York: Harper & Row, Publishers, 1959), pp. 5-6.
[52]1. A; 2. A; 3. F; 4. F; 5. A; 6. F; 7. A; 8. F; 9. A; 10. A; 11. F; 12. F; 13. F; 14. A; 15. A.
[53]Charles E. Dull, H. Clark Metcalfe, and John E. Williams, *Modern Physics* (New York: Holt, Rinehart & Winston, Inc., 1960), p. 144.

7. Like charges repel each other.
8. Uncharged objects cannot be held by the same force which attracts charged objects.
9. Objects will not remain together unless held together by some attractive force.
10. Every object attracts other objects in the universe (Law of Gravitation).
11. The force of attraction mentioned in #10 is calculable.
12. The diameter of a nucleus is calculable and known.
13. The only familiar types of forces are electrostatic and gravitational.

7.7

How are your conclusions related to your initial assumptions?
1. Draw triangles of various sizes and shapes. Find the sum of the angles. Then, make some generalizations on the basis of these observations and measurements. Upon what assumptions do your generalizations rest? List these.
2. Now draw triangles of various sizes and shapes on a tennis ball or an orange or a volleyball. Note the sum of the angles. In what way, if any, would you modify any of your previous generalizations?

7.8

What assumptions are being made?
1. Write the smallest number using only the digits 4 and 1. A student wrote the answer 14.
   What assumptions did he make?[54]
2. Suppose in answer to the above problem, the student had said ¼ or 1/444 or any fraction with the numerator 1 and a denominator of repeated 4's. What assumptions would he have made?
3. How many numbers are there between 21 and 53? A student answered 31. What assumption did he make?[55]
4. Suppose in answer to the preceding problem, the student had answered, "infinite." What assumption would he have made?[56]
5. Three points determine
   Student A wrote *a plane*.
   Student B wrote *many planes*.
   What assumption did each make?
6. Lines that do not intersect are
   Student A wrote *parallel*.
   Student B wrote *skew*.
   What assumption did each make?

[54]Digits could only be used once. Numbers refer to the set of whole numbers.
[55]Numbers refer to whole numbers.
[56]Between any two whole numbers there are many rational numbers.

7. Three planes intersect at
   Student A wrote *a point.*
   Student B wrote *one line.*
   Student C wrote *three lines.*
   What assumption did each make?
8. A train travels 180 miles in three hours. How far does it go in one hour?
   Student A answered *60 miles.*
   Student B answered *x miles.*
   What assumption did each make?
9. A line intersects a plane at a
   Student A wrote *point.*
   Student B wrote *line.*
   What assumption did each make?

7.9

Fill in the sentences below.
1. As pretty as a⎯⎯⎯⎯⎯⎯⎯⎯⎯⎯⎯⎯⎯.
2. All the world's a ⎯⎯⎯⎯⎯⎯⎯⎯⎯⎯⎯⎯.
3. Life, liberty, and ⎯⎯⎯⎯⎯⎯⎯⎯⎯⎯⎯⎯.
4. There's no place like ⎯⎯⎯⎯⎯⎯⎯⎯⎯⎯⎯⎯.
5. War is⎯⎯⎯⎯⎯⎯⎯⎯⎯⎯.
6. First in the hearts of his ⎯⎯⎯⎯⎯⎯⎯⎯⎯⎯⎯⎯.
7. Nice day if it doesn't ⎯⎯⎯⎯⎯⎯⎯⎯⎯⎯⎯⎯.
8. Eat, drink and be ⎯⎯⎯⎯⎯⎯⎯⎯⎯⎯⎯⎯.
9. Variety is the ⎯⎯⎯⎯⎯⎯⎯⎯⎯⎯⎯⎯.
10. Walk before you ⎯⎯⎯⎯⎯⎯⎯⎯⎯⎯⎯⎯.
Now list the assumptions that you believe are operating.

7.10

A disease which results in certain nervous disorders was common among the population of certain sections of the Orient where the diet consisted chiefly of white rice. People whose diet was chiefly brown rice were not afflicted with this disease. To find out whether or not the disease was related to the diet, a group of scientists conducted the following experiment.

"One hundred healthy pigeons were placed in separate cages. Fifty pigeons (Group I) were fed nothing but white rice and distilled water. The remaining fifty pigeons (Group II) were fed nothing but brown rice and distilled water. Within two weeks, the pigeons of Group I began to show symptoms of nervous disorders. When their diet was changed to brown rice, the pigeons of Group I showed immediate improvement and were well in a few days. The pigeons of Group II remained in good health throughout the experiment." The scientists concluded that a change from a diet consisting chiefly of white rice to one consisting chiefly of brown rice would reduce the occurrence (incidence) of the nervous disorders among these Oriental people.

Conclusion: A change from a diet consisting chiefly of white rice to one consisting chiefly of brown rice would reduce the occurrence of the nervous disorders among these Oriental peoples.

Assumptions — *If the conclusion is judged to be False or Probably False*

1. The diet of the Oriental peoples contained many other factors besides rice that are significant in terms of preventing or facilitating the development of nervous disorders.
2. A remedy prescribed as appropriate for a nervous disorder in pigeons would not be appropriate as a remedy for nervous disorders among Oriental people.
3. The effect of diet on the complex human nervous system is influenced by many different, significant factors and cannot properly be equated with the effects of the same diet on a different kind of nervous organization, such as that of pigeons.
4. A single factor such as the presence of white rice in the diet is not the sole cause of a nervous disorder.
5. The two groups of pigeons were not comparable in terms of susceptibility to the nervous disorder.
6. The nervous disorders developed by pigeons under conditions of extremely limited diet (white rice with distilled water) were not equivalent to the nervous disorders developed by the Oriental peoples.

7.11

Below are some student answers to the following question:
"If we could remake history, in your judgment would it have been wiser to have held open sessions at the Constitutional Convention of 1787?"

1. People would have found fault with the Constitution.
2. The Constitution might never have been written.
3. There would have been disturbances.
4. Our present-day government would not be as strong.
5. It would just make things more confusing and nothing would be accomplished by the interference.
6. No, the people wouldn't want the new idea.
7. The Constitution would never have been passed.
8. The federal government wouldn't have had a chance.
9. Nothing would have gotten done.

List the assumptions upon which the above statements rest.

7.12

What assumptions are being made?

1. Ed, a non-swimmer, saw a sign on a pond which said, "Average depth, 3 feet." He reasoned that it would be safe for him to wade in the pond since he was five feet tall.

What assumptions did he make?

2. Tom, a good swimmer and diver, saw a sign at a lake edge which said: Average depth, 9 feet." He reasoned that it would be safe for him to practice diving there.

     What assumptions did he make?

3. Here are some weights of boys in a fifth grade class:

Henry	88 lbs.	James	86 lbs.
Albert	86 lbs.	Robert	84 lbs.
William	82 lbs.	Richard	82 lbs.
John	78 lbs.	Andrew	78 lbs.
Edward	76 lbs.	Ronald	74 lbs.
Stephen	74 lbs.	Gerald	72 lbs.

     From these figures John concluded that on the average a boy in fifth grade in this school weighs 80 lbs.

     What assumptions is he making?

4. If A is 10 miles from B and B is 15 miles from C, how far is A from C? Here is the way Ed solved the problem:

     A_____ B _____ C
         10 mi.   15 mi. $10 + 15 = 25$ miles.

     What assumption is Ed making?

5. A man arrived in Chicago 10 hours after a crime was committed in New York. The fastest train from New York to Chicago makes the trip in 15 hours. Tom concluded that the man did not commit the crime in New York.

     What assumptions is Tom making?

We have said that in communication certain assumptions are continually made. Communication breakdowns occur sometimes because what is assumed may not be assumed. Our annoyance is frequently increased by failure to recognize that someone else can possibly operate from a different set of assumptions. The phrase "how stupid or how blind can you be" seems to indicate this lack of awareness. Perhaps communication breakdowns could be avoided if we were to recognize and take into account the nature of language with its assumptions already built in. *Each* time we say something, assumptions undergird our statement. Yet, there are some of us who think that assumptions are part of the terminology of the experimental laboratory or that they typically belong to the rhetoric of metaphysicians.

Somewhat similar is the popular view of the science of semantics. It is almost as if semantics were one thing and language another! This dichotomy is evidenced in the colloquialism: "That's *just* a matter of semantics." Few know exactly what this is supposed to mean, but it seems to quell discussion. Similarly, if assumptions are lifted out and explained, one runs the risk of being labeled "picky" or technical or hypercritical. Yet, to understand the necessary assumptions supporting a given conclusion is to increase understanding; it is to think deeply and penetratingly. Teaching can hardly be just casually concerned with the important skill of analyzing assumptions.

From the illustrations presented, it may be observed that no one subject area possesses a monopoly of suitable content for use. At one time, assumptions were thought to be within the domain of science or mathematics. That this is not so is probably apparent. Imaginative teachers will avoid the trivial and artificial materials that might speciously present themselves. Instead, they will look for meaningful materials within their subject areas. It is again emphasized that the operation of analyzing assumptions need not await extensive curriculum revision or the revamping of content. It does, however, require the adaptation of existing content so that an emphasis on looking for assumptions is brought into focus. As this stress is made, it will be seen how interdependent this operation is with all the other thinking operations mentioned thus far.[57]

8. Problem-Solving.

Some have called thinking an adventure into the unknown. Even the adjectives *adventurous, creative,* or *exploratory* thinking are used perhaps to indicate its broadest limits. To explore freely is to liberate oneself from earthbound restraints and to soar to the heights. We do not explore when we have already been over the ground; this is merely to retrace our steps. And to so limit our search is to be concerned with ground-clearing or engineering operations.

Our minds can soar more freely probably when we do not know or do not have an answer in advance of a problem situation. When, however, we do have or do know an answer in advance, our thinking tends toward the lower mental processes of recall, recognition, and association. Then, ground-clearing operations are sometimes merely a matter of mechanical application. For example, the exercises at the end of a chapter of the textbook or the blank spaces in the laboratory manual frequently are in the nature of a mechanical task to be overcome. Since there are no choices, since, in fact, the answers are predetermined, there is little need for inquiry or investigation. The learner has merely to make his answers fit the prescribed scheme.

Now, if teacher and student were to work on questions to which answers were *not* known, what then? They might have to create a method for finding out — that is, learning *how* answers can be arrived at and learning a means for checking results. Perhaps most important of all, they would have to

---

[57]Acknowledgment is made to graduate students for contributions in illustrations 7.1, 7. 2; 7. 3; 7. 4; 7. 5; 7. 6; 7. 9.

acquire the facility of expressing what it is that they do *not* know. This requires the acquisition of skills, and skills are a derivative of practice and drill, hence, the operation problem-solving.

Problem-solving is sometimes equated with research. The latter is often thought of as bibliographic compilation, finding out what other people said. Essentially, such "research" is akin to a literary method, especially appropriate to those fields in which a great body of literature is more or less characteristic of the field itself, e.g., religious writings, collections of legal decisions, mythology and national epics. As a method, it is not suited to those areas of inquiry which rely less on authority.

What is meant here is the problem which is investigated generally through philosophical methods (critical examination), or historical methods (documentary evidence), or empirical methods (experimentation). These methods usually require the use of deductive, interpretive, observational, or statistical techniques in the solution of the problem. Thus, in the operation problem-solving, students are given practice in collecting and organizing data and in carrying through an investigation. This might include such activities as stating problems, devising instruments, proposing solutions, and gathering, interpreting, and evaluating data. What are commonly referred to as projects and investigations may also be included here.

At this point, the reader is referred to Parts 1 and 2 of this book (see pp. 16 and 96) for some suggestions regarding a related operation, *applying principles to new situations*. The reader may also note that two other operations appear in Parts 1 and 2, *decision making* and *hypothesizing*. These are *included* in this discussion, however, they are not given singular treatment.

Here, the term *problem-solving* is used. Essentially, it involves the operation of *collecting and organizing data*. Now, collecting and organizing data seem to be "right down the teacher's alley." "This is what we do *all* the time," say some. The operation appears to be simple: students collect data and organize them! Yet, not infrequently, the operation is carried out as an exercise in penmanship, of transferring material from one book to another. Sometimes, moral obloquy attaches to the results because the youngsters have copied. But why? One reason suggests that teachers expect them to!

Collecting data means gathering together what someone *else* said on a subject. Organizing data means accepting *his* organization. Is it not the nature of the assignment that produces the negative result? If we would expect students to collect data variously, outside of books perhaps, if we would give them some data and have them find some more, if we would ask them to arrange data according to a pattern which they help construct, the results might be different.

Some persons have a notion that collecting data requires a "white jacket," as if an experimental method is the only way of getting data. Certainly an historical where an experimental method applies would be inappropriate, but so would the converse be inappropriate; the method is fitted to the problem. Thus, conducting surveys through polls and interviews, or making observations and reports, or setting up an experimental situation are all methods of acquiring data.

Perhaps a crucial part of the operation lies in a statement of a problem, in setting forth what we do *not* know. It would seem that this is preparatory to collecting data, else why collect it? (Unfortunately, the merely acquisitive instinct is too often operative.) Sometimes, teachers look to guides or books for recipes on the stating of specific problems. Books can offer little more than a general outline of what is to go into a problem statement. Since a problem is personal, the statement of it is personal. A general rule to cover all problems would be exceedingly difficult, if not impossible, to construct; the rule varies with the problem. The comments offered below are then not presented as prescriptions for a specific problem, but as general indications.

1. A problem is not a simple "how do you do it?". A problem implies that alternatives are present. With no alternatives, there is no problem.

2. Problems are always questions; questions, however, are not always problems.

3. A puzzle is not a synonym for the word problem. Solutions to puzzles usually depend on a trial and error procedure. Rarely is there an application of principles that is transferable to other situations.

4. A problem cannot be given to someone. What is a problem to one may not be so to another. Unless there is identification with a problem, it remains a puzzle or a task to the individual.

What is true regarding a statement of a problem — that it is personal — is also true for the working out of the problem. Organization and internal consistency may be expected, but it can be destructive to impose a rigid formula from without. It is up to the individual to organize his project into a coherent pattern.

It is here that formalized steps in problem-solving, like steps in *the* scientific method in the laboratory manual, are positively lethal. It is well to recognize that there is *no* scientific method; there are scientific *methods*. The terms *scientific method* and *problem-solving* have, deplorably, become hortatory formulas, probably more useful to teachers than to scientists. The latter are concerned with *doing;* the former, unfortunately, seem concerned with a credo whose unquestioning acceptance they attempt to ensure catechistically. One is tempted to say that an unscientific method is used to teach science.

Steps in scientific method and in problem-solving are inferences and summaries of the way others have organized the data in their researches. The seeming neatness which becomes apparent only through hindsight can easily be twisted into a Procrustean instrument of constraint. The science of logic is sometimes similarly misinterpreted. As a means of checking thought, it is invaluable as an analytic instrument *post hoc*. It can be a measuring rod for a position already advanced, but it is too often confused with the *means by which* the particular position was originally established.

As one makes an effort in having students engage in problem-solving activities, one may note that several thinking operations will be engaged. As students collect data, they may observe, compare, and analyze. As they organize data, they may summarize, classify, interpret, evaluate. It is well to stress that the hierarchy and priority assigned to each of the foregoing will depend on the nature of the problem. As the individual uses the operation according to a system which he justifies, he is employing *a* scientific method. As he employs an encrusted system taken over from a different problem area and a different problem, he is working out a mechanical task, exercise, or puzzle. Insofar as the operation means the working out of a problem with which one identifies, to that extent it has engaged the interest of the learner. One may observe what happens when there is no identification with the problem; the eagerness with which youngsters fill out the spaces in the lab manual indicates how task-like and chore-like the "problem" is viewed.

Of a different nature, it is hoped, are the suggestions below. Some of them require the *application of principles*. Situations, together with some data, are presented, and a solution is sought. Sometimes the solution itself is presented, and there is an attempt to see how it was arrived at. Other suggestions require some *hypothesizing;* predictions, possible solutions, and hunches are called for. In other instances, it may be seen that decisions are made without regard to fact, generalization, and law; in such *decision-making* there is focus on values which have to be protected.

8.1

The Effect of Concentration on the Rate of the Catalyzed Decomposition of Hydrogen Peroxide.

Hydrogen peroxide is an unstable substance which decomposes spontaneously into water and oxygen. The rate of its decomposition may be increased by the use of a suitable catalyst.

Select a catalyst and devise a procedure by which the rate of the reaction may be followed and measured. Then investigate the effect of changing the concentration of the peroxide on the rate at which it decomposes. If there is a definite relationship and it is of low order kinetics, it may be possible to theorize the mechanism by which the decomposition takes place.

In this activity, the student has to apply principles to new situations. He needs to investigate the literature to look for suitable catalysts of what might be most successful. He would have to devise an experimental procedure to follow the reaction. In order to come to a conclusion about the effect of concentration on his reaction rate, he will record and interpret data. Perhaps most important is the determination of a mechanism by which the reaction proceeds; this requires analysis and evaluation of the concentration effects.

Throughout, the responsibility for selection and organization might well be in the hands of the student.

8.2

Here are some operations in arithmetic: adding, subtracting, multiplying, dividing. How are the operations related to each other? When would you use each?

1. How would you go about finding answers to the following?
   Joe works in a carpenter shop. He has a board ⅜ of an inch thick and 42 inches long that he wants to cut into 2½ inch lengths.
   1. How would you find out how many pieces Joe will have?
   2. How would you find out how many pieces he would have left over?
   3. Do you need all the information you are given here?
   4. Why did you use the operation you used?
2. How would you find answers to the following:
   Jim painted his backyard fence. On Thursday, he painted ¼ of it. On Friday, he painted ⅕ of it. On Saturday he finished painting it.
   1. How would you find out when Jim painted the largest part?
   2. How would you find out when Jim painted the least?
   3. How would you find out how much Jim painted on Saturday?
   4. Fifty yards of the fence were painted on Thursday. How would you find out how much was painted on the other days?

8.3

How would you find out if objects do or do not tend to continue in motion? Compare with Galileo's solution.

8.4

How would you find answers to the following? Can you contruct a problem procedure?
1. Why don't clouds fall?
2. Why do some lawn sprinklers rotate as they sprinkle?
3. Why is it usually more difficult to ride a two-wheel bike slowly than at moderate speed?
4. Why is it usually difficult to write with ink on substances like blotting paper?

8.5

How would you go about demonstrating whether or not living organisms spring from nonliving matter? After you have designed a method, gathered data, and observed results,

1. Compare with Francesco Redi's experiments in 1688.
2. Compare with Lazaro Spallanzani's experiments.
3. Compare with Pasteur's experiments in fermentation.

8.6

Here are some conclusions. How would you construct procedures for arriving at them?

1. Putrefaction is not due to spontaneous generation of germs within a liquid like sugared yeast water.
2. If pure-bred plants of different strains (A + B) are crossed and the resultant hybrids again crossed, then, in the next generation, the plants produced sort out in definite proportions: some are pure A's, some pure B's, and some hybrid AB's.
3. The speed with which an object falls when not impeded is related functionally to the time in which it has been falling. Galileo showed that a falling object accelerates according to a certain rate and the distance it falls is proportional to the square of the time it has taken to fall.

In some of the foregoing illustrations, students have been asked to apply principles learned in one situation to another situation which may or may not be familiar. They are asked to construct procedures. The procedures which they construct may be different from those of the original experimenter, but the students are not led to change them in order to conform to the original design. It is quite possible that similar conclusions can tolerate differences in design. Certainly, the comparison of differences in procedures would seem valuable.

In one instance, students are provided with conclusions and are asked to reconstruct procedures and discover data. In another instance, they may be provided with relevant data (in the above cases or in any other), and they are asked to come up with conclusions. Their conclusions, drawn from the data, are compared with the conclusions drawn by the original investigator.

It might be supposed that seeing how conclusions are arrived at is something that is reserved to the natural sciences alone. Many of us follow the unraveling of a mystery in the detective thriller with careful attention and analysis. Some of this excitement may be captured for the classroom in various subject areas. For example, how does Hamlet come to the conclusion that his uncle is really the murderer of his father? What data does he use? Or, how does Duncan, despite his trusting nature, give evidence that he is aware of Macbeth's intentions?

In the illustrations below the focus is on the collection and organization of data.

8.7

Students are given some data with which to work: suicide rates, car deaths, birth rates, school populations, political preferences. They organize the data to present a picture.

8.8

Students measure some processes — plant growth, amount of heat under given conditions, the amount of light under certain conditions. The data are organized to secure answers to a specific problem.

8.9

Students investigate weather lore by gathering together some common expressions about weather and then grouping them. Or they may investigate weather lore which is based on signs within nature such as cloud formations, winds, dew, frost. Categories are created whereby the data are organized.

8.10

Students may go to the local supermarket to gather data regarding the companies which are represented on the food shelves. Or they may chart the prices of certain foods over a period of weeks.

8.11

Students identify all the products which they buy in their household. They determine which are advertised and which are products that they have never seen advertised. They organize their data in response to a specific problem.

8.12

Stock market trends may be followed for a period of weeks. Data are gathered and organized in response to a specific problem.

8.13

Students examine issues in a local election or a school bond debate or the integration question or the fluoridation question. They gather and organize data in response to a particular problem.

8.14

Where possible, students may attend night court sessions. They write up a summary of a case or they write up a defense for either side.

8.15

The local police headquarters may be visited in an attempt to find out what the most common crimes are and how many persons are arrested for each crime within a given period. The data may be organized in response to different problems.

8.16

Students may collect a list of historical personages who were considered "enemies of the people." Reasons for the designation may be investigated and organized.

8.17

It may be interesting and revealing to find out what the chief sources of amusement of people in the community are. (*How* the data are collected would seem to be important here.)

8.18

Students may do a biography of some person in the community. In addition to collecting and organizing the data, they might have to determine the question of validity and the limits of interpretations that could be made.

It may be instructive for students to see how steps in problem-solving will vary with the problem. They vary also with the amounts of data on hand and with the amounts that *can* be available. In addition, procedures can be affected by values one may want to protect. Then too, when problems that have already been solved are worked out, a false notion of neatness and orderly progression may ensue. In retracing someone else's steps exactly as he finally trod them, his false starts and his peripheral and tangential excursions are not always seen.

In the first example below, students are asked to record all the steps they take in finding the principle which is operative. These records of how each is approaching the problem might very well be compared.

8.19

Here is a simple cipher and its meaning. Find the principle which is operating. Record *all* the steps you take in arriving at your solution.

TIJQ	MFBWFT	BU	NJEOJHIU
Ship	Leaves	At	Midnight

As in the above, the concern in the next illustration is not so much with the solution as it is with what happens as one embarks on the solution. In the example which follows, limited amounts of data are introduced at different intervals of time. On the one hand, one may see that procedures and solutions are far from neat and orderly; they are affected by the amounts of data available. On the other hand, we may see how values can be more important than the logic of the situation; in the interests of protecting certain values, our decision-making procedures are affected. It is better not to use the illustration as content but rather as a model of a way of inducing sensitivity to the limitations of data and the relationship of solutions to incomplete data and to values.

8.20

    Given: The goal of building a sea level canal to unite the Atlantic and Pacific oceans. Of four possible locations, which shall it be? Examine the map below.

'ALTERNATE CANAL ROUTES'

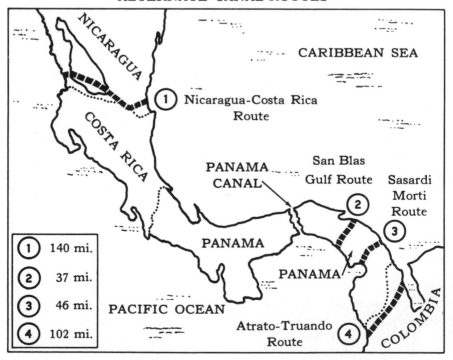

The data may be organized in this fashion:

Name	Country	Length
1. Nicaragua-Costa Rica Route	Nicaragua-Costa Rica	140 mi.
2. San Blas Gulf Route	Panama	37 mi.
3. Sasardi Morti Route	Panama	46 mi.
4. Atrato-Truando Route	Colombia	102 mi.

At this point, there might be lengthy discussion around these two questions: On the basis of the foregoing data alone, where should the canal be built? What other data are needed? Students should write and justify their answers. Then, additional data, below, are introduced.

1. The Nicaragua Route is the most northerly route. It would require draining of Lake Nicaragua.
2. The San Blas Route is a few miles from the present Panama Canal. It is in a heavily populated area.
3. The Sasardi Morti Route is 110 miles from the present Panama Canal. The area is sparsely populated.
4. The Atrato-Truando Route is the most southerly. It is an uninhabited and rugged area.

Again, there is consideration of the question: Where should the canal be built and why? Students are asked to defend their choice. They might also indicate whether they have switched their positions with the introduction of the new data and if so, why. Discussion might also center on how data are typically acquired — are they neat and orderly, are they "helter-skelter," are they at our ready disposal? Then, the following data are presented.

Route	Cost
1. Nicaragua Route	$1.9 billions
2. San Blas Route	$620 millions
3. Sasardi Morti Route	$770 millions
4. Atrato-Truando Route	$1.2 billions

The same questions as before are considered. Heavy emphasis might be devoted to accounting for the switching of positions. The rest of the data below might be presented all at once or may be split up as in the foregoing.

Additional Data

1. Atomic excavation would be less costly than conventional explosive excavation. Engineers have indicated that atomic explosives could be planted so deep that there would be no flames and little radiation.
2. Atomic excavation would require clearance from signers of the nuclear test ban treaty.
3. Unless an additional canal is built, the present canal will be hopelessly jammed by 1980. Many present-day ships, e.g., aircraft carriers, cannot be accommodated.
4. The new canal would probably put the old canal, with its expensive and slow system of locks, out of business.

5. Disposition of the physical assets of the old canal, once a replacement is in operation, would be far from simple.
6. A canal would probably be an economic boon to the nation housing it.
7. The Nicaraguan government has indicated that it would be happy to have the canal built there.
8. The rugged Atrato-Truando Route is through 1000 feet high hills.

Procedures indicated previously may be followed: how data are acquired might be an important consideration and the relationship of the data to the problem may well be explored. As indicated earlier, it is less important for students to "solve the problem," or, more properly "to make a decision," than it is for them to see how problem-solving procedures and processes differ from what is ordinarily mentioned in textbooks. The teacher would also be well-advised to construct his own problems and to adapt some of the procedures indicated.

It used to be thought that scholarship was concerned with the ingorging of information; in medieval times, there were monks who were devoted to the process. In some quarters today, this kind of activity is equated with scholarship; the belief is fed with the nutrition to keep it viable. Perhaps, the notion that knowledge is fixed is still a determinant. It would seem, though, that few would have illusions of what the findings of science would be if the theories of Galen, Eratosthenes, Ptolemy, and the like were accepted as truths of the moment to which nothing was to be or could be added. Yet, scholarship still demands knowing. But knowing what?

Today, the amounts of information are staggering; the phrase, "explosion of knowledge" has become almost as commonplace as "population explosion." Somewhat like the "old woman in a shoe," man has so much knowledge, "he doesn't know what to do." But it is well to point out that the explosion we speak of relates to particulars; we have not been explosive in the invention of theories. Though we have a vast accumulation of information, we do not have much that is new which explains relationships. With the explosion of a miscellany of information, one might suppose that selectivity and teaching for selection would be the order of the day. Yet is it?

Perhaps teachers are necessarily concerned with the miscellany of knowledge and its acquisition. They seem to spend much time in having students gather discrete data and they allot much time to the testing of how well the information has been retained. Most of us know what happens to such information after the testing period is over. There is evidence to indicate that about eighty percent of it is lost. However, data gathered in a context of inter-relationship is retained and strengthened. The gathering of data in response to a problem provides a framework of meaning and understanding. To determine when data are relevant to a problem and thus to select and concentrate on these would be a way out of the dilemma facing "the old woman in a shoe."

But unfortunately, so much of teaching involves an historical emphasis or, more accurately, a focus on chronicle. In a day of science, medieval ideas about scholarship are possessed of remarkable quickening qualities. There is a recounting of what someone *else* did and what someone *else* found out, and less a finding out for oneself.[58] As previously stated, such focus complements a medieval view of scholarship. Indeed, the attitude of the chronicler may be observed among teachers of all subjects, not only in history where it seems to be endemic; one finds an emphasis on chronicle widely employed and tenaciously clung to in the most "scientific" of subjects. Why? Several reasons are suggested:

There is an old saying that one learns from the master and not from the schoolmaster.[59] Perhaps Comenius sired it when he said that "language must be learned not from grammar but from fitting authors."[60] What makes a man a master is his dynamism and his creativity; he searches and experiments. What makes a man a schoolmaster is his codification of the discoveries and explorations of others. Perhaps nowhere can this be seen more clearly than in the formalization, *the* scientific method. Science is what the scientist does; *the* "method" is an *ad hoc* codification by a schoolmaster.

It is being suggested that the handbooks that are thus produced are obsolescent as they are being codified. In attempting to preserve what was at one time new and vibrant, the schoolmaster becomes a conservative. In reality, he fights a losing battle for the concept of learning is properly concerned with the future and not with the past. Francis Bacon reminds us that the amazing contributions of ancient Greece came about because the Greeks had no antiquity of knowledge and no knowledge of antiquity.

It has also to be pointed out that the codification or indices produced by the schoolmaster were logical systems. No doubt, they contributed to an even larger cataloguing; the subject organization of studies by which much of school practice is now governed. Of course, a logical organization of subject matter is *not* the order by which the knowledge of the particular science was arrived at originally. Man did not first discover the cell or the atom or musical scales or grammar. (Yet, some would teach these things *first,* to beginner and advanced student, as a matter of *necessary* antecedence simply because they appear *first* in the logic of the codification scheme.) Hindsight has organized them in this systematic way. What is essentially an administrative convenience is often erected into a concept of *necessary*

---

[58]Whitehead urged that all education begin and end in research. "First-hand knowledge is the ultimate basis of intellectual life . . . The second-handedness of the learned world is the secret of its mediocrity." Alfred North Whitehead, *The Aims of Education* (New York: Mentor Books, 1949), p. 61.

[59]Schoolmaster is here used in its archaic connotation of derision. The schoolmaster was a pedant, a lexicographer, who was concerned with cataloguing and indexing.

[60]*The Great Didactic,* Chapter 16.

antecedence — this *must* come before that. Thus, some teachers impose the external order *because* of its logic. They organize data-gathering activities not in response to a problem but to introduce the learner to the system of the subject, hoping perhaps to store up data against the day when they will be needed to solve some future problem.[61]

A third reason for the chronicle approach of finding out what someone else did is suggested. Much less effort is required of the teacher. Parcels of knowledge may be neatly cut up and distributed for it is much easier to teach product than process. In fact, in some quarters, the product of men's thoughts is sometimes called "teachings;" process is assumed *to be*. Then too, given the prevalent grading system, it is probably easier to test for product. However, when we focus only on the product, the body of knowledge, and not on the process, the method by which it is acquired, inevitably we teach as a consequence, "un-science."

Hopefully, it does not require too much imagination to see that problem-solving is an operation which can be applicable to all subject areas. The curriculum need not be broadened to include yet another subject called Problem-Solving. The existing content can be used as a basis for investigating, for collecting and organizing data, for application of principles, and for decision making even without the addition of special units. What does have to be added is a shift in emphasis.

9. Criticizing and Evaluating.

The Greek word, *kritikos,* means skill in judging. And to judge means to set up a standard by which one chooses or by which one makes a rating or grading on a continuum of superiority-inferiority or appropriateness-inappropriateness. To grade and to rate, from ideas to eggs, is to group and to assign rank; the assigning of rank is defensible only when standards of choice are made known.

In this operation, students are given the opportunity of taking a position and justifying it. Often this is done through an exercise called a debate; sometimes a school newspaper is used as a student forum where criticism of a sort is offered. All too rarely, however, is the classroom made into a place where criticism may thrive. We seem to have an awareness that the amount of criticism allowed in a school is often a fair measure of its intellectual health; yet, who is it who does the criticizing and judging in a school? Surely, students need practice if a critical ability is to be developed; judgment-making is not something that can be taught didactically.

---

[61]Why then is it a crime to discover something new . . . seeing that they, who had none to teach them anything, have handed down such store of knowledge to posterity, shall we refuse to employ the experience which we possess of some things, and possess nought that is not owed to the beneficent activity of others. Quintillian, *Institutes of Oratory,* Book X.

For example, a teacher might assign a paper entitled, "Democracy in the School," wherein students could offer criticism. Cliches of the culture, e. g., the inevitability of progress or the notion of equality, may be examined. Some sacred cows might be put to the test of criticism and evaluation. This would include the untouchables of our day like Darwinian theory, Freudian theory, and the cult of scientism.

The teacher's pedagogic technique will be sure to illuminate the relationship between criticism and evaluation; that is to say, standards are set forth. Criticism builds; it does not tear down. Irresponsible criticism is the negativism with which most of us are familiar; there is a heckling and carping attack which is merely nihilistic. Like the barbarian, what it does not understand, it destroys. How often do our students offer this type of carping criticism? Would there be less extreme manifestations if schools were to cultivate and encourage student evaluation all along the line?

A class was asked to respond to the statement below. Their criticisms follow.

9.1

UN Has Failed[62]

To the New York Herald Tribune:

> During the past weeks in many areas of our country were celebrations in behalf of the United Nations. There is a disturbing element in this type of celebration because during the eighteen years of the United Nations the sovereignty of our country has been constantly encroached upon by this world body.
>
> The original idea of the United Nations may have been an extremely noble one. However, it cannot be said that it has been proved of value because it has not brought the kind of peace which clear-thinking Americans desire. It has not lessened the tension between East and West. Nor has it freed the many Americans that are in the slave labor camps of the Soviet Union.
>
> Did it break the Berlin blockade in 1948? The answer is No. The Berlin blockade was broken by the American Air Force. Did it prevent communism in Asia and Africa? Again the answer is decidedly No. It must be remembered that victory in Korea was not gained by the free world as that country is still in turmoil at the hands of the Communists. In Africa the racial tension has not been eased, but increased during the existence of the United Nations. These are only a few of the destructive elements that the United Nations has indorsed.
>
> Finally, it should not be forgotten that 85 per cent of the United Nations bill is being paid by our country and yet we have less than 15 per cent of the voting strength. The United Nations is weakening the integrity and sovereignty of the United States. For the first time in the history of the United States a foreign ideology has a foothold in the echelon of the United States diplomatic corps.

---

[62]Letter to the Editor, *The New York Herald Tribune*, November 7, 1962.

Now in the last analysis what has the United Nations done to preserve freedom and peace for the individual? Let us as Americans preserve our heritage and freedom and not expend it at the price of an unholy peace.

Some students broke their criticisms down into four groups: the arguments of the writer, his assumptions, some critical questions, and overall evaluation. These are presented below.

The Writer's Argument

1. The sovereignty of the United States has been encroached upon.
2. The U. N. "has not brought the kind of peace which clear-thinking Americans desire."
3. The U. N. has not lessened tension between East and West.
4. The U. N. has not freed Americans in slave labor camps.
5. Eighty-five per cent of the U. N. bill is paid for by the United States.

Some proofs which he offers refer to the breaking of the Berlin blockade and the victory in Korea, which were achieved by other means than the U. N.

The Writer's Assumptions

1. National sovereignty and integrity are important.
2. The U. N. should bring peace.
3. The U. N. should lessen tension.
4. The U. N. should free Americans.
5. The U. N. should break the Berlin blockade.
6. The U. N. should prevent Communism in Asia and Africa.
7. The U. N. should achieve victory in Korea.
8. The U. N. indorses destructive elements.
9. An unidentified foreign ideology has a foothold.
10. The U. N. should preserve freedom and peace for the individual.
11. The amount of money which a nation contributes should determine its voting rights.

Critical Questions

1. What are the purposes of the U. N.?
2. Is the U. N. expected to do what the writer suggests?
3. If the writer's program were adopted, what would be the effect on national sovereignties?

Evaluation of Argument

If one looks at the writer's assumptions, national sovereignty seems to be important. Yet, at one and the same time, he expects the U. N. (1) to be a super-national body, and (2) to reflect the wishes of a single nation, the United States. This basic contradiction makes his argument weak.

Other examples calling for the operation of criticizing are offered below. It may be seen that adaptations within existing subject matter are not difficult.

9.2

Criticize:

1. A new report on cancer.
2. A new report on cigarette smoking.
3. A new book that has become a best seller.
4. A review of a play, concert, or work of art.

9.3

Select a theme and justify:

1. What is wrong with TV programs?
2. Why the younger generation is "going to the dogs."
3. What is wrong with the "new-fangled inventions"?
4. What is right (or wrong) with the world.

9.4

The students write a paper defending a position and then are asked to criticize *their own* position. The following are only suggestions:

1. Beauty contests.
2. The new mathematics (or the old mathematics).
3. Their favorite subject (or their least favorite).

9.5

In this type of exercise, an attempt is made to study one's own reactions. Teachers may take excerpts of political speeches or scientific findings. They are to read such excerpts and omit the illustrious name. Or teachers may present written paragraphs which have high controversy-evoking power. They are to leave them unlabeled and then have students react to them. After evaluations are made, authors may be revealed and students may again evaluate the paragraphs and themselves. The following is an illustration of what is intended.

1. It is the Anglo-Saxon manifest destiny to go forth as a world conqueror. He will take possession of all the islands of the sea. He will exterminate the people he cannot subjugate. That is what fate holds for the chosen people.[63]

2. The struggle is not alone for civil rights and property and home but for religion, for the church, and the gospel.[64]

3. A solemn crisis is at length upon us. The issue is not merely war or peace. It is one far more momentous and alarming than all these—the very existence

---

[63]William Allen White, Kansas publisher, 1902.
[64]Presbyterian Church of the Confederate States of America.

of liberty itself—the continuance or the disastrous overthrow of the great principles of popular rights, constitutional authority, and genuine liberty for which our fathers bled on the battlefield, and has been the pride and glory of all American hearts . . . We repeat, the real and vital issue before our country is the existence or annihilation of freedom.[65]

4. That the synod regards the present war on our part as a war of defense commending itself to our people's efforts, prayer and hearts as a hallowed though stern contest for sacred rights involving our homes and altars, liberty and religion, and to it we solemnly, prayerfully commit our persons and efforts, our energies and property, our sons and lives.[66]

5. Only if we exert all of our strength can we beg the Lord to afford us His aid, as he has done hitherto. We had harmed neither Britain nor France nor the United States; we had made no demands which might have caused enemies to declare war on us.[67]

6. The year 1942—and we pray to God, all of us that it may—should bring the decision which will save our people and with them our allied nations.[68]

9.6

Twelve years passed before Harvey was ready to publish his findings. Why did he delay in reporting his notable discovery to the world? Sir William Osler suggested that "perhaps it was the motive of Copernicus who so dreaded the prejudices of mankind that for thirty years he is said to have detained in his closet the Treatise of Revolutions." Harvey had this to say:

The theory of circulation of the blood "is of so novel and unheard of character, that I not only fear injury to myself from the envy of a few, but I tremble lest I have mankind at large for my enemies . . ."

How would you evaluate Harvey's actions? Does it not seem strange that he should express fear?

9.7

The military problem, psychologically speaking, resolves itself into taking advantage of the herd instinct to integrate the mass . . . This military processing of civilians is a purely empirical thing, but it is an eminently sound one. It has been handed down from past armies . . .

It is useless to try and convince men of the value of military standards by reasoning with them, for reasoning, no matter how brilliant or conclusive, always leaves a suspicion of doubt and uncertainty in the mind of the average man. It is necessary that he be firmly convinced, and the best way of doing this—in fact, the only way—is to indoctrinate him. Constant repetition of the item to be inculcated, unsupported by any reasons, will have an immense effect on the suggestible herd-minded human. An opinion, an idea, or a code acquired in this manner

---

[65]*Chicago Daily Journal,* April 17, 1861.
[66]The Snyod of North Carolina, November 1, 1861.
[67]Adolf Hitler, from a speech on December 1, 1942.
[68]Adolf Hitler, from a speech on December 31, 1941.

can become so firmly fixed that one who questions its essential rightness will be regarded as foolish, wicked, or insane . . .

Parades and reviews are great factors in securing unity. For with pomp and glitter the great unit is massed and to the sound of rhythmic music with flags flying and cadenced step the sub-units pass and render homage to their commander. For the soldier not to be conscious and proud of his identity with his herd is, under these circumstances, almost impossible. Finally, to express its unity, the herd is given a symbol—the colors.

But probably the greatest tool in the hands of the officer for bringing home to the members of the group their basic unity is close order drill . . .

Three things, then, are fostered by close order drill: one, the growth of herd consciousness; two, the development of the habit of automatic obedience; and three, the recognition and acceptance of leaders, and the belief that these leaders have herd approval behind their action.[69]

How would you criticize the above selection? Now read the selection below and criticize.

Of all political questions, that [of education] is perhaps the most important. There cannot be a firmly established political state unless there is a teaching body with definitely fixed principles. Except as a child is taught from infancy whether he ought to be a republican or a monarchist, a Catholic or free thinker, the state will not constitute a nation. (Napoleon Bonaparte)[70]

Question: What are the duties of Christians towards those who govern them, and what in particular are our duties towards Napoleon I, our emperor?

Answer: Christians owe to the princes who govern them, and we in particular owe to Napoleon I, our emperor, love, respect, obedience, fidelity, military service, and the taxes levied for the preservation and defense of the empire and of his throne. We also owe him fervent prayers for his safety and for the spiritual and temporal prosperity of the state . . .

Question: What must we think of those who are wanting in their duties towards our emperor?

Answer: According to the Apostle Paul, they are resisting the order established by God himself and render themselves worthy of eternal damnation.[71]

9.8

Evaluate and Criticize:

1. Galileo constructed a thermometer in 1593. It consisted of a glass bulb an inch or two in diameter with a long tube for a stem. To use the thermometer, the bulb was slightly heated and the end of the tube immersed in water. When the bulb cooled, the water rose to a small height. It indicated

---

[69]Captain John H. Burns, "The Psychologist Looks at the Army," *Infantry Journal*, 33:4 (December, 1928), 593ff.

[70]W. H. Kilpatrick, *Source Book in the Philosophy of Education* (New York; Crowell-Collier & Macmillan, Inc., 1934), pp. 17-18.

[71]C. J. Hayes, *A Political and Social History of Modern Europe* (New York: Crowell-Collier & Macmillan, Inc. 1919), I, 535.

higher temperatures by a fall of the water in the tube and lower temperatures by a rise.

Criticize:

2. In 1639, Dr. Jean Rey filled the bulb and part of the stem with water and pointed it upward. Changes of water level in the stem indicated changes in temperature.

Criticize:

3. Approximately twenty-five years later, the upper end of the tube was sealed.

Criticize:

4. Later, alcohol or mercury was used as the thermometric substance.

Obviously, had not the original thermometer been criticized, there might not have been improvement in it. Had the improvements not been criticized, there might not have been other improvements. Is the one we have now a finished product or can it be criticized?

9.9

Here are some data. If you were to write a critical summary, how would you use them? What would you criticize?

In the 16th U. N. General Assembly sessions, up to December 10, 1961, a total of eight resolutions on nuclear testing and disarmament were debated and approved:

Resolution 1: The appeal to Russia not to detonate the 50 megaton bomb.

For	87
Against	11
Abstained	1

Resolution 2: The Indian Resolution asking a moratorium on all nuclear tests.

For	71
Against	20
Abstained	8

Resolution 3: The U. S.-U. K. Resolution asking for continued negotiation to conclude a test ban treaty.

For	71
Against	11
Abstained	15

Resolution 4: The Ghanian Resolution urging an atom-free Africa.

For	55
Against	0
Abstained	15

Resolution 5: The Ethiopian Resolution urging that all nuclear weapons be outlawed by an international convention.

For	55
Against	20
Abstained	26

Resolution 6: The Indian Resolution urging the U. S. and the U. S. S. R. to negotiate on the composition of a committee to continue disarmament negotiations.   Unanimous approval

Resolution 7: The Swedish Resolution urging the exploration of the possibility of a non-nuclear club.

For	57
Against	12
Abstained	32

Resolution 8: The Irish Revolution urging the nuclear powers not give their weapons to non-nuclear nations.

For	95
Against	0
Abstained	4

Here is the voting record of some of the countries on the preceding resolutions:

Country	Resolution 1	2	3	4	5	6	7	8	Total Yes	No	Abstentions
U. S. A.	Y	N	Y	A	N	Y	N	Y	4	3	1
United Kingdom	Y	N	Y	A	N	Y	N	Y	4	3	1
France	Y	N	A	A	N	Y	N	Y	3	3	2
Canada	Y	Y	Y	A	A	Y	Y	Y	6	0	2
Japan	Y	Y	Y	A	Y	Y	Y	Y	7	0	1
Argentina	Y	Y	Y	A	A	Y	Y	Y	7	0	1
Sweden	Y	Y	Y	Y	A	Y	Y	Y	7	0	1
Nigeria	Y	Y	Y	Y	Y	Y	Y	Y	8	0	0
India	Y	Y	Y	Y	Y	Y	Y	Y	8	0	0
Ghana	Y	Y	A	Y	Y	Y	Y	Y	7	0	1
Cuba	N	A	N	Y	Y	Y	Y	Y	5	2	1
U.S.S.R.	N	N	N	Y	Y	Y	Y	Y	5	3	0

9.10

At the end of the 16th century, the accepted theory of the earth in its relationship to the universe was known as the Ptolemaic theory, named after the philosopher Ptolemy, who lived 1500 years earlier. Briefly, this theory suggested that the earth was stationary, for if it turned, it would break into pieces and fly off into space. Moreover, anything floating in the air, such as a cloud or a bird would be left behind, and an object tossed into the air would descend a considerable distance westward.

How would you criticize this theory?

Now evaluate the following:

In the 16th century, the philosopher Copernicus maintained that it was more logical to assume that the earth turned, instead of the entire universe, for if the earth did not rotate, the sky would have to revolve to produce day and night.

With few exceptions, this idea was violently opposed by the general public and by scientists alike. According to one story, the printer's shop where Copernicus's book was being printed was attacked by university students who tried to destroy the press and the manuscript. The printers had to barricade themselves to finish the job. A burlesque play which depicted Copernicus as having given his soul to Satan was produced by a group of players. Below are some selections which may help to indicate how the Copernican system was received:

1. ". . . the new astronomer who wants to prove that the Earth goes round, and not the Heavens, the Sun, and the Moon; just as if someone sitting in a moving wagon or ship were to suppose that he was at rest, and that the Earth and the trees were moving past him. But that is the way nowadays; whoever wants to be clever must needs produce something of his own, which is bound to be the best since he has produced it! The fool will turn the whole science of astronomy upside down. But, as Holy Writ declares, it was the sun and not the Earth which Joshua commanded to stand still." (Martin Luther)

2. "The world also is established, that it cannot be moved." (Psalm 93) "Who will venture to place the authority of a Copernicus above that of the Holy Spirit." (John Calvin)

3. "He stopped the sun and set the earth in motion." (Philip Melancthon)

4. "The first proposition, that the sun is the center and does not revolve about the earth, is foolish, absurd, false in theology, and heretical, because expressly contrary to Holy Scripture. The second proposition, that the earth revolves about the sun and is not the center, is absurd, false in philosophy and from a theological point of view at least, opposed to the true faith." (Roman Catholic Church)

5. Francis Bacon, one of the leaders of the scientific movement, argued against the idea that the earth rotated on its axis and circled in an orbit around the sun.

This is the way Copernicus's theory was criticized. How would you criticize it?

Now here are some of the results of the Copernican theory:

1. In 1616, the writings of Copernicus were placed on the Index of prohibited books "until they should be corrected" and "all writings which affirm the motion of the Earth" were condemned.

2. Giordano Bruno, a follower of Copernicus, suggested the theory that space was boundless and that the sun and its planets were but one of many similar systems. He also suggested that there might be other inhabited worlds with rational beings equal or superior to ourselves. Bruno was tried before the Inquisition for blasphemy, condemned, and burned at the stake in 1600.

3. In 1633, the astronomer Galileo, under threat of torture and death by the Inquisition, was forced on his knees to give up belief that Coper-

nicus's theories might be sound. He was sentenced to imprisonment for the remainder of his days.

What seems to be wrong with those people in those days? How would you criticize the above?

9.11

In the following exercise, critical questions are raised by the teacher for the students to respond to. It is perhaps best to give all the excerpts to the students at the outset.

Excerpts from the Monroe Doctrine

Paragraph 1. With the movements in this hemisphere we are of necessity more immediately connected, and by causes which must be obvious to all enlightened and impartial observers.

1. What are the causes by which we are connected with the movements in this hemisphere and which are obvious to all enlightened and impartial observers?
2. It says that the causes must be obvious to all. What if they are not obvious?

Paragraph 2: We owe it, therefore, to candor and to the amicable relations existing between the United States and those powers to declare that we should consider any attempt on their part to extend their system to any portion of this hemisphere as dangerous to our peace and safety. With the existing colonies or dependencies of any European power we have not interfered and shall not interfere, but with the Governments who have declared their independence and maintained it, and whose independence we have, on great consideration and on just principles, acknowledged, we could not view any interposition for the purpose of oppressing them, or controlling in any other manner their destiny, by any European power in any other light than as the manifestations of an unfriendly disposition towards the United States.

1. The statement reads: "We owe it to candor . . ." What is it that we owe?
2. The statement reads: "those European powers." Who are *those?*
3. Does the statement, "any portion of this hemisphere," really mean *any* portion of this hemisphere?
4. Why would "any interposition" be viewed as the "manifestation of an unfriendly disposition towards the United States"?
5. Interposition for oppression or controlling their destiny—can there be interposition for any other purpose? Why cannot the U. S. view *interposition* in any other light?
6. Would the doctrine promote "amicable relations" between the United States and "those European powers"?

Paragraph 3. It is impossible that the allied powers should extend their political system to any portion of either continent without endangering our peace and happiness; nor can anyone believe that our southern brethren, if left to themselves, would adopt it of their own accord. It is equally impossible, therefore, that we should behold such interposition in any form with indifference.

1. How does the political system of the allied powers endanger our peace and happiness?
2. Was the political system which these powers had different from the political systems in Canada, Mexico, and Brazil?
3. Why can anyone not believe that our southern brethren if left to themselves would adopt it (the political system) of their own accord?
4. In paragraph 2 above, interposition for the purpose of oppression or controlling their destiny was referred to. In paragraph 3, interposition in *any form* is mentioned. What does *this* mean? Why is a distinction made?

9.12

Resistance met Harvey's discovery of the circulation of the blood, Pasteur's work on microbes, and Semmelweis's discovery that physicians spread the infection of childbed fever from one mother to another. Resistance also met the discoveries of anesthesia, the work of Darwin and the work of Freud. "That seems to be the way it is," we say. How would you evaluate the following:

1. Francis Bacon said: "We have set it down as a law to ourselves that we have to examine things to the bottom; and not to receive upon credit or reject upon improbabilities, until these have passed a due examination."
   (Bacon could not believe that the earth goes around the sun.)
2. Galileo could not persuade physicists and astronomers of his day to look into his new invention, the telescope. He thought they had closed minds.
   (Galileo could not accept Kepler's evidence that the planets move in an elliptical orbit around the sun. Nor did he believe that people accused of witchcraft suffered from mental illness.)
3. Pasteur waged a battle against physicians for the acceptance of the germ theory of disease.
   (At the height of his fame, Pasteur addressed a distinguished group of scientists and told them that scientific methods could *never* be applied to the study of the emotions.)

As we have said before, criticizing and evaluating do not mean being fussy or carping at things, but being able to account for thoughts and feelings. Creating a rationale for one's likes and dislikes is the essence of criticizing. This is not to suggest that passion should acquire reason; the reverse is intended. It does suggest that likes and dislikes be reviewed critically and periodically. It is well to emphasize that criticism that is really expert is done within the framework of existing knowledge. That is to say, the critic learns to use the vocabulary of the given knowledge area, whether art, science, music, history, or literature. It is then that positive alternatives to what exists are more defensible.

Some imagine that special courses in "critical thinking" are needed or that massive curriculum revision is required to carry on the operation of criticizing and evaluating. Neither is the case. Existing content can be adapted to accommodate exercise of the operation.

10. Imagining and Creating.

Painting, dramatic activity, musical activity, and the subject areas of home economics and industrial arts typically come to mind when one speaks of imagining and creating. But, a different approach to a problem—instead of repeating tried and true remedies—calls for imaginativeness and invention too. A teacher invites students to ideate, to create, to change old ways, to invent new ways. Sticking to the old formulas, doing it "the way we've always done it," is a prescription for routine and for dullness. Instead, the accent is on invention and departure from what is known. Two pass keys which can release student imaginativeness and creativity are invitation and encouragement.

It is well to emphasize that, in this operation, there is a release from rules and regulations. Where, in interpreting, for instance, the interpreter is bound by the data, where his inferences may not be unrestrained, where, as in applying principles to new situations, one follows the laws and restrictions contained in the principles, in imagining and creating, one invents *new* laws, *new* principles, and *new* rules.

Activities in this operation would include make believe ("pretend you're a . . ."), guessing, intuiting, inventing, creating—the desert island type of situation. Where students in the lower grades may invent new games or modify old ones, older children are encouraged to find new scientific rules, new language rules, new formulas, to make an ideal world, if they can. Essays like "What Would We Do Without Language," or, "If the South Had Won the Civil War," typify what is intended. Students might try to create different types of languages: gestural, facial, signal-type (whistling, clapping), pictographic, stenographic, each with a systematic alphabet. It is being suggested that imagining and creating activities be an extension of an existing curriculum, an adaptation of present subject matter to accommodate a shift in emphasis. Below are some suggestions.

10.1
Devise a system whereby you can locate a point on an orange. Compare it with the latitude, longitude system.

10.2

Using one of the art forms, express a formula, rule or law in science, mathematics, or language.

10.3

Student response is elicited for the following:
1. How would you, a student, make an interesting speech on the function of the ear, the bones, the circulatory or digestive systems, or the meaning of photosynthesis or the meaning of feudalism?
2. How would you, a student, interest someone in this topic? (The topic might be equations, poetry, or conjugations.)
3. Of what value is *this* particular part of the subject?

10.4

Imagine that you are Newton, Darwin, Einstein, Galileo, Pasteur, Freud, Shakespeare, Beethoven, Bismarck, Gandhi, Charles I of England, Columbus, Mohammed, Luther, Napoleon. Write a diary account of one day.

10.5

Imagine that you have absolute power over a country and forty-eight hours to exercise that power. What would you do?

10.6

Invent some proverbs. Compare them with a list of existing proverbs.

10.7

Find some analogies which will illustrate a particular concept in mathematics or any other subject.

10.8

What is the most vital problem facing man?

10.9

Whom would you most like to be?

10.10

Respond to: "If I had three wishes . . ."

10.11

Change the lines of a poem from tragic to comic or the reverse.

10.12

Change the beginning or ending of a story.

10.13

Change the character of the tune, "Yankee Doodle."

10.14

Imagine happiness. How would you express it musically, artistically, or in an essay?

10.15

Create some parallels: "An arrow is a missile."

Frequently, we hear the exhortation that the primary function of the school is to transmit the culture (as if it were an easy matter to discern which of the competing cultures one is to transmit). Often juxtaposed to this proposition is a truism (honored more at the verbal level than at the *knowing* level), the idea of the inevitability of change. Change, however imperceptible, whether referring to a biological organism or to a massive social institution, is continuous. To say that the school will be "concerned with change" is hardly enough. If there is recognition of the inevitability of change, the school then teaches *for* change. But how?

The school helps to cultivate vision in students, vision being the capacity to see that which *is not* yet but that which *might* be. We seem to know intuitively that a crucial quality of leadership is the capacity to see beyond what others see, to look forward not backward, to see in the future possibilities for improving the present. For a teacher, then, to deal only with that which *is* is to deprive students of the opportunity for developing vision. On the other hand, for a teacher to provide rich materials in imagining and creating is to help equip students for change, for the desire to greet change with hope and expectation and not with fear and resistance.

In the operation of imagining and creating, as with the other operations, the idea is to make school a thoughtful place instead of just a place to find out what other people thought. Montaigne once said, "To know by heart is not to know."[72] It is to know what others have found out and what others have done. This might properly come after knowing and doing first-hand. Thus understood, school would be a place for the development of the curriculum, not the mere imparting of it. To this end, the cultivation of imagination is surely an important means.

SOME FINAL CONSIDERATIONS

If one were to ask a teacher how to teach punctuation, the Pythagorean theorem, the song "Yankee Doodle," the operation of a lathe, the conjugation of regular verbs, or the teaching of a sonnet, the chances are that he would respond with a list of specifications. On the other hand, if one were to ask him how he might teach for thinking, some of the following responses might be forthcoming:

1. "I don't know."
2. "It can't be done."
3. "It's an automatic result."
4. "It's learned by imitation."
5. "I don't want to; it's dangerous."
6. "I don't have time; I have to cover the subject."[73]

Some believe that there is magic to the word *thinking*; "some have it and some don't"; it is a mysterious process accorded to the select few. The view presented herein is that there is no mystery and no magic. As teachers provide for reacting to coding, for comparing, classifying, observing and reporting, summarizing, interpreting, analyzing assumptions, problem-solving, criticizing, and imagining, thinking can ensue. Not all mental processes or operations have been presented in this part; only ten have been identified here. Surely, there are other operations, and there certainly are other ways of ordering them. In this regard, the reader is invited to consult other parts in this book.

It has, however, been said that thinking consists of at least these many processes. It has also been asserted that it is perhaps better to conceive of thinking in terms of these processes since the word *thinking* is so broad a concept under which so much may be described. For example, it is suggested

---

[72]Montaigne, *Of the Education of Children,* Chapter 26.
[73]Teachers of science were asked how they trained pupils to do "scientific" thinking. Five types of answers were forthcoming: "1) The study of science results automatically in this ability; 2) It it is not possible to train a pupil to think; 3) We had a lesson on that last week, or we'll have a lesson on that next week; 4) We take that up in the introduction to the course; 5) The pupils learn the method by watching the procedure of the teacher." Wilbur L. Beauchamp, "Instruction in Science," *National Survey of Secondary Education, Monograph #22,* United States Office of Education, Bulletin #17, pp. 57-58.

that some may be concerned with knowledge of the *forms* of thought; as found in the field of logic, these are not infrequently confused with a total emphasis upon thinking. Sometimes, there is a faith that practice in forms of thought, via a given formula such as the syllogism, will result in a generalized habit.

In this regard, it is well to distinguish between teaching *what* to think, teaching *how* to think, and teaching *for* thinking. Teaching *what* to think is often viewed as indoctrination and a typical reaction is one of almost automatic recoil. On the other hand, there is the notion that teaching *how* to think should be the main concern of teachers. Indeed, student criticism of a teacher's efforts is sometimes expressed as: "I want to learn *how* to think and he's teaching us *what* to think."

Learning *how* to think may be, and frequently is, viewed in a technical sense. One speaks of *logical* thinking, by which is usually meant an emphasis on the deductive process. Or one may hear the terms *critical* thinking, and this is often applied to an ability to analyze and criticize the underlying assumptions of a given position. Sometimes, the phrase *reflective* thinking is employed and here there may be reference to suspended judgment, the widening of the gap between the stimulus of a problem or issue and the response to it. Occasionally, one encounters the phrase *experimental* or *scientific* thinking, which may relate to the setting up of a research design. Then, too, there is the phrase *artistic* thinking. Under this heading, one may find such expressions as *adventurous* thinking, *creative* thinking, *imaginative* thinking, *inventive* thinking, *intuitive* thinking.

In the grouping logical, critical, reflective, and experimental thinking there seems to be concern with the *forms* of thought. Moreover, in the "types" of thinking enumerated above, in only a few is a verb implied and it is the *verb* that is important for teaching and learning; that is to say, without a verb it is unclear as to what one is to *do*. Maybe "adventurous" thinking and "logical" thinking would be more widespread if, as these terms are held forth as goals, students knew what teachers were asking them to do.

Perhaps learning forms of thought is important for an advanced student or for a specialist. One may wonder whether, in such learning, there is actual instruction in *how* to think. Sometimes, instruction in *how* to think blends in imperceptibly with teaching *what* to think. If there is such a thing as learning *how* to think (as distinct from learning forms of thought), it would appear to be a lifetime goal. Sometimes, the best of us go from the sublime to the ridiculous, from maturity in thinking to a sophomoric display.

Be all this as it may, the concern here has *not* been with teaching *thinking* or teaching *how* to think. Nor has there been concern with a particular *kind* of thinking, like "critical" thinking or "intuitive" thinking. The focus has been on ways of providing opportunities *for* thinking. What is it that teachers

might do that will emphasize its incidence? The theory has been put forth
that as we stress a wide variety of thinking operations, greater skill and maturity will be a consequence.

At this point, some persons may retort: "What's all the shouting about?
We have been doing these things all along." Perhaps so. What may be new
here is the focus. The teacher is being asked to be conscious of the parts
which contribute to a composite whole. Frequently, as in the assignment of
a project, there is an easy assumption that certain operations and processes
are *necessarily* engaged. In this regard, a guide has been provided, a checking point and a check-list for the teacher: if there is a desire to provide
opportunities for thinking, how may this be done? Then too, what may be
new here is the theoretical frame, the relating of thinking operations to
behavior.

It has not been intended to suggest that thinking is by any means a simple
act. Recourse to an analogy may be helpful here. Somewhat like thinking,
speaking is a process that appears to be effortless. Yet, if one had to describe
the neural function, the muscular function and the co-ordination which go
into speaking, it would be seen as a complicated procedure. Indeed, there
are speech and voice teachers who indulge themselves in the abstractions of
vocal physiology as a means of showing the learner how to correct his faults,
but it is rare that the learner can benefit from knowledge concerning theoretical function. Moreover, if one had to pause and reflect on the *description* of
the mechanism before one spoke, there might ensue some halting and uncer-
tain sounds. Perhaps the individual would feel inhibited or possibly overcome
at the wonder of it all. Monsieur Jourdain, the unlettered bourgeois in
Molière's, *The Would Be Gentleman,* comes to mind. Astounded at his
sudden discovery of a difference between verse and prose, he declared: "On
my conscience, I have spoken prose these forty years without knowing anything of the matter."

The concern here is with the manifestations of thinking and their pedagogic implications. While a teacher may know or may want to know a good
deal about the neuro-physiological structure of thinking or about forms of
thought, he does not teach *these,* for he is not teaching the theoretical bases
of thinking; he is, however, concerned with providing *opportunities* for the
exercise of mental processes.

The question, then, put in the form of "what *is* thinking" is similar to the
question "what *is* electricity?" It is unanswerable and it is not even pertinent. As has been said, to teach speaking skills one need not classify the bones
and muscles involved. One does supply the appropriate settings, and one does
help to remove obstacles. When behavioral expectations have been described
and when the circumstances under which thinking takes place have been set
forth, that which needs be told has been told.

Should there be an order of priority, of preference for certain mental
processes? Which ones might a teacher seek to engage? Earlier in this part

it was indicated that mental processes have been catalogued into lower and higher divisions. Those which are lowest include the functioning of the sense organs. Slightly higher, but still within the category *lower,* are those sense experiences which involve remembering, recognizing, and recalling. Still "higher" mental processes have been identified as comparing, classifying, interpreting, evaluating.

The designation *higher* has been used for several reasons. One reason suggests a distinction between man and lower animals. While animals perform lower mental operations like recognizing and recalling, as far as is now known, they do not perform the higher ones. A second reason for the distinction lower-higher relates to the amount of contribution required. Recall, for instance, requires no special contribution. The test of how well one can recall something may be seen in how faithful he is to the original. While it may be a sign of "undigestion" for a man to throw up his meat exactly as he has swallowed it, the ability to *re*-produce and to *re*-cite material unchanged is the measure of quality as far as recall is concerned. On the other hand, the measure of quality of a higher mental process is the amount of *change* which is introduced by the individual, *his* contribution to the original.

A third reason for using the terms lower-higher has to do with complexity. The lower process is simple and unrefined; there is little impingement on other processes, whereas in the higher process, impingement is unavoidable. In the lower process, memory furnishes the raw material. However, when memory serves up such raw material or data, it presents the several items in a very loose series, in what is no more than a temporal sequence. It remains for a higher mental process to set up a connection between one loose item and another, to integrate and to link them together into a new subjective entity. For example, it may readily be seen that interpreting in the light of past experience something which is experienced *now* is quite different from recalling something which has been experienced in the past.

Perhaps the matter of impingement of one process on another, which occurs only among the higher mental processes, may be viewed in yet another light. As there is engagement of *one* of the mental processes, e. g., evaluating or interpreting, it may be observed that evaluating involves comparing, analyzing, criticizing, and judgment-making. Similarly, interpreting involves translating, comparing, inferring, deducing, and predicting; they are complicated processes. In fact, lines between them become so blurred that it is difficult to set up a classification scheme or taxonomy simply because of the matter of complexity, of impingement of one process on the other.[74]

This impingement of processes is even more sharply seen in the relation

---

[74]B. S. Bloom's *Taxonomy of Educational Objectives, Cognitive Domain* is a case in point. While it is a laudable attempt, this writer has found his students troubled by a fixation on lines of distinction between processes. The very attempt to isolate one process from another, *i.e.,* to abstract its pristine qualities, is almost an attempt to deny its very nature, the fact of its *necessary* impingement on other processes.

between higher and lower processes. As one compares, analyzes, interprets, and evaluates, the lower processes of recognition, recall, and association *must* be involved. However, the reverse is *not* true; the lower processes do not automatically envelop the higher processes. There is abundant research evidence to indicate that the lower processes are engaged and strengthened as there is concentration on the higher processes. Despite this, many teaching practices seem to continue the emphasis on the lower processes. If one were to judge from tests which are administered from grade school through college, the lower processes of recall and recognition engage an entirely disproportionate amount of attention.[75] One reason for this state of affairs suggests that there is a paucity of materials which are directed to the higher processes. It is hoped that the illustrations included in this text may serve as inducement and stimulus to the classroom teacher in pointing out a direction towards which he can move. The assumption is made that as opportunities for the exercise of the operations are provided, greater skill will accrue.

Earlier in this part, it was recommended that the materials included herein *not* be made into a syllabus or a test of achievement. If one must evaluate responses to thinking operations, one way to do it would be to observe behavior. (In this regard, see Parts 1, 2, and 5 for details.) For example, how often are extremes and *either-or's* used? How impulsive are the students? How often is judgment suspended? How free is thought in the classroom? These are some questions worth asking, and the answers are worth evaluating.

It is recommended that, as teachers extend and develop their subjects and as they invent materials and exercises after the patterns indicated here, they do so in a context that will suggest a relationship to what is real. That is to say, exercises and problems need not be a type of puzzle, intellectually remote and sterile. Elsewhere, it has been emphasized that puzzle solving, while providing for mental acrobatics and pyrotechnics, has little value in terms of transfer. Certainly, puzzles and riddles do promote mental activity, but little of it is of consequence. To maximize the possibility of transfer, the exercise might be one that is closely related to situations actually encountered. Surely, the inventive teacher will search out variety and will avoid situations tending towards artificiality and triviality.

A final caution is sounded. Sometimes, one may observe the neat teaching of things that are not so. In addition to presenting the collected knowledge of mankind, it might help to teach *how* the collection came to *be*. As well as possessing other virtues, the emphasis may be an effective safeguard since it implies selection on the basis of validity and relevance. It may not, then,

---

[75]As the philosopher Schopenhauer observed: "The majority of mankind, however, who study to fill their memory with facts, do not use the steps of the ladder to mount upward, but take them off and lay them on their shoulders in order that they may take them along, delighting in the weight of the burden they are carrying. They ever remain below because they carry what should carry them."

be possible to include all that is now included. As so many teachers say: "We won't be able to *cover* the course." This is fine! It is time that we stopped covering courses and started *uncovering* them. Besides, there seems to be enough time to do that which is considered important.

As teachers provide opportunities for thinking, some beneficial by-products can emerge. Economical learning—learning which will be retained over a longer period of time—is promoted. There will tend to be an increase in teacher zest and enthusiasm; presentations may have more interest and vitality in them. Probably a concomitant, can be the resulting alliance between teacher and learner. Children will be less apt to fight the process of learning, for there is challenge to the individual when he is asked to see how knowledge may be created. "What do you think?" is a compliment to the psyche. "Listen to what others think" may or may not arouse response since less directly and perhaps only incidentally does it personalize learning. We know how admirably well schools have served as teaching and testing places—places to find out what someone else has thought. Can they be made into learning and thinking places?

part four

APPLICATION: THE TEACHER

INTRODUCTION

In recent years schools have been subjected to a barrage of criticism, suggestions, and ideas. Administrators, teacher training institutions, classroom teachers, and others have felt the sting of criticism. Some of this criticism has been justified, some of it irresponsible.

Vast changes in our schools are under way. Curriculum reorganization has become almost commonplace. There is the "new math," the "new science," "linguistics," new approaches to the teaching of reading and foreign languages, and to almost all other curricular areas. Teachers have been expected to "re-tool" through in-service training, National Science Foundation Institutes, graduate study, wide reading, and other activities. Frequently, an edict is handed down from the central office saying, "Beginning next September, all teachers will teach the new curriculum . . ."

Teachers are experiencing growing pressure to change. Sometimes the pressure comes from administration, sometimes from the students, sometimes from the community. Often teachers may be criticized for changing too slowly; yet at the same time they may be criticized for changing too fast.

Through all the pressure, concern, controversy, and anxiety, the classroom teacher stands as a convenient and vulnerable scapegoat for the ills of society and the problems of individual students. Even while curriculum changes are being introduced, the teacher is expected to stand before his class and teach — whether or not he agrees with what he is asked to do — or has even had a chance to really study and understand the official changes. Frequently the teacher is not permitted to take part in building the curriculum nor in the significant curriculum decisions that affect him and his students. Some teachers are inundated by the demands placed upon them and by the inconsistencies of many of these demands. Literally hundreds of efforts are underway to change curriculum. Is it any wonder there are teachers who feel overwhelmed and insecure?

This book, therefore, does not concern itself with curriculum but rather with a method of developing a curriculum. Its purpose is to improve teaching techniques. It offers a framework and a series of suggestions which focus on thinking in the classroom. The assumption is being made that most classroom teachers *are* concerned with the education of their students and that most classroom teachers *want* to improve their teaching. If teaching for thinking is to flourish and have an impact on our schools, individual classroom teachers are the key to the effort.

In one sense this is an educationally conservative position. It goes back to the idea that some learning is enhanced when the teacher, like Mark Hopkins, is at one end of the log and the student at the other. Learning is an act of the learner, not of the teacher. Since no two human beings are exactly alike, learning is encouraged when the teacher is aware of differences and teaches in a variety of ways to provide for these differences.

Teaching for thinking means the student has opportunities to do the thinking. There is no panacea, no easy way, no final answer. This book offers a theory which suggests guide lines so that teachers may provide opportunities for students to become involved in thinking. In a way, what is being suggested is similar to what Winston Churchill said when he offered, "Blood, toil, tears, and sweat." The job is not easy, nor is there a guarantee of success. Yet, on the basis of the evidence available, as teachers emphasize thinking in their teaching over a period of at least one semester, changes take place in the thinking-related behavior of students.[1] It is therefore suggested that teachers focus on the behavior of individual students, especially in relation to their thinking.

Experienced teachers find that they have been using thinking-related operations in their classroom for years. Comparing is certainly nothing new. It has gone on in the schools for a long time. Data collecting is not new, nor is hypothesizing, nor are the other operations presented in this book. What is new is the theoretical framework which links thinking with behavior and the idea that, as teachers concentrate on teaching for thinking, the behavior of students in relation to thinking will change. In order to concentrate on thinking, teachers, by design, provide opportunities for thinking each day. It is not enough just to be aware of thinking operations and to use them once in a while, by chance.

It has been claimed by some that the teaching of a particular subject lends itself to the improving of thinking. Geometry is one of the subjects that is presumed to improve thinking. Through the study of postulates, definitions, axioms, theorems, and proofs, students are supposed to become thinkers.

---

[1]See part 5, pp. 290, 291.

During the 1930's, Harold P. Fawcett undertook a study of geometry and its effect on thinking.[2] Fawcett found that *traditional geometry did not improve students' thinking.* However, when the teacher emphasized thinking in connection with teaching geometry, the students' thinking did improve. In the 1950's, Harry Lewis conducted another investigation of geometry and thinking.[3] Lewis also found that the study of geometry does not improve thinking unless the teacher places an emphasis on thinking. E. M. Glaser found that in 12th grade English classes certain thinking abilities improved when they were emphasized.[4] Several studies[5] have been conducted in connection with the thinking theory presented in this book. One of the interesting by-products of the studies is the follow-up interviews conducted with some of the teachers who had been emphasizing thinking in their teaching. During the experimental period of the studies, these teachers kept careful records of what they did each day in relation to thinking. When the experimental period was over, the teachers in the study had the idea that they knew how to emphasize thinking in their teaching and that they no longer needed to keep records of thinking activities. Many of them were surprised to find that they were not incorporating thinking operations as much as they had been during the experimental period. A number of teachers suggested that brief records of thinking activities be kept as an aid for helping the teacher emphasize thinking. We mean to focus on thinking but unless we stop at noon or after school each day and ask ourselves, "What have I done today and what should I do tomorrow to emphasize thinking?" we tend to have lapses in teaching for thinking.

This part of the book deals with the role of the teacher. Occasions for teaching for thinking, thinking in various fields, process and product, the classroom and thinking, selecting activities, teaching guidelines, thinking operations, focusing on particular behaviors, and implications of teaching for thinking will be discussed.

OCCASIONS FOR TEACHING FOR THINKING

Those who formulate curriculum do so for many purposes. Thinking is one of these purposes. Physical health, emotional health, appreciation of beauty,

---

[2] Harold P. Fawcett, *The Nature of Proof* 13th Yearbook of the National Council of the Teachers of Mathematics (New York: Bureau of Publications, Teachers College, Columbia University, 1938).

[3] Harry Lewis, "An Experiment in the Development of Critical Thinking Through the Teaching of Plane Geometry" (Unpublished doctoral dissertation, New York University, 1950).

[4] E. M. Glasser, *An Experiment in the Development of Critical Thinking,* Contributions to Education #843 (New York: Bureau of Publications Teachers College, Columbia University, 1941).

[5] See Part 5, page 302.

and the development of certain mechanical skills are other purposes. Should everything that is taught emphasize thinking? Probably not. Our purposes help us decide whether or not thinking is to be emphasized in our teaching.

Certain kinds of learning are based more on reflexes than they are on thinking operations. After we have learned to type, our fingers find the keys without our consciously thinking where they are. The action is automatic. Some of what is taught, when it is finally learned, does not require thinking operations to be used. The response is automatic or a reflex action. When we walk we do not think about nor plan each step. For the most part the act of walking is automatic. However, after a leg injury we may become very conscious of each step and very deliberate about our efforts to walk. At such times walking involves thinking rather than reflex action. There comes a time in the upper elementary grades when children are expected to know their multiplication tables by rote. At such times teachers want the youngsters to know that $7 \times 8 = 56$ without stopping to think — without pausing to say, "Now, let me see, seven eights is eight added seven times. Eight plus eight is sixteen . . ." There are times when teachers *do* wish to teach the meaning of multiplication. But if the emphasis is on sheer knowing by rote, the operation is one of quick recall. As a matter of fact, the objective is to put the child in a position where he responds quickly and automatically. He is encouraged to come right out with the answer. When a child learns to ride a bicycle and gains skill, his riding becomes automatic. He does it seemingly without thinking. Pedaling a bicycle is more related to reflexes and practice than it is to thinking operations. However, when it comes to safety on a bicycle, or where to go when riding a bicycle, then thinking becomes appropriate.

Where aesthetic appreciations are involved, it is sometimes appropriate to decrease the emphasis on thinking operations. A concert violinist once told of being unable to enjoy listening to violin music. She was continually analyzing and comparing it to the way she felt it should be played. For her, there was no beauty in violin music. There are times when knowledge and analysis of music enhance enjoyment. How far one should go in thinking about a particular area is an individual matter and is influenced by many factors. One could analyze the sunset to the point where the beauty of it pales. On the other hand, in connection with the study of weather, it might be very appropriate to analyze a sunset.

As teachers decide whether or not teaching for thinking is appropriate it becomes important to make the distinction between *belief in* and *belief that*. If one *believes that* Johnny is a good athlete, it is an opinion which can be supported by evidence and so is subject to analysis. However, when a student *believes in* something, he accepts it as true without evidence. It is an act of faith. If one *believes in* the fundamental goodness of man, it is an act of faith requiring no evidence and so is not subject to analysis in the thinking sense. When a student accepts something as an act of faith, a teacher may help him clarify his belief and see his basis of acceptance. In this instance, teaching for thinking is not appropriate. When mores, certain superstitions and traditions are based on acts of faith, they are not appropriate areas for thinking. However, there are occasions when the purpose is to teach for thinking. There are times when students are encouraged to inquire, to examine, to analyze, to challenge. On such occasions it is appropriate to teach for thinking.

Therefore, let it be clearly understood that the authors are not advocating the teaching for thinking in all circumstances and at all times. It is important to recognize opportunities to teach for thinking when they occur, but it is equally important to recognize occasions when teaching for thinking is inappropriate.

THINKING IN VARIOUS FIELDS

The thinking operations described in this book may be adapted to each of the subject matter fields or disciplines. Thinking operations may be used in almost all fields of human knowledge. However, the application of the operations varies in each field.

The laboratory scientist may emphasize observing. Frequently, precise measurements and carefully regulated controls are paramount in his work. He usually will not accept an hypothesis unless it is supported almost 100 per cent of the time. Classification is important in many branches of science, particularly zoology and botany. In order to classify, one must have a large collection of data and make numerous comparisons. The scientist rarely, if ever, accepts a theory as being proven. Rather, theories are left open-ended so that, as more data become available, the theory may be altered in the light of the new information. The development of the Copernican Theory regarding the solar system took over 150 years. In addition to the work of Copernicus, contributions were made by Kepler, Galileo, Descartes, Newton, and others before the theory was generally accepted. Even now, in the space age, the Copernican Theory is being subjected to slight modifications as more data become available. For example, the satellite, Vanguard I, sent back data to indicate that the earth is ever so slightly pear-shaped. Can those of us who teach science bring data to our students? Are there things worth comparing? Do students have opportunities to make and test hypotheses? Examine assumptions? Evaluate evidence? Apply principles?

The social scientist is usually not in a position to measure as precisely as the physical scientist. He must be content with less exact data. Frequently the social scientist searches for trends, patterns, or tendencies in events. The social scientist may be satisfied with a correlation between two happenings which is as low as .30 for it shows some kind of association even if not a very high one.

Assumptions play a role in the social sciences. Marxism and free enterprise are based on different assumptions. If one is willing to accept the assumptions that Marx made, his structures and reasoning tend to follow. On the other hand, if one rejects Marx's assumptions, then his ideas do not hold together. Certain basic assumptions are made in relation to free enterprise. They can be made known and examined. If one accepts them, the ideas of capitalism tend to follow. Do those of us who teach social studies make data available to our students? Are there primary sources such as diaries, newspaper articles, documents, eyewitness accounts, and others that we can use? Do we provide opportunities for students to compare: two colonies, two governments, two economic systems, two countries, and more? Are there assumptions that our students can examine? Are there dates, events, ideas, and other information that our students can classify? Can we provide data which our students can interpret?

The mathematician is often concerned with recognizing patterns in abstract material. This would involve collecting, comparing, and organizing data usually in the form of numbers and making generalizations in the form of equations. The mathematician is also concerned with precise definitions. He is very careful to state and examine his assumptions. The matter of assumptions often is the basis of differing areas of mathematics such as Euclidean and non-Euclidean geometry. Basic assumptions in the form of definitions, axioms, and postulates differ in these geometries. If one accepts the assumptions of Euclidean geometry, its structure and reasoning in the form of theorems tend to follow as far as this geometry is concerned. To work in non-Euclidean geometry, one must accept a different set of assumptions. There are many geometries, many algebras, and many arithmetics. They differ basically in the kinds of assumptions that are made. Can we provide opportunities for our students to examine assumptions? Are there patterns that our students can discover? Are there things that our students can compare? Numeration systems? Proofs? Theorems? Axioms? Are there possibilities in the field of mathematics to teach for thinking?

What about art, music, drama, literature, physical education, and other curricular areas? Are there things that students can compare? Two pictures? Two songs? Two plays? Two poems? Two books? Two games? Are there possibilities to gather data, examine assumptions, review alternatives, make generalizations? Teachers in almost every curricular area can find opportunities to teach for thinking.

PROCESS AND PRODUCT

The teacher who would teach with an emphasis on thinking may need to be aware of the differences between process and product in relation to education. In short, the process is the experience (plus the efforts) that a student goes through *as* he learns. The product is the end result or the "answer." The process is an on-going, uneven psychological kind of activity about which too little is known because it functions in the mind of the student. The product, on the other hand, is definite, tangible, and relatively easy to identify. As a generalization, educators are too concerned with the product of learning and not enough concerned with the process. There are a number of reasons for this situation. The product, since it is tangible, can be seen and dealt with. The product may be a score on a test, a bulletin board, a report, a speech, or an answer to a question. It is usually the result of an assignment given by the teacher. The assumption is often made that when a student can answer a question correctly, he has learned what it is that has been taught. Frequently, this assumption is valid. However, there are times when the assumption is not valid.

A child may do a page of arithmetic and answer the examples correctly yet he may not understand the process involved. Perhaps he has learned a "trick." Perhaps each example is so similar that he is mechanically following some kind of routine. Perhaps a child has been "lucky" in guessing the right answers. Perhaps he has even copied the answers from someone else. Teachers cannot tell whether the child really understands the process on the basis of his answers alone. This requires deeper probing into his understanding and ability to apply the processes involved. Sometimes this is done by asking him to apply the process to a new situation. Sometimes the assignment is varied. Sometimes questions are asked about what he is doing. He may be asked to describe his processes.

In a sense, process and product are similar to means and ends. Sometimes the concern with ends is so paramount that little is cared about the means by which the ends are achieved. "The end justifies the means." Frequently, efforts to evaluate overlook the means or the process. Sometimes evaluation techniques are misapplied so that what is being measured is what is easily measured rather than what we really want to know.

When swimming is taught, the evaluation should be given while the student is in the swimming pool so that the teacher can observe how the student swims. What does it matter how well he can write a paper on swimming if he cannot actually coordinate his breathing and arm and leg motions in the water? However, if the teacher wants to know what a student knows *about* swimming, then a paper and pencil test may be appropriate.

When driving is taught, the evaluation should be of the student's driving. A paper and pencil test cannot reveal what the driver's reflexes will be in an actual situation. A paper and pencil test may be appropriate to find out what the driver knows about the rules of the road, safety, and laws.

When schools depend too greatly on inappropriate techniques of evaluation, peculiar and embarrassing things may happen. From time to time a scandal involving doctoral students occurs in some institutions of higher learning. Occasionally doctoral students will hire someone to write their dissertations for them. Sometimes they "get away with it." A possible reason for this condition is that not enough attention is paid to the candidate as he prepares his dissertation, in other words, while the *process* is going on. Many who have been doctoral candidates in well-run universities find it almost inconceivable that a stranger could successfully write a dissertation for a doctoral candidate. There is usually a committee of faculty advisors who work so closely with the candidate that no one else could possibly have written the dissertation. The doctoral committee pays enough attention to the preparation of the dissertation (process) so that the dissertation itself (product) is a natural outgrowth.

From time to time in our colleges and universities cribbing or cheating scandals break out. Frequently, so much emphasis is placed on test results as a measure of learning that when answers become available some students are sorely tempted to cheat. What seems to matter most is not what the students have learned but what they score on the test. But *these are not necessarily the same thing.*

Evaluation techniques ought to measure what it is we want to know rather than what it is convenient to know. Often what we want to know the most cannot be measured. Paper and pencil tests do not measure desire or motivation to learn, nor do they predict to a high enough degree a person's future success in learning. College admission officers frequently complain about the low correlation between test scores and success in college. Frequently students are concerned almost solely with their marks or grades. For these students learning takes a back seat. They seek courses which are "easy" and teachers who are "high markers." There is a confusion of means and ends. High school guidance counselors and college advisors often deplore this condition. Some high schools are dealing with the problem by weighting their courses so that a difficult course counts more than an easy course. A grade of C in an honors course may be worth a B or even an A in another course. Other institutions of learning are even beginning to give up grades as a form of evaluation. *Time Magazine* states that high schools

> . . . are under pressure to eliminate grades as marks. New York's influential and reform-minded Public Education Association argues that in some cases marks spur bright, college-bound students to take easy courses just to inflate their academic record. Colleges are also getting leery of grades-are-everything competition. The first major school to act is California Institute of Technology which eliminated freshman grades . . . at the end of the freshman year. Students will simply pass or fail. With grades 'unattainable', Faculty Chairman Ernest H. Swift hopes that freshmen will find it easier to concentrate on the content of their courses. This, in

turn, may enable them to make more sensible choices as to the investment of their time and energy.[6]

Carried to too great a degree, emphasis on product alone in the form of marks and test scores may lead to stifling of thinking and creativity in a particular field. C. P. Snow has taken a dim view of the effects of the old Mathematical Tripos on the field of mathematics in England. The Tripos was an examination given in English colleges such as Cambridge.

> The competition for the top places had got fiercer and careers hung on them . . . A whole apparatus of coaching had grown up. Men of the quality of Hardy, Littlewood, Russel, . . . Keynes, went in for two or three years' training for an examination which was intensely difficult . . .
>
> In every respect but one, in fact, the old Mathematical Tripos seemed perfect. The one exception, however, appeared to some to be rather important. It was simply — so the young creative mathematicians, such as Hardy and Littlewood, kept saying — that the training had no intellectual merit at all. They went a little further, and said that the Tripos had killed serious mathematics in England stone dead for a hundred years.[7]

Given the conditions in American education as they exist today, class sizes becoming larger and acute shortages of teachers in some areas, the temptation is to deal mainly with the product of education particularly in the form of easily administered machine-scored tests. When teaching for thinking, it is necessary to pay close attention to the processes involved along with the product. The product, although certainly important and often a worthy objective, is not the sole basis of concern. As teachers teach for thinking, as they emphasize process, as well as product, as they focus on individual children, education in their classrooms tends to become custom-made rather than a result of mass production.

THE CLASSROOM AND THINKING

The teacher himself and the way he runs his classroom are at the core of teaching for thinking. The classroom atmosphere must reflect profound respect for individuals as unique human beings. As the teacher respects the students, he encourages them to respect each other as well as himself. This does not mean that there are no limits to behavior in the classroom. Surely there must be limits that are clearly and fairly established. The limits reflect the purpose of the activity. As the purposes vary, the activities may vary, and the behavior of students may vary with the activities. When teachers and students agree on purpose, then purpose can control behavior. Students can be asked the

---

[6] "New Views on Grades" *Time,* December 25, 1964, p. 30.
[7] C. P. Snow, *The Two Cultures and the Scientific Revolution* (New York: Cambridge University Press), pp. 21-22.

relationship between *their* behavior and *their* purpose. Within the limits there is basic respect for children. James Raths has written of the dignity of children in the classroom. He observes that ". . . all men are worthy of respect and dignity . . . many children suffer indignities at the hands of teachers . . . What are some of the ways today's teachers treat children that essentially contradict our deep-rooted beliefs in the dignity of man?"

James Raths answers his questions as follows:

First, some teachers have difficulty refraining from making judgment about children's expressed ideas and overt behaviors. Almost every act or word is judged audibly by teachers as "good or bad," "right or wrong," "plus or minus." . . . When teachers judge children in an excessive manner, using primarily their own personal and private feelings and convictions as a basis for criticism, they tend to communicate to their students a disrespect for a basic element of human dignity — the right to hold differing ideas and to behave in unique ways . . .

A second tendency on the part of the teachers constituting a threat to the human dignity of students is one of attributing to students . . . that children don't care, that they are dull, that they won't amount to anything . . .

A third way that teachers may show a basic disrespect for the worth of their students is by drastically limiting the alternatives from which children may make choices . . . By limiting the choices of children, teachers tend to deprive them of self-direction — a major factor that makes up their humanness.[8]

The teacher who respects students is willing to listen to students. Listening is a time-consuming activity, but it is one of the ways that a teacher can get at the processes of thinking. Classroom procedures have to be planned in a way that will give students opportunities to be heard. Along with respect for students is an underlying faith in operations of intelligence as a reservoir within people. If students are looked upon as ignorant fools who are in school solely to sop up the "pearls of wisdom" that come from the text, it is doubtful that much thinking will result.

Teachers who insist that students conform at all times are showing a lack of respect for them and their intelligence. When students are comparing, it is conceivable that no two of them will work in exactly the same way. There may be as many different comparisons as there are students in the classroom. Which one is "right"? Which one is "best"? The answer depends upon the purpose of the activity. Why were the students asked to compare? Was it to produce the most brilliant comparison? Or the most clever? Or the funniest? Or the most trivial? Or, was it to provide *each* student with an opportunity to compare—to participate in a thinking act? When thinking is involved, there is an openness, not a finality. There are possibilities for the "new" and the "unique" which may not always be anticipated. Each student's contribution is a precious thing, for it represents an effort to think. If

---

[8]Reprinted by permission of the Association for Childhood Education International, 3615 Wisconsin Avenue, N.W. Washington, D. C. "The Dignity of Man in the Classroom" by James Raths. From *Childhood Education,* March 1964, Vol. 40, No. 7.

each student were to compare in the same way, or if the teacher were to have a list of expected outcomes, then the processes of thinking would be sacrificed for some kind of a guessing game with the correct answer as the goal.

Respect for students and their efforts at thinking are enhanced by discussion. Pupils need opportunities to discuss with the teacher and with each other *their* thinking, *their* viewpoints, and *their* attempts at analysis. Pupil-teacher planning may encourage discussion and give students opportunities to make decisions, to examine alternatives, and to act in accord with their decisions.

Traditionally, teachers have used the expository mode of teaching. This involves explaining, telling how, and showing. Teaching in this mode is an active process engaged in by the teacher. The student listens passively for what is presented in the class. Frequently, there are a series of assignments and periodic testing of the student's knowledge of what has been presented. The expository mode of teaching is a very useful way of presenting ideas and information. As a matter of fact, this book is written in the expository mode. John Dewey, himself, although critical of the expository mode, used it in the form of lectures and books to present his viewpoint. Yet, teaching for thinking means that the students *actively do* thinking. The objective is not primarily for the students to learn *about* thinking but for the students to be given opportunities *for* thinking.

Where opportunities for thinking are provided, where there is acceptance and discussion of the thinking of students, where students are supported and liked, they are encouraged to think. There is an absence of authoritarianism on the part of the teacher. Students are not told, "Compare because I say compare," but rather something like, "Can you see any similarities or differences between these two objects?" As the student embarks on comparing, the teacher does not say, "And then what?" or, "What else?" or, "This is not enough, give me more." Rather, the teacher may prod ever so gently in the form of, "Can you see anything else?" or, "Is there another way you might look at this?" If the student says, "No. This is all I can do," the teacher may say something like, "Thank you very much," and accept the efforts of the student. This is particularly important when first getting started with thinking activities. Learning, and particularly learning which emphasizes thinking, is a fragile thing. It is influenced by emotions, pressures, the health of the student, the dynamics of the class, varying experiences, varying degrees of self-confidence, teachers' attitudes, and countless other factors. Teachers, aware of the many variables, yet wanting to foster thinking, function as catalyst, control, leader, friend, guide, and authority.

It is frequently threatening to a student to question basic knowledge or understandings that may have been with him for a number of years. The teacher helps a student probe but is very gentle about it. When a student becomes threatened or upset in relation to thinking, it is advisable to back off and stop the activity. There is time to return to thinking activities at a later date. As T. S. Eliot observed, ". . . there will be time . . ."

> Time for you and time for me,
> And time yet for a hundred indecisions,
> And for a hundred visions and revisions,
> Before the taking of a toast and tea . . .
>
> Do I dare
> Disturb the universe?
> In a minute there is time . . .[9]

Students need time to think, time to assimilate, and even time to change their patterns of behavior.

When thinking is going on, errors occur. When one thinks, one makes leaps, one makes guesses, one tries ideas to see if they will work. In a sense, one is experimenting. Thinking does not always proceed in an orderly way, step by step. When students make errors in their thinking, teachers can use these as opportunities for learning. When the processes of thinking are prized, students' chances of learning from their errors are enhanced. If students get the idea that correct answers are prized, they may answer only if they *know* they are "right." An incident involving errors and over-cautiousness occurred during World War II. American Secretary of State, Cordell Hull, ". . . was extremely jealous of his reputation as one officer of the Administration who had been guilty of no conspicuous blunders and who had been spared the criticism lavished on all the others, including the President himself. However, in times of desperate emergency when drastic action had to be taken quickly, Roosevelt was bound to become impatient with anyone whose primary concern was the maintenance of a personal record of 'no runs—no hits —no errors'."[10] If one is to accomplish something, one must be prepared to make errors. How many attempts did Edison make before he perfected a filament for the electric light bulb? Students are not encouraged to make errors, but alert teachers use errors, when they occur, as opportunities for teaching for thinking.

If we *are* to think, we must *dare* to think. Daring implies confidence in ourselves and in our abilities. When we have confidence, we often succeed in doing tasks far beyond our expectations. When confidence is missing, we frequently fail in tasks that seem well within our grasp. Even ability and talent require confidence. Those who follow the sports pages in newspapers find many examples involving professional athletes. Each season there are

---

[9]T. S. Eliot, "The Love Song of J. Alfred Prufrock," *Collected Poems 1909-62* (New York: Harcourt, Brace & World, Inc., 1963), p. 4.
[10]Robert E. Sherwood, *Roosevelt and Hopkins* (New York: Harper & Row, Publishers, 1948), p. 135.

stories about great hitters in baseball who earn as much as $100,000 a year. At one time or another, these hitters may come to bat twenty-five or thirty times in a row without getting a base hit. When asked what is wrong they may answer, "Nothing. All I need is a couple of base hits and I'll get my confidence back." Great pitchers in baseball might go for a series of games without pitching well enough to win. Frequently, the pitcher says, "One or two good games and I'll regain my confidence." During the football season, a huge 250 pound lineman may say that he approaches each game with apprehension or even fright. As soon as he makes his first tackle or block, he regains his confidence and is able to play well. If professional football players and highly paid baseball players are concerned about *their* confidence, surely confidence plays a part in the performance of a *child* in school. Gaining confidence is associated with success experiences. It would seem important for teachers to provide opportunities for their students to succeed. Students need to experience success each day in school so that they can gain in their confidence. As confidence grows, ability often improves. Students become more secure. Tasks should be assigned at the student's level of ability. If the student shows growth or improvement, teachers compliment him. Compliments should be genuine in that they reflect real progress; otherwise the student might tend to look upon them as a joke.

If a student is working on a particular process and the teacher feels he can do better work, the teacher might say something like, "This is a good beginning, Sam. I wonder if there is anything else you can add?" Or, "Sam, you did a fine job on your assignment last week. I get the idea that perhaps this piece of work you just gave me does not reflect your real ability. How do you feel about it?"

Sometimes, when teaching for thinking, a teacher may be carried away by his own enthusiasm. He may try to teach for thinking all day, or arrange a special "thinking period," e.g., Monday, Wednesday, and Friday—9:15 to 9:45 a.m. In his enthusiasm, a teacher may lose sight of the research that says that the best results are obtained when thinking is emphasized in connection with the subject matter under study. At times, a teacher may be so intent on getting students to think that he becomes an interrogator and a heckler and may unintentionally bully his students. Sometimes, a teacher may put students "on the spot," belittle them, and chastise them for "poor" thinking. Even though the intentions are good and the "right words" are used, a tone of voice may degrade students, threaten them, and put them on the defensive. The words themselves may not be as important as the tone in which they are said. Unless care is exercised, instead of teaching *for* thinking, thinking may actually be stifled.

As thinking is encouraged in the classroom, teachers may be amazed at the high quality of students' work. Occasionally, a student from whom not much is expected, comes up with a brilliant idea or shows real insight into a situation. At such times teachers may well experience renewed feelings of humility and perhaps say, "I never thought of that" or, "I'm glad you brought this up." As students become aware of clarity of expression, they may catch the teacher using a word such as *all* when he meant *most*. At such times it is probably a good idea to acknowledge the use of *all* and change it to *most* if the clarity of the idea is enhanced. Sometimes students may catch the teacher in an out-and-out mistake. If the teacher has a relationship with his students which includes mutual respect, he can say, "I made a mistake" without fear of belittling himself in the eyes of his students. By the same token it is possible, no matter how great a teacher's competency in a particular area, for a student to ask a question which the teacher is unable to answer. In such a case, an honest reply might be, "I don't know." As teachers prize thinking processes, as they become familiar with the materials and procedures of thinking, as they are thoughtful, patient, supportive, and careful, as they provide many and varied opportunities for thinking, classrooms become thoughtful places.

As we teach for thinking, some of us are eager for constructive supervision which will help to improve our teaching. Sometimes no help is available. We are left to help ourselves. One way in which we can observe ourselves as teachers is to make tape recordings of our classes. If we let a period of time pass after the tape is made, we can then listen to it more or less objectively and analyze our efforts to teach for thinking. Perhaps we can arrange with a colleague to visit in each other's class to determine to what extent thinking is being promoted. The following questions are suggested for both methods of analysis:

1. Is there purpose for the activities?
2. Are thinking-related activities going on?
3. Who is doing the thinking activities, the students or the teacher?
4. Who is asking the questions?
5. Is the teacher encouraging his students or is he being too critical? Are students being put "on the spot"?
6. What is the teacher's tone of voice? Regardless of the words used, does the voice reflect encouragement, reassurance, security?
7. Is the teacher being too domineering?
8. Is there enough time allowed for students to engage in thinking activities?
9. What is the significance of each activity?
10. Does the teacher censure or use words of praise?
11. Is the teacher "angling" for the "right answer"?

As we gain experience in teaching for thinking, we can add more questions to the list.

SELECTING ACTIVITIES

A number of thinking-related activities which can be used in the classroom have been suggested in Parts Two and Three of this book. The activities are not presented as a prescription or a "cookbook," but rather as examples of what teachers have done to encourage thinking. Probably among the most appropriate materials used in the classroom are those developed by the teacher himself, since the teacher is the final authority as to what is appropriate for his classroom. It is suggested, however, that as the teacher plans for teaching for thinking, he bear in mind some overall criteria. It is left for the teacher to determine which criteria are appropriate when planning particular activities.

CRITERIA FOR DEVELOPING THINKING-RELATED ACTIVITIES:

1. Related to Purpose
   Is there a purpose for the activity?
   What purpose guides the selection of the activity?
2. Related to Operations of Thinking
   Is the activity significant in relation to thinking?
   Does the activity have intrinsic value?
   Is the activity intended to lead to other operations of thinking?
   Will the activity help students improve their abilities to discriminate, *i.e.*, fact and fancy, fact and opinion?
   Does the activity represent a wide sampling or variety of experience?
   Does the activity give the student the opportunity to interpret?
   Are ample data available, *i.e.*, reference books, measuring devices, resources, others?
   Are there data that students can see, hear, smell, taste, or touch, *i.e.*, living things, plants, soil, animals, clay, others?
   Do students have opportunities to measure things such as weight, diet, length, height, time, force, pressure, and others?
3. Related to Students
   Does the activity lead to choice or preferences on the part of the students?
   Does the activity lead to insights such as, "I never noticed this before"?
   Does the activity provoke curiosity on the part of students?
   Is the activity interesting for the students?
   Is the activity being repeated too often? Are the students bored by it?

Is the activity too tedious?

Is the activity appropriate for the student who is doing it? Too easy? Too difficult?

Will the activity lead to sharing on the part of students?

Are students' reactions to activities used to suggest future activities?

Do students have opportunities to raise questions?

Can they say, "I'd like to find out if . . ."?

Are provisions made in case students make errors?

Are students prepared to face errors?

If errors occur, can students evaluate and analyze them? Are records of students' participation being kept?

4. Related to Curriculum

Is the activity appropriate for the subject matter under study?

Does the activity have significance in relation to the subject matter under study?

Is the problem area too broad or too difficult to study?

If so, can it be broken down into smaller questions?

Will the activity lead to future activities?

Is the thinking operation being done too infrequently?

Are opportunities to teach for thinking being lost?

Are provisions made for sharing activities?

Are careful records being kept of the activities?

THINKING ACTIVITIES

As teachers plan thinking-related activities, in the light of some of the above questions, they may recognize many opportunities for incorporating these in their own classrooms and in connection with the curriculum that they are teaching.

Comparing.

Comparing activities may vary in sophistication depending upon the maturity and ability of the student who is doing the comparing. In kindergarten, it may involve greater than or less than, lighter or heavier, more or less. In high school, it may involve two plays, two novels, two political theories.

Comparing is closely related to the student's ability to observe differences which are critical and to generalize when he recognizes similarities. As students gain experience with comparing, their skill becomes more highly developed.

At first, comparing can be approached as a kind of game in which easily compared things are involved. As skill develops, students may apply comparing to more and more challenging things. Teachers can be alert for opportunities to use comparing as an aid in the subject matter being taught.

Teaching Guidelines:

Aids:
(Ways that may enhance thinking)

1. The student does the comparing.
2. The teacher accepts the student's comparison as his contribution.
3. Opportunities are provided for students to discuss each other's comparisons.
4. Student's compare significant things in relation to the curriculum.
5. Students compare a wide variety of things in various subject matter areas.
6. Many different schemes of comparing are expected and accepted.
7. Students are asked if they care to add to their lists.
8. The teacher reacts to comparisons.

Obstacles:
(Ways that may stifle thinking)

1. The teacher does the comparing.
2. The teacher rejects the comparison.
3. Each student keeps his comparison to himself.
4. Comparing is confined to trivial matters.
5. Comparing is limited to one or two areas of inquiry.
6. Only one way of comparing is acceptable.
7. The teacher heckles and demands, "What else? What else? What else?"
8. The teacher does not read comparisons.

As activities are conducted in the classroom, a number of questions may arise in connection with teaching and students. How these questions are dealt with may further enhance or stifle the processes of thinking.

Questions to Consider:

1. Is bias expressed by the students in their comparing?
2. Are *all-or-none* statements used?
3. Is fancy or imagination introduced into the comparing?
4. Are value judgments expressed in the comparing, e.g., which item is better?
5. Do any words need defining?
6. Can the similarities and differences be classified?
7. Is a summary made of the comparisons?
8. Are any problems raised by the discussion of comparisons?

9. Are any conflicts or disagreements raised during the sharing of the comparisons? How are these resolved?
10. Does anyone question whether there is a basis for comparing?
11. Are aesthetic qualities mentioned?
12. Do the students draw any conclusions from their comparisons?
13. Do students criticize or evaluate comparisons?

Summarizing.

The ability to summarize is closely related to the ability to generalize or abstract. It has to do with being able to recognize significant ideas, characteristics, or concepts, and differentiating them from less significant or trivial ones.

In the elementary school opportunities to summarize occur at such times as the end of the morning or at the end of the day. At these times the youngsters can look back at, "what we did today." Sometimes the whole class may summarize in the form of a discussion. Sometimes individual children may summarize orally or in writing. In the secondary school, summaries are useful at the end of a unit, when preparing for an examination, or reviewing information, occurrences, and ideas.

The showing of a film is an example of an opportunity for summarizing. When a film is planned, the teacher might appoint two or three committees ahead of time and say to them, "You are going to be asked to summarize the film. When it is over suppose you meet and list the points you want to make." Each committee could then report to the class, which might then compare the summaries.

During discussions it might be possible to have a secretary at the blackboard. As each new topic is discussed and as each point is made, the secretary could record it on the board. When a summary of the discussion is made, it might be around the points that have been listed.

Sometimes the entire class may be asked to make an outline of a common experience as a preparation for a summary. From the outlines an oral summary can be made. At other times, the class, working as a whole, may make an outline on the board.

A caution about summarizing is raised by some teachers working closely in such areas as "new math" and "new science." They maintain that a summary done at the end of a class or before new material is learned may tend to resolve the material under study and thus inhibit students' reflection and inquiry. They would rather leave questions unanswered.

Nevertheless, summarizing *is* an important operation of thinking, and the classroom teacher, if he wishes, can find appropriate places to introduce summarizing into the curriculum.

Teaching Guidelines:

Aids:	Obstacles:
(Ways that may enhance thinking)	(Ways that may stifle thinking)
1. The student does the summarizing.	1. The teacher does the summarizing for his students.
2. Students are encouraged to summarize in many ways.	2. Only one way of summarizing is considered "correct."
3. The student's summary is accepted as his contribution at this time.	3. The student's work is rejected as "not good enough."
4. Students have opportunities to discuss each other's summaries.	4. The summaries are confined to the teacher's eyes alone.
5. Students are asked if they care to change any part of their summaries.	5. The student is told he is "wrong" and made to feel "stupid."
6. Students are asked to summarize significant things in relation to their lives and their studies.	6. Summaries are confined to minutia.
7. Students summarize in many different subject matter areas.	7. Summaries are limited to one subject area, such as English.
8. The teacher helps the student see what is relevant in his summary. Sometimes students can rank their points in order of importance.	8. Students are encouraged to be too parsimonious with their summaries.
9. The teacher reacts to the student's summary.	9. The teacher does not read the summary.

Questions to Consider:

1. Do some students bring in matters that are truly extraneous? How can this be handled?
2. Do some students indicate that there is only one way to summarize? Chronological sequence, for example?
3. Some students associate each point they summarize with the person who made the point. Does this procedure—where it occurs—contribute to the smoothness of the summary?
4. What about omissions of significant points? If they do not emerge, how can teachers stimulate the group toward further reflection? Can students be asked why certain points were omitted?
5. When relatively trivial points are mentioned again and again, how do other students react? How can a situation like this be handled?

6. Does the summarizing experience suggest that it is beyond or below the maturity level of the students?
7. Does "memory" sometimes play the students false? Is there some way of helping students see the fallibility of our senses, and possible or probable errors in our memories? Should notes be taken in preparation for summaries?
8. If two or more summaries are made of the same experience, in what respects are they alike? Different?
9. Is aesthetic content emphasized or neglected?
10. Is the summary much too brief?

Observing.

Behind the idea of observing is the point of view that the accumulation of information which may lead to knowledge comes primarily from what we see, hear, smell, taste, or touch. Schools can offer a rich environment of things to observe such as animals, plants, water, people, clothing, games, events. As students have experiences in observing, they may gain accuracy in observing and recording their findings.

Teaching Guidelines:

Aids:
(Ways that may enhance thinking)

Obstacles:
(Ways that may stifle thinking)

1. The student does the observing.

1. The teacher does the observing for the students.

2. The student observes for some purpose.

2. Students observe just to "keep them busy."

3. Students have opportunities to discuss and compare observations.

3. Students see only their own observations.

4. Appropriate measuring devices are available when needed.

4. Students are restricted to guesswork.

5. Students observe a wide variety of things in many subject matter areas.

5. Observations are confined to one subject area, such as science.

6. Students are asked if they want to add anything to their observation.

6. The teacher demands, "What else did you see? . . . What else? . . . What else?"

7. The student's observation is accepted by the teacher.

7. The observation is rejected by the teacher.

8. Students are encouraged to use a variety of their senses.

8. Only the eyes are used.

9. The teacher helps the student see the difference between what is observed and what is "read into" the observation.

9. Students' observations are unexamined.

Questions to Consider:

1. How shall students be trained, or prepared for an exercise which involves "observing"? What should be noticed?
2. How do observations differ? Any probable reasons for these differences?
3. What about attentiveness? The particular spot where we are standing? Possible obstructions? Hearing difficulties? Noise? Distractions?
4. Do some students read their own ideas or values into their observations? Can these be written on the board and comments invited?
5. What about the scope of the comments: Wide—narrow? Focused—restricted? How many different sense impressions are included?
6. Are matters pertaining to beauty, form, function, mood, color, space relationships mentioned?
7. What assumptions are made?
8. Are there any blind spots? Why?
9. How can observations be discussed so that students gain additional insight into the operation?

Classifying.

Classifying is a way of organizing data or information for some purpose. There are literally dozens of examples of classification in everyday life. The dictionary is an example of classifying words according to alphabetical order. Sometimes words are classified by parts of speech. A rhyming dictionary has words classified according to their endings. Sometimes words are classified according to their usage, such as in a thesaurus. The carrying out of a classifying activity might involve placing a list of names of prominent people from American history on the board. The question might be raised, "How can these be grouped?" Perhaps the replies might include: according to their political persuasion, by occupation, or according to the period in which they lived. A teacher might place a list of forty cities on the board and ask, "How should these be grouped?" There might be suggestions from the class to group them by size, country, whether or not they are capitals, etc. Students might have to consult almanacs, atlases, and other sources of data to aid them in their classifying. The alert teacher will find many opportunities for students to classify in relation to what is being learned.

Teaching Guidelines:

Aids:
(Ways that may enhance thinking)

1. The student does the classifying.

2. Students classify for some purpose.

3. Many different schemes for classifying are accepted and prized.

4. Students are encouraged to find many categories for their classifying.

5. Students have opportunities to discuss their classifications.

6. Students classify many different kinds of things in many subject areas.

7. Truly unique classifications are applauded by the teacher.

Obstacles:
(Ways that may stifle thinking)

1. The teacher does the classifying for the students.

2. Classifying is confined to inconsequential matters.

3. One and only one way of classifying is allowed.

4. The miscellaneous category contains most of the things being classified.

5. Only the teacher sees students' work.

6. Classifying is limited to one or two subject areas, such as social studies and science.

7. Unique classifications are belittled.

Questions to Consider:

1. Are the pupils greatly dependent upon the teacher for headings or categories?
2. Are the purposes for the classification clear?
3. Can teachers ask different students *why* they put certain things together (basis for their categories)?
4. If different systems of classifying emerge, do pupils think that *one* only can be correct?
5. What is done with the things "left over" which cannot be classified within the system being used?
6. How are inconsistencies between things which were placed in the same category treated?
7. Do some pupils like the activity? See it as a game? See it as a way of organizing their work? Their time?
8. Are any students doing this on their own when it is not an assignment?
9. Do the students' categories invite further thinking? Is everything excessively pigeonholed?
10. How are inconsistencies treated in headings? What if a student classified books into fiction, nonfiction, and animal stories?
11. What is the relationship of purposes to classifying?
12. What conclusions can be drawn from the classification?

Interpreting.

Learning is the discovery of meaning. There are many kinds of meaning. There is scientific meaning, social meaning, artistic meaning, mathematical meaning, philosophical meaning, and others. When we interpret, we recognize meaning. Sometimes the meaning is of a highly disciplined and regulated nature as in the natural sciences. In these cases interpretations follow guidelines for acceptable evidence that are widely agreed upon. When clear patterns of occurrences are established, a certain amount of interpolation and extrapolation are accepted provided they do not go too far. Even so, results of interpolation and extrapolation are seen in degrees of probability rather than unmodified "truth" or "falsehood." In the arts, interpretations are sometimes made on a symbolic level where the reviewer is free to "read into" and attribute meaning far beyond what would be permissible in one of the sciences. Students need varied experiences in interpretation. Maps, charts, graphs, and tables lend themselves to interpretation as do works of art, sculpture, dance, literature, poetry, and scientific investigations.

Students need opportunities to examine the basis of their interpretations and to compare their interpretations with others. Sometimes teachers give students opportunities to interpret scientific evidence and compare their work to the interpretation of a scientist. A student might be asked to interpret a play or a novel and then read an essay on the play or novel so that he can compare the interpretations. When a student states a point or fact, the teacher might ask, "How sure are you that this is so?" Students might be encouraged to use words which express their degree of certainty such as, *probably, likely, perhaps,* where they are appropriate.

Teaching Guidelines:

Aids:
(Ways that may enhance thinking)

1. Students do the interpreting.

2. Students interpret in a wide variety of subject matter areas.

3. Students are encouraged to use precise language to indicate their degree of "sureness."

4. Students are encouraged to see the difference between reporting and interpreting.

5. Students discuss and compare interpretations.

Obstacles:
(Ways that may stifle thinking)

1. The teacher does the interpreting for the students.

2. Interpretations are limited to charts, graphs, and maps.

3. Words such as *true* and *false* go unnoticed when *probably true* and *probably false* are more appropriate.

4. Reporting is misunderstood as interpreting.

5. Students are limited to one interpretation.

6. Students interpret significant things from their lives and studies.	6. Interpretations are limited to trivia.

Questions to Consider:

1. Do the students go away from the data saying things that have almost nothing to do with the given evidence?
2. Do the students make statements which attribute *cause* in their interpretations? Do they make analogies?
3. Do they ascribe more truth to their inferences than the data warrant?
4. Do they tend to rely on authorities who may not be experts in the area?
5. Do they impute motive, or attribute purpose to the evidence, or to those who gathered the evidence?
6. Can teachers ask students to bring materials to class for interpretation? What do students bring ?
7. What kinds of data are students very much interested in? Indifferent to?
8. Can the students be questioned about certain assumptions they may be making as they go beyond the available evidence?
9. Should certain terms be defined?

Criticizing.

In criticism, there is judgment. There is some kind of standard to compare with that which one is criticizing. Perhaps the standard is a value: good or bad. Perhaps the standard has something to do with whether or not something works or is useful. Perhaps the standard has something to do with whether or not an activity is fun. Perhaps the standard has something to do with how successful a writer or speaker is in communicating ideas. Regardless of the standard, there are criteria established as bases for making judgments.

Students often enjoy giving their opinions of things. Very young children, as they first begin to read, can compile lists of books. One might be, "Books I Like." In this case the standard may be, "What I Like." The teacher can help the child see what it is he likes. Perhaps it is dinosaurs, horses, or other animals. The child begins to establish some kind of a standard for criticizing, even at this early level.

As students establish standards for criticizing, they become aware that they are not necessarily finding fault but rather indicating what is good about something, what is bad, and what can be improved. Opportunities to criticize occur in relation to many activities in school. There are editorials, letters, and news articles in newspapers, plays, assembly programs, books, and many other sources. When students are given opportunities for criticizing, the chances are good that they will assume a more active role in relation to their learning.

Teaching Guidelines:

Aids:
(Ways that may enhance thinking)

1. The student is permitted to do the criticizing.
2. Students have a wide variety of opportunities to criticize books, plays, magazines, letters, editorials, newspaper stories — in many subject matter areas.
3. Meaningful and important things are criticized.

4. The establishment of standards is encouraged, identified, and stated.
5. Criticism is constructive in that it contains suggestions for improvement.
6. Students have opportunities to discuss their criticisms.

Obstacles:
(Ways that may stifle thinking)

1. The teacher does most of the criticizing.
2. Criticism is limited to very select areas, such as English literature.

3. Criticism is confined to prepared exercises having little or no relationship to the student.
4. Criticism is random and without a basis.

5. Criticism is mainly finding fault.

6. Few opportunities are provided for discussing criticisms.

Questions to Consider:

1. Are the comments overly negative or even cynical? Overly positive?
2. Are some of the comments of the heckling, niggling kind? Are some too skeptical?
3. Do the students seem to be looking only for what was wrong? Is there any personal animosity?
4. Do students sometimes say, "It's good" when they mean "I like it"? What can be done to clarify these expressions?
5. Are criteria developed as a basis for evaluating? Can students apply these to critical appraisal of their own work?
6. Are the comments narrowly restricted?
7. Do the students examine the *purposes* underlying the critical appraisal? *Why* are they asked to criticize?
8. Can the teacher write on the board some of the value terms which are expressed by students? Can he ask for underlying assumptions?
9. In what ways may the criticisms be used to improve what is being appraised?
10. Who will criticize the critics?

Looking for Assumptions.

Assumptions in and of themselves are neither good nor bad, but they often are very important. We make assumptions daily, and we live according to them. Usually our assumptions are tacit. Often teachers require children to make tacit assumptions. Arithmetic is one of the curricular areas where this occurs. "If two cans of dog food sell for 30¢ how much will one can of dog food cost?" Answer: 15¢. Here the pupil makes a number of tacit assumptions: 1) Both cans cost equal amounts of money. 2) Both cans are the same size. 3) There is not a 1¢ sale going on. 4) The store is willing to sell one can at a time. When "word problems" in arithmetic are studied, the student is usually able to make tacit assumptions and find the correct answer. But are opportunities to look for and examine assumptions being missed? After the student finds the "correct answer," can the teacher then say, "If your answer is 15¢, what else has to be true?" By examining assumptions, students are given opportunities to gain skill in recognizing assumptions.

Teaching Guidelines:

Aids:
(Ways that may enhance thinking)
1. Students look for assumptions.

2. The attempts of students to find assumptions are accepted by the teacher.
3. Students discuss assumptions they have found.
4. Students look for assumptions in various subject matter areas.

Obstacles:
(Ways that may stifle thinking)
1. Tacit assumptions pass by unexamined.

2. Students are derided and made to feel "stupid" for not identifying assumptions.
3. Discussion of assumptions is denied.
4. Assumptions are only examined in one field, such as arithmetic.

Questions to Consider:

1. Can teachers ask students to write down some general statement which they will read aloud later? The students may discuss some assumptions underlying the statement.
2. Can teachers ask students to judge the reasonableness of any assumption that has been identified? Ask them to give support to their judgments?
3. Can teachers ask students if a particular assumption is absolutely necessary? Or can one accept the generalization as true without accepting the assumption? Is it *necessary?*
4. If it *is* necessary, is it sufficient? Or do two, three, or more assumptions have to be accepted before the generalization can truly be accepted?

5. Do certain key words need defining?
6. What about the place of facts in accepting a particular generalization?
7. How do facts differ from assumptions?

Imagining.

Imagining is pretending, letting the mind leap beyond the here and now. To imagine what it is like to live on Mars, to imagine what the world looks like through the eyes of a worm, to imagine what it would be like to be a serf — these activities do not need great quantities of data in support of ideas.

Once a fifth-grade teacher asked her class to imagine what it would be like to sail around the world in the sixteenth century. The children were to write a journal of their travels. One girl wrote that she would sail across the Atlantic Ocean and through the Panama Canal. The teacher questioned the girl as to whether the Panama Canal existed in the sixteenth century. The girl replied that the canal was not completed until the twentieth century. The teacher asked if it would be possible for the girl to sail through the canal in the sixteenth century. The girl replied, "Of course I could. You told us to imagine!"

Teaching Guidelines:

Aids:
(Ways that may enhance thinking)
1. The teacher accepts the student's fancies.
2. Students discuss their imagining activities.
3. Students have access to many examples of fiction, fantasy, and creative forms.
4. Students have opportunities to imagine in many different areas such as creative writing, poetry, art, music, history, literature, *et al.*

Obstacles:
(Ways that may stifle thinking)
1. The teacher rejects the student's fancies.
2. There are no opportunities for students to discuss the activities.
3. There are few examples of imagining in the curriculum.
4. Imagining is limited to fairy tales.

Questions to Consider:

1. How far away from reality is imagination?
2. Should imagining be criticized in the same way as evidence or products are criticized?
3. Should the question of fairy tales, fables, and parables be raised? Do these have any value?

4. When we say "fantastic," or when we use the word "fantasy," what do we mean?

5. How is fantasy sometimes used as an escape from reality, e.g., Walter Mitty?

6. If we are *aware* that we *are* imagining, does this make a difference? Think of someone who is unaware that he is imagining or fantasying. How do we describe his behavior?

7. Do we sometimes suggest to growing children that it is the artists and poets who display imagination? What does this mean for the rest of us?

Collecting and Organizing Data.

An oak tree grew outside of a first-grade classroom. In the morning when the sun was out, the tree cast a shadow on the wall in the classroom. Every week or two the children and the teacher would put a piece of masking tape at the top of the shadow at 11:00 a.m. They put the date on the tape. Each time they marked the shadow they noticed that it was in a different place on the wall. From this experience in collecting and organizing data, the teacher was able to illustrate to the children what happens as the axis of the earth tilts in relation to the sun. The shadow on the wall helped the children see the relationship of the sun to the seasons.

There are many opportunities to collect and organize data in schools. Sometimes the data may be in the form of daily attendance. Sometimes they may be in the form of collecting information from several books. The mother of an eight-year old boy in third grade proudly told the story of her son who was gathering information on the rings of Saturn. The boy went to five books and found three different explanations of the rings of Saturn. One said they were very small moons; one said they were tiny ice particles; a third said they were meteorites. The mother was pleased that her son was dealing with an area where much is unknown even to the greatest scientists.

There are many ways to organize data. Often the organization depends upon the use for which the data are intended. If the data are part of an oral report or speech, it may be necessary to highlight the main parts. If there is ample opportunity to prepare tables or graphs, students might go into great detail in presenting the data. Sometimes when counting individual occurrences, it is convenient to use tally marks. Sometimes it may be necessary to use a stop watch if timing is important. Rulers or yardsticks may be needed. Reference books such as dictionaries, atlases, encyclopedias, card catalogue files, and indices are often sources of data.

Before students embark on collecting data, teachers might ask, "What do we want to find out? How will we find it out? Should we use books, people, movies?" These and other questions might be listed on the board and form the basis of a plan to collect the data. The plan might include the identification of various jobs in connection with collecting data, and answer the questions, "Who will take the responsibility for this job and that job?"

Data are probably best collected for a specific purpose such as a project, report, paper, or other assignment.

Teaching Guidelines:

Aids:
(Ways that may enhance thinking)
1. Students have many opportunities to gather data.
2. Students collect and organize data in a wide variety of areas and subject matter fields.
3. Students have opportunities to discuss the data they have collected and organized.
4. Appropriate measuring devices are available.
5. Students plan their procedures before starting to gather their data.

Obstacles:
(Ways that may stifle thinking)
1. The teacher presents the data to the students.
2. Data gathering is limited to one subject area such as science.
3. Data gathering opportunities are limited to individual experiences of individual children.
4. Appropriate devices are not available.
5. Students leap helter-skelter into data gathering.

Questions to Consider:

1. How will data be collected, *i.e.,* questions, interviews, books, experiments?
2. What purposes are being served by the data to be collected and organized? Why are the students doing this work?
3. How good, or reliable, are the data? Will they be worth the work? Do they help to answer some important questions?
4. What planning has been done about the whole project *before* any data are gathered? Was an outline developed? Are students participating in the total study?
5. Most often relevant evidence can be gathered from more than *one* source. What sources and how many are being used? Are there any that are first-hand, or primary sources? Can the secondary sources be relied upon? How is this known?
6. What plans are being made for organizing the materials? Tables? Charts? Summaries? How will this be done? Do the individual students know for sure that evidence is *available to them* from the suggested sources?
7. How will the data be presented? Orally? Written? Both? A panel? A visual aid?
8. What conclusions can be drawn from these data? Do these data support the conclusions? Are students going "beyond the data" in drawing conclusions? How can this be handled?

Hypothesizing.

An hypothesis is an educated guess or a hunch. It is a possible solution to a perplexing situation. It is a possible explanation of a happening. It is often accompanied with an *if-then* statement. *If* something is done, *then* something will happen. Often two occurrences are linked by an hypothesis in some kind of relationship. *If* we let the ball go, *then* it will fall. *If* we reduce the temperature of water below 32°F., *then* it will freeze. Usually an hypothesis implies a prediction. When a perplexing situation is encountered in a classroom or when the opportunity arises in connection with subject matter under study, it is frequently a good idea for teachers to ask students to list as many possible solutions as they can. The students can then try to predict, "What will happen if we do this?" or "What will happen if we do that?" Then the students can test their hypotheses and go back and ask such questions as, "Did this solution work? Can it be improved? Did it explain?"

Teaching Guidelines:

Aids:
(Ways that may enhance thinking)

1. Students make and test hypotheses.
2. Ample time is provided to examine and judge hypotheses.
3. There is rigorous testing of hypotheses.

4. Students make hypotheses in areas where the teacher is prepared to allow them to act on the basis of their hypotheses.
5. Hypotheses are made regarding areas of perplexity that are significant in the lives and studies of the students.
6. Opportunities for hypothesizing are faced in many curricular areas.

Obstacles:
(Ways that may stifle thinking)

1. The teacher tells the class the solution.
2. Students act without examining hypotheses.
3. Hypotheses are accepted solely on the basis of faith in an authority.
4. Students are not allowed to act on the basis of their hypotheses.

5. Making hypotheses is limited to games and trivia.

6. Hypothesizing is restricted to science problems.

Questions to Consider:

1. Is the question or problem clearly stated so that some hypothesis can be attempted? (A fuzzy, vague statement interferes with success in formulating hypotheses.)

2. Does the hypothesis suggest an explanation for the problem? "If we do this, then the situation will be better."
3. Are there rival hypotheses? Can these be listed on the board? Which ones seem more reasonable and why so?
4. How can a particular hypothesis be tested? Does the suggested plan *really* test the hypothesis? How can we tell?
5. Do some words in the hypothesis need defining?
6. What resources are needed to carry out a test of the hypothesis? Equipment? Materials? People? Time?
7. Are there some school problems which could be looked at in these patterns? Can hypotheses be formulated and then tested?
8. Are there neighborhood or community problems which could be treated like this?
9. What about personal problems? Can they also be approached in terms of hypotheses to be tested?
10. Do students see any differences between assuming and hypothesizing? What is taken for granted? What is tested?

Applying Facts and Principles in New Situations.

Mathematics and science textbooks contain many examples of questions in which students are asked to apply some principle that has been learned to answer the question. The student may be given extraneous information to see if he can disregard it in favor of pertinent information. As students see relationships, understand meaning, apply rules and laws, they gain ability in answering questions correctly. Principles can also be identified, learned, and applied to such areas as social studies, English, mathematics, and any body of knowledge where the information is organized into some kind of structure.

Teaching Guidelines:

Aids:
(Ways that may enhance thinking)
1. Students break down large questions into smaller ones when appropriate.
2. Questions are on a reading level that the student can handle.

3. Students have opportunities to discuss and explain their reasoning.
4. Students use many different methods of answering questions.

Obstacles:
(Ways that may stifle thinking)
1. No attempt is made to analyze questions.

2. Students are expected to understand questions regardless of the students' reading ability.
3. Discussion is denied.

4. Only one method of answering questions is permitted.

5. Answers are tested on the basis of the principles and the questions asked. Answers make sense.	5. No effort is made to understand the answers.
6. Students apply principles in various areas of the curriculum.	6. Principles are not applied or they are limited to one area of the curriculum, such as mathematics.

Questions to Consider:

1. When students are asked to explain the "hows and whys" of their solution to a new problem, do they do so in terms of principles? Or do they say they did it "just like they did the others"?
2. When students offer a "principle" in support of their solution, is it precisely stated?
3. When students give the right explanation but have the wrong solution, how may this be handled?
4. When they have the correct solution and give the "wrong" reasons, how may this be handled?
5. If a correct solution requires more than one principle, and the student gives *only one,* how may this be handled?
6. Where students offer hunches, guesses, intuitions, how do teachers relate this to a knowledge and application of principles?
7. How are principles being selected?

Decision-Making.

Decision-making involves making choices and selecting among alternatives on the basis of laws, principles, generalizations, and rules. Decisions are made in such a way as to protect values. We ask: "What *should* be done? Where will it lead? Is it good or bad?" Students need opportunities to make real choices which involve comparing, observing, imagining, and other operations of thinking. The role of the teacher is to help the students clarify those values which they prize, affirm, repeat often, think about, and allow to penetrate their lives. In a sense, the teacher holds up a verbal mirror to the student and asks, "Is this you? Is this what is important to you? Is this the way you see it?"

Teaching Guidelines:

Aids:	Obstacles:
(Ways that may enhance thinking)	(Ways that may stifle thinking)
1. Opportunities are provided for students to make choices.	1. The teacher makes the choices for the students.

2. When students make decisions the teacher asks such questions as:
   a. Is this something you prize?
   b. Is this good?
   c. Would you do this often?
   d. Have you thought a lot about this?
   e. Are you willing to organize your life so that you can do this?

3. Students have opportunities to discuss their decisions.

2. Little attention is paid to values in connection with students' decisions.

3. There is almost no discussion of students' choices.

Questions to Consider:

1. What *values* do the students assert as reasons for their decisions?
2. Could these be listed and examined? Are any important values left out? Have certain *facts* been disregarded? Are all the values important?
3. Which values should be protected no matter how the problem is to be solved?
4. How can one test whether the desired values will be protected by the proposed solution? Can it be tried out?
5. Who should participate in making decisions? If time is short, should one consult fewer people? How important is this?
6. Are values as important as facts? Is there a difference? How significant is the difference, if any?
7. Do minority groups or groups of low prestige figure in the decision-making process? What happens if they are left out?
8. When students disagree on a decision, can teachers ask them to state the opposing viewpoint?

Designing Projects or Investigations.

Projects involve formulating problems, planning, framing questions, gathering data, analyzing the data, forming conclusions, and reporting. Projects usually require an extended period of time. Sometimes students work together in committees, sometimes the student works alone. The data gathering may involve the use of libraries, experiments, interviews, polls, questionnaires, newspapers, and many other sources. Projects tend to give students opportunities to use many operations of thinking for some purpose. Often, students are most interested in projects where they play a role in the planning and selection of the topic.

Teaching Guidelines:

Aids:	Obstacles:
(Ways that may enhance thinking)	(Ways that may stifle thinking)
1. Students have a voice in determining their topic.	1. Topics are assigned.
2. Students participate in selecting, planning, and designing their project.	2. Students are told what to do each step of the way.
3. Ample time is provided to carry out the project.	3. Time is severely limited.
4. Students have opportunities to discuss their projects.	4. Projects are not discussed.
5. Students have access to libraries, newspapers, and equipment needed to gather data.	5. Students have very limited access to data.

Questions to Consider:

1. Can students choose their projects?
2. In what ways must these assignments be controlled? Should much time be spent on planning?
3. Should plans have teacher approval before the work is started?
4. Can the total project be subdivided and certain tasks chosen by subgroups or individuals?
5. Should a school ever have projects? Is reliance on the textbook safer and better?
6. What about due-dates for reporting progress? For the completion of the job?
7. What steps must be taken so students will make definite day and hour appointments if they are to interview adults in the community?
8. When one or a few students are shirking their share in the larger task, what may teachers do to insure the success of the project?
9. How will the total task be evaluated?
10. In any public, cooperative task, students and teachers reveal much of themselves to each other. Revealing is at least a two-edged sword. The less favorable characteristics may become the subject of comments. How can the teacher anticipate and how can he diminish the possible negative aspects of public criticism?
11. How can the projects be presented in a dynamic and interesting way?
12. What productive role (not managerial) does the teacher play in the project?
13. Is the time spent on project work worth-while? Do students have oppor-

tunities to compare, observe, summarize, classify, and make decisions in their project work?

Coding.

When teachers read students' writing they may wish to call to their attention the relationship between their thinking and their writing. When students write, their thinking is often revealed. Sometimes they use words and phrases more out of habit or whim than out of a desire to write what they really mean. Teachers can call students' attention to certain words and phrases and inquire, "Is this what you mean to say?" Such words as *all, always, everybody, never, none, nobody,* and other extreme statements may be coded on students' papers. Phrases such as *either-or, if-then, qualifying words, value statements, attributions,* and others might be coded by placing a mark near the word or phrase under examination. The student can then be asked to list the words or phrases that have been coded. Are there similarities? Are there differences? Then the student can be asked if he wishes to change any of the words or phrases. If the student does not wish to change any of his statements, the teacher accepts the student's judgment. The classroom atmosphere is one of acceptance and give-and-take. When a teacher codes a paper, it is not "wrong." The purpose of coding is to give the student an opportunity to examine what he wrote and to assume responsibility for his writing.

At first perhaps only extreme statements might be coded. As the student gains awareness of his use of extreme statements, the teacher can begin to code other expressions. Often the student's first reaction to coding is to attempt to eliminate all extreme statements from his writing. When this occurs, the student has missed the meaning of coding. The elimination of *all* extreme statements from a student's writings is not the goal of this operation. It is rather to call the student's attention to what he is writing, to help the student become responsible for what he writes. If he wants to use *all, always,* or *never,* he may realize what he is doing and affirm it. It is important that he knowingly stands by what he writes.

Teachers might gently try to question oral statements of students. If a student says, "never", the teacher might ask, "Never?" If the student affirms his use of *never,* the teacher accepts his decision *even if the teacher disagrees.*

It is probably not a good idea to code everything a student writes. Too much coding may become boring or monotonous. But when teachers do code, it is important to mark *all* extreme statements whether or not they are appropriately used, whether or not the teacher agrees with the student.

Students might be given newspaper articles, editorials, books, and other writing to code. Students might write an analysis of the papers they have coded based on extreme statements, value-loaded phrases, attributions, and other statements.

Teaching Guidelines:

Aids:
(Ways that may enhance thinking)

Obstacles:
(Ways that may stifle thinking)

1. The teacher carefully reads and codes the student's writing.

1. The teacher reads the paper only for the purpose of assigning a grade.

2. The student examines the coded words and phrases. He changes those he wishes to change. The teacher accepts the student's decision *whether or not* the teacher agrees with the student.

2. The teacher requires the student to change coded words and phrases.

3. When coding a particular category of words, the teacher marks *all* words in the category.

3. The teacher's coding is inconsistent.

4. The coding on a student's paper is not considered right or wrong, good or bad.

4. The student is led to believe that the code marks refer to incorrect statements.

Questions to Consider:

1. Do students "miss" many of the words which should be coded?
2. Are students defensive about the codings on their papers? How can teachers anticipate this sensitivity? How can they treat it if it does arise?
3. Do the students react by trying to hide their own judgments of values? Do they react by seemingly writing or speaking in such a way as to say nothing?
4. Does paying attention to the things coded make the students overly self-conscious? How should this be handled?
5. When students themselves code an advertisement, then a "letter to the editor," then a news story, are they asked to compare the three samples?
6. Does coding (used now and then) help to develop a more mature and confident self-concept or does it detract?
7. When teachers code, do they try to code too many things at the same time? How do students react when many things are coded?

Summary of Guidelines

Teaching guidelines have been discussed in connection with a number of operations of thinking. Many of the guidelines apply to various efforts to emphasize thinking. The following is a summary of the guidelines:

Aids:
(Ways that may enhance thinking)

Obstacles:
(Ways that may stifle thinking)

1. The student does the activity.

1. The teacher does the activity.

2. The teacher accepts the student and his efforts to do the activity.
3. The activities have a purpose or a significance.
4. Students do the activities in many different ways.
5. Students have opportunities to discuss the work they have done.
6. Students are asked if they wish to make any changes in their work. The teacher accepts the students' wishes whether or not he agrees with the student.
7. Particular activities reflect a variety of subjects and curricular areas.
8. The classroom atmosphere is one of mutual respect, acceptance, and give-and-take.
9. The activities frequently combine various operations of thinking, *i.e.,* as students classify, they are encouraged to observe, compare, and summarize.

2. The teacher rejects the student and his efforts.
3. The activities are almost always trivial.
4. Only one way to do each activity is permitted.
5. Discussion is not permitted.
6. The teacher heckles, bullies, and intimidates the students. Changes are made in response to teacher demands.
7. Particular activities are confined to one area.
8. The classroom is autocratic.
9. The focus on each thinking operation is so sharp that no other operation may be employed.

THINKING EXPERIENCES

One important way of looking at an activity is to ask: Will it stir a student's sympathy, his involvement, his participation? Will it influence his behavior, his life?

When Dewey talks about the concept of activity, he uses two major headings. One of them is *enduring.* The other is *suffering.* When he talks about *enduring* he means "going through" the activity. The activity is passive, quiescent, often "unthinking." In a sense, the activity is tolerated by the student, but it does not have a real effect on the student's life. When Dewey talks about *suffering* he means that our lives are *affected* by the activity. There is personal involvement, purpose, and direction. The activity might stimulate deep intellectual analysis. It might produce exhilaration, inspiration, projection into the future. In other words, the activity which involves what Dewey calls *suffering* may be referred to as an *experience.* It penetrates the student's life and involves his active participation. When teachers plan to incorporate thinking activities into the curriculum, they might choose the ones which seem likely to become *experiences,* to have *meaning* in the lives of the students.

Many events and tasks undertaken during the day may accomplish a variety of important purposes without becoming experiences. Routine undertakings like repeating multiplication tables, reciting answers to questions, and drilling may contribute to such important functions as promoting vital skills, but under ordinary circumstances the student is only "going through something," he is *enduring* in a quiescent, "unthinking" way. Yet, even such mundane tasks, upon reflection and analysis, may become experiences. Sometimes school activities are passive in nature for the student. The student who is *taking* math, *taking* physics, *taking* history, from a teacher who is *covering* the text, *covering* the lab manual, *covering* the syllabus, may well be passively tolerating school rather than actively experiencing learning.

On the other hand, the concept of experience has a wide range of possible involvements. Exhilaration, elation, joy, happiness, frustration, failure, anxiety, sorrow, grief, misfortune, mischance, achievement, accomplishment, progress, commitment, the facing of unhappy contexts, being around people who reject you, having the feeling that what you are doing isn't worth much, having the feeling that no matter how hard you try you will not succeed — these are part and parcel of the concept. In addition, there are the experiences of sharing with larger and larger numbers of people, experiences of responsibility and irresponsibility, of feeling a great responsibility for fellow students, for the rights of fellow citizens, for people in war torn countries; the experience of standing up for what you believe, of taking a public responsibility for what you have said; the experience of being in the minority, sometimes a minority of one; the experience of conforming, and in the act of conforming, going against your conscience and being troubled by what you are doing.

If one looks at the doing of something as casual, as automatic, as habitual, it hardly enters the domain of experience. When someone says, "I had an experience this morning," it seems to connote something out of the ordinary. Perhaps students should have many experiences during the day with a number of them worth retelling so that there need not be the notion that it is exceptional to have an experience. Sometimes schools are over-protective of students. Things are arranged so that students will not experience failure, frustration, difficulty, complete exhaustion. Yet, a scheme is set up whereby students can fail, can repeat a class, can be berated publicly. With foresight, difficulties can be anticipated. Students can be prepared to face frustration. They might learn how to meet difficulties through experiences in school that are carefully prepared, planned, and coordinated with the student so that he knows something about himself and how he faces difficulties.

The concept of experience as a guide for curriculum development is not taken seriously by enough people. As teachers who seek to emphasize thinking in our classroom, let us ask ourselves: Are we providing *activities* or *experiences?* Are our students passive or are they personally involved? Are our students only "covering" activities or do they often have experiences which become part of their lives?

FOCUSING ON PARTICULAR BEHAVIORS

As teachers provide opportunities for students to have experiences with thinking operations, they may have several objectives in mind. The intent may be for each student in the class to have experiences with thinking operations. In addition, there may be concern with the thinking-related behavior of particular students. How may teachers help the student who is impulsive in his thinking? What may be done with students who are overly-dependent upon the teacher, who can't concentrate, or who miss the meaning? If teachers say to them, "Think for yourselves," very probably their behavior will not change. What these students need are many experiences with thinking operations — day in and day out — over a period of about a semester in order to effect a change in their behavior. Some of the thinking operations may be particularly appropriate as we concentrate on working with students with specific thinking-related behaviors.

Impulsiveness.

This student needs to be slowed-down so that he does not go off "half-cocked." He might be asked to write four ways of doing something — four ways of comparing, four ways of answering a question, four ways of making a summary. When this student makes a generalization, he might be asked to take a few minutes and write out some ideas that support the generalization. As the student starts to work on an assignment, project, or question, the teacher might ask, "What are three or four ways of going at this? Give some reasons that might support each of them. Choose the one that you believe is best." Then the student might be asked to plan ways of doing the assignment. He might observe a committee at work without being a member of it. He might record what the committee did first, what it did next, and so on. As the impulsive student is provided with opportunities to gain experiences with the thinking operations, he is being given opportunities to slow down, to deliberate, to become less impulsive.

Over-dependence upon the teacher.

The objective is to help the student become independent. The teacher might ask the student to plan the way he will spend a half-hour of a study hall. What books will he need? What materials? After the study hall, the student might be asked to evaluate his plan. Was he able to follow it? Did it have to be modified? What changes would he make in future plans? Can he observe other students working on a task? Did they take the initiative? Did they ask for help? What kind of help did they need? Did they do it by themselves? This student might make a list of things he can do independently, *e.g.*, ride a bicycle, make deliveries. As he becomes more independent, we might ask him to enlarge the list.

Inability to concentrate.

These students seem to miss the connection between means and ends. They start out to accomplish something and seem to get sidetracked. Sometimes students do not concentrate when they are not interested in a topic. Sometimes we say a student *can't* concentrate when we mean he *doesn't* concentrate. If a student *can't* concentrate, he might be asked to talk into a tape recorder as he begins an assignment. If he gets lost, he might listen to the tape and see where he left the topic. As he begins to work on an assignment, the teacher might ask what he plans to do to complete the task. Where will the plan lead? How is it related to the topic? When directions are given, the student might be asked to take notes and to make a plan. Then, the teacher might ask, "Are you following the plan?" Sometimes isolation or a quiet place helps keep outside stimuli from interfering with concentrating. Teachers might ask students who can't concentrate to focus very sharply on a task for a short period of time, perhaps as little as five minutes. As they gain skill, the time can be lengthened. Planning probably is an important experience for students who can't concentrate. They might plan in such areas as assignments, projects, homework, study halls, and ways to spend free time outside of school. Planning implies that we can influence our world, that we can do things we like to do, that we can accomplish things.

Missing the meaning.

Students who miss the meaning probably need many experiences with interpreting. After the class has seen a film, read a book, or completed an assignment, teachers might ask, "What was it all about?" Perhaps the answer will be, "South America," or some other broad statement. The teacher would then say, "Thank you," or something to that effect, and wait for another opportunity to ask for an interpretation. The student might be asked to write two or three sentences which give the main idea of a story or a newspaper article. A row of prices might be listed on the board and the students asked, "Which is the highest? Which is the lowest?" After the student has read a book he might be told, "You have one minute to tell the main idea of the book." He might be asked to take notes on a class discussion, identifying the topics which were discussed, the points which were made, the main idea of the discussion. He might look at a political cartoon with the caption covered and make up a new caption. He could then compare his caption with that of the cartoonist. He might even try drawing his own cartoon.

Dogmatic, Assertive Behavior.

When the dogmatic student makes assertions, he might be asked to support his statements. What evidence does he have? The teacher might code his writing and speaking. If he uses extreme words such as *all, always, never, nobody* the teacher might inquire about his degree of certainty about them. Is he absolutely positive? Pretty sure? Reasonably sure? Or doesn't he know? He might be asked to code other people's writing with which he agrees, disagrees, or has no opinion. He might compare his coding. Is he "objective" where he agrees, where he disagrees, where he has no opinion? He might examine assumptions: which seem reasonable, which are hard to accept? Can he support his assumptions? The purpose here is to put the dogmatic student in a position where he is aware of what he is saying and will take the responsibility for what he says and writes.

Rigidity, inflexibility of behavior.

These students need experiences with new ways of doing things, with reviewing alternatives, with hypothesizing. When an assignment is given, the teacher might ask the students to plan three or four different ways of completing it. If an arithmetic example is given, they might be asked to do it with two or three different algorisms. They might do a lot of comparing: of various algorisms, of various ways that classmates have made summaries, of outlines, of classification schemes, of various accounts of events, of various points of view. When opportunities for hypothesizing occur, these students need to consider a number of possible solutions.

Extreme lack of confidence in one's own thinking.

These students need success experiences with thinking, operations, opportunities to share their thinking, and opportunities to make errors without fear of ridicule. As they embark on a thinking operation, it would be important for the teacher to eliminate value judgments such as, "good" and "bad," "right" and "wrong." Instead, the teacher might inquire, "Did it work?" If not, "Is there anything else you might try?" As other students in the class make statements, the teacher might ask those students with a lack of confidence in their thinking, "Do you agree?" Whatever their response, it is important to accept it with respect which dignifies their efforts at thinking.

Unwillingness to think.

These students need large, but gently applied, doses of thinking operations. They need to be put into a position where they are *expected* to do thinking.

They need opportunities to gain experiences in interpreting, in doing independent work, in projects, in hypothesizing, in gathering data, in classifying, imagining, coding, summarizing, and comparing. If these students are expected to do thinking, and if opportunities are provided for them to participate in thinking operations — day in and day out — over a semester, the chances are good that students who don't want to think will change their behavior.

IMPLICATIONS OF TEACHING FOR THINKING

The application of some of the ideas in this book may have far-reaching results. It may lead to situations similar to the opening of Pandora's box. When students apply thinking to their lives and studies, in a sense they are set free. German students have an expression for this freedom. *Die Gedanken sind frei* — Thoughts are free. Freedom to some implies lack of control of behavior. To others it means extreme skepticism, cynicism, or even rudeness. To some it means free use of obscenity. There is a degree of unpredictability about thinking. There is no assurance as to what conclusions our students will reach. There is no way of knowing how students will act in relation to their thinking. It might be well to pause and examine some of the possible implications of teaching for thinking.

1. The openness of thinking may present a threat to teachers.

In thinking, there is examination. There is looking for assumptions, attributions, extreme statements, bases of belief, and evidence. As students scrutinize, they may very well begin to criticize each other, their teacher, their textbooks, their principal, and even their parents. Prejudices, values, and tabus may be revealed. There may be contempt for some textbooks. Is this bad? One answer is that it depends upon the way they do it. One needs to distinguish between freedom to think and license in behavior. Does freedom mean we can do anything we want? Oliver Wendell Holmes said that freedom of speech does not give a person the right to yell "fire" in a crowded theatre. We have said that students can examine assumptions in arithmetic "word problems" and still find the "correct answer." A fourth-grade boy took a reading test. One of the questions was: Through the night the truck driver drove his truck. In the morning he felt a) happy b) tired c) sad d) rested. The boy said, "I answered *tired,* but he might have been happy. Maybe he was rested. Driving *can* be relaxing." Despite his examination of the problem, the boy was able to answer the question. Perhaps the writers of tests might pay more attention to assumptions.

Students may be critical of textbooks. A fourth-grader read about Columbus. According to the book, Columbus would wander over to the docks as a boy wishing to become a sailor. There was conversation quoted between Columbus and the sailors. Some of the children asked how the author was able to record actual conversations. Even nonfiction books that children read for their factual content contain products of the author's imagination. Are there primary sources we can use with students? If the class is studying Columbus, can parts of his diary be read? A writer of children's nonfiction trade books told of a disagreement he had with the children's editor of a large publishing company. The editor wanted the manuscript "spiced up" with dialogue and anecdotes. The author refused to so fictionalize the book. The book was published with no dialogue and when legends were used they were identified as such. According to the author, the book received good reviews but none of the reviewers commented on the care that had been taken to separate fact from fancy, history from fiction. Should all books that are carelessly written be discarded? Of course not. They can be used as opportunities to teach for thinking. Why shouldn't children be told the charming story of George Washington and the cherry tree? Why can't children be told it is a legend and part of our folk heritage? Legend or not, it is still a very good story. When teachers find books that may be questioned because of too much license, do they let the publishers know their feelings? Do they let librarians and reviewers know the kinds of books they want?

As thinking is emphasized, we are helping establish a *universe of discourse* which helps us to work together and understand each other. This does not necessarily mean that people will agree just because they are thinking. But where there is disagreement, differences can be pinpointed by examining assumptions, beliefs, evidence, and values. There can be disagreement without personal attacks, calling names, using insults, being rude, or becoming emotional. Sometimes a profound respect can grow for the other fellow even though we do not agree with him completely. If teachers expect them to, students can function within a universe of discourse where the teacher maintains his control over the class and where students respect each other and their teacher. In the search for knowledge each of us may well be humble. In the broad scheme of things each of us is rather insignificant. However, teachers sometimes assume the role of a god. They know what is "right" for their students. They know all the answers. They are the ultimate authority. Are they really that well endowed? Will the students' respect be lost if teachers admit that they, too, are searching for knowledge, that they, too, can make mistakes? Can teachers do these things and still use to their advantage their maturity and experience?

2. A set for thinking.

As a person becomes committed to thinking as a way of getting at facts, of testing, and of projecting ideas, he frequently comes to expect more from what he reads. For example, when he reads a history book and there is little or no corroboration of the data, he might say, "I want primary data and I want a way for it to be attested to as primary." Such phrases as "I think," "I feel," "everybody knows," "it is a well-known fact," become annoying. When books do not reach our expectations in connection with thinking, we tend to reject them.

Sometimes a body of knowledge may be looked at from a theoretical point of view. When we read about space and the solar system, we are disciplined by a Copernican outlook. When an idea does not jibe with this outlook, we want an explanation or we want the idea recognized as a deviation from the theory. Whoever uses the Copernican scheme is aware of some of the basic underlying assumptions such as the origin of the system. These assumptions are taken on faith, but they are examined and clearly stated. As we read another theory where underlying assumptions are not examined, we tend to conclude that the theory is not disciplined. Our "set" for thinking disciplines our outlook and our expectations.

3. The behavior of students in other teachers' classes.

Sometimes students who have learned something new become "hot-shots" or "show-offs." They may seek to confound their friends and bait adults. In a departmentalized school they may try to put one of their teachers "on the spot." One of the realities of education is that different teachers emphasize different things. Sometimes the student only seeks to find out what the teacher wants and "gives it to him." The more teachers the student comes in contact with, the more it may become necessary for him to "shift gears" from class to class. One teacher may emphasize thinking, another concepts. One teacher may emphasize product, another process. Sometimes these teachers do not have first hand contact with each other. Is it any wonder why there are so many "crazy mixed up kids"? As students have the idea that thoughts are free but behavior is not always free, as they use thinking operations, as they examine differences of opinion, perhaps they become better able to cope with the realities of the differing expectations of teachers.

4. Effects of learning.

A teacher cannot get into a student's brain to find out what is going on and is, therefore, faced with the necessity of using indirect means of evaluation. One way of evaluating what is happening to students as a result of their being given experiences with operations involving thinking is to examine their behavior. In this text, a theory which links experiences in thinking operations with behavior has been presented. It has been suggested that as teachers provide opportunities for thinking—day in and day out—students' behavior will change. Students will become less dogmatic, less rigid, and less impulsive. They will suspend judgment, deliberate and examine alternatives before reaching a conclusion. Thinking cannot be observed, but behavior can. If behavior changes in connection with efforts to emphasize thinking, there is the idea that students' thinking is improving. (Part 5 contains some examples of ways of observing behavior.)

What happens to the rest of the curriculum when thinking is emphasized? We have indicated that the available research suggests that there is no loss in academic achievement as teachers emphasize thinking in connection with the regular curriculum. Actually, the data in some studies of thinking indicate that not only were there no losses in academic achievement, but in some cases there were dramatic gains. The individual children being studied *and* the classes of which they were members showed gains in achievement test scores. (Part 5 contains a further discussion of research on the Thinking Theory. Suggested Readings contains a listing of the research.)

5. Relations with other teachers.

As teachers teach with an emphasis on thinking what will happen to their relations with other teachers? The answer probably depends upon the quality of the relationships before teaching for thinking is emphasized. A teacher who had good professional relationships before probably will continue to have them. Of course, if teachers become boastful, arrogant, and claim to have solved the problems of the world, they may not endear themselves to their fellow teachers. On the other hand, if teachers are truly humble, searching in their attitude toward knowledge, and if they do not become emotional when differences of opinion occur, they may well find that their relationships with fellow teachers are actually improved.

6. Relations with administrators.

Administrators are primarily concerned with the smooth running of the school. When teachers are teaching well, when students are eager about attending classes, when parents believe the school is doing a noteworthy job, when problems are at a minimum, administrators are usually pleased.

Almost everybody is *for* "thinking" and administrators are no exception. Most of them are in favor of a curriculum in which thinking is emphasized. Therefore, as teachers incorporate thinking activities into their program, as students become more challenged by their educational experiences, it is likely that the teachers' efforts in behalf of teaching for thinking will be welcomed. As students gain skill in using the thinking operations to some purpose, the results will speak for themselves. The saying, "Nothing succeeds like success," is most appropriate when looking at teaching for thinking. A poor teacher teaching poorly is often a source of much concern to an administrator. A good teacher teaching well is often a source of security to an administrator.

7. Reactions of parents.

A primary concern of most parents in relation to school is whether or not their children are learning. Anxiety over learning is expressed in many ways. "Will my child succeed?" "Will he pass?" "Will he get into college?" "Will he be a success in life?" In one way or another, these questions are related to learning. When parents have the idea that their children are *not* learning, problems may well develop. When parents have the idea that their children *are* learning, they tend to support schools and their child's teachers. There is much to support the notion that teaching with an emphasis on thinking enhances learning. As students gain skill in the thinking operations, they grow in enthusiasm toward school, their studies, and their teachers. The anxiety of parents towards school tends to diminish as parents see their children learning.

8. Rationalizing of teachers.

As teachers read about emphasizing thinking, a frequent reaction is, "This makes sense to me. I do it all the time." Sometimes a teacher is asked, "What did you do today to emphasize thinking in your classroom?" The response is, "I do it all the time in so many ways I just can't think of any examples." Sometimes teachers tend to look at themselves through rose-colored glasses. Teachers believe that because they mean well, they do well. But do they always do as well as they mean to do? How can they be sure? It has been suggested that the use of tape recordings of classes is one way to step back and evaluate teaching. Some teaching guidelines have also been suggested. Questions for teachers to consider have been raised. It is hoped that these suggestions will lead to fruitful introspection and soul-searching on the part of teachers.

9. Teaching for thinking as a "fad."

It often seems as if society is searching for easy answers or panaceas. Each year publishers come out with *the answer* to "all" our problems. Of course, the publisher wants to sell his books, so he is inclined to overstate his case. Too frequently the answers become fads which are discarded as *new* answers become available. Teaching for thinking is not offered as a panacea nor as the solution to "all" educational problems. It has been indicated that there are some occasions when thinking may not be appropriate. It is not suggested that teaching for thinking be the sole objective of the school. The authors see teaching for thinking as an approach to the curriculum, needing effective and judicious application at the kindergarten through twelfth grade level and beyond.

10. Expectations and purposes.

Sometimes people have the idea that, "You should always be at your best." The idea is a worthy one but does it always apply? Probably not. What is "best"? Students do not usually wear their *best* clothes during a gym period. On the contrary, they tend to wear clothes that will give them freedom of movement for their arms and legs. The clothes may not be their *best* but hopefully they are appropriate for gym. In other words, the purpose of the activity influences the expectation in relation to clothes. What is *best* to wear to gym is not necessarily what is *best* to wear to a party.

As students participate in activities, teachers' expectations concerning outcomes depend upon the purposes of the activities. If one wished to paper a wall, it would not be necessary to measure the length to the nearest 1/128th of an inch. There is no need to do one's *best* job of measuring. Teachers may want students to have experiences with measuring the area of a circle. In the elementary grades this may involve making circles out of paper. The children cut the circle into wedges (sectors) and then fit the wedges together to make a crude rectangle. From the rectangle they can get a rough idea of the area of a circle. As students study algebra and geometry, they will discover a more accurate way to find the area of a circle. But, probably not until they study the calculus will students come in contact with a rigorous proof of the formula for the area of a circle. Does this mean that all experiences with the area of circles should be postponed until students study the calculus? Of course there are better ways to find the area of a circle than cutting it into wedges but are they appropriate for young children? Do they reflect the purposes of the curriculum?

The authors of this book have taken the position that students need opportunities for thinking. Many ways of inquiring have been presented. Classifying constitutes inquiring into what goes together. Comparing involves inquiring into likenesses and differences. Summarizing means inquiring into order and coherence. To apply principles is to inquire into why something did or should happen — the rationale and the expectation. The preoccupation has not been with rigorous testing, precision of measurement, research design, formal logic nor proof. Not that these are considered unimportant, but there is the idea that children need experiences with thinking operations as early as possible in their school lives. As children become experienced in using operations of thinking, and as they gain knowledge of subject matter, opportunities for more rigorous thinking can be provided.

11. Recognition of learning problems.

The saying, "Ignorance is bliss," may apply to teaching for thinking. If a teacher's only contact with his students is as a lecturer to a large class, the chances are that he will neither recognize nor identify learning problems. He probably will not notice his students as individuals. It is when teachers associate closely with students that they become aware of their problems. It is when teachers give students opportunities to reveal their behavior that behavioral symptoms may be identified. When learning problems emerge, it may well be an indication that teachers have become more acutely aware of their students as individuals.

12. Problems.

It has been indicated that there are a number of possible implications growing out of teaching for thinking. It is very possible that problems may develop. No matter what teaching method is used or what curriculum is taught, problems will develop. Emphasizing thinking is no exception. It, too, will produce problems. If teachers are autocratic and rigid in their teaching, problems will develop. If teachers are democratic in their teaching, other problems will develop. If teachers are permissive in their teaching, still other problems will develop. No matter how classes are taught, teachers will face certain problems. If teachers are very successful, they may be the object of envy. If teachers are very inept, they may be the object of contempt. Furthermore, teachers may be subjected to a certain amount of criticism no matter what they do in the classroom. In extreme cases, on a single day, a teacher may be criticised for being too strict, too lenient, too easy, too hard, giving too much homework, boring his class, telling too many jokes, and so on. Sometimes the school and the teacher become the scapegoat for the frustrations of the public. Life itself involves problems, challenges, striving, difficulties. As long as problems and criticisms are part of life let us accept them. They do not diminish the satisfaction that comes from teaching with an emphasis on thinking.

CONCLUSION

The authors have made the assumption that readers of this book really want to emphasize thinking. Sometimes the effort is a lonely one. It is very hard to do something when a person is the only one in the school doing it. At such times a teacher needs inner strength, fortitude, a strong sense of purposefulness, confidence, and faith in what he is doing. Even under the most ideal circumstances problems develop. Teachers need the courage to see them through. Sometimes they seek aid from supervisors, expressing their doubts about themselves and asking for help. Some supervisors respond by saying, "You're doing just fine. You are a good teacher." Even good teachers sometimes seek help and suggestions. In this chapter some guidelines and questions have been presented so that teachers may help themselves if no other help is available. Occasions when it is appropriate to emphasize thinking and when it is inappropriate have been discussed. Thinking in various curricular areas, process and product, and the importance of thinking in connection with process were stressed, as were the atmosphere in the classroom and the importance of a close relationship between teacher and student. It has been suggested that teachers use tape recordings of their classes in an effort to supervise themselves and improve their teaching. Specific guidelines and questions to consider were presented in relation to fourteen thinking operations. These operations in and of themselves are not thinking, but when used they provide opportunities for students to think. When students think, their solutions are not always sound and teachers do not necessarily agree with them. Students' conclusions alone are not the test, but the processes by which the conclusions were formulated are. Can students recognize assumptions? Formulate and test hypotheses? Gather data? Summarize? Can they use the various thinking operations to some purpose? Does their behavior associated with thinking change? Are they less impulsive?

Emphasizing thinking requires hard work in the form of observing children, planning activities, "digging up" material, and paying much individual attention to students. Teaching for thinking is not easy, yet it may lead to much satisfaction. The reward for the effort is seeing changes in students' behavior and enjoying increased stimulation in teaching.

It is the teacher who is the key to emphasizing thinking in the classroom. Explicitly and implicitly the role of the teacher is the theme of this part of the book. It is easy to stifle thinking. It is much harder to encourage thinking. It is easy to think for the students. It is much harder to give the students opportunities to think for themselves. Yet, if the emphasis on thinking is one of our goals, we, as teachers, must dedicate ourselves to providing opportunities for our students to think.

part five

RECAPITULATION

THEORY AND HYPOTHESES

If colleges, universities, or special schools set themselves up as responsible agencies for the preparation of teachers, it must follow that there are principles or theories which are to be taught. Ideally these principles or theories give direction to what the teacher will do in the classroom as he meets those situations which are in some way related to his theoretical preparation. We need to assume also that the preparation of teachers is directed toward the kinds of problems which are present in typical teaching situations. Those problems of concern to teachers are almost always related to behavior of one kind or another on the part of students.

In some circumstances the student behaves in such a way that makes it difficult for him to learn. Sometimes his behavior makes it difficult for other students to learn. The teacher who takes seriously his responsibilities to promote learning tends to be frustrated when learning is inhibited. The teacher wants help in these situations. He wants to know how to help the student who is in difficulty. If there is sound theory in the field he accepts this as a guide. If his efforts along this line do not succeed he may want to try another theory, and still another. There have been relatively few *theories* in the field of education which are helpful to teachers in the solution of behavior problems related to learning. The available evidence is fairly clear that we do not accomplish very much in our efforts to modify the values of children or of young adults. The same might be said of thinking-related behaviors. If one examines the textbooks which are used in the college courses directed toward the preparation of teachers, one finds that theory, as defined in this volume, is conspicuous by its absence. In this same connection it should be said that in the area of education, theory tends to be thought of as something that is nebulous, up in the clouds, away from reality, something almost irrelevant to the practical concerns of the day. It is almost never conceived as a clear statement of relationships between two or more variables. It is almost never seen as something that suggests hypotheses which can be tried by the classroom teacher.

For years people have talked about progressive education as a theory. If there is something called "progressive education" it probably includes numbers of theories. The concept itself is so elusive that practically no one understands what it means. Those who write about "progressive education" usually do not clearly describe a theory; they do not state the variables which are supposedly related. If they do, they do not clearly define what they are talking about and it becomes very difficult indeed to assess the theory. In this volume, on the other hand, a statement has been made to the effect that certain behaviors of children are related to the child's lack of experience with thinking. It has been stated that where characteristic behaviors exist— such as impulsive behavior in thinking situations, overly dependent behavior in thinking situations, missing the meaning in thinking situations, failing to concentrate in thinking situations, over-assertiveness and dogmatism in thinking situations, rigidity in thinking situations — there are indications that the child has failed to develop the habits which are appropriate to successful conduct in the same situations.

Also in this volume, a wide variety of operations which give students opportunity for thinking was presented. These included comparing, summarizing, classifying, interpreting, criticizing, and others. Many illustrations of fifteen such thinking operations were presented that had bearing upon early primary grades, later primary grades, and the upper grades of the elementary school; these same operations relating to teaching in the secondary school were also presented and discussed.

The most significant hypothesis derived from the theory suggests that as students engage in these thinking operations regularly and consistently for at least one semester, the behaviors indicative of immaturity tend to decline. Given students with behavior like that described and given a teacher who wants to test the theory, thinking operations may be easily carried out with methods that are appropriate to the guidance of students at that age level. Under these circumstances the teacher does not have to take materials on faith. He is in a position *to test* what has been offered. Here is an hypothesis which can be tested by the teacher who uses it, and as he tests it with different students in different situations, he will be testing the soundness of the theory as it operates in his own classroom with the students he teaches.

In deciding to test the hypothesis with respect to particular students, the teacher is warned to make a two-pronged investigation before he starts. One should make sure, first of all, that some disability in the area of physical health is not operating. It is wise to consult whatever medical records are available. One may find out from parents if something is wrong. In some cases the results of an annual physical check-up may be available. We need to take more seriously the idea that ill health affects behavior and particularly those behaviors related to learning. In the second place, a teacher would be wise to make some assessment of the student's emotional stability. If a student has deep worries, these would probably inhibit him from making important adjustments. The surface manifestations which are significant indicators of emotional problems include persistent and unusual aggressiveness, persistent and unusual withdrawal from group activities, unusual meekness or submissiveness to other students, symptoms of psychosomatic illness which are confirmed by the physician, and patterns of behavior which regress to earlier age levels. Where physical or emotional illness is involved, these need attention before any great program for an emphasis on thinking is launched.[1]

If we could assume that the questions of physical and emotional illness have been answered, the next step would be to identify some students who— according to the theory — are very much in need of intensive work. Below is a Teacher Rating Instrument which was developed by Wassermann. In using it the teacher writes the names of students who seem, without doubt, to be characterized by the descriptive paragraphs in the first group of blank spaces following the paragraph. In the second group of blank spaces, teachers are asked to write the names of those students who are *possible* candidates for inclusion in the category.

TEACHER RATING INSTRUMENT

1. *The Impulsive Type*

This is the child who jumps to conclusions and hurries into action without considering alternatives. He often says that he should have given more thought to his activity. Where judgments are made about a value it is the immediacy of the satisfaction that determines the judgment; reflection and consideration might change the judgment but as a matter of habit, the impulsive child does not engage in this reflection.

Associated with impulsiveness is the idea of rapid and random movements; of acts directed by little more than whim or caprice. Action itself seems to be much more important than deliberation on possible modes of action. To be *up and doing* is so prominent in this child's behavior that the significance or purpose or goal of the doing is neglected.

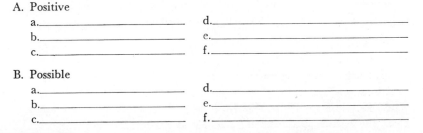

A. Positive

a._____   d._____
b._____   e._____
c._____   f._____

B. Possible

a._____   d._____
b._____   e._____
c._____   f._____

---

[1]Louis E. Raths and Anna P. Burrell, *Understanding the Problem Child.* (South Orange, New Jersey: Economics Press, 1951).

2. *The Overly Dependent Type*

This is the child who wants help at practically every step in the work that he is doing. He finds it hard to begin a task and when you help him get started, he does get started; but in no time at all, he asks for help in the next step. When you arrange to help him with that part of the procedure, he carries it out and then wants more help. He often says, "I am stuck," or "I don't know what to do now." As a matter of fact, he never really understands what he is doing or the relationships of a current activity to a long range goal. For the thinking processes he seems to be almost wholly dependent upon others. Unless he gets practical help for each step he is apt to do nothing or is apt to complain a great deal to the effect that the problem isn't clear or that he doesn't know what he is supposed to do.

A. Positive

     a._____   d._____

     b._____   e._____

     c._____   f._____

B. Possible

     a._____   d._____

     b._____   e._____

     c._____   f._____

3. *The Loud, Dogmatic and Overly Assertive Type*

We think of this child as insensitive to the feelings of others. Such words as *rude, abrupt, brash* frequently appear in descriptions of him. In his own defense he sometimes says, "Everything I said was true, wasn't it?" He doesn't see that the single criterion of truth may be inadequate to the total situation. He seems to have all the answers. He is unyielding. He doesn't seem to listen to alternatives; in fact, he seems reluctant to acknowledge that there are alternatives.

He is apt to impugn the motives or the purposes or the concepts of anyone who opposes his views. There is a quality of rigidity and inflexibility about his convictions. He is apt to be loud in his assertions, but this is not always the case. His language is frequently studded with *always, everybody, nobody,* or *never.* He generalizes loosely about races or nations or religious groupings. Frequently his defense of his utterances is restricted to his personal experience and this seems to be an adequate basis for him to generalize. We sometimes say that he is authoritative; that he tries to dominate other people; that he is rash in his judgments, intemperate or unreasonable in discussion.

A. Positive

     a._____   d._____

     b._____   e._____

     c._____   f._____

B. Possible

     a._____   d._____

     b._____   e._____

     c._____   f._____

4. *The Rigid "In-a-Rut" Type*

In facing practically any situation, this child wants to do things in the same old way. The fact that the problem is somewhat new and perhaps slightly different does not call forth new solutions. He tries to force old methods to fit new problems. He doesn't want to modify the rules of any game. He doesn't want new or different kinds of assignments. If something new is proposed he is apt to say "Can't we do it the way we used to?" Group discussion is apt to bother this child because of the variety and novelty of suggestions which come forth. He himself has gotten used to some authorities, and he wishes a continuation of what he is already used to and what he already knows.

He is happiest when carrying out routines; what he has already learned is good but the prospect of learning something new is not inviting. There is an insensitivity to alternatives and a disinclination to consider them even when they are brought to his attention. We say of this child that he is in a rut. Sometimes we say that he is a "lesson-learner."

A. Positive

    a._____   d._____

    b._____   e._____

    c._____   f._____

B. Possible

    a._____   d._____

    b._____   e._____

    c._____   f._____

5. *He Misses the Meaning*

In a learning situation after what seems to be a very clear situation, this individual will say that he doesn't understand. He does not seem to comprehend relationships. He does not discriminate the relevant or the irrelevant; he does not interpret his experiences in a way which seems sound and adequate to others who have participated in the same experience. When he is asked to summarize a brief discussion he is apt to put emphasis upon what is irrelevant, to introduce things that were not there, or to repeat almost every little detail.

We sometimes say that he doesn't listen properly or that he doesn't hear, that he doesn't pay attention, or that he doesn't read with discrimination. What we do understand very well is that he doesn't comprehend, that he does not get rich meanings out of his experiences, that he does not interpret sensory data intelligently, that he has poor powers of discrimination. He doesn't absorb, interpret, or synthesize his experiences effectively.

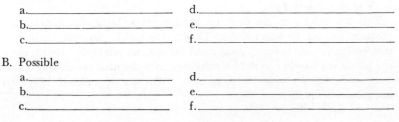

A. Positive

    a._____   d._____

    b._____   e._____

    c._____   f._____

B. Possible

    a._____   d._____

    b._____   e._____

    c._____   f._____

6. *Cannot Concentrate*

The outstanding characteristic of the child in this group is his tendency to use means which are either inconsistent, inappropriate or inadequate to the ends he seeks to achieve. He can't seem to concentrate on the matter at hand. He seems to select procedures or activities which do not lead to successful achievement. Sometimes he has fantastic goals for which there seems to be no practical means. Consequently, the results of his efforts are very frequently unsatisfying. He is not *impulsive,* and is not *stuck* in the sense in which these patterns have been previously described. This child has ideas and seems to be trying, but the ideas do not lead him to achievement that is consistent with his aims. There is an element of inconsistency in the way he chooses means to achieve ends; sometimes there are no means which would be productive, or there is a lack of logic in the relationship between means and ends.

A. Positive

a._____ d._____
b._____ e._____
c._____ f._____

B. Possible

a._____ d._____
b._____ e._____
c._____ f._____

7. *The Under-Confident Type*

This child is characterized by a lack of respect for and a lack of confidence in his ability to think. During class or group discussions, he is apt not to volunteer information, not because he is shy, but because he is afraid to risk exposing his thoughts. He is apt to say, at the close of the meeting, that he wanted to suggest something, but he didn't know how it would be received. Perhaps he might be laughed at or ridiculed. He feels that he is safe when neither he nor his ideas are exposed to possible criticism.

A. Positive

a._____ d._____
b._____ e._____
c._____ f._____

B. Possible

a._____ d._____
b._____ e._____
c._____ f._____

8 *The Anti-Think Type*

This is a child who just does not want to think. He avoids thinking in every situation; instead, he wants action. Thinking to him is "way out," and he rejects the process. He wants things spelled out for him, on principle. "Isn't it the teacher's job to tell us what to do?" Confronted with the need for making some plan, alone or in concert with others, he says, "Why all the talking? Why don't we just go ahead and do something?"

A. Positive

    a._____ d._____

    b._____ e._____

    c._____ f._____

B. Possible

    a._____ d._____

    b._____ e._____

    c._____ f._____

While filling out these forms, the teacher may have some doubts about relying upon his memory for such an important judgment. To check on the validity of his memory, he might take the students whom he identified in the *Positive* and *Possible* categories and make observations of them each morning and afternoon for a period of about a week. When he finds corroborating evidence, he will be more confident about proceeding.

The teacher may also find that the school records contain anecdotal materials or behavioral judgments. The teacher or teachers who worked with the student the preceding year may have indicated some judgments relevant to thinking-related behavior bearing upon the student being identified. The teacher may consult with other teachers who had the child previously. If there are other teachers *now* working with the child (such as the music teacher, the physical education instructor, and other subject matter teachers), the classroom teacher may solicit comments from them. The principal of the school may have some information that is relevant. One can be more certain when the same kinds of testimony come from different sources.

A *second* way of getting evidence is to have all of the students in the room use some form of self-rating instrument. Here again, use may be made of the materials employed by Wassermann in her research. An attempt was made to write this instrument at the reading ability level of upper elementary school children, and there is a paragraph descriptive of the behavior of each of the eight types discussed in this volume. The student signs his name to this record and indicates whether the paragraph describes him, whether it describes him sometimes, or whether it describes him not at all. Behavioral types listed in parentheses at the beginning of each paragraph are for the teacher's information only and should not appear in the instrument.

SELF-RATING INSTRUMENT

Name_____

(Can't Concentrate)

1. A lot of times, when I want to get something done, I can figure out what it's got to be like when I'm finished, but nothing I do seems to get me there. I can't seem to figure out the way to do it. I'll think a little and try one way. When that doesn't work, I'll think some more. Then I'll try another way, and that won't work

either. There seems to be a lot of ways to start, but I'm never sure which way will get me where I want to go. Somebody will try to explain the way to do it to me, but it's hard for me to understand, even when they say it a few times. It always looks as if everybody gets things done before I do.

This is me._____   This is me sometimes._____
                        This is not me at all._____

(Misses the Meaning)

2. When somebody is explaining something, a lot of the time I think that I understand what he said, but when I try to say it back or explain it to somebody else, I find that I missed the point. Sometimes I'm trying to figure out what something means I don't get anything out of it, while everybody else gets it easily. Sometimes the gang laughs at some joke and it doesn't sound funny to me at all. A teacher can tell us carefully what we have to do, but I'm never sure I'll get it right. When I have reading for homework I read every word, but still sometimes I don't have any idea of what the book is saying. I try to study hard, but I don't seem to get out of it what other people get out of it.

This is me._____   This is me sometimes._____
                        This is not me at all._____

(Rigid, "In-a-Rut")

3. When something has to get done, I like to do it the way I've done things before. I don't like new ways of doing things. I know that if something has worked before, it will work again. I don't like it when I'm in a group and everybody is trying to figure out a different way of doing something. It seems to me nothing ever gets done that way. Somebody will say, "Let's try it this way." I will answer, or I would like to answer, "What's wrong with the old way?" With all the things there are to do, I don't think we'd ever get anywhere if we didn't have some kind of a regular way of doing them.

This is me._____   This is me sometimes._____
                        This is not me at all._____

(Overly Dependent)

4. When I get stuck in my work, I look around for somebody to help me. Sometimes it's hard to get started, because I'm not sure about what I'm supposed to do. Then somebody explains it to me and it's all right—I go ahead till I get stuck again and need more help. Everything always seems to work out for me after it's been explained, but I need a lot of help. Sometimes somebody tells me that I should try to figure things out for myself, but what can you do when it won't work out? You have to ask for help. If people want to help you, I don't think there's anything wrong with asking them for help.

This is me._____   This is me sometimes._____
                        This is not me at all._____

(Loud, Dogmatic and Overly Assertive)

5. I like to come right out with what I think. People tell me that I think I'm always right about everything I say. Also, they say I'm pretty loud about it, and even yell sometimes. Once in a while, that hurts somebody's feelings, but I can't help that, if what I'm saying is the truth. Truth is the important thing.

Maybe I should be nicer to people, but if I think something is true, I have to say it, don't I? Sometimes that means that I really have to argue with them, but I want to show them what my ideas are. I know what I know.

This is me._____   This is me sometimes._____

This is not me at all._____

(Impulsive)

6. When I want to do something, I always like to get to it right away. When I have to decide about anything, I make my decision quickly. Sometimes when I think about it, I decide that I might have done it another way, but that doesn't matter the next time. I'll still do the first thing that comes into my head, usually. It does turn out, once in a while, that I've done something the wrong way, or that it could have been done better, but I don't like sitting around. I like to do things all the time.

This is me._____   This is me sometimes._____

This is not me at all._____

(Under-confident)

7. I don't talk much in class. When I get an idea, I don't like to talk about it. Maybe its a wrong idea and people will laugh at me. When the teacher asks a question I sometimes think of a good answer. But I am afraid to say it. I'm afraid that the teacher and the other children will think that I'm not very smart.

This is me._____   This is me sometimes._____

This is not me at all._____

(Anti-think)

8. I like doing things. I don't like to think about why I'm doing them, or how I'm doing them. A lot of people like to think about everything before they do it. This makes me mad. It's a waste of time, and can even get you all fouled up. I always say, "If you have a job to do, just go ahead and do it."

This is me._____   This is me sometimes._____

This is not me at all._____

If teachers are to select students for a trial of the theory it is suggested that there should be some consistency between the ratings of adults and the self-rating of the child. On the other hand, where a student is of the opinion that he is "not at all like this" and where this is contrary to several other sources of evidence, it might be wiser *not* to exclude him as an experimental subject.

A third way of getting evidence about the behavior of students is to make use of the judgments of the other students in the classroom. This represents a kind of GUESS WHO test and is here called a Peer Rating Instrument. Once again the paragraphs are written on the assumption that the students will understand the behavior that is being pointed to. Beneath each paragraph representing a behavioral category, the student is asked to write down the name or names of students to whom it applies. In this instrument a student is directed not to write his own name and the instrument can be used without the signature of the person filling it out. Where the judgments of students tend to converge, where there is agreement about students who are "like this," this evidence is then merged with that from other sources. It makes a contribution to the total picture and from it the teacher makes a judgment as to whether a particular student should be singled out for intensive work in the area of thinking. Again, the behavioral types listed in parentheses at the beginning of each paragraph are for the teacher's information only and should not appear in the instrument.

PEER RATING INSTRUMENT

Name_____

(Can't Concentrate)

1. A lot of times, when he wants to get something done, he can figure out what it's got to be like when it's finished, but nothing he does seems to get him there. He can't figure out a way to do it. He thinks a little, and tries one way. When that doesn't work, he'll think some more. Then he'll try another way, and that won't work either. There seems to be a lot of ways to start, but he's never sure which way will get him where he wants to go. Somebody might try to explain to him the way to do it, but it is hard for him to understand, even when he is told a few times. Everyone gets things done before he does.

This is_____.
This is_____.
This is_____.
This may be_____, but I'm not sure.
This may be_____, but I'm not sure.
This may be_____, but I'm not sure.

(Misses the Meaning)

2. When somebody is explaining something, he thinks that he understands what is said, but when he tries to say it back, or to explain it to somebody else, he finds out that he missed the point. Sometimes he tries to figure out what something means, but he doesn't get anything out of it, while everyone else gets it easily. Sometimes the gang laughs at some joke and it isn't funny to him at all. When he is reading he reads every word, but sometimes he doesn't have any idea of what the book is saying. He tries to study hard, but he doesn't seem to get out of it what other people get out of it.

This is_____.
This is_____.
This is_____.
This may be_____, but I'm not sure.
This may be_____, but I'm not sure.
This may be_____, but I'm not sure.

(Rigid, "In-a-Rut")

3. When something has to get done, he likes to do it in the same old way. He doesn't like new ways of doing things. He knows that if something has worked before, it will work again. He doesn't like being in a group where everybody is

trying to figure out a different way of doing something. Somebody will say, "Let's try it this way." He will answer, "What's wrong with the way we always used to do it?"

This is_____.
This is_____.
This is_____.
This may be_____, but I'm not sure.
This may be_____, but I'm not sure.
This may be_____, but I'm not sure.

(Overly Dependent)

4. When he gets stuck in his work, he looks around for somebody to help him. Sometimes it's hard for him to get started because he is not sure about what he is supposed to do. Then somebody has to explain it to him. He goes ahead until he gets stuck again and needs more help. Things usually seem to work out for him after they have been explained, but he needs a lot of help. Sometimes we try to tell him that he should try to figure things out for himself. He feels that if people want to help you, there is nothing wrong with asking for help.

This is_____.
This is_____.
This is_____.
This may be_____, but I'm not sure.
This may be_____, but I'm not sure.
This may be_____, but I'm not sure.

(Loud, Dogmatic and Overly Assertive)

5. He likes to come right out with what he thinks. He also thinks that he is always right about everything he says. Sometimes he is pretty loud about expressing his opinions, and, at times, he will even yell. Once in a while, he hurts someone's feelings, but he says that he can't help it, because what he is saying is the truth. He thinks that maybe he should be nicer to people, but if he feels that something is true, he has got to say it. At times he really gets into a big argument. He says, "I know what I know." He has to show everyone what his ideas are.

This is_____.
This is_____.
This is_____.
This may be_____, but I'm not sure.
This may be_____, but I'm not sure.
This may be_____, but I'm not sure.

(Impulsive)

6. When he wants to do something, he always likes to get to it right away. When he has to decide about anything, he makes his decision quickly. Sometimes when he thinks about it, he decides that he might have done it another way, but that doesn't matter the next time. He still does the first thing that comes into his head. It does turn out, once in a while, that he has done something the wrong way, or that it could have been done better, but he does not like sitting around. He likes to keep doing things all the time.

This is_____.
This is_____.
This is_____.
This may be_____, but I'm not sure.
This may be_____, but I'm not sure.
This may be_____, but I'm not sure.

(Under-confident)

7. He doesn't talk much in class. When he gets an idea, he doesn't like to talk about it. Maybe it's a wrong idea and people will laugh at him, he thinks. When the teacher asks a question, he may think of a good answer, but he is afraid to say it. He is afraid that the teacher and the other children will think that he is not very smart.

This is_____.
This is_____.
This is_____.
This may be_____, but I'm not sure.
This may be_____, but I'm not sure.
This may be_____, but I'm not sure.

(Anti-think)

8. He likes doing things. He doesn't like to think about why he does them, or how he does them. He says, "A lot of people like to think about everything before they do it. But this makes me mad." He thinks that thinking things out and planning is a waste of time, and that they can sometimes get you all fouled up. He feels that if you have a job to do, you just go ahead and do it.

This is_____.
This is_____.
This is_____.
This may be_____, but I'm not sure.
This may be_____, but I'm not sure.
This may be_____, but I'm not sure.

Still another way might be employed to get evidence about some behavior related to thinking. There are some tests which are appropriate for children in the elementary school and some which may be used in the secondary school. At the level of the elementary school THE VAN PIT THINKING TEST could be used as a source of evidence. This was developed by Raths and others, and has been used quite widely to get some evidence about thinking. Another instrument much more widely used for secondary school students is the WATSON-GLASER CRITICAL THINKING APPRAISAL.[2]

These testing instruments are of the pencil and paper kind. As a matter of preference the authors of this volume prefer to rely upon observation of

---

[2]WATSON-GLASER CRITICAL THINKING APPRAISAL (Yonkers, N. Y.: World Book Company, 1952).

behavior. Excellent teaching helps a student to mature, and as he matures he behaves differently. We think it is much more important to know that a child is excessively dependent upon the teacher than it is to know what score he makes on a pencil and paper device which supposedly measures one or more aspects of thinking. Fortunately, an *either-or* choice need not be made. In the section following dealing with research, the reader will find evidence indicating that an emphasis on thinking along the lines suggested actually does produce increases in test scores which relate to thinking. Moreover, there is a concomitant change in the behavior of these students relating to the eight categories which have been presented.

In this respect another factor deserves emphasis. Many statements of educational objectives indicate changes which teachers want to make in the behavior of students. There is the implication that the teacher changes the student. Hopefully, these procedures leave the decision for change in the hands of the student. According to these procedures a teacher does not urge or exhort the student to change his ways or to mend his manners. The theory requires that a student be given many, many opportunities to think, to think under the guidance of an informed, competent, compassionate teacher. The hypothesis is made that under these conditions the student does change his behavior. As he gains skill in comparing, as he practices summarizing, as he learns to classify, as he criticizes, as he learns to interpret materials, as he learns to hypothesize, he is forming habits of behavior which are ordinarily called *thoughtful*. He begins to develop habits of responding which are at variance with those characterized as immature. The change in behavior may be directed by the teacher but it is the student who chooses the expressions he will use.

Thus far there has been a restatement of the theory. Suggestions have been made for ways of identifying students whose behavior is related to the thinking theory. Brief mention has been made of curriculum materials and operations by which teachers may provide many opportunities for thinking. The next step is concerned with the collecting of evidence after a semester of exposure to these learning activities.

The same instruments could be used again at the end of a semester's trial. Evidence from the classroom teacher's observations may be obtained, in addition to relevant evidence from other teachers: the music teacher, the physical education teacher, the art teacher and other subject matter teachers. Each student might fill out the self-evaluation blank. We could again have judgments by each student's peers. Thinking tests could be administered again. All of the evidence thus collected could then be pooled and a judgment made about progress, lack of progress, or uncertainty as to whether progress was made. In terms of the researches thus far connected with this theory the evidence indicates that more than 80 per cent of the students reveal significant changes in their behavior.

RESEARCH RELATED TO THE THEORY

One of the earliest researches bearing upon the theory was conducted by Rothstein.[3] He undertook an investigation to test the hypothesis that with the use by teachers of some of the thinking operations presented in the present volume, the test scores on thinking would change significantly, and that thinking patterns in essay-type materials would show a shift in favor of the experimental group. In his study Rothstein used a number of assignments which related to comparing and interpreting, and he utilized coding techniques. He had exercises which dealt with problem-solving and decision-making as these applied to the area of social studies in the secondary school. His experience in the utilization of these operations supported the idea that these are ways to stimulate thinking and that actual increases in thinking test scores take place. In addition, Rothstein reported an increased interest on the part of students in classroom work and in the area of social studies generally. One or two students, accustomed to more conventional types of assignments, were persistent objectors to questions which involved thought. These exceptional cases wanted work that could be "learned" in a homework assignment. They wanted to read and reread such assignments, and they wanted to be asked information type questions the following day about what they had read.

Shortly after the completion of Rothstein's work, a more controlled type of study was initiated by three elementary school teachers who were working together in the same building. One of them taught at the level of grade three, another at grade four, and the third at grade five. Machnits[4], Jonas[5], and Martin[6] undertook to study the relationship of certain behaviors of children to thinking. As a matter of fact, each of them included cases that related to areas other than thinking, but each also had individual children who were taught as if an emphasis upon thinking were clearly needed. The results of three studies supported the general notion that when there was an emphasis upon thinking, the behavior of the experimental children changed during the work of one semester. These three investigators also undertook to determine

---

[3]Arnold Rothstein, "An Experiment in Developing Critical Thinking Through the Teaching of American History in the Secondary School" (unpublished Ph.D. dissertation, School of Education, New York University, 1960).

[4]Ernest Machnits, "A Study of the Relationship of Certain Behaviors of Children to Emotional Needs, Values and Thinking" (Unpublished Ph.D. dissertation, School of Education, New York University, 1960).

[5]Arthur H. Jonas, "A Study of the Relationship of Certain Behaviors of Children to Emotional Needs, Values and Thinking" (Unpublished Ph.D. dissertation, School of Education, New York University, 1960).

[6]Donald Martin, "A Study of the Relationship of Certain Behaviors of Children to Emotional Needs, Values and Thinking" (Unpublished Ph.D. dissertation, School of Education, New York University, 1960).

whether there was any loss in the usual subject matter achievement if thinking were emphasized. The various standardized tests which relate to reading, study skills, and other subject areas indicated that the experimental children, *and* the children in the classes in which thinking was stressed, made more than the average gains achieved by several previous classes at the same level of instruction.

As this work is going on, Cartwright[7] undertook the development of a comprehensive resource unit for use at the college level which would include a heavy emphasis upon thinking operations. His collections of criteria and illustrative examples represented a further contribution to possible trials of the theory under more controlled conditions.

In 1962 Wassermann[8] completed "A Study of the Changes in Thinking-Related Behaviors in a Selected Group of Sixth Grade Children in the Presence of Selected Materials and Techniques." She tested the hypothesis that when materials and techniques designed to stimulate thinking are applied, a change will result in thinking-related patterns of behavior. At the beginning of her investigation, the children were identified by their former teachers, by their peer group, by themselves and by the investigator. An objective test relating to thinking was also used as a basis for estimating certain thinking abilities.

Nine children identified as thinking-related behavioral types at the close of the previous school year were placed in Wassermann's sixth grade classroom the following September. The children were provided with frequent opportunities to participate in activities involving comparing, classifying, criticizing, summarizing, and other operations of the kinds illustrated in Parts 2 and 3 of this volume.

At the close of the semester the behavior of these experimental children was once more assessed by their teachers, by their peers, by the children themselves, and by the thinking test which was administered again. The results were very conclusive. In the terms of before-and-after scores on the thinking test there was an improvement that was significant at the 2 per cent level. The behavior patterns changed in very significant ways. Each of the nine children showed a positive change in the behavior by which he was initially identified by teachers, and in his total behavior. These results were significant beyond the 1 per cent level, and the evidence clearly supports the theory which has been put forth in this volume. The same kind of positive change

---

[7]Roger Cartwright, "An Account of the Development and Application of a Resource Unit Stressing Thinking for a Course: ETA 2: Values, Teaching, and Planning" (Unpublished Ph. D. dissertation, School of Education, New York University, 1961).
[8]Selma Wassermann, "A Study of the Changes in Thinking-Related Behaviors in a Selected Group of Sixth Grade Children in the Presence of Selected Materials and Techniques" (Unpublished Ed.D. dissertation, School of Education, New York University, 1962).

was revealed in the peer ratings and this, too, was significant beyond the 1 per cent level.

In addition to the before-and-after scores and ratings, Wassermann's research includes case studies of the nine "experimental" children. This is a valuable, almost day-by-day, record of the way in which each child participated in thinking activities. These cases are rich in suggestions for other teachers. It is unfortunate that limitations of space make it impossible to include them all in this volume. Two such cases are here presented.

CASE STUDIES

Eddie

Eddie is a boy of medium height and weight with dark brown gleaming hair and dark shining eyes. His brusque manner and short, staccato speech mannerisms, coupled with his sardonic comments, belied the really sensitive child underneath.

Eddie, born in September, 1949, was admitted to first grade, at Lincoln School, at the age of six. His first grade teacher described him as "quite immature—noisy, restless, annoys the other children." Reports from his third grade teacher read, "I find Eddie to be a friendly and communicative child in class. He tends to rush through written assignments—accuracy is affected, and he makes careless, thoughtless mistakes. In his work, speed rather than accuracy seems to be his goal." The fourth grade teacher surveyed her year with him by writing, "He is easily diverted from any task—as a result he jumps from area to area without completing the assigned material. He seems to need special attention and encouragement constantly. There appears to be a lack of concentration. It has been pointed out to him that we cannot accomplish a great deal by doing three or four things at one time— but this seems difficult for Eddie to understand. He does not follow directions, written or otherwise." Eddie's fifth grade teacher indicated similar problems. "Eddie has difficulty in following directions and this causes him to sometimes do the wrong work and other times to misinterpret new facts." The sixth grade teacher wrote, after the first quarter of the term, "His independent work is not well self-directed. It is haphazard and impatient. He cannot be consistent about following specific guidelines."

Eddie's score on the *Pintner-Cunningham Primary Intelligence Test* administered during Eddie's first year in school, showed his I.Q. to be 115. The *California Test of Mental Maturity*, administered during the first month of sixth grade, measured his I.Q. at 106. On achievement tests given during his second, fourth and fifth years in school, Eddie was found to be achieving on grade level. However, on the *Stanford Achievement Test* given in April of his sixth grade term (the close of the experimental period), Eddie achieved scores of two years above grade level in reading ability, one year above grade level in arithmetic reasoning ability and showed slightly better than grade level ability in the other academic areas.

As part of the school's health program, the school nurse-teacher gave Eddie a complete physical screening at the beginning of the sixth grade. She reported that she had found no medical problem. The school psychologist found, on the basis of his observations and Eddie's performance on the *H-T-P* test, that Eddie seemed to be basically a suspicious and distrustful child who compensated for his feelings of inadequacy with a façade of compliance and a happy-go-lucky attitude. The psychologist concluded that although the drawings indicated that Eddie manifested some difficulties with respect to his social and emotional development, there was no evidence of psychosis or severe emotional disturbance.

In the initial assessment of behavior, Eddie was strongly identified by the teacher group as having behaviors representing both the "loud, dogmatic" type and the rigid "in-a-rut" type. Only the latter identification was strongly supported by the peer group, and Eddie himself added to this support by rating himself strongly in this category on the self-identification instrument. On the VAN PIT THINKING TEST Eddie made a total of eighteen errors in eighty responses. These data appear in the table on page 315.

For the purposes of the study, Eddie was classified as the child who is "in-a-rut," a characteristic of lack of experience with thinking. Eddie participated in thinking activities which involved the operations of comparing, classifying, observing, collecting and organizing data, summarizing, criticizing, looking for assumptions, suggesting hypotheses, self-analysis, applying principles, and analyzing the writings of others.

Eddie kept his own planbook, a record of his daily school activities. Although these were not difficult for him to formulate initially, he consistently reminded the investigator that, "this wasn't the way we did it last year," thus revealing suspicion of innovations in teaching methods and techniques. This type of comment almost became a trademark of Eddie, since it was attested to strongly by peer group responses as an identifying feature of Eddie's behavior.

Eddie had no academic problems which involved the need to structure curriculum material at a lower grade level. Nor did he appear to have any consuming interests at first. He seemed unable to comprehend the reasons for his being removed from the sixth grade group of children with whom he had been associated since the fourth grade. The true reason which reflected the purpose of the investigation was not given to him. It was explained as an administrative decision. He quite frankly admitted on numerous occasions, that the boys in the other group were still his "buddies" and that the boys in his present class were a bunch of "fairies." (This was a term used by some boys to denote those boys who were possibly more interested in school activities than in after-school activities.) These clues about Eddie were instrumental in aiding the investigator to develop thinking activities and value-questions for him.

Dec. 19 — Because Eddie had quoted an "assumed authority" to substantiate some information he had obtained, we discussed the question of supporting factual information with suitable documentation. He made up three examples of reasoning by "assumed authority" for practice.

Dec. 20 — He compared two films shown in class. He wrote:

Birds	*Asterisk*
1. About birds	1. About stages of growing up
2. Colorful	2. Bright colors

The investigator asked whether he felt that he had done a comprehensive comparison. He groaned, shrugged his shoulders and said that he didn't think so.

Dec. 20 — He compared the life of a boy in the Congo to the life of a boy in Forest City. He wrote:

(I am referring to a primitive boy in the Congo.)

1. An 11 year old boy in Forest City is much more civilized than an 11 year old boy in the Congo.
2. An 11 year old boy in Forest City is much smarter in arithmetic, spelling, reading, etc., than an 11 year old boy in the Congo.
3. An 11 year old boy in the Congo knows how to hunt better than an 11 year old boy in Forest City.
4. An 11 year old boy in Forest City has a much more balanced diet than an 11 year old boy in the Congo.
5. An 11 year old boy in the Congo lives in a hut but an 11 year old boy in Forest City lives in a house.
6. An 11 year old boy in the Congo can take care of himself better than an 11 year old boy in Forest City.
7. An 11 year old boy in the Congo is much more interested in survival than anything else.
8. An 11 year old boy in the Congo hasn't as much opportunities as an 11 year old boy in Forest City.
9. An 11 year old boy in Forest City has more entertainment and activity than an 11 year old boy in the Congo.

The investigator asked Eddie to look for assumptions he had made in the above comparisons. This was extremely difficult for him to do. He was asked to define the words "civilized," "smarter," and "survival" as he had used them in context.

Dec. 21 — Eddie compared two recorded popular songs.

Jan. 4 — He classified twenty-five geographical locations according to cities, countries and continents.

Jan. 9-10 — He collected and organized data about the contents of a newspaper.

Jan. 16 — He classified animals according to species.

Dec. 8-Jan. 16 — Eddie participated in group work and research on the topic "Primates" which was one part of a larger class science unit. This group work involved several thinking operations before its termination in group sharing of research and demonstration of projects. Eddie, as a member of his group, classified, observed, and collected and organized data, looked for assumptions, suggested hypotheses and did problem-solving. Eddie was highly motivated by this group work and showed a high degree of interest in the research. At one point, four boys in the group, including Eddie, decided they would take a Saturday trip into the city to the Museum of Natural History to use the Hall of Man as reference. They later summarized their trip experiences in the class.

Jan. 16 — During the time in which the various groups were sharing their research, Eddie questioned the children of the group who had studied the theories of the creation of the earth, asking, "Some scientists think that Pluto may be a part of another solar system. If this is true, was Pluto then formed the same way as the earth? I just want to know what you think."

Jan. 27 — Eddie criticized the class' reaction to an air raid drill.

Jan. 27 — Eddie evaluated "A Good Teacher." He wrote:
"To me a good teacher must fit the following classifications. She or he must have a good personality and a good way of teaching. To me those are the important (things). Then there is some that are less important such as a good patience and a good sence (*sic*) of humor. There is a lot more, but these are the ones I will be talking about. In all of my years of school I have never had a teacher who did not fit the classifications. Before each new school year I wonder if my teacher will fit the classifications, but so far no sweat."

Feb. 3 — As a self-analysis activity, Eddie was asked why he wanted to learn. He frankly said, "It's very simple. I really don't know what I want to be when I grow up, so I want to have a good chance later on in life when I choose my occupation."

Feb. 6 — Eddie came to the investigator and said that he had a good idea for a science project that he wanted to do. When questioned about it, he proceeded to explain how he would use the design and title of a project which his class had done last year. He was given permission to carry out the project, but he did not complete it.

Feb. 9 — Eddie, sent on an errand, was asked to write what he had observed. Later, when he handed in his paper, he said, "I don't like doing this. When I first sat down, I didn't know what I saw. Then I thought for a while and I could have written three pages."

Feb. 10 — Eddie, speaking in class on the subject of whether to use a pen or pencil for a given assignment, said, "I know when you (referring to the investigator) say a pencil is all right. Then I start to use a pencil, I look at the guy next to me and he's using a pen. The guy next to him is using a pen, too. So I rip up my paper and start again with a pen."

Feb. 14-24 — Eddie was involved in planning activities, in collecting and organizing data and in group discussion as part of social studies committee work.

Feb. 16 — In class discussion on current events, Eddie volunteered this information: "If you ask me, I think that the crash (referring to the Boeing 707 jet crash in Belgium) was fixed. You know, a Russian could always go up to a man and say, 'I'll give you a few thousand dollars if you make the plane crash and parachute out.' " The investigator wrote this statement down and gave it to Eddie to re-examine. He maintained his original position.

Feb. 27 — Eddie was asked to compare two of the murals done in class. When the assignment had been made, he began working, discarded his paper, took another, discarded that and took a third. He said, then, "It's pretty hard when it's your own mural that you're comparing, because you think that it's the best."

Investigator: "Well, do you think you could make your comparison without making any value judgments?"

Eddie: (Smiling broadly) "Oh, I see what you mean.'" He then made the comparisons on the points of color, type of media used, information contained and content.

Feb. 28 — Eddie compared group reading and individualized reading.

Feb. 28 — He compared *The New York Times* with *Newsday*. He found fifty-four points to compare in this activity.

Mar. 1 — Eddie compared two boys in the class. His choice of boys was interesting, since he had selected for comparison two boys whom he had previously considered "fairies." His admiration for these boys was evident in his comparison.

Mar. 1 — Eddie compared two teachers. On the point of discipline, he wrote that one teacher made use of "capital punishment." The difference between capital punishment and corporal punishment was brought to his attention. He grinned and said, "I know the difference and I *mean* capital punishment!"

Mar. 1 — Eddie was given a simulated stock certificate for 100 shares of stock in a *bona fide* company. He developed a method for tabulating his daily and weekly profits and losses on the stock market.

Mar. 2 — Eddie compared the life cycle of a frog to that of a butterfly. Added to his written comparison were illustrations which he drew for each stage of development.

Mar. 2 — He compared two of his daily plans.

Mar. 3 — He compared two books he had read.

Mar. 3 — He compared the school library with the public library.

Mar. 6 — He summarized an article on the U. N.

Mar. 6 — Eddie changed his seat so that he could sit with his new friends. These new friends consisted of the children he had chosen to work with in the ongoing social studies unit and who, in the investigator's opinion, manifested maturity and who functioned on a high level of self-direction.

Mar. 6 — Eddie summarized his day in class.

Mar. 7 — Eddie summarized an assigned article about airplanes.

Mar. 7 — He summarized a film which he had seen in class.

Mar. 8 — He summarized his evening's activities.

Mar. 8 — As a self-analysis activity, he wrote on the topic, "Who I would Like to be Like When I grow Up." He wrote:

"When I grow up I would like to be like Albert Einstein. One reason is that he is a great celebrity. Oh, I know there are many more celebrities in the world but none as smart as him. I would make a lot of money and many jobs would be open to me. There are a lot more reasons but I am just an average boy who has to finish his lunch in a candy store!"

Feb. 1-Mar. 17 — Eddie's choice of a group in the new social studies unit was a surprising one to the investigator. He chose to work with a group of children whom he had openly criticized at the beginning of the school year for their interest in school and in learning. This group did research on the American Negro, and showed in dramatic form, with music and dance, a history of the American Negro in this country from the arrival of the slaves. Eddie's group probed deeply the problem of racial prejudice and presented a poignant picture of how children were affected by this. This choice of a group was a surprise from another point of view. Although not previously recorded, Eddie had displayed feelings of racial prejudice on several occasions. Therefore, his choice of group was doubly interesting. During the group work Eddie was spirited, enthusiastic and highly involved. The group project, the dramatic presentation, was deemed a creative and successful experience by those who were invited to attend the production.

Mar. 22-28 — During this week, Eddie classified types of foods, manufactured goods, cities, musical instruments, famous people, numbers, words, the books he had read during the term, and sports.

Mar. 29 — Eddie summarized his experiences at the U. N.

Mar. 30-Apr. 9 — Easter Holidays

Apr. 10 — Eddie participated in an activity in observing and interpreted data based upon his observation.

Apr. 11 — Eddie wrote his definition of thinking:

"What is thinking? Thinking is what you do before you do it. In other words you stop and say — What am I doing? Why am I doing it? and How am I doing it?"

Apr. 13 — Eddie summarized a story which he was assigned to read.

Apr. 14 — He summarized a television program he had seen.

Apr. 17 — Eddie analyzed a piece of literature distributed during the school board election campaign by one of the factions supporting candidates for election. He underlined words which he felt were "emotionally charged" and which tended to slant the facts. His evaluation on this leaflet was, "I think that this paper is trying to make up YOUR mind by using colored words and possibly false facts."

Apr. 19 — As a self-analysis activity, Eddie was asked to list the things which he felt prejudiced against. He enumerated the following:
1. classical music
2. Communism
3. Eichmann
4. long car rides
5. corderoy

6. velvet
7. grouchy people
8. bossy people
9. spinach
10. plums
11. peaches
12. peanut butter
13. untidiness
14. love stories
15. small print
16. big shots
17. pies
18. physical discomforts
19. short hair
20. greasy hair
21. poor manners
22. gardening
23. housework
24. red hair
25. rude people
26. unkindly people
27. sauerkraut
28. pickles
29. sad music
30. diseases
31. shots

After he had done this, he classified the above list. And finally, he wrote the following:

"My prejudices are few but the thing that disturbs me the most is "Characteristics of People." (Here he was referring to a category which he had set up.) In my life I have come across many types of people such as grouchy people, bossy people, rude people, etc., but when I stop to think, I find I have judged some of my prejudices very unfairly, such as red hair. This bothers me badly because it is not the person's fault but the person was born that way. Doing this essay made me stop and think about my prejudices and I find that I was very, very wrong, therefore, I think that this assignment was very interesting and good."

Apr. 20 — Eddie criticized the individualized math program.

Apr. 20 — Eddie criticized his day in school.

Apr. 21 — Eddie criticized his self-discipline.

Apr. 21 — He criticized the school's safety patrol.

Apr. 22 — Eddie wrote a criticism of his teacher during the weekend and submitted it to her on Monday.

Apr. 24-28 — Eddie participated in various teacher-developed activities involving the interpretation of data.

Mar. 24-May 4 — Eddie participated in group planning and research of the nervous system, as part of a larger class science unit. Included in this group work were activities in observing, collecting and organizing data, interpreting data, applying principles, and suggesting hypotheses. During the time in which the projects were shared with the entire class, Eddie was also involved in criticizing.

May 1-11 — Eddie collected and organized data on the following topics: bacteria, Louis Pasteur, Marie Curie, Alexander the Great, Hippocrates, Euclid and number systems.

May 11-19 — As a part of the self-analysis activities, Eddie wrote what he felt on the following topics. Value clarification was carried out by the investigator with Eddie for each of these papers:

"I am a boy of 11 years old. I have many likes and dislikes in the world but I find that I have to live with them. Some things I just can't apply myself to and some things I just don't give a chance. In school I think I am an average student and I find it very easy to get along with people."

"From the time I was born till now I was told what was right and what was wrong by my parents, my grandparents, my relatives, my friends and everyone else who was older than me. But now my brother gets all the attention and I am left on my own until I really do something very bad. But I do think that 11 year old children should be left alone.'

"I think cheating on a test is a bad thing to do because a test just tells how much you learned. But I also think that cheating isn't the worst thing to do."

"If I had $5.00 and my mother's birthday was this coming week and I needed a bicycle tire for a bicycle trip also this coming week and my mother said that she would not mind if I didn't get her a present, what would I do? I still would buy my mother the present. Why? 1. I would not feel right. 2. There will be other bicycle trips."

"I think stealing is very bad thing to do and is caused by jealousy or poor up bringing. But I must admit that years ago when I saw an open bag of toy soldiers I would take maybe one or two of them. I feel that I have outgrown that stage a long time ago. One reason why I think I stopped was that I started reading the papers and hearing about these terrible things that people do."

June 1-8 — Eddie participated in several exercises which involved suggesting appropriate hypotheses for problem situations. In general, his suggestions were logical and imaginative.

May 8-June 15 — For the large class social studies unit, Eddie chose to do group work and research on the Middle Ages. He was instrumental in assigning duties to the members and directing group operations. Many of the ideas for the project came from him. He selected films in this area from the audio-visual library which were shown in class. He also arranged for the scheduling of the films. The group activity, under Eddie's direction, was well-organized, and well presented. The project, a scale model of a feudal manor, was well designed and well executed.

June 8 — It was apparent to the investigator, by this time, that Eddie had some different feelings about himself than he had had at the beginning of the year.

Several specific incidents supplied evidence to support the investigator's observation. On this day, the class was visited by a graduate student from a nearby college who questioned the children about their sixth grade experiences. She was concerned about how they would adjust to a departmentalized junior high school program the following year, and she asked the children how they felt about this. Eddie volunteered his thoughts and said, "This type of sixth grade program has taught us to have self-discipline and to think for ourselves. I feel that I could face any kind of seventh grade and do a good job, because thinking for yourself teaches you how to handle any new situation."

June 13 — Eddie wrote the following assessment of his sixth grade work:

"My Evaluation of My Year's Learning. This year I think was the best school year I have ever had and possibly the best year I will ever have. I also think I have learned a great deal in this program. It really amazes me to think that last year I was almost under grade level and I worked to learn. Whereas this year I am over grade level and I find that I enjoy learning."

June 14 — Eddie evaluated himself on a simulated report card. He rated himself above grade level in reading, oral expression, math and social studies. This was in close accord with the investigator's evaluation of his progress.

June 15 — In a class discussion of a problem which the children were facing, Eddie made this comment about himself and another boy in the class:

"We came from the same class and should have gone to Mr. S's sixth grade. B. (referring to the child) is still very much like those boys in that class. I used to be that way, but somehow, I'm just not myself anymore.'

Behavioral Changes

Eddie was originally identified by the teacher group as exhibiting behaviors indicative of the "loud dogmatic" type and of the "in-a-rut" type. He received a score of $+12$ for each of these identifications. In the final assessment by the teacher group, Eddie was only tentatively identified by two teachers as "in-a-rut" giving him a total score of $+2$ for that category, and he was not identified as the "loud, dogmatic" type by any of the teachers in the group, giving him a zero score for that category. The final ratings by the teacher group showed a behavioral gain of $+10$ for the "in-a-rut" behavior, and a gain of $+12$ for the "loud, dogmatic" behavior. The peer group identification of Eddie's behavior at the beginning of the investigation gave him a rating of $+23$ for the behavior associated with the "in-a-rut" type. The final rating by this group was $+10$, showing a behavioral gain of $+13$ for this category. Eddie's rating of his own behavior as the "in-a-rut" type was originally $+3$. His final rating of his own behavior in this category was zero. Finally, Eddie's performance on the VAN PIT THINKING TEST showed a total of fourteen errors out of eighty responses, compared to the eighteen errors made on the first administration of this test. An analysis of the original eighteen errors showed that fourteen of these were errors made by his having gone beyond the data, two were cautious errors and two were gross errors. On the final test, an analysis of the fourteen errors showed that six were errors in having gone beyond the data, seven were cautious errors and one was a gross error. These data are presented in the table on this page.

Although the validity of the investigator's observation may be open to challenge as evidence to attest to behavioral change, it is her opinion that Eddie was the child in the study whose behavioral change was the most dramatic.

TABLE I

EDDIE

CHANGES IN RATINGS

Group	"Rigid — In a rut" Behavior				Total Ratings			
	Maximum Possible	Initial	Final	Change	Maximum Possible	Initial	Final	Change
Teachers	15	12	2	+10	120	40	4	+36
Peers	45	23	10	+13	360	51	17	+34
Self	3	3	0	+ 3	24	11	4	+ 7

CHANGES IN VAN PIT SCORE TEST SCORES

	Maximum Possible	Initial	Final	Change
Total number of errors	80	18	14	+4
Number of "going beyond the data" errors	60	14	6	+8
Number of "cautious" errors	20	2	7	−5
Number of gross errors	20	2	1	+1
Number not answered	80	0	0	0

Bobby

Bob, a superbly tall and well built boy, towered head and shoulders above the other children in the class. It seemed to him that all of his life he had been bigger and stronger than those children in his peer group. Atop his head was a rich crop of light brown wavy hair. His bright eyes seemed to encompass his surroundings quickly. His upper lip protruded above the lower, a result of an extreme malocclusion, yet he exhibited no apparent self-consciousness about either his height or his teeth, both extremely prominent physical characteristics.

Bob's cumulative records showed that he had had difficulties in school from first grade upward. His first grade teacher wrote that his work habits and general attitude were poor. She added, "Although he has done adequate work to go into second grade I feel he could be near the top of the group if he would only apply himself." Notes from the second grade teacher read, "I am constantly after him to get to his lessons. He talks aloud and gets on the floor so much that he is very disturbing to the rest of the class. He is a large boy and likes to push the other children around. His work isn't as good as it should be. He just isn't trying." From the third grade teacher — "Robert is a boy who is capable of doing much better work. However, due to his emotional insecurity (?) and other factors which I am not too sure of, he is functioning on a below average level in all of his subjects." Bob's third grade teacher recommended that he repeat third grade. Before this recommendation was acted upon by the administration, a survey of opinion of the special subject teachers was made. The school nurse-teacher indicated that "previous conferences with teachers revealed he was a behavioral disturbance in class." The art teacher wrote that "Robert seems overly aggressive." Bob was promoted to fourth grade. His teacher wrote, "He wanders about the room, does not come to class prepared. He is capable of doing his work quickly but procrastinates and then is the last to finish. I feel that he is capable of doing very good work, but he finds it difficult to do one thing too long or to stay put for long." Bob's fifth grade teacher, a male, exercised considerable control over him, with the threat of severe punishment. He recorded that "Robert is no longer a behavior problem in school." At the beginning of sixth grade, the investigator made the following observations: "He needs close supervision and structuring; he seems totally unequipped to function independently. He attests to the importance of learning, yet will not (or rather *can* not) extend himself totally into the learning situation. There appears to be very little inner motivation for learning. Bob needs to conform and he resists and resents having to function as an individual. There appears to be a great conflict within him — brain vs. muscle — and since he is so well equipped with the latter, this is usually his choice. Bob reflects some deep rooted bias toward minority groups. He is very adamant about his point of view and rarely allows himself to see another."

Bob was given a group intelligence test in the first, third and sixth grades. His I. Q. scores on each were 117, 114, and 116 respectively. Achievement tests administered in second, fourth and fifth grades indicated that he was achieving on or slightly below grade level. On his sixth grade achievement test, administered in April (the close of the experimental period) Bob showed a remarkable gain in his score. The battery median measured his achievement at 7.8, with individual test scores of 8.7 in reading, 7.2 in arithmetic, 7.7 in science and 9.5 in social studies.

A routine physical screening administered by the school nurse-teacher indicated that Bob was in good physical health. He was being treated by an orthodontist for his teeth, and during the course of the year Bob began to wear a temporary appliance. The speech teacher who worked with Bob because of his lisp, felt that little could be done for his speech until his teeth were corrected. The school psychologist, on the basis of his observations and Bob's performance on the H-T-P test, reported that he found Bob to be a "bright, aggressive boy, who, in spite of his large physical stature, showed a lack of masculinity. In addition, Bob's pictures showed a conflict between expansiveness and conservatism with extreme standards of propriety and morality. However, there is no evidence of psychosis or severe emotional disturbance."

In the initial assessment of behavior, Bob was classified in three categories by his previous teacher as the "loud-dogmatic-assertive" type, the "impulsive" type and the type "who actively resists thinking." In each case these identifications were supported with a rating of +3 by the investigator. Each teacher gave him a positive rating of +3 for each identification. The peer group strongly supported the identification of Bob as the "loud-dogmatic-assertive" type, with the highest score recorded by the investigator for any child in a single category. This group also strongly supported the "anti-think" identification. On the self-identification form, Bob rated himself as "impulsive" and one who "misses the meaning," but only tentatively supported the "anti-think" identification and gave no support to the "loud-dogmatic-assertive" identification. Bob's performance on the VAN PIT THINKING TEST was twenty-six errors out of eighty responses. These data are found in the table on page 328.

For the purposes of the study, Bob was classified as the child who actively resists thinking, or the "anti-think" type. Because of the strength of the teacher group and peer group ratings in the "loud-dogmatic" category, Bob was classified as belonging within the category despite the fact that his own rating did not support this identification. Procedures were then initiated to provide Bob with frequent opportunities to engage in thinking activities. He participated in activities which involved the operations of comparing, classifying, observing, collecting and organizing data, summarizing, criticizing, looking for assumptions, suggesting hypotheses, self-analysis, applying principles and analyzing the writings of others.

Bob kept his own planbook of his daily school activities. At first, he made every effort to avoid writing his plans. After several weeks, he finally shouted, "I can't do this stuff. I need you (referring to investigator) to tell me what to do. I need you to put arithmetic, page so and so, on the blackboard. I need you to do that for me." It was at this point that the investigator realized that the pace she had set for Bob was too rapid; that he was not yet ready for this type of independent activity; that he needed more time to make the transition between a program which was completely structured for him and one which he designed for himself. Immediately, Bob was taken back to the teacher-controlled program, and a step-by-step procedure of helping him to gain his independence in this activity was carried out.

By the beginning of December, Bob was able to do a competent job of writing plans and showing purposes for his daily school activities. His problem at that time became carrying these plans out, or accomplishing what he had set out to do. Again the investigator had to assume the role of director, checking Bob's activities against his plans many times during the day. This technique, however, was one that was agreed upon by both the child and the investigator. Finally, to gain added support and control, Bob moved his table and chair to a position adjoining the teacher's desk. He remained there for many weeks, and when he felt ready, he moved to join a group on the far side of the room. This occurred on February 8 and was looked upon by the investigator as a positive indication of Bob's feeling about himself.

Bob's consuming passion was drawing and he used almost every free moment for this activity. His art usually depicted scenes from the middle ages (knights in combat, feudal castles, ancient war implements) or scenes from his fantasy world of the future (large ultra-modern city structures, mechanized city life, space craft, motor vehicles). His exceptional talent and his ambition to become an architect served the investigator as means for developing thinking-related activities which had both purpose and meaning for Bob.

Dec. 15 — As an activity in self-analysis, Bob wrote on the topic, "What Makes Me Mad":

> "It's odd but half the time I am mad and half the time I am not. But most of all I am mad because of my brother Gary! It begins in our room in the morning when we are dressing. I sing a song (mostly *Whistle While You Work*) and my brother says I sing like an old cow, and I say he can't even sing, and he says oh sure, and he says listen and he sings. So I hold my ears and he gets mad and says to me get off my bed fatso. I look at him and say get your clothes off my chair and he says no, so I throw them off and he puts (the clothes) them back on, etc., etc., etc. And we keep it up until he knots *(sic)* something down (mostly models) and I punch him and he crys *(sic)* and gets my mother and we both get whiped *(sic)* and I say I'll never give him another thing and I go out of the room and ram the door shut. Another thing that gets me mad is girls. They are always running across my lawn so I get mad and make holes in their lawn etc., etc. So they get there *(sic)* mother and my mother comes out and everybody is on the girls' side. And the only ones on my side are my friends and the only thing I can say is rats!"

Dec. 19 — Bobby compared two recorded songs.

Jan. 4 — He classified a list of cities according to location in countries.

Jan. 7 — Bob was asked to compare the structure of a news article to that of an editorial. Instead, he summarized the content of an editorial and the content of a news article. At the end of his paper he wrote: "My thought: As you can see there is much difference between the articles."

Jan. 10 — Several boys who were working on a science project using plaster of Paris washed the residues of the plaster down the sink, causing the sink to clog. Bob, observing the situation, commented, "You know why this thing's clogged — it's cheap!"
Investigator: "Is that the only reason you can think of?"
Bob: "Well, everybody left a mess at the sink!"

Investigator: "Do you mean everybody in the class?"

Bob: "Yeah, everybody always leaves a mess!"

Investigator: "Do you really mean everybody in the class, without a single exception?"

Bob: "Well, almost everybody."

Jan. 16 — During the sharing of the science projects, one of the boys explained to the rest of the class about one-celled animals. Bob made the following observation:

Bob: "We eat protozoa."

Investigator: "What do you mean, Bob?"

Bob: "Well, you said that meat has cells and we eat meat, so we eat protozoa."

Jan. 17 — Bob classified a list of animals according to species.

Jan. 18 — Bob analyzed advertisements in magazines for those which led the public into making assumptions.

Jan. 19 — Bob: "See, I was right," (showing investigator a picture in a reference book illustrating pre-historic life).

Investigator: "What do you mean?"

Bob: "Dinosaurs are not reptiles."

Investigators: "Why do you say that?"

Bob: "It says here, "There are about 5,000 kinds of dinosaurs. The word *Dinosaur* means *terrible lizard*. But dinosaurs were not lizards. They were not even close relatives of the lizards. So you see, they're not even reptiles."

Jan. 20 — During a class discussion of a television program which had dealt with the desegregation of a public school in Arkansas and its effects on a Negro family, Bob made the following comment:

Bob: "Do you know what I would do if I had to go to school like that Negro boy? I would go through those people with a gun and would shoot my way through!"

Investigator: "Why would you do that?"

Bob: "I'd show them that they couldn't push me around!"

Jan. 23 — Bob, listening to a report on amphibians, retorted, "What's the use of their laying eggs if they're going to be eaten? That doesn't make any sense."

Investigator: "What would happen if the amphibians stopped laying eggs completely, Bob?"

Bob: "They'd die out."

Investigator: "What would you do if you were an amphibian — lay eggs, knowing that some would be eaten, or stop laying eggs completely, knowing that the species would then die out?"

Bob: "I see what you mean. I guess it's better to have some eggs than none at all."

Dec. 8-Jan. 23 — Bob participated in investigations and group work (discussion, planning and construction of project) on the topic of Reptiles, as part of a larger class science unit. Bob was very highly motivated to do the research, which dealt primarily with pre-historic reptiles and secondarily with current reptile species. He was also very much absorbed in working on a mural, which served as a background scene for a table-top diorama. During the sharing of results, Bob's group demonstrated a simulated volcanic eruption, much to the delight of the class. The group work involved thinking operations of classifying, observing, criticizing (much of this was done by Bob and was directed toward the behavior of the three other boys in the group, who in turn, had their opportunities to criticize Bob's behavior both to him and to the investigator), collecting and organizing data, suggesting hypotheses, problem-solving and self-analysis.

Jan. 25 — Bob was extremely interested in a visitor to the class — a Korean teacher from the University of Hawaii's Laboratory School — who told the children about Korea, about Hawaii and about herself and her family. After she left, Bob, visibly upset, asked, "Why did she have to tell us about her husband? (She had told the class that he had died several years ago.) I wonder why she told us that?"

Jan. 27 — Bob criticized the class' performance on an air raid drill.

Jan. 27 — Bob wrote the following, analyzing his feelings about "A Good Teacher":

"A good teacher must have patients *(sic)* with the children and parents (at conferences) when they don't understand something. They must have good humor and laugh when something is funny, but they have to be strict sometimes. They must always have confidence in the children, show them and lead them on the right road to succes *(sic)*. They should be able to hold their temper and treat the child in a nice way. Not only do they teach from book but in ways of making it fun to do it. They must know what work a child needs otherwise it makes it bad for him or her. They must always have love even for the bad ones."

Jan. 30 — Bob was given the responsibility of caring for the newly arrived art supplies. He stored the supplies in cabinets and on shelves and presented the investigator with a tentative plan for distribution. He issued orders to the children about taking supplies and about keeping the supply cabinets neat.

Feb. 1 — Bob: (After the investigator had been absent for one day) "Don't be absent any more. I need you here. Something happens to me when you're not here."

Investigator: "What do you mean, Bob?"

Bob: "I don't know. I just fall apart."

Investigator: "What makes it different when I'm here?"

Bob: "I don't know. The substitutes they send are just plain mean. They just don't understand kids. They pick on me for every little thing. Then I get mad and before I know it I'm in trouble again."

Investigator: "Who takes care of you when you're out playing with the boys?"

Bob: "What do you mean? I take care of myself. I can take care of myself. You should see me."

Investigator: "I can see that all right. And who will take care of you when you go into junior high, and into college?"

Bob: "You know, I know what you mean. I guess I have to learn to get some good self-discipline in school."

Investigator: "I think you are learning that, Bob."

Feb. 1 — Bob did some exercises in reasoning from the universal to the particular. He was then asked to try to make up some similar exercises, but he was unsuccessful at this.

Feb. 2 — During a class discussion on "good human relations" Bob commented, "What's this about the Moslems who believe in the sacredness of the cow? Cows running loose and being worshipped? Isn't that pretty stupid?"
Investigator: "Why do you think that's stupid?"
Bob: "It's ridiculous to worship cows!"
Investigator: "How do you know that?"
Bob: "We don't do that in our religion."
Investigator: "Might the Moslems think that some religious rites which you practice are silly?"
Bob: "What? Don't be silly. At least my religion is sensible. I wouldn't care if I had any other religion as long as it was a Christian religion. That's the only sensible religion."

Feb. 2 — Later during the same discussion which had now come to the problem of discriminating against the Negro, Bob made a reference to the fact that the white population of the world was in the majority. This was contradicted strongly by several children, while one girl went to a reference book for the facts. Presented with population figures, he still looked incredulous and shook his head in disbelief.

Feb. 3 — Bob analyzed his feelings about learning.
He wrote:
"I want to learn because . . . Well let's put it this way. I have to learn if I want to be an architect (and that's what I want). I like to learn sertin *(sic)* subjects and others (ugh) I don't like. I like language because of themes, but then again I don't like spelling because it drives me nuts with all the words. And then theys *(sic)* subjects I only like half and half like arithmetic. I like to learn how to do a problem, but certain exzamples *(sic)* drive me battey *(sic)*. I like most of the subjects and what you have to know to do it, but others are out of orbit. I like to learn and I have to learn, so I can't fight, can I?"

Feb. 6 — During class discussion on problems existing for the African in the Union of South Africa, Bob raised the following question:
Bob: "There's something I don't understand."
Investigator: "What's that, Bob?"
Bob: "Well, when there was a slavery problem down south in our country, the north fought them and won the war and the slaves were freed. So why don't the people in North Africa go to war against South Africa and free the slaves there?"

Feb. 9 — Bob observed the teacher and wrote his observations. He looked for assumptions in his observation.

Feb. 10 — Bob wrote his observations of his walk from the gymnasium to class. He looked for assumptions in his observation.

Feb. 14 — Bob compared two films shown in class. His comparison centered about the artistic quality of the films.

Feb. 15 — Bob classified cities relating to the group studies of the social studies unit.

Feb. 16 — Bob's social studies group was having internal difficulties. The investigator asked the six boys in the group to suggest possible means of solving their problems.

Feb. 20 — Bob compared *The New York Times* and the *Newsday*.

Feb. 21 — Bob criticized the art work in a newly arrived children's book.

Feb. 22 — Bob observed rock formations and terrain of southwest United States from slides.

Feb. 23 — Bob compared two paintings of women, one by Matisse and one by Toulouse-Lautrec.

Feb. 27 — He compared two murals done by children in the class.

Feb. 28 — Bob compared individualized and group reading. He listed the following points:

Self Reading

1. You can read better
2. You pick your own book whenever you want
3. You read as much as you want
4. You can read A.M. or P.M.
5. You can stop in the book whenever you want
6. You can tell others about the book
7. You have a conference anytime

Group Reading

1. You have a hard time reading
2. You have to read the book you're given and read it at a certain time
3. You can only read a certain amount
4. You have to read it in the morning
5. You read the whole book
6. You can't sell a book because the other children have already read it
7. You don't have a conference with the teacher

Bob looked for value judgments he had made in his comparison.

Mar. 1 — Bob compared butterflies and frogs. He did a comprehensive ten point comparison.

Mar. 1 — Bob compared two teachers. He looked for assumptions in his comparison and found one.

Mar. 2 — Bob compared two boys in the class.

Mar. 3 — Bob compared the school library with the public library.

Mar. 3 — Usually very active in class discussion, Bob began to preface his comments with the phrase, "This has nothing to do with it, but ..."

Mar. 6 — Bob compared two books he had read.

Mar. 6 — Bob summarized an article on the U. N. He summarized a film shown in class. He looked for assumptions in his summary.

Mar. 7 — He summarized his day's activities in class.

Mar. 7-10 — Bob was actively involved in criticizing and evaluating skits presented by children working in social studies groups.

Mar. 8 — In class discussion concerning the possibility of presenting the social studies skits for the school in an assembly program, Bob was very adamant about his feelings. He said, "The other kids will make fun of it."
Investigator: "Which other kids?"
Bob: "There are about twenty kids who will act up — I know them. I don't want them to be making fun of me."
In the discussion that followed, Bob seemed to be making the point that he did not want to expose not only himself, but the class to possible ridicule by others in his peer group (specifically other sixth grade boys). Bob seemed to associate the singing and dancing in the skits with the type of program which is often done by primary grade children.

Mar. 8 — Bob summarized his evening's activities.

Mar. 9 — He summarized a television program.

Mar. 13 — Bob was extremely uncooperative during the afternoon rehearsals for the program. When his behavior was discussed with him, he sometimes shrugged it off, and other times indicated that he was embarrassed by the performances.

Mar. 14 — Bob summarized a film shown in class.

Mar. 14 — He summarized a book he enjoyed.

Mar. 15 — He summarized a story he had read in class.

Feb. 1-Mar. 17 — Bob was involved in group work, as part of a larger class social studies unit which focused upon the improvement of human relations. Bob's group studied the Irish immigration to America and the hardships which these people encountered when they settled in this country. The result of the group study was a dramatic presentation which was written and acted by the six children in the group. Although, on several occasions, Bob voiced disapproval of this type of production, he entered into the last week of preparation and rehearsal of his own group's work very spiritedly. While participating in this unit, Bob carried on activities in collecting and organizing data, self-analysis, suggesting hypotheses and problem-solving.

Bob voiced many negative comments which were chiefly directed to the recorded Russian folk music being used for the Central European group's dances. Because the record was labeled "Russian," Bob scorned it contemptuously. It was his feeling that the use of a Russian song implied favoring Communism. Although the investigator discussed this with Bob, there did not seem to be a change in his attitude.

On the evening of the performance, however, Bob approached the investigator during the intermission and suggested that it might be a good idea for us to play the music on the Russian record as background music, to entertain the parents during intermission time. Several days later, he asked:
"How much does that Russian record cost?"
Investigator: "Oh, about four dollars, I guess."
Bob: "Gee, that much? I'd like to buy it. but I only have two dollars saved."

Mar. 20 — Bob classified cities appropriate to the social studies unit work.

Mar. 21 — He classified the types of musical instruments used by his group in the play.

Mar. 21 — He classified types of foods according to meals.

Mar. 23 — He classified the books that he had read during the term.

Mar. 23 — Bob classified the names of people in the news according to nationality.

Mar. 23 — He classified numbers according to odd and even numbers.

Mar. 24 — He classified sports according to team and individual participant sports.

Mar. 27 — He classified a list of manufactured goods according to which stores they could be purchased in.

Mar. 28 — Bob wrote a comprehensive observation of his trip to the U. N.:

"I learned that there are a lot of different places in New York City. I never heard of Washington Square but I saw it on the day of the field trip. I also learned that a bookshop run by a beat is the same as one run by a business man. I thought that beatniks only like jazz, but they like folksongs too (and they sing pretty good). I learned that the United Nations was planned by eleven men (from different countries). I saw gifts given to the U. N. by Holland, Russia, and Greece. I saw all the flags of different countries and the U. N. garden. I learned what all the rooms were for and the countries that took parts in the meetings and why they took parts in the meetings. I learned that there was a dark room for anyone who wanted to think or pray before meetings. I learned who planned the different rooms and furnished them. I learned that the U.N. has all kinds of people working for it. And I learned there are four rooms, but I forget their names. I also learned that the U.N. has a very expensive gift shop."

Mar. 29-Apr. 9 — Easter Holidays

Apr. 10-11 — Bob recorded his observations in performing science experiments, exploring respiratory and muscular functions of his body.

Apr. 12 — Bob gave his definition of thinking:

"A use of the brain, a learning in life: a learning in school, adult work and science, a learning in the world and space. To examine your worrying and conscience."

Apr. 13 — During class discussion on school budget (community was to vote on budget the following day), Bob commented: "When I was in Mrs. V's (4th grade) class, she tried to explain to us how important it was to support schools and school budgets. The whole class was won over, all but me. She tried to help me understand, but I wouldn't be swayed. I kept to my own point of view, which was my parents' point."

Investigator: "How do you feel about it now?"

Bob: "The same, I guess."

Apr. 17-21 — Absent, due to illness.

Apr. 24-28 — Bob participated in activities involving the interpretation of data. Bob was elected president of the class. After the nominations had been made, several children spoke to support a particular candidate (while the candidates were out of the room). Those speaking on Bob's behalf said that they felt his behavior had improved considerably and that the honor of serving as class president might further help him. (These comments were unsolicited by the investigator. As a matter of fact, although the investigator did not doubt the good intentions of the children supporting Bob's candidacy, she was, at that time, unconvinced as to Bob's ability to "handle" this kind of responsibility.)

May 1 — Bob looked for assumptions in problems in his math text.

Mar. 24-May 4 — Bob participated in group work, doing research on and preparing a project showing the major organs of the human body. This study challenged Bob's interest, and his drawings and clay models of the body organs were excellent. It is interesting to note at this point, that there were few major behavioral crises in the group work, as compared to the two previously described group activities which took place during December, January, February and the early weeks of March. It is also interesting to observe that on a culminating evaluative test made up by the various groups of children who worked on this science unit, Bob received a score of 91. He was especially delighted by this, since he had previously felt that science was one of his poorest subjects, and on a similar test given at the end of November, his mark had been 29.

May 2-11 — Bob collected and organized data on the following topics: Louis Pasteur, the wheel, Marie Curie, Alexander the Great, Greek architecture, Frank Lloyd Wright.

May 15-19 — Bob analyzed his thinking on the following topics:

"Myself. I think I'm tall and long. I think I'm a normal thinker, what I mean is, I'm not dumb and I'm not brilliant. I am a good drawer sometimes, but there are days when I can't even draw a straight line. I think I'm good in social studies and off and on in science (it all depends on the subject), but in spelling, oh brother! I like most sports and enter most events, but there are times I can't even kick a ball. I like hobbies such as putting together models and collecting odds and ends which my mother calls junk! I like to read about famous generals of the past and wars and countries. I like school for one reason. I learn there and another is if there were no school I wouldn't have anything to do and I would soon get bored. I like to travel and I've gone to a lot of places in the country. I like animals and once in a while I find an animal I like in the woods or the pet store (but that's very rare that I get one). I like my friends (that's because I've been playing with them for ten years) and go to many places with them. I like many things, but best of all I like my parents and brothers."

"What I Think of Cheating on a Test. I cheat very rarely, but when I do, I know why I'm doing it, mainly because I don't know the answer and it's the biggest question (with the most points). My conchience *(sic)* never bothers me when I do cheat but the big problem is keeping it to myself without opening my big mouth. Sometimes I'm caught but that's very rarely. I feel there's nothing wrong with cheating a little, but if you do it constantly, it's not doing you a bit of good."

"If I had to choose between buying my mother a present or a bicycle tire for myself, I would buy my mother a present, because, well, your mother's birthday only comes once a year and you can get a bike tire any old time. And also, does a bike tire look after you until you're full grown, does a bike tire feed you, clothes *(sic)* you and give you shelter, (of course the father does too) is a bike tire alive and understanding when you're in dutch? Well all I can say is there's nothing like a mother and what she does for you, so in return I would give her a present."

"My Successes. I like self discipline because I don't feel like I'm in an army. I feel like I have a little air to breathe and I like it when I can pick the subject I want to do first and take as much time as I like. I like it because I can try to control myself without the help of anyone.

"My Failures. I don't like it because, well, I come from a family that believes in discipline. And I when I come to a situation like this I sorta *(sic)* fall apart and having a teacher that believed in discipline last year didn't help any. And sometimes having freedom I get carried away and do anything I please. I even get in trouble sometimes from doing it, but all in all I have my faults too."

"The kindest thing I ever did was when my mother wasn't feeling good and I went home for lunch that day, I went into the house and my little brother came running up to me and said, 'Mommy isn't feeling good and is in your room.' So I went into the room and my mother was laying on my bed and said, 'Bobby my throat hurts and I've got a headache, so you will have to make your own lunch.' So the first thing I did was help my mother make her bed and let her lay down on it. Then I did a few chores for my mother (mainly because she asked me to), then I made my lunch and fixed something for her. After that I washed the dishes and went to school. The thing that was kind is that I did everything without putting up a big fuss."

"I can't say what's right and what's wrong because there's too many things to cover, there's billions and trillions of things that are right and wrong. And also what I may think is right and wrong other people might think the opposite. I can't cover any of it and I don't think anyone can come up with the right or wrong answer."

"Why I'm a Conformist. I'm a conformist because I do (and like) most of the things my friends do. For instance, I like to play basketball, baseball, softball, football, soccer and kickball. Also I like running, jumping, and climbing sports and games. And my friends like these games too. I like going places with my friends. And well, I do a lot of things my friends do and I do it for two reasons: To keep my friendship and because I like to do certain things and go to certain places."

"I have two things that are important in my life and they are drawing and thinking of the future. First, I started drawing when I was in kindergarten and practiced through the years and now I'm pretty good and I think I will keep on drawing to my last days. Second, I'm hoping that someday I will become an architecture *(sic)* and have a good family and the best of everything."

(The value clarification procedures described on pages 79-80 of Wassermann's dissertation were used with each of Bob's themes.)

May 22-26 — Bob did exercises in suggesting hypotheses for several problem situations.

May 8-June 15 — Bob actively participated in group work, doing library investigations of the Roman Empire. His enthusiasm for this area of study was typified by the comment he made during a reading conference, when he brought his book, on this topic, to the investigator and said, "When I get a book like this I just get buggy about it and I can't put it down." He made a series of drawings depicting clearly and graphically Roman life and times. These studies were applauded by the children in the other groups and on several occasions Bob was asked by children to help out in the project work of their groups.

June 22 — Instead of a final class party, the children decided that they would rather have a trip, and a swimming party was arranged at an indoor pool. Accompanying the investigator, as an additional supervisor, was the physical education instructor, who made this comment on the return trip to the school: "I watched Bob approach Mark, who was standing at the edge of the pool. Bob had his hands out, grinning, ready to push. Then he seemed to give it a second thought, and turned away. Is this the same Bobby I used to know?"

Behavioral Changes

In the initial identification of his behavioral characteristics by the teacher group, Bob was rated +15 for "loud-dogmatic-assertive" behavior, +12 for "impulsive" behavior and +12 for "anti-think" behavior. In the final assessment of his behavior by this group, Bob was rated +4 for "loud-dogmatic-assertive" behavior, a gain of +11; +3 for "impulsive" behavior, a gain of +9; and +2 for "anti-think" behavior, a gain of +10. Comments made by both the school nurse-teacher and the music teacher during the interviewing were, "He used to be like that, but he's not that way anymore." The peer group rated Bob initially +39 for "loud-dogmatic-assertive" behavior and +13 for "anti-think" behavior. The final assessment by this group rated Bob +23 for "loud-dogmatic-assertive" behavior, showing a behavioral gain of +16, and gave him a zero rating for "anti-think" behavior, showing a behavioral gain of +13. Bob's self-identification was most interesting. Initially, he rated himself strongly (+3) as "impulsive" and as the type who "misses the meaning," and tentatively (+1) in the categories of "overly-dependent," "means-ends confusion," and "anti-think." He rated himself zero in the categories of "loud-dogmatic-assertiveness," "in-a-rut," and "under confident." His total combined rating on this instrument was +9. In the final assessment of his own behavior, Bob rated himself with a +3 for "overly-dependent," "misses the meaning," and "anti-think" behavior; +1 for "loud-dogmatic-assertive," "means-ends confusion," and "under-confident" behavior; and

TABLE II

BOB

CHANGES IN RATINGS

Group	"Loud-Dogmatic-Assertive" Behavior				"Anti-Think" Behavior				Total Behaviors			
	Max. Poss.	Initial	Final	Change	Max. Poss.	Initial	Final	Change	Max. Poss.	Initial	Final	Change
Teachers	15	15	4	+11	15	12	2	+10	120	48	9	+39
Peers	45	39	23	+16	45	13	0	+13	360	91	24	+67
Self	3	0	1	− 1	3	0	3	− 3	24	9	12	− 3

CHANGES IN VAN PIT THINKING TEST SCORES

	Maximum Possible	Initial	Final	Change
Total number of errors	80	26	13	+13
Number of "going beyond the data" errors	60	25	4	+21
Number of "cautious" errors	20	1	8	− 7
Number of gross errors	20	0	1	− 1
Number not answered	80	0	0	0

zero for "impulsive," and "in-a-rut" behavior, giving himself a total combined rating of $+12$.

Several questions can be raised at this point concerning self-identification:

1. Might Bob's particular behavioral characteristics cause a loss of objectivity in self-identification?
2. What might be the reasons for the extreme discrepancy between the initial ratings on the peer and teacher scales and the ratings on self-identification?
3. Does Bob begin to see himself more objectively in the final assessment?
4. Is he more severe on himself in the final assessment?

Bob's final score on the VAN PIT THINKING TEST showed a total of thirteen errors out of eighty responses, compared with a total of twenty-six errors out of eighty responses on the first test. An analysis of the errors on the first test showed one cautious error and twenty-five errors in going beyond the data. On the second test there were four errors in going beyond the data, eight cautious errors and one gross error. These data appear in the table on page 328. The direction of change moved from going beyond the data to caution, and for an impulsive type, this shift was regarded as being in a favorable direction.

ADDITIONAL RESEARCH FINDINGS

Wassermann's investigation was a before-and-after study of nine children. No outside controls were employed. There was the idea that if anything of great significance happened in the course of engaging in thinking activities, the results would be immediately visible in rather significant changes in the behavior of the children. As was stated earlier, the results were unusually significant. Behavior changed significantly, and so did the scores on the thinking test.

At this point in the testing of the theory, there seemed to be need for a more closely controlled study, and this was undertaken by Ruth R. Berken[9] in 1963. Berken was a member of the Bureau of Curriculum Research of the New York City Schools and received permission from the Director of the Bureau and an Assistant Superintendent of Schools in New York to conduct the study. With some slight revision, she used the same techniques for identifying children as had been used by Wassermann. Nine *teachers* participated in this study, and they represented fifth and sixth grade classrooms in several elementary schools on the West Side of Manhattan. These teachers were

---

[9]Ruth R. Berken, "A Study of the Relationships of Certain Behaviors of Children to the Teaching of Thinking in Grades Five and Six in Selected Schools in West Side Manhattan" (Unpublished Ph.D. dissertation, School of Education, New York University, 1963).

members of a seminar course in which Berken carried on in-service training with respect to the use of thinking-related assignments. When these teachers began the process of selecting children, they identified twenty-seven matched sets, one child for the experimental group, and one for each of *two* control groups. In addition to the matching of thinking-related behavior, the sets were also matched on grade level, sex, academic achievement, I. Q. level within five points, and economic status of the family. Each such matched trio typified one of the thinking-related behavior patterns. The children selected for the experimental group were encouraged to carry on extensive work in experiences which emphasized thinking-type opportunities. With the control groups, which were made up of children from each of the classes that included the experimental children, no single effort or intensive work in thinking-type experiences was undertaken.

As was mentioned previously, a second control child was chosen who matched the other two, but who was in *another classroom* at the same grade level. The results thus have bearing upon "control" children in the same classroom, and "control" children outside of the experimental classroom. Berken reports that there was a significant difference between both control groups and the experimental group. On the rating scale used there was a gain of three or more points by twenty-four out of the twenty-seven experimental pupils; a similar gain was achieved by only three out of the twenty-seven control-in-class pupils. These results are significant at the 1 per cent level and support the theory.

In terms of the before-and-after self-ratings of the same students, there was again a very significant difference of the same order as has been described. In the self-ratings, twenty out of the twenty-seven experimental students thought they had shifted, and none in the control group thought they had improved. The peer ratings demonstrated again a significant difference between the control and experimental groups, and this evidence is also consistent with the theory expressed in this volume. Berken's study gives added support to the idea that where children with certain behaviors are helped to focus on assignments which involve thinking, their behavior changes. The students themselves report awareness of change; their peers assess them more positively in the specified areas, and teachers see positive changes in their behavior.

Still another kind of research has bearing on this theory. Stern[10] undertook a study of "The Perseverance or Lack of it of Specified Behaviors Among Children in Selected Elementary Schools in Nassau County, New York." Among the behaviors were those which in this volume are described as *thinking-related*. In one of his schools there was a perseveration of identifica-

---

[10] Ira Le Roy Stern, *"The Perseverance or Lack of it of Specified Behaviors Among Children in Selected Elementary Schools in Nassau County, New York"* (Unpublished Ph.D. dissertation, School of Education, New York University, 1962).

tion of 84 per cent in the many behaviors relevant to this study. If two or more of the behavior patterns were chosen for comparison, two of the schools in his study showed a perseveration rate of 80 per cent. He notes that even if one takes the 71 per cent level (the average) of perseveration, this is relatively high if we are to think of the elementary school as a place which has significant influence on the growth and development of children. In other words, where little or no emphasis is placed upon developing appropriate thinking exercises, there is much less likelihood that significant change in the thinking-related behavior of children will take place.

Rothstein's study indicated that where there was a focus upon thinking and the use of materials such as are presented in this volume, the experimental group made significant change. The work of Machnits, Jonas, and Martin indicated that in the cases which they studied, there was also very significant change in the behavior of the children. Wassermann's before-and-after study revealed very significant differences in the behavior of children. Berken's more controlled study showed the same results. Stern has some data which indicate that where little or nothing is done for students who reveal these rather distinctive thinking-related types of behavior, they tend to be identified the following year as having the same kind of behavior.

What has been proved by all of this? A theory is not something which can be proved in the absolute sense. In almost all of these studies the investigators have operated on the hypothesis that there *is* a relationship between consistent and persistent exposure to thinking-type situations and resultant behavior. On the basis of these studies we can be reasonably sure that if one works with children in ways that put an emphasis upon thinking (and these have been described), changes will take place in the behavior of children. We cannot be specific in attributing the cause of the change. It can be said that as teachers work in these ways with children, certain kinds of behavior will diminish in frequency and certain other kinds of behavior will come into being.

What about the element of chance in all this? If the results of only one study were available, we might be tempted to say that these represented the unique responses of an enthusiastic teacher, or that the so-called Hawthorne effect was operating. That is, that almost any "new" procedures would produce a change. The testing, however, has been tried out with a number of teachers. It has been tried out in a variety of situations where students did not know that they were in an experiment. The final ratings which were made by teachers and by children were done in circumstances where no knowledge was available as to who the experimental children were. Stern's study supports the findings which relate to the control groups, in the sense that from 70 per cent to 80 per cent of the children characterized with these behavioral characteristics tended to be similarly characterized a year later. The experimental children in the several studies not only made significant changes; nearly all of them did. It is reasonable to infer that teaching which is characterized by the use of these thinking-related materials will, in other situations with other children, produce positive and welcome changes in the behavior of school children, and it is predicted that this "emphasis on thinking" will receive wide attention in the years ahead.

FINAL COMMENTS

This entire volume has been concerned with a theory which relates behavior to thinking activities. Great emphasis has been put upon the importance of thinking in our daily lives. Literally hundreds of examples of ways to emphasize thinking at three levels of elementary education have been given, and many examples have been given which are pertinent to the secondary levels.

Why all of this emphasis on thinking? There are a number of ways to go about making a decision. Sometimes we do it by hunch or intuition. Sometimes we do it by consulting an authority. At times we do it by consulting what has been done in the past. A number of people seek divine guidance when they are in the presence of a problematic situation of great consequence. However few they are, some people seek advice in the stars and from fortunetellers. Some people look for help in established policies or rules and regulations.

Of all the methods that are known for solving problems in terms of human needs, human values, and human concerns, *thinking* represents the one best method available. This is not to say that the processes emphasized here will inevitably lead to a correct or even to the most appropriate conclusion. Thinking is not an absolute guarantee for an adequate solution of a problem. Where hundreds of problems are to be solved, and a higher average of success is sought, then thinking is the single best approach. Where there is freedom to think, there is also freedom to correct past errors. Where there is freedom to think, there is the possibility that new and better hypotheses will be proposed for testing. Where there is freedom to think, ideas not yet heard of may have opportunity to be heard, to be discussed, to be modified, and to be tried. Our faith is in a process which is to be used by man in solving the problems which he faces and in identifying problems to which man has been insensitive heretofore.

Some critics will point out that the position taken here is idealistic. It will be said that our society is characterized by economic conflicts between social classes, that people of a social class tend to think of the materialistic advantages for themselves, that the strife between classes inhibits the possibility of clear thinking for the good of the society or of the community. This is not altogether sound. One has only to look at the development of medicine as a science and as an art to see how much progress can be made in a society where class conflicts are supposed to exist. It may be assumed that one hundred years ago much the same criticism was leveled at those who saw opportunities for the application of thinking processes to the realms of human illness. Still, much has been accomplished; many people can be trained as doctors to look at evidence regardless of social class biases. The gap is not entirely closed. There remain, perhaps, many individuals whose social class consciousness may inhibit them from this wider perception of what is human, but they represent a decreasing number in the profession of medicine. Can one say that those in the profession of teaching cannot achieve similar progress?

Another argument put forward to dampen the enthusiasm of those who seek a greater emphasis upon thinking is that we live in a dog-eat-dog world, a world so competitive that each person is seeking to take advantage of others, and that in this context it is quite impossible to develop an attitude that is favorable to thinking. Still, it must be acknowledged that definite progress has been made in legislation, in hours of work, in conditions of work for women and children, in the social controls that have been placed upon factors which are inimical to public health. There is increased concern for the training of social workers, of government workers, of engineers, and of psychiatrists. There has been a rise in the amount of thinking which is directed toward common concerns. Schools at all levels have a contribution to make to this humanizing of knowledge, to this concern for the other person, to this moral awakening which concerns itself with the quality of our culture as it impinges upon every man. In other words, the competitive aspects of our culture do not constitute a permanent barrier. An emphasis upon thinking in our schools can make a contribution to a consideration of what is good for humanity.

Much also is said about the monopolistic characteristics of our culture, its associated bureaucracy, and its accompanying emphasis on automation. The more pessimistic outlook suggests that these elements control us, that these *determine* our thinking, that we can do nothing but drift with the times. Throughout time man has reconstructed his environment. He is still capable of doing it. Where we can clearly see what it is that we want for our culture and where deliberate processes of thought are employed, our culture can be modified in ways that more nearly represent our heart's desire.

There has been a tendency in the past thirty years to associate almost all learning difficulties with emotional disturbances. If children lean heavily on authority figures for guidance, an inference is drawn about relationships with parents at the time of infancy. If children "cannot concentrate," it is suggested that psychological therapy is needed. There is an analogy here with the medical profession. Not so very long ago physicians tended to believe that all, or almost all, illness was caused by germs. We now acknowledge the presence of many causes. Some will say that this book deals with profound emotional problems and does so superficially, because of its orientation to thinking processes. We must be clear about this matter. We agree that emotional security is very important and that some behavior disorders may be traced to emotional insecurity. We do *not* believe that all, or *almost all,* behavior problems have their roots in emotional imbalance.

Research evidence clearly associates some behavioral tendencies with experiences that put an emphasis on thinking. These experiences are not narrowly intellectual or cognitive. They involve the organism as a functioning unity, but the emphasis is on thinking in a broad sense. Those who urge that emotional disturbance is *the* cause of nearly all behavioral problems are more vulnerable to criticism in this area. *They* oversimplify these situations. New conceptions are needed, a new look, the testing of new hypotheses, inquiry into new situations and a focused trial of thinking operations at all levels of instruction.

We do *not* see the teacher as a therapist. He is a person who facilitates learning through an intelligent emphasis upon emotional, physical, social and intellectual components in curriculum and instruction. This book emphasizes thinking operations which have been found to contribute to self-directed changes in behavior.

What about the argument *that there is so much* wrong with the structure, the organization, and the curriculum of our schools that the ideas proposed in this volume are altogether impractical, so far as a significant contribution to the improvement of education is concerned? Throughout these pages it has been said that no profound reconstruction of the curriculum is necessary in order to employ these thinking operations. Over and over again, it has been said that practically all of these thinking operations could be employed within the framework of an existing curriculum. With ever so many other students of education we should like to see less emphasis placed upon textbooks; we should like to see more of a concern with large generalizations, with *meanings* which would help each child to understand himself better and to understand the world in which he lives. The materials in this volume were not designed to replace a curriculum. They were designed to help in developing curriculum materials which would put an emphasis upon thinking. Would it have been better to write a different book about ways of improving the curriculum?

While we might wish for a different kind of curriculum in which to place these operations, it seems reasonable to expect that more concentrated use of them in present programs may, in fact, improve the curriculum.

Some have said that all of these approaches represent gradualism in circumstances where speed is vitally necessary. Neither *gradualism* nor *speed* is good or bad in the abstract. In particular situations, the possibilities for going faster might be particularly inviting. In other situations where essential data are missing and where there are great divergences in points of view, a thoughtful analysis might urge us toward caution and inaction. Those who sometimes stand most strongly for speedy action often favor revolutionary action. Very few people would say that *all* revolutions are bad, or that *no* revolution had any good qualities about it. Even so and notwithstanding, most would argue for an exchange of thinking, for the deliberate processes of thought, for a deep consideration of the values that we want to protect no matter what the final decision would be. As these ways of trying to solve problems are adopted, revolution will probably be delayed, in defense of the one best way to handle the problems which divide us, which disunite us, and which make life less worth-while.

Something too, should perhaps be said about a sizable group which believes that it is quite alien to human nature to embrace thinking approaches to life. Within this group there are some who believe that the intellectual elite might learn to use these processes, but that for the vast majority, there is little hope that *they* can learn them or will use them. So many changes have been brought about in the practices of the vast majority, so many changes have been brought about in terms of their beliefs that the evidence is really most supporting of a contrary view. Given our release from the burdens of backbreaking labor, given our opportunities for a great system of public education, given the resources which will soon be ours for a great increase in the service occupations, given an increasing concern for a good life which goes beyond the amassing of things, there is ground for optimism in the extension of the thinking processes to many more areas of human living.

What will we say about those people who assert that we are *now* doing all of these things and that they do not work? It is difficult to find evidence that these processes of thought have been given a fair trial. There is not much emphasis upon these thinking processes in the day-by-day operations of public schools today. Evidence from many sources points in the direction that thinking as an aim is given much lip service, but very little practical application in the classrooms. It is to be regretted that this is so, and while many reasons are given to explain the existing situation, there is little doubt that great changes in emphasis can and should take place. Criticisms of thinking as a method for solving problems should be postponed until a widespread emphasis has been given to the processes. Moreover, personal opinions, may well be deferred to a time when hypotheses will have been tested.

CONCLUSION

The United States, as a nation, is very proud of its public schools. True, it criticizes them severely at times, but beneath the criticism there is also a close identification with these schools. In no other country of the world are fathers and mothers as closely affiliated with what goes on in the schools as they are in the United States.

For the administrators of our schools, professional training is required. Teachers also are required to secure an understanding of students at the several age levels, in addition to an understanding of the curriculum as a body of subject matter. A majority of the public is convinced that our schools have made a great contribution to the welfare of the nation and to its resources in terms of identifying and solving the many problems which now confront the nation.

Yet, while there is commitment on the part of teachers to excellence in the educative processes and to furthering the growth of children, there seems to be a lack of commitment to mobilizing the resources which would help these teachers in the achievement of their purposes. For example, if an emphasis upon thinking is an objective, one would expect that the graduate schools, the colleges, and the trained supervisors would be helping the teachers day-by-day in very specific and concrete ways to build a curriculum which would reflect this emphasis on thinking. As a matter of fact, however, the emphasis is *not* upon the operational procedures which would help to carry out purpose, but rather on formulation of statements of purpose themselves. This Book emphasizes operational procedures which are consistent with the purposes of emphasizing thinking in teaching.

In a larger sense, the book attempts a significant contribution to what may be called "a way of life." As a country we are committed to a deep respect for the individual; we are also committed to a doctrine that is best expressed as "faith in intelligence." We have indicated in our constitution that we believe in sharing our problems and our ideas in the widest possible manner, thus insuring the participation of all our people in decisions which affect their lives.

Thinking often adds to tensions already experienced. Society is threatened in many ways by freedom of thought. The very structure which is cherished becomes a subject of reflection and possible change. Consequently, it takes more than "freedom to think" to handle the tensions which are created by such a society as ours. It takes competence in thinking. It requires excellence as an ideal for those who emphasize thinking. As we continue to pledge ourselves and each other to the great ideals of democracy, we must also pledge that we will use every resource to provide that excellence in the education of children. Just as we want them to be free to identify the problems of concern to them, so do we want them to have those experiences which can contribute greatly to the competence of people in problematic situations.

To translate these majestic purposes into classroom practices which involve experiences of a kind best calculated to further these goals, to present educational theories relating to the achievement of these noble purposes, and to do it in ways that suggest hypotheses which can be tested in any or every school of the country, represents the major contribution of this text.

As we see it, the good life is associated with zestful living, and zestful living is, over and over again, associated with a life that both creates problems and creates opportunities for working with the problems. Man may be a reed, but as has been said, he is a thinking reed; and where he can think, and where ideas can be put to test in the market place, life is richer, and life is better. Where our schools have these aims, and where teachers have the competence to put these aims into operation, school life too will be richer and better for teachers and for chidlren.

SUGGESTED READINGS

BOOKS

1. Bartlett, Sir Frederic, *Thinking*. New York: Basic Books Inc., 1958.
   The book represents a thorough and detailed analysis of thinking by an eminent psychologist. The author deals at length with experiments in the mental processes of interpolation and extrapolation. He delineates everyday thinking* and adventurous thinking, the thinking of the artist and the thinking of the experimental scientist.

2. Black, Max, *Critical Thinking*. New York: Prentice-Hall, 1946.
   This is a college text with a heavy emphasis on logical analysis. It provides many fine illustrative materials on fallacies.

3. Bloom, Benjamin S., *Taxonomy of Educational Objectives, Part I, Cognitive Domain*. New York: Longmans, Green and Company, 1956.
   This is an attempt at classifying the goals of teaching: knowledge, comprehension, analysis, synthesis, application, and evaluation. Essentially, the work is derived from an analysis of the materials used in the PEA Eight Year Study.

4. Bruner, Jerome S. *The Process of Education*. Cambridge: Harvard University Press, 1961.
   The author sets forth the thesis that it is the structure of a subject that should be taught. It is his contention that how the discipline came to *be* should occupy a central role in the process of education.

5. Bruner, Jerome S., Goodnow, Jacqueline J., and Austin, George A., *A Study of Thinking*. New York: John Wiley and Sons, Inc., 1961.
   The book inquires into the processes of categorizing and conceptualizing. Man's capacity to categorize is seen as necessity. He groups things into classes and responds to them as classes. Concept attainment, a result of categorizing, enables man to learn more readily.

---

*Adjectives describing the term thinking like adventurous, empirical, reflective, autonomous, represent the terminology of the particular author. They do not represent the usage of the authors of this book.

6. Bury, J. B., *A History of Freedom of Thought*. London: Oxford University Press, 1922.

The author traces the history of man's emancipation from passion and prejudice. He indicates that there is no linear progress but merely illuminating flashes of freedom of thought. (The books of Robinson and Russell listed below deal with similar themes.)

7. Conant, James B., *On Understanding Science*. New Haven: Yale University Press, 1947.

Through the presentation of case histories from the diaries of famous scientists, the author offers an historical approach to the understanding of science with the hope of acquainting the non-scientist with the tactics and strategy of the scientist. The book is an inquiry into the methods of science. "Understanding science" is, according to the author, acquiring a special point of view, knowing what science can or cannot do.

8. Dewey, John, *How We Think*. Boston: D. C. Heath and Company, 1910.

The book is now a classic. It was a pioneering and systematic examination of thinking — the method by which things acquire significance — and its relationship to teaching and learning.

9. Dimnet, Ernest. *The Art of Thinking*. New York: Fawcett World Library, 1955.

This is a highly literary presentation of thinking as art. The author's sparkling pen and engaging style make for pleasurable and enlightening reading.

10. Hullfish, H. Gordon, and Smith, Philip G. *Reflective Thinking: The Method of Education*. New York: Dodd, Mead and Company, 1961.

Reflective thinking is presented as the method of teaching and learning. Leaning heavily on epistemology, the book offers a theory of learning and suggestions for the promotion of reflection.

11. Keyser, C. J. *Thinking About Thinking*. New York: E. P. Dutton and Company, 1926.

The book is a highly analytical discussion of empirical and autonomous thinking described as human thinking. Other kinds of thinking, whether by humans or not, are characterized as sub-human. The book is the scientific counterpart of Dimnet's presentation of thinking as art.

12. Raths, Louis E., Harmin, Merrill, and Simon, Sidney B., *Values and Teaching*. Columbus, Ohio: Charles E. Merrill Books, Inc., 1966.

This book creates new concepts for guiding children's learning toward the clarification of their values.

13. Robinson, James H. *The Mind in the Making*. New York: Harper Brothers, 1950.

The author sees the collective rational efforts of man to solve his problems as an historical development of mind. He regards creation of more mind as a distinct function of the school.

14. Russell, Bertrand. *Understanding History*. New York: The Wisdom Library, 1957.

Written with an acid pen, the book contains a valuable essay on free thought. It makes a good companion to Robinson and Bury above.

15. Russell, David H., *Children's Thinking*. Boston: Ginn and Company, 1956.

This is a compilation of research findings in thinking from various fields. The author attempts to combine child development, educational psychology, and the psychology of thinking into a possible structure from the developmental point of view.

16. Thomson, Robert. *The Psychology of Thinking.* Baltimore: Penguin Books, Inc., 1959.

This is a lucidly written psychological inquiry. It presents thinking as a collection of skills (among which is reflection), which is the coordinated result of simpler functions. How the higher-level functions are developed is not yet clear. The book makes a good companion to Bartlett and Judd.

17. Whitehead, Alfred N. *The Aims of Education.* London: Williams and Norgate, Ltd., 1950.

The "book" is actually a collection of lectures written in elegant style by the eminent philosopher. The author is concerned with educational goals and their means of attainment.

BOOKS WRITTEN IN A POPULAR STYLE

1. Carroll, Lewis. *Alice's Adventures in Wonderland and Through the Looking Glass.* New York: Macmillan and Company, 1930.

This literary gem, enjoyable in its own right, is sometimes overlooked as a resource in thinking materials.

2. Chase, Stuart, *Guides to Straight Thinking.* New York: Harper Brothers, 1956.

The book is very easy to read. The author builds the book around an analysis of fallacies drawn from formal logic.

3. Hayakawa, S. I. *Language in Action.* New York: Harcourt, Brace and Company, 1947.

There is a heavy emphasis on semantics and problems of communication. With an engaging style and highly readable prose, the author analyzes language as the expression of thought.

4. Huff, Darrell. *How To Lie With Statistics.* New York: W. W. Norton and Company, Inc., 1954.

This small volume in soft cover is well illustrated and humorous. The author draws attention to common errors in going beyond data, especially those data presented in the form of charts and graphs.

5. Keyes, Kenneth S. *How To Develop Your Thinking Ability.* New York: McGraw-Hill, 1950.

This is an easy to read and profusely illustrated book. The author draws heavily from semantics to offer a popular guide to thinking. He attempts to teach moderation in the use of language.

6. Stebbing, L. Susan. *Thinking to Some Purpose.* Baltimore: Penguin Books, 1959.

This is a more serious treatment of a guide to thinking in the Chase and Thouless vein. The author, a logician, talks about moderation, propaganda, illustration and analogy, and stereotypes.

7. Thouless, R. H. *How To Think Straight:* New York: Simon and Schuster, 1947.

Like the preceding, the book is a popular guide to informal logic. It is an early work in its field being a revision of an older title. It gives the reader a chance to practice avoiding fallacies.

RESEARCH LITERATURE

1. *Berken, Ruth R., *"A Study of the Relationships of Certain Behaviors of Children to the Teaching of Thinking in Grades Five and Six in Selected Schools in West Side Manhattan."* New York University, 1963.
   The thinking theory outlined in this book was tested in a controlled study with nine teachers. The results of this investigation are consistent with the theory.
2. Bloom, B. S. and Broder, L. J. *Problem-Solving Processes of College Students.* Supplementary Monographs #73. Chicago: University of Chicago Press, 1950.
   This is an investigation into thought in-process. The study involves an analysis of transcripts of students who were thinking "out loud" in response to selected problems.
3. Brownell, W. A. *Problem Solving—The Psychology of Learning.* Forty-First Yearbook of National Society for the Study of Education, Part II. Bloomington, Illinois: Public School Publishing Company, 1942.
   This classic work offers a presentation of the characteristics of problems. The author distinguishes between problems seen as applications of principles to new situations and puzzles and exercises.
4. *Cartwright, Roger. *"An Account of the Development and Application of a Resource Unit Stressing Thinking for a Course: ETA 2: Values, Teaching, and Planning."* New York University, 1961.
   This study develops a resource unit for college teachers which would put an emphasis on thinking. There is a comprehensive statement regarding the making of the resource unit with its emphasis on thinking operations and on the making of thinking-type assignments.
5. *Chess, Edith. *"The Manner in Which Two Samples of Ninth Grade General Science Students Analyze a Number of Selected Problems."* New York University, 1955.
   The investigation is somewhat similar to the Bloom and Broder Study. It attempts to analyze thought-in-process as recorded on tapes by children as they worked out loud in solving specific problems presented to them. Some implications of the study are worth noting: similarity of mental product does not mean similarity of mental process; instead of failing to learn, students sometimes learn something different from that which is intended; teacher delineation of problems is not necessarily meaningful since different problem statements persist in the thought processes of the student.
6. Fawcett, H. P. *The Nature of Proof.* Thirteenth Yearbook of the National Council of the Teachers of Mathematics. New York: Teachers College, 1938.
   This was a pioneering investigation which focused on the use of non-mathematical materials in the teaching of mathematics. The author was concerned with those aspects of demonstrative geometry which served to illustrate the nature of proof rather than the content as traditionally organized. Fawcett demonstrated that even for the so-called "thinking subjects," there is little gain in thinking ability unless there is direct focus. His work antedates latter day champions of having students discover rules rather than memorize them.

---

*Also available on microfilm from University Microfilms, Ann Arbor, Michigan.

7. Glaser, E. M. *An Experiment in the Development of Critical Thinking.* Contributions to Education #843. New York: Teachers College, 1941.
The well-known *Watson-Glaser Critical Thinking Appraisal,* used in this study for the first time, is a distinct contribution of the work. The experiment, somewhat staged, is less convincing than the materials used. The latter are heavily weighted in the areas of propaganda analysis and syllogistic reasoning.

8. *Jonas, Arthur, "A Study of the Relationship of Certain Behaviors of Children to Emotional Needs, Values, and Thinking." Unpublished doctoral dissertation. New York University, 1960.
*Martin, Donald, "A Study of the Relationship of Certain Behaviors of Children to Emotional Needs, Values, and Thinking." Unpublished doctoral dissertation. New York University, 1960.
*Machnits, Ernest, "A Study of the Relationship of Certain Behaviors of Children to Emotional Needs, Values, and Thinking." Unpublished doctoral dissertation. New York University, 1960.
These three separate but closely related studies were conducted in grades three, four, and five in a suburban New York School. Fifteen children were studied in relation to their behavior associated with thinking. As the teachers of the three experimental groups emphasized thinking over a four-month period, the behavior of the experimental children changed significantly in comparison to the control children. There was no loss in academic achievement both for the experimental children and the experimental classes.

9. Judd, C. H. *Education as Cultivation of the Higher Mental Processes.* New York: Macmillan and Company, 1936.
This is an outstanding classic on the subject of thinking. It provides one of the earliest psychological discussions on mental processes, their definition and distinctions. In addition, it is illustrative of ways of putting emphases on higher mental processes.

10. *Lewis H. "An Experiment in the Development of Critical Thinking Through the Teaching of Plane Geometry." New York University, 1950. Also available in *Mathematics Teacher,* Volume 43, 1950.
Teachers of geometry cannot teach the subject in a traditional way and expect growth in thinking ability in non-mathematical areas. The author gets students to discover and even to create geometric principles. This study, as also demonstrated in the Fawcett, Glaser and Rothstein investigations, reveals that experimental groups, while showing marked growth in achievement in thinking abilities, also do better on traditional tests than do control groups. The belief of teachers in the necessity of fact coverage in order to pass the examination is not supported by the evidence.

11. *Obourn, E. "Assumptions in Ninth Grade Science." Unpublished doctoral dissertation. New York University, 1950.
This was an experiment similar to those of Fawcett, Glaser, Lewis, and Rothstein. It emphasized science as discovery and as method rather than as content. The major thinking operation stressed was assumption finding.

---

*Also available on microfilm from University Microfilms, Ann Arbor, Michigan.

12. Marcham, F. G. "Teaching Critical Thinking and the Use of Evidence." *Quarterly Journal of Speech.* Volume 31 (October 1945).
    With the field of literature as a base, the author offers a description of how he provided students with practice in comparing and interpreting sources and using evidence.
13. Professional Reprints in Education, Charles E. Merrill Books, Inc.
    These loose leaf articles are excellent for strengthening instructional materials in introductory courses and higher levels in social foundations, psychological foundations, curriculum and methods, nature of teaching, and nature and interrelation of knowledge.
14. *Rothstein, A. "An Experiment in Developing Critical Thinking." Unpublished doctoral dissertation. New York University, 1960.
    This work confirms earlier investigations that there is no loss in subject matter when emphasis is put on thinking, while there is distinct gain in thinking achievement. A great part of the work is devoted to illustrations of curricular materials emphasizing thinking, and guidelines for ways in which materials may be constructed and used are set forth.
15. *Stern, Ira Leroy, "The Perseverance or Lack of It of Specified Behaviors Among Children in Selected Elementary Schools in Nassau County, New York." New York University, 1962.
    This investigation relates to the behaviors set forth in Part I of this book. Where nothing specific is done for the students exhibiting the "thinking-related" behaviors, the behaviors tend to preserve in the following year and are so identified.
16. *Wassermann, S. "A Study of the Changes in Thinking-Related Behaviors in a Selected Group of Sixth Grade Children in the Presence of Selected Materials and Techniques." Unpublished doctoral dissertation. New York University, 1962.
    In this investigation, certain behavioral patterns, which relate to thinking, were identified in a group of nine sixth grade students. It was found that after day-by-day exposure to "thinking tasks," these nine children modified their thinking-related behaviors significantly.

---

*Also available on microfilm from University Microfilms, Ann Arbor, Michigan.

INDEX

INDEX

Abeken, Heinrich, 134-135
Analysis, in classification, 9
Assumptions, defined, 199n

Bacon, Francis, 219
Behavior, immature, described, 2
Berken, Ruth R., 329-330

California Institute of Technology, 248
California Test of Mental Maturity, 306
Cartwright, Roger, 305
Change, schools' concern with, 233
Curriculum reorganization, 241
Curriculum revision, and coding, 131

Democratic society, cornerstone of, 1
Dewey, John, 251
Drill, stress on, 3

Emotion, "pure," 117
Experience,
  and maturing, 2-3
  and summary, 7

Facts
  importance of, 11
  defined, 199n

Fawcett, Harold P., 243

Glaser, E.M., 243
Goals, and decision-making, 17
Good judgment, in criticism, 99
Grades, 248
Gradualism, 334
Grouping, 9-10

Hawthorne effect, 331
Higher mental processes, concept of, 29
Historical emphasis, 219
Homework, stress on, 3
Hypothesis, defined, 94

"Independent work," defined, 15
Inference, 10
Institutions, social, 1
Interpretation, 10

James, William, 120
Jonas, Arthur H., 304, 331

Learning, and maturing, 2
Lewis, Harry, 243
Lewis, John L., 137
Lincoln, Abraham, 137

McCarthy, Joseph, 137
Machnits, Ernest, 304, 331
Martin, Donald, 304, 331

Maturing process, 2-3
Maturity
    and criticism, 12
    and imagination, 14
Memorization, stress on, 3
Mill, John Stuart, 181
Mnemonic device, 168

National Science Foundation In-
    stitutes, 241

Order, and classification, 9

PEER RATING INSTRU-
    MENT, 300-302
Pitner-Cunningham Primary In-
    telligence Test, 306
Poe, Edgar Allen, 168, 171
Problem-solving, 210
"Progressive education," 292
Public Education Association of
    New York, 248

Raths, James, 250
Reading, post-war stress on, 4-5
Reason, "pure," 117
Recall, ability to, 168
Reflex action, 244
Rothstein, Arnold, 304, 331

St. Wapniacl, 169
Schools, social contribution of, 2

Scientific method, 210
SELF RATING INSTRU-
    MENT, 297-299
Semanticists, 122
Snow, C.P., 249
Social problems, creation of, 1
Stanford Achievement Test, 306
Stern, Ira LeRoy, 330
Swift, Ernest H., 248
Synthesis, 9

TEACHER RATING INSTRU-
    MENT, 293-297
Theories, educational, 289
Thinking
    importance of, 1, 3
    lack of emphasis on, 3-5
    and hypotheses, 16
    types of, 235
    mentioned, 26-29
Three R's, the, stress on, 3
Tyler, R.W., 29

VAN PIT THINKING TEST,
    302, 307, 329

Wassermann, Selma, 305-306, 331
WATSON-GLASER CRITICAL
    THINKING APPRAISAL, 302
Wert, James E., 29
Wilde, Oscar, 168
Words, attention to, 121